# THE HUMAN
# PERSON
## IN THEOLOGY *and*
## PSYCHOLOGY

# THE HUMAN PERSON

## IN THEOLOGY *and* PSYCHOLOGY

A BIBLICAL ANTHROPOLOGY
*for the*
TWENTY-FIRST CENTURY

JAMES R. BECK

BRUCE DEMAREST

Kregel
*Academic & Professional*

The Human Person in Theology and Psychology: A Biblical Anthropology for the Twenty-First Century

Published by Kregel Publications, a division of Kregel, Inc., P.O. Box 2607, Grand Rapids, MI 49501.

**Library of Congress Cataloging-in-Publication Data**
Beck, James R.
   The human person in theology and psychology: a biblical anthropology for the twenty-first century / by James R. Beck and Bruce Demarest.
       p.     cm.
   Includes bibliographical references and indexes.
       1. Theological anthropology—Biblical teaching. 2. Bible—Psychology. 3. Theological anthropology—Christianity. 4. Christianity—Psychology. 5. Psychology and religion.
   I. Demarest, Bruce A.  II. Title.
BS661.B43              2005              233—dc22              2005023263

ISBN 978-0-8254-2116-7

Printed in the United States of America

⌐ 07 08 09 10 11 / 6 5 4 3 2

*To*
*Vernon C. Grounds,*
*esteemed philosopher, theologian,*
*counselor, colleague, and friend*
*who taught us that it's*
*all about people.*

# CONTENTS

# ABBREVIATIONS

| | |
|---|---|
| ACW | Ancient Christian Writers. Edited by Johannes Quasten et al. 60 vols. London: Longmans, Green, 1961–. |
| *ANF* | *Ante-Nicene Fathers.* 10 vols. Peabody, Mass.: Hendrickson, 1994. |
| *CD* | *Church Dogmatics,* by Karl Barth. Edited by Geoffrey W. Bromiley and Thomas F. Torrance. 14 vols. New York: T. and T. Clark, 1936–77. |
| *DSM*-IV | *Diagnostic and Statistical Manual.* 4th ed. Text Revision. Washington, D.C.: American Psychological Association, 2000. |
| *EDT* | *Evangelical Dictionary of Theology.* Edited by Walter A. Elwell. 2d ed. Grand Rapids: Baker, 2001. |
| *FOTC* | *The Fathers of the Church: A New Translation.* 109 vols. Washington, D.C.: The Catholic University of America Press, 1947–. |
| LCC | Library of Christian Classics. Edited by J. A. Baillie et al. 26 vols. Philadelphia: Westminster, 1953–69. |
| *LW* | *Luther's Works.* Edited by J. Pelikan and H. T. Lehman. 55 vols. St. Louis: Concordia; Philadelphia: Fortress, 1955–56. |
| *NDT* | *New Dictionary of Theology.* Edited by Sinclair B. Ferguson and David F. Wright. Leicester: InterVarsity, 1988. |
| *NIDNTT* | *New International Dictionary of New Testament Theology.* Edited by C. Brown. 4 vols. Grand Rapids: Zondervan, 1975–85. |
| NIVSB | *The NIV Study Bible.* Edited by Kenneth Barker. Grand Rapids: Zondervan, 1985. |

*NLEKGNT*    *The New Linguistic and Exegetical Key to the Greek New Testament.* Grand Rapids: Zondervan, 1998.

*NPNF*[1]    *Nicene and Post Nicene Fathers: First Series.* Edited by Philip Schaff. 14 vols. Peabody, Mass.: Hendrickson, 1994.

*NPNF*[2]    *Nicene and Post Nicene Fathers: Second Series.* Edited by Philip Schaff and Henry Wace. 14 vols. Peabody, Mass.: Hendrickson, 1994.

*ST*    *Summa Theologica,* by Thomas Aquinas. 22 vols. London: R. and T. Washbourne; New York: Benzinder Brothers, 1912–25.

*TDNT*    *Theological Dictionary of the New Testament.* Edited by Gerhard Kittel and Gerhard Friedrich. Translated by Geoffrey W. Bromiley. 10 vols. Grand Rapids: Eerdmans, 1964–76.

*TWOT*    *Theological Wordbook of the Old Testament.* Edited by R. Laird Harris et al., 2 vols. Chicago: Moody, 1980.

WAIMH    World Association for Infant Mental Health

# INTRODUCTION

EARLY IN THE BIBLICAL HISTORY, while wrestling with issues of profound loss and pain, Job offered the following rumination with respect to the Almighty: "What is man that you make so much of him, that you give him so much attention . . ." (Job 7:17). Centuries later the psalmist David posed a similar question: "What is man that you are mindful of him, the son of man that you care for him?" (Ps. 8:4; cf. 144:3). Beyond the pages of the Bible, the human person has remained an enigma, a paradox, both to himself and to his fellow human beings. Pascal expressed in classic fashion the surd that is the human person: "What sort of freak then is man! How novel, how monstrous, how chaotic, how paradoxical, how prodigious! Judge of all things, feeble earthworm, repository of truth, sink of doubt and error and refuse of the universe!"[1]

A study of the human person is fitting because men and women represent the pinnacle of God's creative activity and the most complex of living beings. The center of Scripture and human experience is the human being. Otto Weber expresses this point tersely: "The issue in the Bible and in the message of the Church is really man."[2] Yet the nature and functioning of the human person has given rise to a multiplicity of views in both scholarly and popular discourse. Such breadth of perspectives, both from the past and in the present, requires thoughtful clarification.

---

1. Blaise Pascal, *Pensees* (Baltimore, Md.: Penguin Books, 1966), no. 131.
2. Otto Weber, *Foundations of Dogmatics*, 2 vols. (Grand Rapids: Eerdmans, 1981–83), 1:530.

Some thirty years ago the Old Testament scholar, Hans Walter Wolff, observed that "no field has been subject to such little research as contemporary man. . . ."[3] Yet in the decades since the publication of Wolff's book, many studies dealing with the human person have come forth from the fields of philosophy, theology, psychology, sociology, biology, medicine, and brain science. In these studies fundamental, ancient questions have been revisited, such as the origin of the human person, the reality of the soul, and the afterlife. In addition, new and complex issues have been raised by modern science, such as the genetic foundation of personality and how brain functioning relates to what we have always labeled "mind." Nevertheless, as one authority avers, "There are many indications that anthropology is the weak point of evangelical theology today."[4]

One foundational issue of debate today concerns the essential nature, or constitution, of the human person. In late modernity and postmodernity—particularly in the fields of philosophy and theology—a discernible "turn to relationality" has occurred. This shift involves a rejection of classical substance ontology and faculty psychology in favor of a relational ontology, wherein the person, or self, is said to be constituted *in relationship* with another or others. The present work explores whether this growing paradigm shift represents a more authentic way of viewing the human reality, or whether it constitutes a capitulation to sub-Christian disciplines such as existential philosophy and evolutionary biology.

The present study represents an interdisciplinary engagement with the complex phenomenon that is the human person. Principal topics relating to the human person will be examined from biblical, theological, and psychological points of view. Conclusions from the classical disciplines of biblical studies and theology, freshly examined, will be integrated with responsible findings from the newer discipline of psychology, and vice versa. We are pleased to welcome psychology into the conversation, for this modern discipline contributes much to our understanding of the nature and functioning of the human person. Paul Bloom, a professor of psychology at Yale University, offers an appropriate observation in this regard: "The great conflict between science and religion in the last century was over evolu-

---

3. Hans Walter Wolff, *Anthropology of the Old Testament* (Philadelphia, Pa.: Fortress, 1974), 1.
4. Jeffrey H. Boyd, "Self-Concept: In Defense of the Word *Soul,*" in *Care for the Soul,* ed. Mark R. McMinn and Timothy R. Phillips (Downers Grove, Ill.: InterVarsity, 2001), 116.

tionary biology. In this century, it will be over psychology, and the stakes are nothing less than our souls."[5]

As we have been working on this project, we both have been aware of a large, inspiring shadow influencing our work. This shadow is cast by the classic work, *A System of Biblical Psychology* (1855, 1861), written by Franz Delitzsch (1813–1890), professor of theology at the University of Leipzig in the mid-nineteenth century.[6] Dr. Delitzsch used his considerable Old Testament skills to produce a comprehensive survey of the Bible's teachings regarding the human person. His linguistic work in both Hebrew and Greek, coupled with careful exegesis, makes the book a useful resource for anyone interested in theological anthropology.

Delitzsch began his quest to understand the relationship between soul and spirit in 1846 when he produced a dissertation in Latin that argued for the essential unity of soul and spirit. In other works (1845, 1852, and 1853) he defended a dichotomous position regarding the human person. By the time Delitzsch finished the two editions of his *System of Biblical Psychology*, he had adopted a trichotomous view, wherein the human person is said to consist of body, soul, and spirit.[7] This intellectual approach that considers all the evidence, that is willing to change position when the evidence demands it, and that bases one's position solidly on responsible exegesis has served as a useful model for us as we have endeavored to produce a theological anthropology for the twenty-first century.

The content of Delitzsch's work, as valuable as it is, is matched in value by the frank discussion he provides in the prefaces to the first and second editions of his book (1855, 1861) concerning the methodology he used to go about his work. We have concluded that his methodology is sound and that it provides a helpful model for us and for all others attempting an integration of theological and psychological concepts. Delitzsch described for his readers ten methodological principles that guided his work.[8]

---

5. Paul Bloom, "The Duel Between Body and Soul," www.NYTimes.com (accessed September 10, 2004).
6. This classic has appeared in many editions over the last 150 years. Franz Delitzsch, *A System of Biblical Psychology* (1855; reprint, Eugene, Ore.: Wipf and Stock, 2003).
7. Ibid., iii–vii.
8. Ibid. Delitzsch refers to these principles in the preface to the first edition (1855, vii–ix) and the second edition (1861, x–xiv).

- *The biblical scholar must investigate how the teachings of the Christian Scriptures relate to relevant non-Christian systems.* In Delitzsch's case, he sought to understand how the teachings of the Old and New Testaments related to Platonic categories and to the Indian Vedanta. In our case, we are exploring with our readers how biblical teaching relates to twenty-first century psychology.
- *The teachings of the Bible will be non-self-contradictory and will not be inferior to any "late anthropologic researches."*[9] We likewise affirm the integrity, inspiration, and full authority of the Bible. When biblical material appears to present contradictory pictures of the human person, we seek to find the underlying and unifying principles that resolve those apparent problems. And when material from secular research arenas contradicts the clear teachings of Scripture, we prefer to suspend judgment rather than to conclude that the Bible is incorrect. Further work in the specialties of social science often clears up the problem over time. Delitzsch likewise, when confronted with an apparent contradiction between science and the Bible, did not see the problem as evidence for the absurdity of Scripture. Instead he adopted an apologetic tone and let the contradiction stand.[10]
- *Scripture's central revelatory focus on the drama of redemption presumes and is built upon a foundation of material regarding the nature of the human person.* We affirm that the Bible is an important source of information about how God created and designed the human race. Without this information we are adrift in a world of less than satisfying anthropologies and psychologies. The biblical picture of human nature is not only an important component of God's revelation to us, but it also is useful in knowing how to understand and process information coming to us from current secular research.
- *The biblical perspective on the nature of humans should be of interest to those outside the discipline of theology.* Delitzsch hoped that his work would attract the attention of "inquirers into natural science and philosophy."[11] While we would not presume that our current work will make a large impact on secular researchers, we do agree with Delitzsch that anyone interested in understanding human na-

---

9. Ibid., viii.
10. Ibid., 24.
11. Ibid., viii.

ture ought to consider seriously the perspective contained in ancient sources such as the Christian Scriptures. A historical perspective can enrich one's approach, which too often is impaired if we are only aware of current or contemporary information.

- *Psychological controversy rages both within the church and in the academic arena, and Christians need to be informed about these substantive issues.* Delitzsch worked in a context of controversies swirling about within the Roman Catholic Church and within nascent psychology. He wrote that psychological literature dealing with these controversies is "deserving of consideration, both old and recent."[12] We agree. Doing theology in our own small corner of the world while trying to ignore the great social science debates and competing claims around us is both unwise and dangerous for the future of the church. Christianity makes eminent intellectual sense, but we must articulate its credibility to a skeptical world if we as Christians want to participate in these important discussions.

- *We need to investigate the depths of Scripture in an intelligent and exegetically careful manner.* Delitzsch regarded the creeds of the church as providing a restraining barrier but not a circumscribing measure guiding his work. For him, the creeds helped establish for his enquiries a mean between a false bondage and a false freedom. In contemporary terms, we similarly feel that the theological convictions of contemporary evangelicalism provide for us a legitimate context in which to do our work, a climate that provides both freedom and limits.

- *The book of Holy Scripture and the book of nature are both part of God's revelation to us, although Scripture is the primary authority on all matters it addresses.* We concur with Delitzsch's approach to special revelation (the Bible) and to natural or general revelation (creation). He included in his work information from physiology, empirical psychology, and medical psychology (academic disciplines of his day). Delitzsch reminded his readers that we find truth in the book of Holy Scripture and "empirical facts which have a biblical relation and require biblical examination" in the book of nature.[13] God still expects us to read and understand the message He has

---

12. Ibid., ix.
13. Ibid., 19.

sought to communicate to us in both the book of Scripture and the book of nature. We are told to explore His message of special revelation (2 Tim. 3:14–16) and also to learn the lessons of general revelation (Ps. 19; Rom. 1:19–21). Nowhere in the Bible are we told not to investigate God's creation.

- *Delitzsch opposed the position that "biblical views ought to be modeled according to the results of natural science" or the latter according to the former.*[14] Delitzsch was careful not to collapse the teachings of one discipline into the categories of the other. We too believe that the integrity of both disciplines should be respected and that both should be allowed to speak with their own voices. In our day, both theology and psychology have important material to contribute to the public debates regarding the nature of the human person; and we wish to facilitate the message that comes from both of these disciplines. We seek to avoid a theologized psychology as well as a psychologized theology.

- *Delitzsch was aware that his approach might not be the final word on the subject.* We also want to assure our readers that, while we are confident that the positions we take throughout this book are defensible, we do not expect every reader to agree with every one of our conclusions. We do hope, though, that our approach might be at least considered by those who come to different conclusions.

- *Delitzsch invited his readers to watch for nondemonstrable fancies that might creep in to his work, to dismiss them, and to consider the clearer passages in his work as atonement for these weaknesses.* This also is our wish.

## THE CURRENT SCENE

The evangelical church of our day abounds with ignorance of, and indifference to, theology. To make matters worse, many evangelicals remain skeptical of, or opposed to, psychology. Many people question whether the church should be engaged in the integrative task of bringing these two disciplines together. We have devoted some space in this introduction to the example of Franz Delitzsch and his integrative work between the psychology of his day and the truths of Scripture as he understood them in order to challenge

---

14. Ibid., xiii.

the contemporary church with the appropriateness of this type of integration. The context in which Delitzsch worked bears some similarity to the current scene we face. One could observe within the church of his day a dead and nearly lifeless orthodoxy and a "miserable ignorance of natural science."[15] People "had no eyes to see clearly and without prejudice the rays of truth which shone outside the range of their own confessions of faith."[16]

The integration of psychology with theology is not a new invention of twentieth-century Christian psychology. It is not a diversion promoted by those who would seek to undermine the integrity of Bible-based faith. It is not the first step toward heresy and unfaithfulness to God's Word. Instead, it is a time-honored task of the church that predates the modern movement of psychology and that has engaged the minds and hearts of countless of our predecessors in the faith. "In a real sense there has never been a period when science and theology have not been in dialogue. The reflections of such significant figures as Augustine and Aquinas were as much influenced by the 'science' of their day as were later thinkers. . . ."[17]

Psychology meanwhile has increasingly come under the influence of postmodern thought. This new paradigm presents us with many challenges, such as the attack it makes on the possibility of propositional forms of truth. But in other ways the postmodern mind-set provides a context for integration in the twenty-first century that is at least open to the idea of religion and to the possibility of its importance and relevance. Rychlak admits that the study of humanity must explore concepts that exist beyond the limits imposed by engineering and medicine. "This realm of 'something beyond' has been implied whenever people refer to topics like religion, mysticism, spirituality, emotionality, or simply faith. Such attributions suggest to me that there is a side to human nature that is impossible to explain in the hard sciences and materialistic philosophies of our time."[18] Our hope is that Christians will be present in this arena to represent the truths of God's Word as this postmodern openness to things of the spirit conducts its work in the public sphere.

---

15. Ibid., 7.
16. Ibid.
17. G. R. Peterson, *Minding God: Theology and the Cognitive Sciences* (Minneapolis, Minn.: Fortress, 2003), 13.
18. J. H. Rychlak, *The Human Image in Postmodern America* (Washington, D.C.: American Psychological Association, 2003), xii.

Meanwhile science continues to make substantial progress in understanding human systems related to psychological process. Alexander reminds us that every indication points to substantial scientific gains in the decades to come, advances that will raise questions many scientists by themselves are very ill-equipped to answer.[19] Science is increasingly laying "bare our biological constitution."[20] As more and more of these secrets of creation are uncovered, some Christians will be tempted to retreat in fear or threat. But we must not abandon the task facing us as people of faith. Again, will informed Christians be prepared to advance biblically based, theologically informed perspectives into the debate? If not, we will again face the prospect of losing our voice in the academic issues our generation and the next will surely face.

## NATURAL (GENERAL) REVELATION

Athanasius (c. 296–373), bishop of Alexandria, is one example of an early church father who recognized the value of studying nature and all of creation for the purpose of learning what God intends for us to know about His purposes and character. In his treatise *Against the Heathen,* Athanasius affirmed that we see God's sovereignty and oneness in the order, proportion, and arrangement of creation.[21] "Creation, as though in written characters, declares in a loud voice, by its order and harmony, its own Lord and Creator."[22] Based on the teachings of Romans 1:20 and Acts 14:15, Athanasius was convinced that creation displays order because the Creator has implanted it there. "For often the artist even when not seen is known by his works."[23] To this list of what we can learn about God from carefully observing creation, John Calvin (1509–64) adds God's eternality, goodness, power, and wisdom.[24] The knowledge we can gain from observing creation is available,

---

19. D. Alexander, *Rebuilding the Matrix: Science and Faith in the 21st Century* (Grand Rapids: Zondervan, 2003), 7.

20. Alexander, *Rebuilding the Matrix,* 472. Franz Delitzsch was uncharacteristically pessimistic as he looked ahead. He realized that science had uncovered the secrets of human vision by tracing it to the retina at the back of the eye, but he declared that "it can go no further." (Delitzsch, *System of Biblical Psychology,* 22). In this judgment, of course, he was wrong.

21. Athanasius, Bishop of Alexandria, "Against the Heathen," in *NPNF*[2], 4:24 (3.38.1–2).

22. Ibid., 4:22 (3.34.4).

23. Ibid., 4:22 (3.35.1).

24. John Calvin, *Institutes of the Christian Religion,* ed. John J. McNeill; trans. Ford Lewis Battles, 2 vols., LCC, vols. 20–21 (Philadelphia: Westminster, 1960), 1:69–71 (1.5.6–7).

said Calvin, to believer and nonbeliever alike. The secrets of creation belong to God, but those that are revealed in Creation are there for humans to
analyze and learn from.[25]

Ironically, many Christians can accept this line of argument with regard
to those parts of creation declared "good" by the Creator (the planetary
system, the rotation of the earth, and so forth) but have a difficult time
applying the same argument to that part of creation declared "very good"
(the human race) by the same Creator. Studying the human person to discover the orderliness and harmony that exists in neurologic functions, cognitive processes, and the operation of the human brain (mind) will yield a
testimony to God's sovereignty and oneness every bit as powerful as the
witness of the rest of nature.

Scripture affirms that Athanasius was correct. The Bible claims that God's
covenants are as sure and certain as are the fixed orders of creation, and
that these evidences of God's power are expressions of God's wisdom. Wisdom was the Master Craftsperson or Artisan that was present at creation to
implant "natural cause-effect laws, boundaries, and overall structure to the
natural order (Prov. 8)."[26] "God's wisdom not only creates but is itself im-
printed upon and embedded within nature as its pattern, way, and dynamic
law-like structure of things."[27] Thus God makes known principles for living
well in propositional form (such as the book of Proverbs) and in the structure of the organic and inorganic created world (the subject matter explored
by the natural and human sciences). "The Old Testament sage is convinced
one can discover facts about values from facts about nature, particularly
from facts about human behavioral, interpersonal, and intrapsychic phenomena."[28] Living in harmony with this discovered wisdom is essential for
the wise person and provides a means whereby people can avoid the self-
injury that inevitably comes from the pursuit of foolishness, the opposite
of wisdom. One example of the sage's admonition is found in Proverbs
24:30–34. Here the sage makes an observation about a human behavioral

---

25. Eugene T. Mayhew, "God's Use of General Revelation in His Response to Job: A Critique of 2000 Years of Interpretation in Judaism and Christianity" (paper presented at
   the annual meeting of the Evangelical Theological Society, Santa Clara, California).
26. John Coe, "Why Biblical Counseling Is Unbiblical" (unpublished manuscript,
   1991), 17.
27. Ibid., 18.
28. Ibid., 12.

pattern with its problematic underlying motivation and the consequences of this pattern:

> I passed by the field of one who was lazy,
>     by the vineyard of a stupid person;
> and see, it was all overgrown with thorns;
>     the ground was covered with nettles,
>     and its stone wall was broken down.
> Then I saw and considered it; I looked and received instruction.
> A little sleep, a little slumber, a little folding of the hands to rest,
>     and poverty will come upon you like a robber,
>     and want, like an armed warrior. (NRSV)

In Proverbs 24, the sage reveals his methodology for pursuing wisdom as one would attempt to discover silver (cf. Prov. 2:1–4). He first utilized keen observation (24:30–31) followed by reflection upon what he observed (24:32). "As a member of the school of sages he ventures out into the natural order of things—with Scriptures in hand and God in mind—in order to discern the wisdom available as well in natural and human phenomena."[29] As the heavens shout out these wordless messages about the character of God, "Nature drenches consciousness with an awareness of God. Interestingly, most of us are standing in this downpour and hardly seem to notice it."[30]

The following caution must be noted with respect to natural, or general, revelation's contribution to our knowledge of the human person, particularly its nature and destiny. The truth content mediated by general revelation proves less perspicuous in these regards than the truth content mediated by special revelation. Thus disciplines that build largely on the former are exposed to varying degrees of error. The Swiss theologian Emil Brunner offers a helpful insight here in his "law of closeness of relation," which states: "The nearer anything lies to . . . man's relation to God and the being of the person, the greater is the disturbance of rational knowledge due to sin; the farther away anything lies from this center, the less is the disturbance felt, and the less difference is there between knowing as a believer or as an unbeliever."[31] The principle inherent in Brunner's law infers that disciplines such

---

29. Ibid., 29.
30. John Coe, "Natural Revelation, God Images, and Psychopathology: The Unsympathetic Voice of Creation" (unpublished manuscript, 1995), 3.
31. Emil Brunner, *Revelation and Reason* (Philadelphia, Pa.: Westminster, 1946), 383.

as psychology and philosophy—that deal with core issues of the human person—contain insightful truths mixed with misjudgments or errors. This means that the pronouncements of these disciplines must be carefully evaluated in the light of authoritative Scripture insofar as it addresses such issues. Our task as responsible investigators is to welcome all that is true in psychology (or any other discipline) while rejecting what is inconsistent with biblical teaching.

## STYLE OF INTEGRATION

Peterson suggests three possible styles of integration when considering theology and the cognitive sciences (of which psychology is one).[32] The first is *reduction,* reducing one completely into the categories of the other in either a friendly or hostile manner. For obvious reasons we reject this approach. The second style is *challenge,* calling things in one discipline into question from the perspective of the other discipline. This style of challenge exists within the evangelical world, mainly in the form of critiquing psychology with scriptural principles but doing little else with the findings of this social science.[33] We can find many examples in the church of people who take the following view: "Scientists are viewed as dangerous meddlers, wresting secrets from nature that are best left well alone, playing God as they pry into the sequence of the human genome and uncover the fundamental forces that hold the universe together."[34] The third model Peterson suggests is using the cognitive sciences as a lens through which to view theology or using theology as a lens through which to view the cognitive sciences. The lens model is superior to the first two, but it too ultimately proves unsatisfactory since the integration involved is minimal and incomplete.

We suggest a fourth approach in the methodology we have used in writing this book: *engagement.* We think germane and relevant information flows out of the work of both theology and psychology when we come to

---

32. Peterson, *Minding God,* 18.
33. For information about integrative challenge and conflict, see J. R. Beck and J. W. Banks, "Christian Anti-Psychology Sentiment: Hints of an Historical Analogue," *Journal of Psychology and Theology* 20 (1992): 3–10; J. R. Beck, "Questioning the Intermediate State: A Case Study in Integrative Conflict," *Journal of Psychology and Christianity* 10 (1991): 24–35; and J. R. Beck, "*Sola Scriptura:* Then and Now," *Journal of Psychology and Christianity* 16 (1997): 293–302.
34. Alexander, *Rebuilding the Matrix,* 7.

the task of understanding the human person. We need to lay out data from both sources, compare and contrast them, and seek to develop means of helping people through the various branches of ministry. These means must be in harmony with the clear teachings of the Word of God and must represent responsible use of scientific data that emerges from psychology. The two disciplines are different: theology is ancient and changes little; psychology is recent and constantly in a change mode. Both contain a vast amount of information about humans. We are wise to use trustworthy material from both disciplines in our quest to understand and thereby serve people better.

In many ways, an engagement style of integration allows each discipline to do what it does best. Psychology continues to display a restless impulse to understand human behavior and function more accurately and more completely. Theology serves as a masterful guiding and corrective force. "Theism provides a unified worldview that does a remarkably effective job in providing a matrix for science in which the validity of scientific knowledge is justified and in which the fruits of scientific discoveries are channeled in ways that affirm human value, justice, and care for the environment."[35] Delitzsch likewise noted the value of theology to enrich psychology. When the Reformation opened up new opportunities for inquiry, "Psychology could then bring its traditional store of knowledge into the light of Scripture, and thus it advanced into a new phase."[36]

The engagement style of integration as we envision it does not create new and permanent amalgamations of truth. Instead it builds working alliances between the findings of science and the teachings of the Bible—alliances that can foster effective ministry with people. We propose maintaining these working alliances for as long as they are useful rather than enshrining them as fairly permanent paradigms of truth. Psychology changes too quickly for such a style of integration to make any sense. No doubt some of these working alliances that we build will be useful for a considerable length of time; others will lose their usefulness as better data emerge from psychology. Delitzsch gave his readers an example of the wisdom of this approach. If we should find in the Bible indications supporting the theory of magnetism or nervous fluids, and if we should integrate this biblical "support" with nineteenth-century understanding of

---

35. Ibid., 472.
36. Delitzsch, *System of Biblical Psychology*, 6.

magnetism and nervous fluids, what are we to do when science abandons these approaches and moves on to other theoretical approaches?[37]

## ORGANIZATION OF THIS BOOK

Franz Delitzsch organized his exploration of biblical teachings about the human person around a salvation history outline: creation, fall, redemption, and eternal state. This type of arrangement would have given us a convenient way of organizing our material from the Bible by weaving related psychological topics into the redemptive outline. Or we could have selected an outline that reflects the organization and branches of the academic discipline of psychology: clinical, cognitive, developmental, neuropsychological, and so forth. In this instance we could have woven into the psychological outline relevant material from the Bible. Instead of using either of these approaches, however, we developed a list of four major categories that are directly related to the study of the human but do not directly come from either discipline: origin and destiny, substance and identity, function and behavior, and relationality and community. In each of these four parts, we have written a chapter that deals with biblical, historical, and theological considerations (Bruce Demarest) and a chapter dealing with the psychological dimensions of that topic (James R. Beck).

Separating the material as we have done in the book into theological and psychological chapters respects the natural separation seen in academia. We might wish that the two disciplines were more fully integrated in seminaries and secular graduate schools, but the reality is that they are primarily separate in the academic world at the present time. The separation respects the differences inherent in each discipline as it pursues its work, and it ensures that we will give as comprehensive treatment of each category as we can. We do not suggest that each discipline is of equal authority or of equal truth-value. Theology with its base in special revelation is by definition distinct from psychology with its roots in general revelation. But each discipline can make a substantial contribution to the discussion table where the topic is the nature of the human person. And we urge our readers to give serious consideration to both types of input to this discussion.

Readers will quickly realize a distinction between how we have composed the theological chapters and how we have composed the psychological

---

37. Ibid., 21.

chapters. In the former instance, the material seeks to summarize the vast range of theological, historical, and biblical material spanning both scriptural Testaments and numerous centuries of scholarly work. By taking this approach, we feel that we can summarize material regarding the human person as it reflects a conservative, or orthodox, understanding of the Bible. In contrast, the psychological chapters primarily focus on contemporary approaches to these four topical areas. We do not seek to trace the development of these psychological concepts as they emerged from philosophy and as nineteenth- and twentieth-century scholarship shaped and developed these ideas. In other words, the theological chapters give us a panoramic view of the material, whereas the psychological chapters give us a snapshot view. We trust that this distinction will not disorient readers but will help them as they gather material for the integrative task.

At the conclusion of each part, we have written a brief integrative essay giving our conclusions as to how the two disciplines relate to each other in that area. We hope that the conclusions we draw will inform our readers as well as illustrate to them how they can build their own integration of the material. We are quite convinced, though, that the only way to approach the integrative task properly is to set forth material from both the disciplines as completely as we can so that we have a comprehensive pool of data from which to create our integration. As readers will frequently see throughout this book, not all of the material covered in either one of the disciplines is reciprocated in the other. But there are many important areas of overlap that we attempt to handle in our integrative essays.

We envision this book to be a handbook for those interested in a Christian view of human persons. We have sought to document our material carefully so that readers can pursue particular areas of interest for further study. Embarking on an integrative approach to the task of understanding humans is indeed both challenging and intimidating. In the words of our distant mentor, Franz Delitzsch, "May God bless our going out and our coming in" as we journey on this road of inquiry.[38]

---

38. Ibid., 25.

# PART 1

# THE ORIGIN *and* DESTINY *of the* HUMAN PERSON

# CHAPTER 1

# ORIGIN *and* DESTINY *in* THEOLOGICAL PERSPECTIVE

PART 1 OF THIS WORK ADDRESSES matters of origin and destiny foundational to the anthropological issues that will be treated in parts 2–4 (human nature, functioning, and relationships and community). We humans cannot adequately comprehend our present without understanding our past and our future. The core concern of human value and worth is profoundly related to where we came from and what is our end. Christians believe that these crucial points are addressed on the pages of inspired Scripture. Indeed, the Bible presents the human person as created by God "a little lower than the heavenly beings" (Ps. 8:5) and intended for a glorious destiny.

## BEGINNING OF HUMAN LIFE *(BIOS)*

Life for an organism involves the ability to metabolize, grow, react to stimuli, and reproduce. Clearly the zygote-embryo-fetus of a woman possesses biological life. But is the unborn a human life? Is the zygote-embryo-fetus properly a person, or human being? The Fourteenth Amendment to the United States Constitution states, "Nor shall any state deprive any person of life, liberty, or property without due process of law, nor deny to any person within its jurisdiction that equal protection of the laws." Then what does the Constitution understand to be a person? When does personhood begin? Abortion, for example, would be permitted by the Constitution only if the zygote-embryo-fetus is not a human person.

## Historical Perspectives

Christian and non-Christian thinkers have defined human life's beginning in quite different ways.

### Human Life Begins During the Gestation Period Following Conception

The *late ensoulment* or *delayed animation* view holds that life begins at some threshold point during gestation. The implication is that the soul is infused into the developing physical material following conception but prior to birth. Often this infusion was identified with the time of "quickening" or physical animation or with the first brain wave activity when the major organs initially develop.

Stoic philosophers claimed that the soul enters the fetus before the time of viability. "They say the human seed is deposited *ex-concubiter* in the womb and then starts to form like bread rising in an oven. Somewhere along the way the soul drops in."[1] Aristotle (384–322 B.C.) also held to late ensoulment by drawing a distinction between the unformed and the formed fetus; only the formed fetus is a proper human person. Aristotle figured that forming, including the development of a rational soul, occurs at forty days for a male fetus and at ninety days for a female fetus.[2] His ethics allowed for taking the life of an unformed fetus. Plato (428–347 B.C.) went farther (see p. 30).

Augustine (354–430), as we shall see in chapter 3, vacillated on the soul's origin. Following Aristotle, he generally distinguished between the unformed and the formed, animate human embryo.[3] For Augustine, aborting a formed fetus is murder. Destruction of an unformed fetus, although immoral, is a lesser crime. He insisted that even the unformed fetus is a highly valued work of God. Augustine was reluctant to specify the time at which the fetus becomes a human being.[4]

---

1. Robert L. Wise, *Quest for the Soul: Our Search for Deeper Meaning* (Nashville: Nelson, 1996), 171.
2. See Michael J. Gorman, *Abortion and the Early Church* (Downers Grove, Ill.: InterVarsity, 1982), 22.
3. Ibid., 70.
4. Augustine, *On Marriage and Concupiscence*, NPNF², 5:271 [1.17]; cf. idem, *Faith, Hope and Charity*, ACW, 3:83–84[23].

Also drawing on Aristotle's thought, Thomas Aquinas (1225–1274) distinguished between *potential* humanness and *actual* humanness. The difference between the two is an *essential* difference, not merely an *accidental* one. Aristotle judged that the substantial, rational soul can be infused only in a well-organized body. Hence the soul is implanted in the fetus, making it human, at the time of quickening. Aquinas, with Augustine, allowed for abortions during the first trimester. Although some later Roman Catholic theologians adopted Aquinas's view, the church officially has discarded it.

Canadian biologist and ethicist N. J. Berrill judges that the rudiments of personhood can be identified by eight weeks, when all organs are present in rudimentary form. "By the end of the second month . . . we can say with some assurance that the person in the womb is present, with all the basic equipment and some sensitivity, although with a long, long way to go to be fully human."[5] According to Berrill, "It is the human birthright to be born whole in body, brain and senses."[6] Thus if a fetus is discovered to be malformed, its termination is justified.

Berrill defends abortion on other grounds, including the woman's unwillingness to bear a child and as a response to planet overcrowding.

The late professor of theology and ethics at Fuller Seminary, Lewis B. Smedes (1921–2002), held that the fetus is *"only* potential" human life and not a proper human person. "Fetal life is person-becoming life."[7] The fetus gradually develops into a full-fledged human being over time. "The fetal life gradually develops from the fertilized egg toward personal life as the organism becomes more complex and enters ever more complex relationships with its environment."[8] Precisely when the fetus becomes a person is obscure. Smedes, however, allows for abortion during the first six weeks of pregnancy, since "no one can reasonably be sure that the fetus is a person during the first six weeks."[9] Abortion, however, should be severely restricted between weeks seven and twelve. "This allows ample time for . . . the discovery of serious—even monstrous—defects in the fetus."[10] Abortion is permissible during this period for reasons of threat to the mother's physical health, conception by rape, or identification of serious congenital disease

---

5. N. J. Berrill, *The Person in the Womb* (New York: Dodd, Mead and Co., 1968), 45–46.
6. Ibid., 5.
7. Lewis B. Smedes, *Mere Morality* (Grand Rapids: Eerdmans, 1983), 134.
8. Ibid., 132.
9. Ibid., 143.
10. Ibid., 144.

in the fetus. Insists Smedes, "Abortion after the third month should be a crime."[11]

## Human Life Begins at Birth

The view that human life does not begin until birth, posits that transition with the first breath of the newborn. Christian theologians who affirm this position draw a parallel between God's action of breathing the breath of life into Adam (Gen. 2:7) and the first breath of a newborn baby.

Plato judged that the fetus becomes a human person upon leaving the womb, when the umbilical cord is cut and the newborn takes its first breath. Plato allowed for the killing at birth of deformed infants and offspring of inferior parents.[12]

The U.S. Supreme Court in its 1973 *Roe v. Wade* decision [410 U.S. 113 (1973)] adopted this position. The question before the United States Supreme Court in the *Roe v. Wade* case was the following: *Is the unborn a human person entitled to protection under the Fifth and Fourteenth Amendments?* The court's seven-to-two opinion, written by Justice Harry Blackmun, states that the term *person,* as used in the U.S. Constitution, applies only postnatally. The court ruled that the fetus is a potential person that becomes a fully human person at birth. Since the Constitution does not protect those who are not "persons in the whole sense," the unborn are excluded from protection against abortion. The court further declared that it is unconstitutional for any state to forbid abortion during the first trimester of life. Whether a life should be terminated thereafter should be a medical decision based on health considerations, not a prerogative of government. Abortion is permissible even in the third trimester "where it is necessary, in appropriate medical judgment, for the preservation of the *life* and *health* of the mother" (emphasis added).[13] Since the latter in practice can be interpreted to include a range of physical, emotional, and familial factors, *Roe v. Wade* came to guarantee abortion on demand.

Likewise, Canada's Supreme Court in 1988 decided that "a child becomes a human being" only after it is born—when the umbilical cord is cut and

---

11. Ibid.

12. Plato, *Republic,* in *Great Books of the Western World,* ed. Mortimer J. Adler, 2d ed., 60 vols. (Chicago: Encyclopedia Britannica, Inc, 1990), 6:362. [bk. 5, no. 460].

13. *Roe v. Wade,* 410 U.S. 113 (1973), 165.

the child no longer is part of its mother's body.[14] Abortion had been banned in the provinces in 1869 and made a criminal offense in 1892. A 1988 decision declared the country's abortion law unconstitutional, in violation of Canada's Charter of Rights and Freedoms, which upholds the woman's right over her own body. Similarly, Francis Crick (1916–2004), who won the Nobel Prize in biology for DNA research, states, "We should wait until children are at least two days old before we legally declare them persons; by that time we will be able to certify that they are healthy."[15] A proponent of eugenics, Crick wants to ensure that the newborn is free from physical deformities and genetic diseases before declaring it to be a human person.

The social ethicist Joseph Fletcher (1905–1991) judges that conception begins biological life, or makes the fetus a member of the species *homo sapiens.* The developing fetus, however, is only a potential person. According to Fletcher, the fetus lacks two essential indicators of personhood, some "minimal level of intelligence" and "individual or separate existence."[16] Fletcher avers that a life is not a human person unless it has an IQ of at least twenty (or possibly 40) on the Stanford-Binet scale. A fetus does not meet this condition, nor does a grossly senile person. "Humans without some minimum of intelligence or mental capacity are not persons, no matter how many of their organs are active, no matter how spontaneous their living processes are."[17] According to this criterion, an animal theoretically could be a human being. Fletcher adds other qualities that define personhood, including "curiosity, affection, self-awareness and self-control, memory, purpose, conscience."[18]

Fletcher favors Plato's view of the beginning of life: "The nearest thing to a specifiable 'moment' for *becoming* human is when the fetus is respirated after birth—that reflexive and explosive gulp of air starting the lungs to work."[19] Since the life in the uterus is not human, Fletcher claims that its termination is not murder. Thus abortion, infanticide, and euthanasia represent merely the taking of biological life, not acts of homicide.

---

14. See http://www.knightsite.com/kc9496/unborn17.htm (accessed March 27, 2004).
15. Cited in Paul B. Fowler, *Abortion: Toward an Evangelical Consensus* (Portland, Ore.: Multnomah, 1987), 34.
16. Joseph F. Fletcher, *The Ethics of Genetic Control* (Garden City, N.Y.: Anchor Press, 1974), 171.
17. Ibid., 137.
18. Joseph F. Fletcher, *Humanhood: Essays in Biomedical Ethics* (Buffalo, N.Y.: Prometheus, 1979), 12–15.
19. Fletcher, *Ethics of Genetic Control,* 171; cf. idem, *Humanhood,* 136.

### Human Life Begins Post-Birth When Functioning at Some Minimal Level

Others wait even after birth for the point of declaration of personhood. Advocates of the *functioning person theory* generally distinguish between a human and a person. A person has a life that attains a certain level of physical, mental, and social functionality. Within the developmental continuum, proponents argue, time is required for a human to develop the capacities that constitute personhood. Consequently, a fetus and a newborn are potential, not actual, persons. Many proponents of this view subscribe to the naturalistic evolutionary thinking that *homo sapiens* have evolved over time into intelligent animals. Functionality or social value constitutes the litmus test of species personhood.

Philosopher of religion Charles Hartshorne (1897–2000) judges that a person is a living thing that speaks, reasons, exercises moral judgment, and has personal relations. Functioning at this level requires months if not years to achieve. Prior to attaining this level of functioning, the infant is less than a human person. Thus taking the life of a fetus, a prehuman infant, or a hopelessly senile child or adult is not murder.

Michael Tooley, the bioethicist and animal rights advocate, similarly says that the unborn is merely a *potential* person. According to Tooley, a *human* and a *person* are not automatically the same. A human being is simply a member of the biological species *Homo sapiens*. A person, however, possesses self-consciousness or an enduring sense of self ("the property of being an enduring subject of non-momentary interests"[20]). Since a newborn baby does not possess the concept of a continuing self, it is not a person. Its destruction, therefore, is morally acceptable. Tooley's conclusion is that "humans become quasi-persons at around three months" and full persons at approximately one year.[21] "New-born humans are neither persons nor even quasi-persons, and their destruction is in no way intrinsically wrong. At about the age of three months, however, they probably acquire properties that are morally significant, and that make it to some extent intrinsically wrong to destroy them."[22]

---

20. Michael Tooley, *Abortion and Infanticide* (Oxford: Clarendon Press, 1983), 302; cf. 419.
21. Ibid., 424.
22. Ibid., 411–12.

Positing the equality of animals and persons, Tooley believes that the killing of adult animals, like the killing of mature persons, is an act of murder.

The Australian philosopher and founder of the animal liberation movement, Peter Singer, rejects the Judeo-Christian worldview, including belief in the human person's creation as *imago Dei*. The traditional Western ethic has collapsed and must be replaced, he believes, with a more pragmatic system, based on science. Singer distinguishes between a human and a person, the former being a member of the species *Homo sapiens* and the latter being a living entity that possesses qualities such as rationality, autonomy, and self-awareness. Men and women belong to the same family and genus as chimpanzees, orangutans, and gorillas, differing from these animals in degree, not in kind.[23] Singer asserts, "Around fourteen days after conception, once the possibility of the embryo dividing into twins has passed, there exists an individual being who is alive and human."[24] But the fetus at this stage is no more valuable than a nonhuman animal at a similar stage of development. A newborn infant likewise is a living being or a human, but not a person.[25] Thus the killing of a fetus or a newborn is not an immoral or a culpable act. About twenty-eight days after delivery, however, the newborn becomes rational and self-aware and hence can be said to be a person with a right to life. "A period of twenty-eight days after birth might be allowed before an infant is accepted as having the same rights to live as others. This . . . would allow a couple to decide that it is better not to continue with a life that has begun very badly."[26] He adds, "We are less disturbed at the destruction of a fetus we have never seen than at the death of a being we can all see, hear and cuddle."[27]

## Human Life Begins at Conception

At the other pole are those who believe in *immediate animation,* that human life begins at conception. This has been the view of most Christians throughout church history. In this perspective, God's act of forming a person in His own image is not a process but an event that occurs at conception, or

---

23. Peter Singer, *Rethinking Life and Death: The Collapse of Our Traditional Ethics* (New York: St. Martin's Press, 1995), 94, 130, 178, 189.
24. Ibid., 105.
25. Ibid., 210.
26. Ibid., 218.
27. Peter Singer, *Practical Ethics* (Cambridge: Cambridge University Press, 1993), 138.

fertilization. Proponents insist that functions of thinking, willing, emoting, and relating need not be fully developed for the zygote, embryo, or fetus to be a human person. Both the creationist and traducian views of the soul's origin (see chap. 4) support this conclusion.

Strongly opposing the common practice of abortion in ancient Greco-Roman culture, the early church regarded abortion as murder and its perpetrators as worthy of everlasting punishment. *The Didache* or *The Teaching of the Twelve Apostles* (an undated early Christian handbook that could be from as early as the late first century A.D.), commanded, "Thou shalt not murder a child by abortion nor kill that which is begotten."[28]

Athenagoras of Athens (late second century), who defended Christians against accusations of murder, cannibalism, and other crimes, judged that the fetus in the womb is a living person and the object of God's special care. Women who induce abortions with drugs must answer to God for murder.[29] The *Letter of Barnabas* (c. 200) espouses a similar position: "Thou shalt not slay the child by procuring abortion; nor, again, shalt thou destroy it after it is born."[30] It adds, the crooked way of darkness that merits eternal death includes those "who are murderers of children, destroyers of the workmanship of God."[31]

Clement of Alexandria (c. 150–c. 215) appealed to the phenomenon of John the Baptist leaping in Elizabeth's womb (Luke 1:41) to claim that the fetus is a human person developing according to God's plan. As a result, taking the life of a fetus is wanton murder.[32]

A lawyer by profession, Tertullian (160–220) refuted the Roman legal view that the fetus is merely an appendage to the mother and not a human being. The great apologist held that the body and soul of a human person are formed simultaneously through the union of sperm and egg at the moment of conception (a view known as *traducianism*—see chap. 4). Tertullian wrote, "The embryo . . . becomes a human being from the moment when its formation is completed."[33]

Once conceived, Tertullian taught that the human person's body and soul develop together. "That power of the soul which contains all its native potenti-

---

28. *The Didache* 2 [*ANF,* 7:377].

29. Athenagoras, *A Plea for the Christians* 35 [*ANF,* 2:147 ].

30. *Letter of Barnabas* 19.5 [*ANF,* 1:148].

31. Ibid., 20.2 [*ANF,* 1:149].

32. See Gorman, *Abortion and the Early Church,* 52–53.

33. Tertullian, *On the Soul* 37.2 [*ANF,* 3:217].

alities gradually develops along with the body, without any change in the initial substance which it received by being breathed into the man in the beginning."[34] Tertullian stressed that the fetus, while not fully formed and entirely dependent on its mother, is a developing human being or person in process.

Naturally, Tertullian deplored the act of aborting the human fetus in the womb: "We are not permitted to destroy even the fetus in the womb, as long as blood is being drawn to form a human being. . . . It is a human being and one who is to be a man, for the whole fruit is already present in the seed."[35]

In his essay *On the Soul,* Tertullian described in some detail the instruments used to perform an abortion (e.g., "circular knife," "blunt hook," and "brazen needle")—the use of which he judged to be commission of "murder within the womb." He observed that all the doctors witnessing an abortion "were convinced that a living thing had been conceived" and "that they all felt pity for the poor child who must be killed in the womb."[36] Tertullian insisted that abortion is homicide, except in the case of a direct threat to the life of the mother.

The *Constitutions of the Holy Apostles,* a manual of Christian life and conduct composed in Syria about the year 380, testifies that the fetus possesses a soul and thus is a human person. "Thou shalt not slay thy child by causing an abortion, nor kill that which is begotten. For everything that is shaped, and hath received a soul from God, if it be slain, shall be avenged, as being unjustly destroyed."[37]

John Chrysostom (347–407), bishop of Constantinople and a powerful preacher, insisted that the unborn fetus is a human person and the object of God's care. The act of taking the life of the fetus is murder subject to God's righteous punishment.[38]

Jerome (347–420) observed that Roman women who took sterilizing drugs to abort an unborn child were guilty of murdering a human being in the womb. "When they learn they are with child through sin, they practice abortion by the use of drugs. Frequently they die themselves and are brought before the rulers of the lower world guilty of three crimes: suicide, adultery against Christ, and murder of an unborn child."[39]

---

34. Ibid., 37.5 [*ANF,* 3:218].
35. Tertullian, *Apology* 9.8 [*ANF,* 3:25].
36. Tertullian, *On the Soul* 25.5 [*ANF,* 3:205].
37. *Constitutions of the Holy Apostles* 7.3 [*ANF,* 7:466].
38. John Chrysostom, *The Epistle to the Romans,* homily 24 [*NPNF*[2], 11:520].
39. Jerome, *Letter* 22.13 [ACW, 33:145]

The Protestant Reformers Martin Luther (1483–1546), Philip Melanchthon (1497–1560), and John Calvin judged that human life commences at conception, so the developing fetus is a human person. The Reformers believed that this view accords well with original sin and the depravity of the immaterial soul/spirit. Luther naively held that the male semen contains life and that the woman provides only nourishment for that life. For Luther, the male is the source of the fetal soul. The Reformers uniformly believed that abortion is an abomination in the sight of God.

The view that human life begins at conception became Roman Catholic dogma in 1869. Medieval theology upheld the Aristotelian and Thomistic distinction between the "unformed" and the "formed" fetus. Concerning current thinking, Daniel Callahan notes, "While some Catholic moralists are attempting to revive the earlier distinction between formed and the unformed fetus, the general trend in recent decades has been to eliminate the distinction and count as human the immediate product of conception."[40] The Roman Church officially holds that abortion at any point in the gestation period constitutes the killing of an innocent human being. The only permissible exceptions to abortion are an ectopic pregnancy or a cancerous uterus where priority is given to the life of the mother.

The *Catechism of the Catholic Church*,[41] the latest comprehensive promulgation of official Catholic dogma, contains statements regarding the beginning of the human person's existence:

- *2270:* Human life must be respected and protected absolutely from the moment of conception. From the first moment of his existence, a human being must be recognized as having the rights of a person—among which is the inviolable right of every innocent being to life [Jeremiah 1:5 and Psalm 139:15 are cited in support].
- *2274:* Since it must be treated from conception as a person, the embryo must be defended in its integrity, cared for, and healed, as far as possible, like any other human being.
- *2319:* Every human life, from the moment of conception until death, is sacred because the human person has been willed for its own sake in the image and likeness of the living and holy God.

40. Daniel Callahan, "The Roman Catholic Position," in *Abortion: A Reader,* ed. Lloyd Steffen (Cleveland, Ohio: Pilgrim Library of Ethics, 1996), 84.
41. *Catechism of the Catholic Church* (New York: Doubleday Image, 1995).

Within twentieth-century Protestantism, Karl Barth (1886–1968) insisted that personal existence begins at conception. "The unborn child is from the very first a child. It is still developing and has no independent life. But it is a man and not a thing, nor a mere part of the mother's body."[42] Barth added:

> The embryo has its own autonomy, its own brain, its own nervous system, its own blood circulation. If its life is affected by that of the mother, it also affects hers. It can have its own illnesses in which the mother has no part. Conversely, it may be quite healthy even though the mother is seriously ill. It may die while the mother continues to live. It may also continue to live after its mother's death, and be eventually saved by a timely operation on her dead body. In short, it is a human being in its own right.[43]

Concerning abortion, Barth said that "we must underline the fact that he who destroys germinating life kills a man and thus ventures the monstrous thing of decreeing concerning the life and death of a fellow human being, whose life is given by God."[44] The deliberate and wanton act of abortion, which violates the sanctity of human life, "is irrefutably seen to be sin, murder and transgression."[45]

Where one is forced to choose between sparing the life of the mother or the fetus, Barth agreed that the former should take precedence.

In their book *Whatever Happened to the Human Race?* evangelicals Francis Schaeffer (1912–1984) and pediatric surgeon C. Everett Koop also insist that human life begins at conception. "All that makes up the adult is present as the ovum and sperm are united—the whole genetic code."[46] Hence the destruction of the fetus any time after conception constitutes infanticide.

One among Protestant evangelicals who has changed positions is apologist Norman Geisler. In the 1970s he ventured that the embryo is not fully human, but only an undeveloped person. Personhood, he insisted, requires self-awareness and relational ability. Geisler later came to believe that human life begins when the male sperm fertilizes the ovum. "The Bible leaves

---

42. Karl Barth, *CD*, 4.3.415.
43. Ibid., 4.3.416.
44. Ibid.
45. Ibid., 4.3.419.
46. Francis Schaeffer and C. Everett Koop, *Whatever Happened to the Human Race?* (Old Tappan, N.J.: Revell, 1979), 41.

no doubt that the God who makes man in His image and likeness (Gen. 1:27) does this in the womb before birth." From conception onward, the unborn is "a tiny, growing human being," and self-awareness is no test for personhood.[47] Even before the zygote should split (twinning), it is properly human. "What takes place after conception is the growth and development of a particular human individual. The process this individual undergoes continues into infancy, childhood, adolescence, and adulthood."[48]

The Roman Catholic professor of philosophy at the University of Rhode Island, Stephen D. Schwarz, argues persuasively that personal existence begins with conception or at the moment the fertilization process ends (usually after twenty-four hours). The zygote and later the fetus, which develops at eleven or twelve weeks, possess the essential structure of human personhood—a structure that develops over time.

In response to those who argue that the zygote or fetus is not a person because it lacks self-consciousness, thinking, feeling, or a sense of moral obligation, Schwarz responds that the zygote and fetus is a person because it has the *capacity* for exercising these functions. Schwarz illustrates that an adult who is asleep, in a coma, or incapacitated by severe senility remains a human person while in such conditions of latent functioning. Likewise, a young child, whose intellectual, volitional, and moral functioning is far less developed than those of a college-educated adult, is nevertheless a human person. "Human life is a single continuum beginning at conception-fertilization, continuing through the time in the womb, entering a new phase at birth, and continuing from birth to death."[49] The fetus, infant, and adult differ only in degree of development and level of functioning.

Schwarz elaborates on the latter point:

> It is *being* a person that is crucial morally, not *functioning* as a person. The very existence and meaning of functioning as a person can have its basis only in the being of a person. It is because you have the being of a person that you can function as a person, al-

---

47. Norman L. Geisler, "The Bible, Abortion, and Common Sense," *Fundamentalist Journal*, May 1985, 25.

48. Francis J. Beckwith and Norman L. Geisler, *Matters of Life and Death* (Grand Rapids: Baker, 1991), 16.

49. Stephen D. Schwarz, *The Moral Question of Abortion* (Chicago: Loyola University Press, 1990), 81. Emphasis in original.

though you might fail to function as a person and still retain your full being as a person.[50]

Elsewhere he says, "Even a very severely abnormal or handicapped human being has the basic inherent capacity to function as a person. . . . The abnormality represents a hindrance to the actual working of this capacity, to its manifestations in actual functioning. It does not imply the absence of this capacity, as in a nonperson."[51]

## Biblical and Theological Perspectives

### *The Genesis Creation Narratives*

The Old Testament book of Genesis contains two distinct accounts of the creation of the human person. Genesis 1 describes the creation of the universe and "man" (*ʾādām*) in chronological order. Following the creation of light, atmosphere, seas, dry land, and lower forms of life, God on the "sixth day" created the first man from the stuff of the earth and formed the first woman from the side of the latter. This first creation account introduces the human person as the climax of God's creative work. Moreover, it affirms persons' unique identity and unsurpassed dignity as made in the likeness of God Himself. Consider the following, relevant texts from the early chapters of Genesis:

- *Genesis 1:26:* "Then God said, 'Let us make [*ʿāśâ*] man [*ʾādām*] in our image, in our likeness, and let them rule. . . .'" Only after earth was fitted as a suitable habitation did God by divine fiat create *ʾādām*, generic humanity. The word *then* marks the creation of *ʾādām* as something special. Created to resemble God, the human species is distinct from, and superior to, other creatures made on the same sixth day.
- *Genesis 1:27:* "So God [*ʾĕlōhîm*] created [*bārāʾ*] [the] man [*hāʾādām*] in his own image, in the image of God he created him; male [*zākār*] and female [*nᵉqēbâ*] he created them." This pivotal verse describes the creation of humankind as two sexes. Occurring some twenty

---

50. Ibid., 94.
51. Ibid., 97.

times in Genesis 1, *ᵉlōhîm* denotes the Creator God known to the nations. *Bārā*, used three times in this verse alone, is used exclusively of God's creative activity and signifies His work of creating something entirely new. The repeated affirmation that God created persons in His image signifies that both male and female possess a remarkable resemblance to Himself (see chap. 4) and thus are endowed with unparalleled dignity and worth.

- *Genesis 1:31:* "God saw all that he had made *[ᶜāśâ]*, and it was very good *[tôb]*." The descriptor, "very good," denotes that the entire creation, including human persons, perfectly conforms to the divine will and is ideally suited to the purpose for which God created it.

The second account of creation, recorded in Genesis 2, locates the human person at the center of the cosmos ("the heavens and the earth," v. 1) as the object of God's special consideration and favor. The divine Artisan formed the human person from the dust of the earth, breathed life into his material frame, and placed him in a plenteous garden to work it.

- *Genesis 2:7:* "The LORD God formed *[yāṣar]* man *[hāʾādām]* from the dust of the ground and breathed into his nostrils the breath of life *[nišmat ḥayyîm]*, and the man became a living being *[nepeš ḥayyâ]*." LORD *(Yahweh)*—the covenant-making God—formed the man from the materials of earth and animated his frame by an act of divine inbreathing. The verb *yāṣar* points to the divine potter (cf. Isa. 45:9; Jer. 18:6) who skillfully shaped the human person from the stuff of the earth (see Job 33:6). Notice in this verse the play on the words *human being (ʾādām)* and *ground (ʾādāmâ)*—from the common root *ʾdm*, meaning "be red." This underscores the human person's affinity to the earth. This connection is preserved in the Latin, in which *homo* ("man") is etymologically related to *humus* ("ground"). Although *nᵉšāmâ* ("breath") is also used of the life force that animates animals (Gen. 7:22), only in the case of man is there recorded "a direct transfer of the divine breath" that constitutes man "an independent spiritual I" and unique image of God.[52] The outcome of the divine inbreathing is that Adam "became a living being," which simply means that he came to

---

52. Walther Eichrodt, *Theology of the Old Testament*, 2 vols. (Philadelphia, Pa.: Westminster, 1961, 1967), 2:121.

life. Note the similarity of this verse to Job 33:4: "The Spirit of God has made me; the breath *[nᵉšāmâ]* of the Almighty gives me life." The apostle Paul offered the following summary reflections on Genesis 2:7: "The first man Adam became a living being" (1 Cor. 15:45a) and "The first man was of the dust of the earth" (v. 47a). God then placed the man in a luxurious garden where he enjoyed God's good gifts.

- *Genesis 2:18:* "The LORD God said, 'It is not good for the man to be alone. I will make *[ʿāśâ]* a helper suitable for him.'" Solitary Adam was in some respect incomplete without a female companion and helpmate. The animals Adam named could not meet his deepest need; only a complementary human being could complete him.

- *Genesis 2:21–24* describes the creation of the woman, Eve, out of Adam. Verse 22a reads, "Then the LORD God made a woman *[ʾiššâ]* from the rib he had taken out of the man *[hāʾādām]*." God created Eve not from a subhuman life form, but from Adam's side, which argues against the evolutionist's claim that the human race evolved from a subhuman ancestor. This verse also differentiates the female from the male within the unity of humankind, while implying the ontological equality of the man and the woman. Matthew Henry (1662–1714) expressed this point admirably. "Not made out of his head to top him, not out of his feet to be trampled upon by him, but out of his side to be equal with him, under his arm to be protected, and near his heart to be beloved."[53] With this act of forming the woman, creation reached its intended goal: *male and female as equal and complementary forms of human life.* The reference in verse 24 that Adam and Eve were "one flesh" signifies their profound psycho-spiritual-physical unity within the marriage relation.

- *Genesis 3:20:* "Adam named his wife Eve, because she would become the mother of all the living."

- *Genesis 5:1b–2:* "When God created *[bārāʾ]* man, he made *[ʿāśâ]* him in the likeness of God. He created them male and female" and blessed them. And when they were created, he "called them 'man.'" These verses, which three times employ the verb *bārāʾ*, offer a summary recapitulation of God's creation of humanity as male and female in a condition of perfect innocence.

---

53. Matthew Henry, *Commentary on the Whole Bible,* 6 vols. (Old Tappan, N.J.: Revell, n.d.), 1:20.

Rich in anthropomorphisms, the Genesis creation texts clearly teach that the first pair, the noblest expression of God's handiwork, came into being by a nonrepeated act of creation, not by a blind development from some primitive life form. The verbs that describe God's creative work confirm this conclusion: *make* (Gen. 1:26, 31; 2:18; 5:1; 6:7), *create* (1:27; 5:1, 2), and *form* (2:7). The first pair, of whom we read in the early chapters of Genesis, was the result of God's intentional design, not the outcome of blind adaptation to changing environmental forces. Furthermore, just as human beings are not self-originating, neither are they self-sustaining; they are totally dependent upon God for life. In addition, humans are not identical to God (*pantheism*) nor a part of God (*panentheism*), for what is made differs from the One who made it (see Hos. 11:9). Although uniquely fashioned in God's image, the human person as *imago Dei* profoundly resembles God in several important respects (see chap. 4, pp. 147-54). These foundational truths from the creation records unravel the enigma of human beings and their relation to the universe.

Other biblical creation texts include Job 33:6; Psalms 8:5; 100:3; 119:73; Proverbs 22:2; Isaiah 64:8; Matthew 19:4 (cf. Mark 10:6); Acts 17:25–26; and Colossians 1:16.

Scripture indicates that God took great delight in His creative activity (Ps. 104:31). In His sovereign wisdom God judged it fitting to create the cosmos, planet earth, and the subhuman and human life forms that would inhabit it (Ps. 104:24; Jer. 10:12; 27:5). Reflecting on everything He brought into existence, God pronounced it "good" (Gen. 1:4, 10, 12, 18, 21, 25; cf. 1 Tim. 4:4) and "very good" (Gen. 1:31). The entire created order elegantly demonstrates God's majesty (Ps. 8:1) and redounds to His praise (Pss. 104; 148). Creation's ultimate purpose is to bring glory to God, its sovereign and exalted Maker (Ps. 104:31; Isa. 43:7).

## Conception Marks the Beginning of Human Life

Scripture regards the fetus as a proper human person, not merely a potential person. When barren Rebekah became pregnant with twins, "The babies jostled each other within her . . ." (Gen. 25:22). God then said to Rebekah, "Two nations are in your womb, and two peoples [are] within you . . ." (v. 23). This should be understood as two nations in the persons of their respective heads, Jacob and Esau (Isa. 44:24). Job poetically described God forming him in the womb (Job 10:8–11). Later the psalmist David penned this convincing testimony: "My frame was not hidden from you when I was made in the secret place. When I was woven together in the depths of the earth, your eyes saw my unformed body. All the days ordained for me were written in your book before one of them came to be" (Ps. 139:15–16). God called some persons to salvation and/or to service while yet in the womb, for Isaiah testified, "Before I was born the Lord called me . . ." (Isa. 49:1; cf. v. 5). Similarly, God said to the prophet Jeremiah, "Before I formed you in the womb I knew you, before you were born I set you apart; I appointed you as a prophet to the nations" (Jer. 1:5). In the New Testament record, Mary's unborn child was a proper person, for the angel Gabriel stated, "You will be with child and give birth to a son . . ." (Luke 1:31). When Mary visited and greeted Elizabeth, "the baby leaped in her womb . . ." (Luke 1:41; cf. v. 44).

## Biological Considerations

The sperm and ovum—each with twenty-three chromosomes—join in the mother's fallopian tube, fuse nuclei, and unite chromosomes. The result is a fertilized egg, or zygote of a given sex, with a fixed genetic pattern or DNA (the zygote being one-fourth the size of the period at the end of this sentence). Completion of the fertilization process within twenty-four hours appears to mark the moment of conception. As the zygote travels down the fallopian tube, it divides with exponential rapidity. A single ovum may split, producing identical twins during the first three or four days. Multiple ova may form within the same time frame to produce fraternal twins. Implantation in the womb occurs within a week. Hormones introduced will expel a fertilized egg from the lining of the womb up to the second week.

From two weeks to ten to twelve weeks, the life is called an *embryo*. Blood cells form at seventeen days. Eyes begin to form at nineteen days. A rudimentary nervous system is established by twenty days. The heart begins to pulse at four weeks. The vascular system is in place at thirty days. The cerebral cortex that governs motor activity and intellect is formed at thirty-three days. At one month the embryo looks like a distinct human, although only one-quarter inch long. Brain waves and simple reflexes develop at six

weeks. Abortion treatments such as RU-486 plus Cytotec will expel an embryo within the first fifty days of pregnancy. Fingerprints develop at two
months. All organs are formed and functioning by ten to twelve weeks. At
thirteen weeks the nervous system is formed and the fetus can feel pain. At
four months the fetus becomes active (quickening). At twenty-two to twenty-
four weeks, the fetus becomes viable outside the womb. By the end of gestation, some thirteen trillion cells will have been formed.

From conception, human life develops gradually and purposefully:

> At conception a man is called a zygote; at implantation, an embryo;
> at two months gestation, a fetus; at birth, a baby; at fifteen years, a
> juvenile; and at twenty-one years, an adult. Zygote, embryo, and
> fetus are mere descriptions of a man at different stages of develop-
> ment. But throughout all of the developmental stages there is the
> basic continuity of *a man*.[54]

The sequence described involves the *development* of the human person
who is formed at conception. We are aware of the potential difficulties with
this position. Some 70 percent of fertilized eggs disappear. Some Christians
believe that they will be received into heaven without ever having been
known.[55] This is a matter about which we are told nothing, and it must be
left in the hands of the all-wise God. Moreover, twinning can occur for a
few days after an egg is fertilized. But this does not negate the fact that the
conceptus was fully human. "Twinning may be a nonsexual form of
'parenting' or parthenogenesis. . . . Or, twinning may be a case of the existing
human dying to give life to two new and identical human beings like himself
or herself. . . . In any case, they were human before and after splitting."[56]

## In Sum

Although the Bible offers no scientific explanation as to when human
life begins, it does provide a theological basis for identifying the commence-
ment of human life. The theological basis is found in creation in the divine

---

54. Clifford E. Bajema, *Abortion and the Meaning of Personhood* (Grand Rapids: Baker,
   1974), 37.
55. See Herb Spencer, "Contagious Infertility," *Christianity Today,* September 2004, 12.
56. Beckwith and Geisler, *Matters of Life and Death,* 18.

image (see chap. 4). As noted above, there is abundant reason to believe that the Bible teaches that the life within the womb is a human person. The zygote, embryo, and fetus each is a person, not merely a potential person. The fetus, for example, is not subhuman by virtue of its limited level of functioning, any more than a person temporarily comatose is subhuman for the same reason. Essential being must be distinguished from functioning ability. Functioning is a sufficient but not necessary criterion for human personhood. "A person is a being who has the basic inherent capacity to function as a person, regardless of how developed this capacity is."[57] We dissent from the opinion of Norman Anderson, who writes, "It is in fact impossible to fix any particular time when the embryo or fetus 'becomes a little human being,' before which abortion is of little or no consequence and after which it becomes murder. All we can safely assert is that it is, right throughout pregnancy, at least a *potential* human being, and should therefore be treated with all due respect."[58]

It is indefensible to drive a wedge between human beings and persons. A human being and a created person are one and the same. More specifically, all humans are persons, but not all persons are humans. Angels are persons, and God is three persons; but neither angels nor God are humans.

Does abortion constitute an act of murder? For this to be so, four criteria must be satisfied:

1. A person must be killed.
2. The person must be killed intentionally.
3. The victim is innocent.
4. An unlawful or sinful motive must be involved in the killing.[59]

Abortion as commonly practiced today satisfies these criteria. Clifford Bajema, following much Christian conviction, allows for "critical abortion," the outcome wherein the unborn dies as a result of an attempt to save the life of the mother, where it is reasonably certain that unless a critical abortion is performed, mother and child will die.[60] This painful course of action, devoid of a sinful motive, involves saving the one life that can be saved.

---

57. Schwarz, *Moral Question of Abortion*, 100.
58. Norman Anderson, *Issues of Life and Death* (Downers Grove, Ill.: InterVarsity, 1977), 77.
59. Bajema, *Abortion and the Meaning of Personhood*, 44.
60. Ibid., 47.

# ENDING HUMAN LIFE

God ordained an end to human life as well as a beginning. Apart from the Lord's prior coming to earth to gather living saints, death is inevitable. "There is a time for everything, and a season for every activity under heaven: a time to be born and a time to die" (Eccl. 3:1–2; cf. Ps. 89:48; Heb. 9:27). Life is fleeting (Pss. 39:4; 90:10) and uncertain (Prov. 27:1), and death often is sudden (Job 34:20) and always final (Job 7:9–10). One day, according to common Old Testament idioms, we all will "go the way of all the earth" (Josh. 23:14; 1 Kings 2:2), be gathered to our people (Gen. 35:29; 49:33), and return to the dust from whence we came (Gen. 3:19; Ps. 104:29). All that we have accumulated on earth through sweat and toil will be left behind (Ps. 49:17; 1 Tim. 6:7). So Job testified, "Naked I came from my mother's womb, and naked I will depart" (Job 1:21).

What is the meaning of the enigma of death, described in the Bible as "the king of terrors" (Job 18:14)? What happens when the human person dies? The profound question posed by Job millennia ago cannot be dismissed: "If a man dies, will he live again?" (Job 14:14). Woody Allen once flippantly remarked, "I am not afraid of death; I just don't want to be there when it happens." The Bible says much about death as well as what lies beyond the grave for believers and unbelievers.

## Historical Perspectives

The following represent the principal views concerning the ending of human life:

### Continuation of the Human Personality

The *continuation of personality* view borrows the notion of the soul's immortality from Plato and Neoplatonism. It denies the resurrection of the body but affirms ongoing soulish life in heaven. The survival of the individual personality beyond death often is perceived as a new stage in human evolution.

The Baptist theologian William N. Clarke (1841–1912) equates the Pauline "spiritual body" with the human personality set free by death. Concerning Christendom's allegedly mistaken notion of bodily resurrection,

Clarke writes as follows: "The present body, belonging wholly to the material order, has no further use or destiny after death has detached the spirit from the material order, and is abandoned, to be known no more."[61] Clarke adds, "A doctrine of the resurrection that dispenses with the intermediate period of disembodiment has exceptional advantage in power to lift the gloom of death."[62]

H. Wheeler Robinson (1872–1945) taught that the spiritual personality, moral achievement, and fellowship with God endure through death into the spiritual realm. "The term 'immortality,'" Robinson believes, "is preferable to 'resurrection,' because our whole line of thought points to the immortality of the soul and its values rather than to the resurrection of the body. On this point Greek thought contributes more than the Hebrew. . . ."[63] Following Greek philosophy, the liberal theologian Harry Emerson Fosdick (1878–1969) writes, "I believe in the persistence of personality through death, but I do not believe in the resurrection of the flesh."[64] According to Fosdick, belief in the intermediate state, the resurrection of the body, and the final states of bliss and torment entered Judaism and Christianity from Zoroastrianism.

## Termination of Existence

The theories under the heading of *termination of existence* agree that death brings about the dissolution of the human person. A guiding presupposition of all cessationist and annihilationist views is anthropological monism, which signifies that the human person is of but one kind—either wholly matter or wholly spirit.

**Cessationism.** *Cessationists* claim that life naturally ends at death, and the body returns to the earth to be recycled by natural processes. Modern advances in the natural sciences and the secularization of the Western world have advanced this perspective. Proponents claim that *this* world, *this* life, is

---

61. William N. Clarke, *An Outline of Christian Theology* (Edinburgh: T. and T. Clark, 1909), 457.
62. Ibid., 459.
63. H. Wheeler Robinson, *The Christian Doctrine of Man* (Edinburgh: T. and T. Clark, 1926), 286–87.
64. Harry Emerson Fosdick, *The Modern Use of the Bible* (New York: Macmillan, 1924), 99; cf. idem, *The Living of These Days* (New York: Harper and Brothers, 1956), 240–41.

the Garden of Eden and all that exists, hence there is no future heaven or hell. Professing Christians of liberal persuasion who subscribe to this position appeal to scriptural texts such as Genesis 3:19 and Ecclesiastes 3:19–20.

*Humanist Manifestos I* (1933), *II* (1973), and *III* (2003) state that Christianity is an untenable and outmoded faith, that humans are an integral part of nature, and that death ends all. The eighth thesis of *Humanist Manifesto I* reads, "Religious humanism considers the complete realization of human personality to be the end of man's life and seeks its development and fulfillment in the here and now." The second thesis of *Humanist Manifesto II* states, "Promises of immortal salvation or fear of eternal damnation are illusory and harmful. They distract humans from present concerns, from self-actualization, and from rectifying social injustices." The thesis continues, "There is no credible evidence that life survives the death of the body. We continue to exist in our progeny and in the way that our lives have influenced others." *Humanist Manifesto III* reflects the same outlook.[65]

Corliss Lamont (1902–1995), the godfather of modern secular humanism, claims that notions of life after death have been fostered by the loss of loved ones, dreams in which the deceased reappear, and the human tendency to self-preservation. Monistic anthropology forms the basis for the belief that death ends personal existence. "The monistic relation . . . has the standing of a proved psychological law and makes untenable any theory of a worthwhile personal survival after death."[66] Lamont concludes, "Death is an altogether natural thing and has played a useful and necessary role in the long course of biological evolution. In fact, without this much-abused institution of death . . . the animal known as Homo sapiens would never have evolved at all."[67]

**Annihilationism.** *Annihilationists* hold that eternal torment in hell is inconsistent with God's love and goodness. At death or the last judgment, God will destroy the unsaved, so that they will not experience endless punishment in the lake of fire. Christian believers will experience eternal bliss in heaven with Christ. William Temple (1881–1944), archbishop of Canterbury, cryptically wrote concerning those who resist God's will

---

65. For the texts of the Humanist Manifestos see http://www.americanhumanist.org (accessed March 27, 2004).
66. Corliss Lamont, *The Philosophy of Humanism,* 8th ed. (Washington, D.C.: Humanist Press, 1997), 103.
67. Ibid., 111.

throughout their lives: "There is nothing that Almighty Love can do with such a soul except to bring it to an end. That, no doubt, constitutes a failure in God."[68]

The Reformed theologian Philip Edgcumbe Hughes (1915–1990) judges that sinners' everlasting suffering in hell would be incompatible with the triumph of Christ's redemptive kingdom and the renewal of all creation. Hughes understands biblical language of sinners' "destruction" to mean obliteration of existence. Thus "Everlasting death is destruction without end, that is, destruction without recall, the destruction of obliteration."[69] According to the evangelical writer Edward W. Fudge, at the final assize the unrighteous dead will be raised, judged by God, undergo conscious punishment as long as justice requires, and thereafter be annihilated. The wicked "will disappear like smoke," and "nothing will remain of the wicked but ashes."[70] Fudge judges that the biblical lake of fire is a symbol denoting "utter, absolute, irreversible annihilation."[71]

Anglican pastor and theologian John R. W. Stott believes that the idea that all human souls are by nature eternal is an alien Greek construct. Christians must be open "to the possibility that Scripture points in the direction of annihilation, and that 'eternal conscious torment' is a tradition which has to yield to the supreme authority of Scripture."[72] Stott cites three reasons in support of this view: (1) The fire of hell (Matt. 5:22; 25:41; Rev. 20:15) consumes rather than inflicts endless pain; (2) conscious punishment eternally administered would be inconsistent with sins committed during a finite lifetime; and (3) the eternal suffering of many in hell would be incongruent with God's final victory over evil (Eph. 1:10; Phil. 2:10–11).

The Canadian theologian Clark Pinnock argues that God's judgment on the unrepentant involves extinction of being. Pinnock concludes that biblical descriptions of hell (particularly the lake of fire and the second death) suggest termination of human existence. "How can one imagine for a moment that

---

68. William Temple, *Christus Veritas* (London: Macmillan, 1924), 208.

69. Philip Edgcumbe Hughes, *The True Image: The Origin and Destiny of Man in Christ* (Grand Rapids: Eerdmans, 1989), 405.

70. Edward W. Fudge, *The Fire That Consumes* (Fallbrook, Calif.: Verdict Publications, 1982), 116–17.

71. Ibid., 304.

72. John R. W. Stott, "The Gospel for the World: Response," in *Evangelical Essentials: A Liberal-Evangelical Dialogue,* ed. David L. Edwards (Downers Grove, Ill.: InterVarsity: 1988), 315.

the God who gave his Son to die for sinners because of his great love for them would install a torture chamber somewhere in the new creation in order to subject those who reject him to everlasting pain?"[73]

### Soul Sleep

From the perspective of a monistic anthropology, believers in *soul sleep*, or *psychopannychia*, hold that human persons at death sleep in the grave in a state of unconsciousness to await resurrection. Soul sleep denies the existence of a conscious intermediate state between death and resurrection of the body. Advocates note that Scripture often depicts death as an unconscious state of "sleep" (Jer. 51:39; Acts 7:60; 1 Cor. 15:6, 18, 20, 51) and describes the dead as knowing nothing (Eccl. 9:5).

Martin Luther (1483–1546) occasionally described the intermediate state of the righteous and the unrighteous as a kind of sleep. Opposing the Roman doctrine of purgatory, Luther held that following death Christians sleep in the arms of Jesus as they await the resurrection. Wrote Luther, the grave "designates that hidden recess in which the dead sleep beyond this life."[74] The Reformer added, "We shall sleep until He comes and knocks on the little grave and says, 'Doctor Martin, get up!' Then I shall rise in a moment and be happy with Him forever."[75]

Seventh-day Adventists deny that there exists a conscious entity such as a soul or spirit that survives the death of the body. At death the whole person enters the grave, where it sleeps in a state of unconsciousness until the resurrection. "Death is really and truly a sleep, a sleep that is deep, that is unconscious, that is unbroken until the awakening at the resurrection."[76] Seventh-day Adventists fear that the notion of a conscious existence in the intermediate state will lead to the occult practice of communicating with the dead. Anthony Hoekema describes the Adventist position as "soul-extinction."[77]

---

73. Clark Pinnock, "Fire, Then Nothing," *Christianity Today*, March 20, 1987, 40.
74. Cited in Ewald M. Plass, comp., *What Luther Says* (St. Louis, Mo.: Concordia, 1959), 385.
75. Martin Luther, cited in LeRoy E. Froom, *The Conditionalist Faith of Our Fathers*, 2 vols. (Washington, D.C.: Review and Herald, 1965), 2:75.
76. Carlyle B. Haynes, *Life, Death and Immortality* (Nashville: Southern Publishing, 1952), 202; cf. "Immortality," in *Seventh-day Adventist Encyclopedia* (Washington, D.C.: Review and Herald, 1966), 559.
77. Anthony Hoekema, *The Four Major Cults* (Grand Rapids: Eerdmans, 1963), 345.

From the perspective of a monistic anthropology, Oscar Cullmann (1902–1999) believes that the dead in the intermediate state sleep in a dreamlike state. At the resurrection believers and unbelievers will awake to consciousness and will be clothed with bodies. Those who in their lifetimes had no opportunity to hear the gospel will be given a further opportunity to receive Christ.[78] Liberal theologian John Hick writes, "When someone has died he is, apart from any special divine action, extinct. But in fact God, by an act of sovereign power, either sometimes or always resurrects or reconstitutes or recreates him."[79]

## Reincarnation, or Transmigration of the Soul

A pagan perspective, taken over from Buddhism and Hinduism, is widely held. *Reincarnationists* claim that the soul is released from the body following death to inhabit another material form, either human or animal. The nature of a person's reincarnation is determined by fate or by the inexorable law of *karma*—a law of cause and effect. Present deeds determine the course of future lives. By securing sufficiently good *karma*, a person is liberated from the dreary cycle of births, deaths, and rebirths to merge with the *Absolute*. Reincarnation advocates claim that this view is required by the demands of justice, whereby good is rewarded with a favorable reincarnation and evil punished by an unfavorable reincarnation.

Plato held that the preexistent and immortal soul at birth descends to occupy a mortal body, much as an oyster occupies a shell. At death the soul leaves the prison of the body and returns to the world-soul to inhabit another body at a later time. The cycle of soulish reincarnations continues forever.

The soul's reincarnation from one life to another has been a central belief in Eastern religions such as Hinduism, Buddhism, and Taoism. In the Western world the cult of theosophy, under the influence of its leader Annie Besant (1847–1933),[80] promotes reincarnation in its eclectic system. Contemporary movements that subscribe to reincarnation include the occult,

---

78. Oscar Cullmann, *Immortality of the Soul or Resurrection of the Body?* (New York: Macmillan, 1958), 49.

79. John Hick, *Death and Eternal Life* (San Francisco, Calif.: Harper and Row, 1976), 279.

80. Annie Besant, *The Ancient Wisdom: An Outline of Theosophical Teachings* (Wheaton, Ill.: Theosophical Publishing House, 1977) 197–266.

witchcraft, Scientology, and the New Age movement. Today some thirty million Americans believe in the reincarnation of the soul.

Geddes MacGregor, the Scots-born philosopher of religion, writes, "I am inclined to take very seriously the possibility that a form of reincarnation might show how sadly we have neglected what could be an enrichment of the Christian hope."[81] The notion that unbelievers will suffer eternally for sins committed during a short life span supports the theory of reincarnation. The transmigration of souls would allow people multiple chances to work out their salvation—each reincarnation allowing further opportunity for growth. "Surely the working out of our moral and spiritual development must take longer than a few decades of one particular life."[82] MacGregor admits that reincarnation is not explicitly taught in Scripture, but neither, he argues, is the Trinity and other traditional doctrines.

### Entry into the Intermediate State

According to those who believe in an *intermediate state,* at death the undying soul/spirit separates from the body and enters this state. As immaterial spirits, the righteous enjoy preliminary rewards in Christ's presence ("paradise" or "Abraham's bosom"), whereas the unrighteous experience provisional punishments separated from the Savior. Each person's final destiny is settled at the time of death. At Christ's second coming, the bodies of the saved and the unsaved will be raised, united with their immaterial selves, and judged. Christian millenarians believe that believers will reign on earth with Christ for a thousand years. Following the final judgments, the righteous will enter heaven to enjoy endless bliss, whereas the unrighteous will be consigned to hell to suffer everlasting torment.

Informed by the parable of the rich man and Lazarus in Luke 16, the early theologian Irenaeus (c. 130–c. 200) concluded that following death "souls continue to exist, they pass from an earthly to an eternal body . . . and before the final judgment each person's abode will reflect what they have coming."[83] Tertullian insisted that death dissolves the unity of the im-

---

81. Geddes MacGregor, *Reincarnation as a Christian Hope* (Totowa, N.J.: Barnes and Noble, 1982), ix.

82. Ibid., 29.

83. Irenaeus, *Against Heresies,* cited in Robert L. Wise, *Quest for the Soul: Our Search for Deeper Meaning* (Nashville: Nelson, 1996), 170.

material soul and the material body and so ends sensory knowledge. Following death, as a foretaste of things to come, souls apart from the flesh are kept in one of two regions in hades: The righteous are blessed in paradise, and the unrighteous are punished in hell. In these places of temporary detention, souls await resurrection of the body and full accounting at the final assize. "We affirm that thou dost continue to exist after the extinction of life and to await the day of judgment; and that, according to thy deserts, thou wilt be delivered either to torture or to bliss, both eternal."[84] Augustine held that at death the soul separates from the body and enters the intermediate state in a condition of conscious existence. Christian believers, like Lazarus in Luke's parable, abide with Christ in paradise, whereas unbelievers experience the pangs of hell as they await the general resurrection.

Orthodox and Roman Catholic theologies insert purgatory into the intermediate state. They teach that souls who die in a state of grace but short of moral perfection undergo penal sufferings in order to be purified for entry into heaven. The duration of purgatory is said to be proportional to the magnitude of one's guilt. Support for purgatory is alleged in Malachi 3:2–3, 2 Maccabees 12:39–45, Luke 12:59, and 1 Corinthians 3:11–15. Souls in purgatory earn release more quickly through masses, prayers, and the good works of the faithful. When the process of purgation is completed, the soul is released to heaven to await resurrection of the body.

John Calvin taught that the human soul "is a substance, and after the death of the body truly lives, being endued both with sense and understanding."[85] At death the saved leave their bodies to enjoy blessedness in Christ's presence, whereas the unsaved apart from the body experience misery in hades. "Scripture goes no farther than to say that Christ is present with them [believers] and receives them into paradise that they may obtain consolation, while the souls of the reprobate suffer such torments as they deserve."[86] Calvin believed that biblical language concerning the fire of hell symbolically describes the wretchedness of being forever cut off from fellowship with God.

---

84. Tertullian, *The Testimony of the Soul* 4 [*ANF,* 3:177].
85. John Calvin, "Psychopannychia," in Henry Beveridge, trans., *Tracts and Treatises in Defense of the Reformed Faith* (Grand Rapids: Eerdmans, 1958), 3:419–20.
86. John Calvin, *Institutes of the Christian Religion,* ed. John T. McNeill; trans. Ford Lewis Battles, 2 vols., LCC, vols. 20–21 (Philadelphia, Pa.: Westminster, 1960), 2:997 [3.25.6].

The Reformed doctrinal statement, the Westminster Confession of Faith (1647), contains the following statement:

> The bodies of men, after death, return to dust, and see corruption; but their souls (which neither die nor sleep) . . . immediately return to God who gave them. The souls of the righteous . . . are received into the highest heavens, where they behold the face of God in light and glory, waiting for the full redemption of their bodies: and the souls of the wicked are cast into hell, where they remain in torment and utter darkness, reserved to the judgment of the great day.[87]

The Reformed theologian Charles Hodge (1797–1878), reflecting on 2 Corinthians 5:2, wrote, "As soon as our earthly house is destroyed, the soul, instead of being left houseless and homeless, is received in that house which is eternal in the heavens."[88]

## Biblical and Theological Perspectives

### The Meaning of Death

Death marks the end of the human person's temporal existence. Whereas death is a "natural" event in that it passes none by (Ps. 49:12), it is an "unnatural" event in that it severs the God-created body/soul-spirit unity. Existentially the prospect of death strikes fear in the human heart (Heb. 2:15). "Inscriptions on tombs and references in literature show that first-century pagans viewed death with horror, as the end of everything."[89] In the words of Hughes, death "is the annihilating surd that makes no sense."[90] Since God created humans for life rather than death, Scripture regards death as an enemy and a curse (1 Cor. 15:26). Civilized Western cultures attempt to mute this reality by sanitizing death in a variety of ways. The Bible employs vivid imagery to describe this deadly foe: the withering of a flower (Job

---

87. Westminster Confession of Faith, in Philip Schaff, ed., *Creeds of Christendom,* 3 vols. (Grand Rapids: Baker, reprint, 1977), 3:670 [chap. 32.1].

88. Charles Hodge, *Systematic Theology,* 3 vols. (reprint, Grand Rapids: Eerdmans, 1973), 3:729.

89. NIVSB, 1824, note on 1 Thessalonians 4:13.

90. Hughes, *The True Image,* 119.

14:2; James 1:10–11), the vanishing of the morning mist (James 4:14), the fading of an evening shadow (Job 8:9; Ps. 102:11), "water spilled on the ground, which cannot be recovered" (2 Sam. 14:14), and the severing of a silver cord, the shattering of a golden bowl, and the breaking of a wheel at a well (Eccl. 12:6). Death is a hideous and mysterious event.

The Bible identifies three forms of death.

1. *Spiritual death* connotes the sin-caused severance of the human's relationship with God. Unbelievers, who are out of fellowship with God, are said to be in a state of spiritual death. Jesus affirmed this reality when he said that the one who believes in him "has crossed over from death to life" (John 5:24). To the Ephesian Christians, Paul wrote, "You were [formerly] dead in your trangressions and sins" (Eph. 2:1). See also 1 John 3:14 and 5:16.

2. *Physical death* comes at the cessation of biological functioning. Theologically it represents the humanly irrecoverable separation of the immaterial soul/spirit from the material body. In the words of Tertullian, "Even if our last breath is filled with joy, death is still a violent expulsion of the soul from the body."[91] With forceful simplicity, the apostle James wrote, "The body without the spirit is dead . . ." (James 2:26). Elihu said, "If it were [God's] intention and he withdrew his spirit and breath, all mankind would perish together and man would return to the dust" (Job 34:14-15). The Bible describes physical death figuratively as "rest" from temporal troubles (Deut. 31:16; Rev. 14:13) and euphemistically as "sleep" (Ps. 76:5; Acts 13:36; 1 Cor. 11:30). According to the Bible, each person's destiny is settled at the time of physical death (Luke 16:26; Heb. 9:27).

3. *Eternal death* denotes the endless perpetuation of spiritual death. Known also as the "lake of fire" and the "second death" (Rev. 20:6, 14–15; 21:8), eternal death was symbolized in the primordial history by sinful Adam being cut off from the tree of life and banished from the Garden of Eden (Gen. 3:22–24). Eternal death is not the cessation of existence but a different state of existence. The Bible makes clear that Christian believers will not experience eternal death (Rev. 20:6).

---

91. Tertullian, *A Treatise on the Soul,* cited in Wise, *Quest for the Soul,* 134.

## Causes of Death

Physically, vital organ failure due to old age or disease is the immediate cause of death. Ultimately, however, God brings about death by removing the breath of life (Job 34:14–15). Life and death are under God's sovereign control. "The LORD brings death and makes alive; he brings down to the grave and raises up" (1 Sam. 2:6; cf. Job 12:10). Scripture uniformly testifies that God justly judges sin with death. As God promised the first couple in the Garden of Eden, "You must not eat from the tree of the knowledge of good and evil, for when you eat of it you will surely die" (Gen. 2:17; cf. Ezek. 18:4, 20). The moment Adam sinned, he experienced spiritual death and came under the sentence of physical and eternal death. In the New Testament the apostle Paul stated this with forceful simplicity: "The wages of sin is death" (Rom. 6:23a; cf. Rom. 5:12, 15, 17, 21). In the words of the church father Tertullian, death "is the result of a fault or defect. Our own arbitrary choice of sin brings death. If the human race didn't sin, death wouldn't follow."[92]

## The Time of Death

The Bible indicates that death occurs after the last breath is taken. "Man dies and is laid low; he breathes his last and is no more" (Job 14:10). Yet it is God who establishes the boundaries of a person's life. "Man's days are determined; you have decreed the number of his months and have set limits he cannot exceed" (Job 14:5; cf. Pss. 31:15; 139:16). God, therefore, determines the time of a person's death. "You turn men back to dust, saying, 'Return to dust, O sons of men'" (Ps. 90:3; cf. Job 30:23). God often blesses the faithful with long lives and cuts short the years of the wicked (Job 22:15–16).

Modern medical science offers a technically detailed description of the nature and time of death. The brain consists of three parts: (1) a higher brain containing two cerebral hemispheres; (2) the cerebral cortex consisting of the layer of grey matter surrounding the two hemispheres; and (3) the cerebellum. The lower brain is comprised of the brain stem that controls unconscious functions such as heartbeat, breathing, and reflex actions. In most civil jurisdictions death is legally defined as the nonfunctioning of the higher and lower brains (i.e., the absence of brain waves). Some new-

---

92. Ibid.

borns are delivered with much of the higher brain missing *(anencephaly)* but with the brain stem still functioning. An infant in this "persistent vegetative state" can be kept alive for months or years with intensive care. The child's parents and other involved parties (physicians, clergy, and ethicists) usually permit a newborn in such a condition to die. But a few have been kept alive for some time at the parents' insistence, with the support of the courts. All Western countries accept brain death as the indicator of physical death.

### Unnatural Deaths

Since God wills the beginning and the end of personal existence, the taking of a human life other than in cases of legitimate self-defense violates human dignity and usurps God's prerogative as creator and sustainer of life. Murder, or *homocide*—the intentional termination of the life of another—is forbidden by the sixth commandment, which states, "You shall not murder" (Exod. 20:13; cf. 21:12–14). Infanticide, the intentional killing of newborns is forbidden by the same commandment. Infants born grossly deformed with little expectation of living generally are allowed to die naturally, while nourishment is provided and suffering minimized. By the common application of biblical ethics, the life of a newborn with illnesses such as Down's syndrome should be preserved and the child lovingly cared for by its parents and medical professionals.

*Euthanasia,* from the Greek meaning "good death," may be involuntary (without consent and thus a form of murder) or voluntary (with consent and thus a form of suicide). Nineteenth-century utilitarians advocated involuntary euthanasia to eliminate handicapped persons, who were regarded as a burden on society. In one of the most tragic episodes in human history, twentieth-century Nazis "euthanized," or murdered, millions of Jews on ethnic grounds. On the other hand, persons suffering from a painful illness sometimes pursue voluntary euthanasia by self-administered poison. The work of physician, Jack Kevorkian, serves as a recent example of a physician who administered voluntary euthanasia. Seriously ill persons should be reminded of the value of suffering and provided treatment that minimizes their pain. Passive euthanasia, allowing a terminal patient to die by turning off the respirator and withholding IV infusions (following a person's living will, for example) is a common medical decision of last resort. Christians,

Roman Catholic and Protestant, have consistently denounced active euthanasia as a repudiation of God's authority over life and death.

Suicide, the killing of oneself, constitutes self-inflicted murder. The Bible does not speak directly to the subject of suicide, but it does record the successful suicides of several prominent persons, including a judge of Israel (Samson, Judg. 16:30), two kings (Saul, 1 Sam. 31:4–6; and Zimri, 1 Kings 16:18–19), a renegade apostle (Judas, Matt. 27:5), and two less prominent persons (Saul's unnamed armor-bearer, 1 Sam. 31:4–6; and Ahithophel, counselor to Absalom, 2 Sam. 17:23). Suicide may be prompted by intense physical suffering, depression and other mental illnesses, hopelessness and despair, and, yes, the guilt of unconfessed sins (1 Kings 16:18–19). Persons who inflict death upon themselves believe that life holds no meaning or value for them personally.

The sixth commandment ("You shall not murder," Exod. 20:13) implies the prohibition of suicide. Liberal thinkers see in suicide "the signature of freedom,"[93] whereas most Christians perceive it as the ultimate sign of distrust of God and thus a sin.[94] Of course, the laying down of one's life for a noble cause represents an act of love, not a sin (see John 10:15).

The Bible most clearly supports a comprehensive "pro-life" posture, where the so-called right to die rests with God alone. "The Christian believes that life comes to us as a gift from God; that it is to God and for God that we both live and die; and that it is wrong for man to usurp the divine prerogative by cutting life short in the absence of some overriding justification."[95]

### What Lies Beyond Death?

Lacking certain knowledge of their destiny, secular persons can venture only guesses as to the future: "Who knows if the spirit of man rises upward and if the spirit of the animal goes down into the earth?" (Eccl. 3:21; cf. Job 11:8). Since the Hebrew outlook was largely focused on human obligations

---

93. Fletcher, *Humanhood,* 175.
94. Many authorities in Christian history, such as Augustine, Dante, and Charles Spurgeon, believed that all persons who take their own lives will be damned in hell. We disagree with this opinion.
95. Anderson, *Issues of Life and Death,* 99. Dietrich Bonhoeffer, *Ethics* (New York: Macmillan, 1965), 163, adds: "There is no life that is not worth living; for life itself is valued by God. The fact that God is the Creator, Preserver, and Redeemer of life makes even the most wretched life worth living before God."

to live uprightly before God in this world, continuation of life after death in the Old Testament was a vague concept, with only shadowy glimpses into what lies beyond the grave. The New Testament, however, presents a clear disclosure of the destiny of the righteous and the unrighteous. Biblical teaching as a whole reveals that death is not the end of personal existence. Beyond the grave lie the following places and/or states:

**The Intermediate State.** The *intermediate state* refers to the condition of human beings between death and bodily resurrection in states of provisional bliss or punishment. At death the body decomposes in the grave, whereas the soul/spirit lives on in awareness. The Hebrew word *šᵉōl* (sixty-five times in the Old Testament) literally refers to the grave (e.g., Gen. 37:35; Num. 16:30, 33; Job 24:19) and by extension to the shadowy, underworld realm of the departed (Deut. 32:22; Amos 9:2). In the Old Testament *šᵉōl* was regarded as a condition of darkness, gloom, provisional punishment, and no return (Job 7:9; 10:21–22; 17:13–16; Isa. 38:18). The realm of the dead is variously described as "the land of oblivion" (Ps. 88:12), the "pit" (Ps. 30:9; Isa. 14:15), and "destruction" (Job 26:6; Prov. 15:11; 27:20). The New Testament Greek equivalent of *šᵉōl* is *hadēs* (ten times), which signifies the grave (e.g., Acts 2:27, 31) and, in all but one occurrence, the place or state of the wicked dead in provisional torment (Luke 16:23; Rev. 6:8; 20:13–14). The New Testament indicates that the righteous are in paradise, or with Christ, that is, "in the heaven of glory, but this glory is still awaiting an increase," according to Delitzsch.[96]

In the patriarchal history, Job nurtured the faint hope of existence beyond death (Job 14:7–22). Old Testament prohibitions against necromancy—the attempt by mediums or spiritualists to communicate with spirits of the deceased (Lev. 19:31; Deut. 18:10–11)—also support the intermediate state. The account of Saul and the witch of Endor (1 Sam. 28:3–19) suggests that God caused the departed spirit of Samuel to appear to the medium and to Saul, for the latter was convinced that the spirit was Samuel (v. 14) and the text itself identifies the ghostlike figure as Samuel (v. 15).

Israel's psalmists cherished a less ambiguous hope that God would spare them from the terrors of *šᵉōl* and bring them hereafter into His glorious presence. Death and the grave would not have the last word. Consider the following texts:

---

96. Franz Delitzsch, *A System of Biblical Psychology* (Edinburgh: T. and T. Clark, 1869), 486.

- *Psalm 16:10–11:* "You will not abandon me to the grave, nor will you let your Holy One see decay. You have made known to me the path of life; you will fill me with joy in your presence, with eternal pleasures at your right hand." David expresses confidence that *šᵉōl* will not hold him in its grip. Rather, at death he will pass from the grave into God's presence to enjoy spiritual pleasures forever.
- *Psalm 17:15:* "In righteousness I will see your face; when I awake, I will be satisfied with seeing your likeness." The text describes more than an awakening from sleep, for it is set in opposition to the fate of the wicked "whose reward is in this life" (v. 14).
- *Psalm 49:15:* "God will redeem my soul from the grave; he will surely take me to himself." The verb *lāqâ,* "take," is used in Genesis 5:24 of God catching Enoch up to heaven.
- *Psalm 73:24:* Asaph confidently wrote, "You guide me with your counsel, and afterward you will take *[lāqâ]* me into glory."
- *Ecclesiastes 12:7:* "The dust returns to the ground it came from, and the spirit returns to God who gave it."

The coming of Jesus Christ and His resurrection from the dead brought the intermediate state into clearer light, as the following New Testament texts confirm:

- *Luke 9:30–31:* The deceased lawgiver Moses and prophet Elijah appear and converse with Jesus on the Mount of Transfiguration.
- *Luke 16:19–31:* According to this parable, Lazarus was carried at death by angels to "Abraham's side," where he enjoyed comfort and rest (vv. 22, 25). The rich man, on the other hand, wound up in "hell *[hadēs]*, where he was in torment" (v. 23). The text teaches that at death the righteous immediately enter the place of blessedness, whereas the unrighteous are excluded from that place of bliss.
- *Luke 23:43:* On the cross Jesus said to the believing thief, "I tell you the truth, today you will be with me in paradise." Immediately following his death, the repentant criminal, apart from his body, went to be with Christ in heaven.
- *Acts 7:59–60:* After being killed by stoning, Stephen's "spirit" was received into heaven.
- *2 Corinthians 5:1–9:* Paul revealed his anxiety about leaving his body

at death and being "unclothed." But his longing to be with Christ was so strong that he concluded, "I . . . prefer to be away from the body and at home with the Lord" (v. 8).

- *2 Corinthians 12:1–4:* Paul refers to his experience of being "caught up to the third heaven" or "paradise," where he experienced "visions and revelations from the Lord." This ecstatic event might be viewed as an out-of-the-body experience, although Paul himself states that he was uncertain whether he was in his body. The purpose of the experience was to encourage Paul in the midst of his trials and to fortify his belief in the reality of heaven.
- *Philippians 1:22–24:* Paul relates his struggle over whether to remain with the Christians in the flesh or whether "to depart and be with Christ, which is better by far."
- *Hebrews 12:23:* The writer describes Old Testament believers as "the spirits of righteous men made perfect." Henry Alford believes the text teaches that saints who die in Christ "are not sleeping, they are not unconscious, they are not absent from us: they are perfected, lacking nothing . . . but waiting only for bodily perfection."[97]

Protestant confessional statements such as *The Westminster Shorter Catechism* (1647) testify to the reality of the intermediate state. The answer to question 37—"What benefits do believers receive from Christ at death?"—reads, "The souls of believers are at death made perfect in holiness, and do immediately pass into glory: and their bodies, being still united to Christ, do rest in their graves till the resurrection."

**The Resurrection of the Body.** The focal point of the Christian hope is the conquering of death through *bodily resurrection.* When Christ returns in glory at the end of the age, the dead will be raised, the righteous preceding the unrighteous. Lacking knowledge of the empty tomb, Old Testament understanding of bodily resurrection was sparse, limited to the following central texts:

- *Job 19:26:* "And after my skin has been destroyed, yet in my flesh I will see God." Distressed Job expressed hope that by the power of his

---

97. Henry Alford, *The Greek New Testament,* 4 vols. (reprint, Grand Rapids: Baker, 1980), 4:255.

heavenly "Redeemer" (v. 25) he would be reclothed. Note Job's reference to his "skin," "flesh," and "eyes."

- *Isaiah 26:19:* "But your dead will live; their bodies will rise. You who dwell in the dust, wake up and shout for joy. Your dew is like the dew of the morning; the earth will give birth to her dead." The prophet's vision of Israel's restoration embraces also the future resurrection of the body.
- *Daniel 12:2:* "Multitudes who sleep in the dust of the earth will awake: some to everlasting life, others to shame and everlasting contempt." In this clearest of Old Testament texts, Daniel envisages the resurrection of the righteous and unrighteous at the end of the age.
- *Hosea 13:14:* "I will ransom them from the power of the grave; I will redeem them from death. Where, O death, are your plagues? Where, O grave, is your destruction?" Paul quotes from this text as a promise of the bodily resurrection of believers in Christ (1 Cor. 15:55).

The hope of bodily resurrection became clearer in Jewish tradition during the centuries between the Testaments (see Wisd. of Sol. 3:1–9; 2 Macc. 7:9, 11, 14; 14:46) and became accepted belief among the Pharisees. The New Testament, however, teaches bodily resurrection at the end of the age with stunning clarity.

- *Matthew 22:30–32:* "At the resurrection people will neither marry nor be given in marriage. . . . But about the resurrection of the dead—have you not read what God said to you, 'I am the God of Abraham, the God of Isaac, and the God of Jacob'? He is not the God of the dead but of the living." Jesus certified bodily resurrection of the dead, contrary to the Sadducees, who denied that there was a bodily resurrection.
- *John 5:28b–29:* "A time is coming when all who are in their graves will hear his voice and come out—those who have done good will rise to live, and those who have done evil will rise to be condemned." Jesus declared the future raising of the righteous and the unrighteous dead.
- *Acts 23:6; 24:15, 21:* In his preaching ministry, Paul proclaimed his unswerving belief in the resurrection of the dead at the end of the age.
- *1 Corinthians 15:42–43:* "So will it be with the resurrection of the dead. The body that is sown is perishable, it is raised imperishable; it

is sown in dishonor, it is raised in glory; it is sown in weakness, it is raised in power." Paul's teaching on the resurrection of the dead in 1 Corinthians 15 focuses on the raising of Christians' transformed bodies.

- *1 Corinthians 15:51–52:* "Listen, I tell you a mystery: We will not all sleep, but we will all be changed—in a flash, in the twinkling of an eye, at the last trumpet. For the trumpet will sound, the dead will be raised imperishable, and we will be changed."
- *1 Thessalonians 4:16–17:* "For the Lord himself will come down from heaven, with a loud command, with the voice of the archangel and with the trumpet call of God, and the dead in Christ will rise first. After that, we who are still alive and are left will be caught up with them in the clouds to meet the Lord in the air. And so we will be with the Lord forever." Paul teaches that the believing dead will be raised before living believers are caught up in the air to meet Christ at His return.

Scripture triumphantly announces that Christ in His resurrection has dealt death a decisive defeat. The powerful conquest of death is hinted at in the Old Testament and openly proclaimed in the New.

- *Isaiah 25:6–8a:* "The LORD Almighty . . . will swallow up death forever. The Sovereign LORD will wipe away the tears from all faces." Paul quoted from this text in 1 Corinthians 15:54.
- *1 Corinthians 15:25–26:* "For he must reign until he has put all his enemies under his feet. The last enemy to be destroyed is death."
- *2 Timothy 1:10b:* "Christ Jesus . . . has destroyed death and has brought life and immortality to light through the gospel."
- *Revelation 20:13–14:* "The sea gave up the dead that were in it, and death and Hades gave up the dead that were in them . . . Then death and Hades were thrown into the lake of fire."

As a result of Christ's resurrection victory over the grave, death for Christians has been emptied of its terror.

- *1 Corinthians 15:54b–55:* "Death has been swallowed up in victory. Where, O death, is your victory? Where, O death, is your sting?"

- *Hebrews 2:14–15:* "Since the children have flesh and blood, he too shared in their humanity so that by his death he might destroy him who holds the power of death—that is, the devil—and free those who all their lives were held in slavery by their fear of death."
- *Revelation 20:6:* "Blessed and holy are those who have part in the first resurrection. The second death has no power over them, but they will . . . reign with him for a thousand years."

**Final Judgment.** In the end all humans who have ever lived will *stand before the Judge* of the universe (Ps. 50:6; Acts 10:42). On numerous occasions Jesus taught the inevitability of the final assize (Matt. 11:24; 12:36), as did the apostle Paul (Acts 17:31). Without partiality God will examine deeds (Ps. 62:12; Matt. 16:27), words (Matt. 12:36), thoughts (Rom. 2:16), and motives (1 Cor. 4:5). All will give account for what has been done in the body. The final examination of our lives is as inevitable as the reality of death. "Just as man is destined to die once, and after that to face judgment . . ." (Heb. 9:27).

Scripture distinguishes between God's end-time examination of believers and His judgment of unbelievers. To the Corinthian Christians Paul wrote, "For we must all appear before the judgment seat of Christ, that each one may receive what is due him for the things done while in the body, whether good or bad" (2 Cor. 5:10; cf. Rom. 14:10–12). Clothed with the righteousness of Christ, Christians will stand before God the Father freed from condemnation (8:33–34). Unbelievers, on the other hand, will give account of their rejection of Christ and their ungodly lives before the Great White Throne judgment (2 Peter 2:9; Rev. 20:11–13).

**Endless Life in Heaven or Existence in Hell.** Unlike Scripture, little talk about heaven and especially about hell occurs in contemporary religious discourse. The Bible, however, affirms that the righteous will dwell forever in "heaven" (*ouranos,* 272 times), which is a place as well as a state. The enduring home of believers in Christ is variously described as the *Father's house* (John 14:2), *paradise* (a loan word from Persian meaning a pleasure garden: Rev. 2:7), and a *better country* (Heb. 11:16). For Christians "Death is only a grim porter to let us into a stately palace."[98] In a homecoming

---

98. Richard Sibbes, cited in I. D. E. Thomas, ed., *The Golden Treasury of Puritan Quotations* (Chicago: Moody, 1975), 70.

celebration that defies description (1 Cor. 2:9), the children of God will be welcomed into Christ's kingdom (2 Peter 1:11) and realize the full attainment of the eternal life. It is that glorious place of light (Isa. 60:19), reward (Matt. 5:12), joy (Luke 15:7), sight (1 Cor. 13:12), righteousness (2 Peter 3:13), worship (Rev. 4:9–11; 19:4), and healing (22:2). Heaven, in the words of an unknown saint, is "Christmas morning for ever and ever." The indescribable blessedness of the righteous in heaven is without end (Matt. 25:46).

Revelation 21:1–22:5 presents a richly symbolic description of the eternal state. The apostle John portrays the saints' eternal home via three principal images: (1) a city; (2) the Holy City; and (3) the New Jerusalem. Here is the homeland of God's people that will never be snatched away (21:2–21), a temple that becomes the very dwelling place of God (vv. 22–27). Its setting is like a garden that recalls the pristine Eden where the first human pair enjoyed blissful communion with God (22:1–5).

The Bible is not silent concerning the fate of the unrighteous. Jesus spoke more often of the torments of hell than of the joys of heaven (e.g., Matt. 5:22, 29–30; 10:28; 23:15, 33). The future state of the unrighteous is described by the place-terms *geenna* (translated "hell" in the NIV: e.g., Matt. 5:29–30; 10:28; 23:15, 33; Luke 12:5; James 3:6), "lake of fire" (Rev. 20:14–15), and the "second death" (20:6, 14; 21:8). Gehenna, named after a valley south of Jerusalem where a garbage dump smoldered, figuratively describes the place of eschatological judgment. Whatever term is used, hell represents sinners' ultimate separation from the life of God. Hell's ultimate agony is that image-bearers should have missed the lofty purpose for which they were created. Punishment of the unrighteous, Scripture asserts, will be proportional to the degree of light and knowledge one possessed (Luke 12:47–48). God sends no one to hell (2 Peter 3:9); sinners "perish because they refused to love the truth and so be saved" (2 Thess. 2:10).

The Bible teaches that sinners' punishment in hell is everlasting (Matt. 25:46; Jude 7; Rev. 14:11), indeed, of equal duration to the saints' bliss (Rev. 22:5). The Greek phrase describing the duration of sinners' punishment (*eis tous aiōnas tōn aiōnōn*) is the same phrase used for Christ's eternal reign (11:15) and the endless life of the Father and the Son (4:9; 5:13). The everlasting punishment of the wicked—grievous, indeed, to contemplate—is inextricably woven into the fabric of Christian theology. "Think lightly of hell, and you will think lightly of the Cross. Think little of the sufferings of lost souls, and you will soon think little of the Savior who delivers you from them."[99] To this statement of Charles Spurgeon may be added one from Geoffrey Gorer: "If there is no belief in hell the concept of judgment also becomes meaningless and then all that is left of Christianity is a system of ethics."[100]

Biblical language indicating that God will "destroy" (Ps. 94:23; 1 Cor. 3:17) the wicked or bring about their "destruction" (Matt. 7:13; Rom. 9:22), that the wicked will "perish" (Pss. 1:6; 37:20; Prov. 11:10; John 3:16; 2 Peter 2:12), and that God will "consume" His enemies (Heb. 10:27; cf. 12:29) in no wise contravenes the reality of eternal punishment. Such expressions variously signify physical death, loss of fellowship with God, and everlasting perdition—never extinction of being. Moreover, fire in Scripture is a symbol for God's judgment on the wicked (Isa. 29:6; 33:14). "Eternal fire" (Matt. 18:8), the "fire of hell" (Matt. 18:9), and the "lake of fire" (Rev. 20:14–15) refer not to sinners' annihilation but to the soul-wrenching torments of eternal separation from God.

---

99. Charles H. Spurgeon, *Metropolitan Tabernacle Pulpit*, 63 vols. (Pasadena, Tex.: Pilgrim Publications, 1969–80), 12:174.
100. Geoffrey Gorer, cited in Gordon S. Jackson, ed., *Quotes for the Journey* (Colorado Springs, Colo.: NavPress, 2000), 82.

# CHAPTER 2

# ORIGIN *and* DESTINY *in* PSYCHOLOGICAL PERSPECTIVE

SCRIPTURE GIVES US A RICH amount of material describing the origin (From whence have we come?) and the destiny (Where are we headed?) of the human person. The Bible concerns itself with the creation of the human race, the beginning of an individual's life, the meaning of death, and what lies beyond physical death. God could not have fully revealed to us the great drama of redemption without also providing for us a great deal of this information. These truths represent the great parentheses that demarcate both the beginning and the end of human life. The creation of the race and the conception of the individual form the starting points of the redemptive story, and eternal life or eternal death forms the terminus of life as we know it here on earth and the end point of redemption.

Psychology and other related social sciences also concern themselves with the origin and destiny of human life. But they approach it in very different ways. Psychological investigators generally focus on naturalistic explanations for both the origin of the race and the origin of any given individual. And while the theoretical and clinical branches of psychology focus a great deal of attention on the end of an individual's life, the discipline as a whole is appropriately silent about what is beyond death. Psychology is best prepared to address issues related to the natural history of an individual's life and is least prepared to address questions of ultimate meaning and life beyond the grave. We learn about both the natural and the supernatural realm in the pages of God's revealed Word. Psychology, by definition, cannot be so comprehensive. Social science can only describe and seek to explain the natural world and must remain mute regarding the supernatural context that surrounds the world as we know it.

This chapter will first explore several issues related to the beginning of life. We will look at psychology's increasing fascination with evolutionary explanations for the origins of the human mind. Although this emphasis is relatively recent, it has assumed so many variations and is so vast in scope that we can only hope to provide a summary of how the discipline seeks to provide a thoroughly naturalistic explanation for the origins of human cognition and behavior. Regarding the beginning of an individual's life, we will discuss psychology's approach to abortion, the postabortion syndrome, infertility, and prenatal development.

Psychology's interest in destiny questions focuses on death: its meaning to the dying person as well as to those who will survive the death of a loved one. Studies in grief and loss processes that affect all parties touched by death either before or after it has occurred also merit close examination. We will explore two topics closely related to physical death: near-death experiences and suicide. Thus we are able to see that the specific topics related to origin and destiny will vary somewhat when comparing Scripture with modern social science. But both fields regard the beginning and the end of life as vitally important.

## BEGINNING-OF-LIFE ISSUES

### Evolution and Psychology

Most observers of twentieth-century social science would likely assume that evolution and psychology have a long history of interaction together. Somewhat surprisingly, however, their collaboration is quite recent. Sociobiology made its largest impact in the 1970s and 1980s followed by evolutionary psychology (EP), which has exploded in size and impact just since 1990. Why should we be interested in this interaction of evolution with the field of psychology? We believe the influence of evolution on psychology is just beginning, and we can find no good reason to predict the demise of this trend in the foreseeable future. Edward O. Wilson, the Harvard professor most closely associated with the field of sociobiology, has predicted that by the end of the twenty-first century the internalization of evolutionary themes with all of the social sciences will be nearly complete with the result that the social sciences (including psychology) will "come to full flower."[1] Charles Darwin himself predicted the interaction of evolution with psychology in a now-famous passage in the *Origin of Species*. "Psychology will be based on a new foundation, that of the necessary acquirement of each mental power and capacity by gradation."[2] His prophecy is just now coming to fruition.

Instinct psychology was an early attempt to incorporate evolutionary concepts into the field of psychology. But when the estimated number of instincts in humans and animals rose to 1,594, instinct psychology lost its parsimony and soon succumbed to behaviorism.[3] Skinner's approach to learning and reinforcement dominated American psychology until the linguistic work of Noam Chomsky triggered the cognitive revolution. Behaviorism fell into decline.

Chomsky's work with language and how humans acquire linguistic skills demonstrated that general processes and abilities, as favored by Skinner and Piaget, could not adequately explain language acquisition. Language, the creative use of a limited set of symbols to create an almost unlimited number of combinations, develops in children from the age of one to five. Any human infant can learn any one of the 5,500 languages on earth if exposed to that language during this phase of development. Children not only acquire a substantial vocabulary during this time frame, but they also learn the rules of grammar and syntax without being able to articulate the rules they are using.[4] "We are primed by our genes and development to acquire language."[5] Chomsky described this inborn ability as a mechanism or module in the mind that we inherit from our parents. For evolutionists this widely accepted explanation is the product of adaptation and the paradigm for all or most all of the brain's architecture. Advocates of an intelligent design (ID) approach argue that we cannot account for Chomsky's

1. E. O. Wilson, *Sociobiology: The New Synthesis* (Cambridge, Mass.: Harvard University Press, 1975), 574–75.
2. Charles Darwin, *On the Origin of Species* (1859; reprint, Cambridge, Mass.: Harvard University Press, 1964), 488.
3. M. C. Corballis and S. G. Lea, "Comparative-Evolutionary Psychology," in *International Handbook of Psychology*, ed. K. Pawlik and M. R. Rosenzweig (Thousand Oaks, Calif.: Sage, 2000), 348.
4. H. Plotkin, *Evolution in Mind: An Introduction to Evolutionary Psychology* (Cambridge, Mass.: Harvard University Press, 1998), 124–27.
5. Ibid., 134.

discoveries by describing the chance arrangement of evolutionary building blocks.[6]

Chomsky's work figuratively opened the door for a variety of evolutionary influences in the field of psychology. Now that behavior was not the sole focus of the field and now that the discovery of an inborn mechanism for language appeared to be part of universal human nature, advocates of various Darwinian themes began to offer explanations for human cognition. Since its start as a serious discipline in the 1980s, evolutionary psychology has grown greatly in size and influence as evidenced by professional societies, journals, academic posts, textbooks, handbooks, and college courses all dedicated to the subject.[7]

Space will allow us only to refer by way of introduction to some of the general principles of evolution as they have appeared in modern biology and more recently entered the field of psychology. The modern synthesis in biological evolution occurred mid-twentieth century so that now scientists understand the principles of natural selection as originally proposed by Darwin as related to genes and genetic transmission, something Darwin could have known little about. All individuals in a species show variation, some of which is heritable. All individuals compete for scarce resources, an observation that leads to the conclusion that the more successful competitors will have more offspring and thus increase their particular variations in the population. As natural selection occurs slowly over eons of time, some traits disappear and others become more prominent.[8] Evolutionists assert that we can see continuity between the animal kingdom and humans, even though language seems to provide a strong indicator of discontinuity.[9] Animals cannot write books, play instruments, undergo psychotherapy, build skyscrapers, or launch space exploration vehicles, but they do evidence the same natural selection mechanics that evolutionists see in human evolu-

---

6. J. W. Oller, "Languages and Genes: Can They Be Built Up Through Random Change and Natural Selection?" *Journal of Psychology and Theology* 30 (2002): 26–40.

7. D. F. Bjorklund and P. K. Smith, "Evolutionary Developmental Psychology: Introduction to the Special Issue," *Journal of Experimental Child Psychiatry* 85 (2003): 195. Two major handbooks are C. Crawford and D. L. Krebs, eds., *Handbook of Evolutionary Psychology: Ideas, Issues, and Applications* (Mahwah, N.J.: Lawrence Erlbaum Assocs., 1998); and L. Barrett, R. Dunbar, and J. Lycett, *Human Evolutionary Psychology* (Princeton, N.J.: Princeton University Press, 2002).

8. Barrett, Dunbar, and Lycett, *Human Evolutionary Psychology*, 3.

9. "Attempts to teach chimpanzees to actually talk have never been even remotely successful." Corballis and Lea, "Comparative-Evolutionary Psychology," 351.

tionary history.[10] And recent biochemical evidence points to the facts that the chimpanzee has "about 99.6% of its amino acid sequences and 98.4% of its DNA nucleotide sequences in common with our own species."[11]

The process of natural selection is blind; that is, there is no conscious effort to direct the process in any given direction other than to replicate one's genes in the next generation. Some evolutionists describe the gene as immortal because it replicates itself through the generations.[12] Modern evolutionary theory has abandoned the Lamarkian idea that acquired characteristics can be inherited by the next generation. Although Freud was a Lamarkian, other Freudian themes such as instincts, the sexual overtones to development, regression, repression, and libido all fit in well with evolution. Thus evolution has found some common themes in certain branches of psychology.[13]

In recent years scientists have proposed other evolutionary mechanisms to supplement original Darwinian ideas: inclusive fitness, kin selection, reciprocity theory, the evolution of life histories, evolutionarily stable strategies, and optimality theory.[14] In a very short time frame, human evolutionary psychology has become a "surprisingly fractionated field."[15] Some authors, such as Grinde, propose that evolutionary ideas can be the basis for better individual mental health and for better societies in general if we can learn to live in harmony with our nature rather than at odds with it.[16] Colin Tudge argues that evolutionary themes in psychology will help create societies that conform to our nature, societies that will be better because, after all, people are nice most of the time.[17] Yet other authors sound more cynical. Krebs writes that humans evolved "to behave morally when it pays off, to cheat when one believes one can get away with it, and to catch and punish cheaters when it is to one's advantage."[18]

10. Barrett, Dunbar, and Lycett, *Human Evolutionary Psychology*, 2.
11. Corballis and Lea, "Comparative-Evolutionary Psychology," 351.
12. E. Sexton, *Dawkins and the Selfish Gene* (Cambridge: Icon Books, 2001), 12.
13. C. Badcock, "PsychoDarwinism: The New Synthesis of Darwin and Freud," in Crawford and Krebs, *Handbook of Evolutionary Psychology*, 457–58.
14. C. Crawford, "The Theory of Evolution in the Study of Human Behavior," in Crawford and Krebs, *Handbook of Evolutionary Psychology*, 4.
15. Barrett, Dunbar, and Lycett, *Human Evolutionary Psychology*, xi.
16. B. Grinde, *Darwinian Happiness: Evolution as a Guide for Living and Understanding Human Behavior* (Princeton, N.J.: Darwin Press, 2002), 4.
17. C. Tudge, *The Impact of the Gene: From Mendel's Peas to Designer Babies* (New York: Hall and Wang, 2000), 219.
18. D. L. Krebs, "The Evolution of Moral Behaviors," in Crawford and Krebs, *Handbook of Evolutionary Psychology*, 340.

Evolutionists have had three major aims when interacting with psychological themes. First, they have attempted to provide psychology with a metatheory that would help unite this otherwise fragmented field. David Buss describes psychology as a field in "theoretical disarray" with various branches that "proceed in relative isolation from one another, at most occasionally borrowing like a cup of sugar a concept here and a method there from a neighbor."[19] Buss aims at providing the unifying theoretical paradigm that psychology has never had. Frans deWaal is hopeful that just such a unification will occur. "In the end, evolutionary theory may serve as the umbrella idea so desperately needed in the social sciences."[20]

The second aim of evolutionary psychologists is to provide answers for otherwise difficult questions that have defied resolution. "Why do people strive for status? Why does a man who is deeply attracted to beautiful women regard sex with his gorgeous sister as disgusting? Why do women so often marry older men, but have affairs with younger ones? Why do men and women commit adultery, murder, rape?"[21] Perhaps many people would not consider these questions monumental enough to justify a new theory of human behavior. But they do interest evolutionary theorists. Perhaps a more interesting question has to do with snakes. Why do modern people possess an almost universal fear of snakes? Snakes are not part of the experience of most people living in cities and suburbs. Why don't we fear things that are genuinely more likely to hurt us, such as an automobile passing a pedestrian? The answer, say evolutionists, is found in our evolutionary past, a vestige, if you will, of our days spent living in the wild.[22]

A third aim of evolutionists interested in psychological matters deals with the desire to provide a comprehensive and unified explanation for the human mind and resulting behavior. All of the following three main evolutionary approaches recognize the importance of behavior, but they also see cognitive and mind functions as causal and underlying mechanisms. Although evolutionary psychologists often use the word *mind,* they generally

---

19. D. M. Buss, "Evolutionary Psychology: A New Paradigm for Psychological Science," *Psychological Inquiry* 6 (1995): 1.

20. F. B. M. deWaal, "Evolutionary Psychology: The Wheat and the Chaff," *Current Directions in Psychological Science* 11 (2002): 187.

21. C. Stanford, *Significant Others: The Ape-Human Continuum and the Quest for Human Nature* (New York: Basic Books, 2001), 131.

22. D. E. Over, ed., *Evolution and the Psychology of Thinking: The Debate* (New York: Psychology Press, 2003), 3.

are referring to the brain. Modern evolutionary psychologists are monistic physicalists rather than dualists.[23]

Sociobiology was the first movement deeply entwined in evolutionary theory to gain notoriety among psychologists. Edward Wilson's massive 1975 tome on the topic stirred up generous amounts of controversy. In that volume he outlined his hope that sociobiology would someday prove to be a unifying theory around which all the social sciences could work, and he reiterated that same hope nearly twenty-five years later in *Consilience*.[24] By combining ethology, behavioral ecology, and genetics, Wilson attempted to identify the genetically determined bases of human behavior. Wilson's critics were loud and unrelenting, accusing him and his colleagues of indulging in pseudoscience and being purveyors of "just-so stories."[25] Feminist scholars were particularly skeptical that his approach could produce any worthwhile findings. The resulting debate gave sociobiology a bad name, but the debate likely helped sharpen concepts and clarify issues.[26]

Soon sociobiology morphed into evolutionary psychology (EP). A narrowly construed EP first emerged in 1979, and the phrase itself (EP) was first used in 1987.[27] The six major claims of EP[28] are:

- *Adaptation.* The human race has a common descent. The principle of natural selection acted on our ancestors, who manifested traits that facilitated reproduction, survival, and a larger number of heirs. These adaptations became fixed features of human brain architecture. Since these changes occurred at a very slow pace during a time

---

23. Plotkin, *Evolution in Mind,* 122.

24. Wilson, *Sociobiology,* 574; and E. O. Wilson, *Consilience: The Unity of Knowledge* (New York: Alfred A. Knopf, 1998).

25. J. Alcock, *The Triumph of Sociobiology* (Oxford: Oxford University Press, 2001), 217.

26. Rhetoric scholar Leah Ceccarelli argues that Wilson's rhetoric of conquest explains the venomous response critics leveled at sociobiology. Contemporaries who were proposing similarly radical ideas found much better reception by using a rhetoric of negotiation. Leah Ceccarelli, *Shaping Science with Rhetoric: The Cases of Dobzhansky, Schrodenger, and Wilson* (Chicago: University of Chicago Press, 2001), 124. See also U. Segerstrale, *Defender of the Truth: The Battle for Science in the Sociobiology Debate and Beyond* (Oxford: Oxford University Press, 2000), 408.

27. S. J. Scher and F. Rauscher, "Nature Read in Truth or Flaw," in *Evolutionary Psychology: Alternative Approaches,* ed. S. J. Scher and F. Rauscher (Boston: Kluwer Academic, 2003), 7.

28. C. E. Grace, "The Pleistocene Mind: A Critical Review of Evolutionary Psychology and an Introduction to Intelligent Design Psychology," *Journal of Psychology and Theology* 29 (2001): 289–300.

frame we can no longer observe, we must infer these changes from the end-states they produced, i.e., from cognitive and behavioral features of the modern human.

- *Rejection of the Standard Social Science Model (SSSM).* Authors writing in the EP tradition accuse the previous generations of social scientists of studying the human mind from the standpoint of content-independent, general purpose mechanisms (learning, intelligence, rationality, capacity for culture), whereas the mind is better explained by identifying content-dependent mechanisms. EP scholars insist that the SSSM specializes in *ad hoc* explanations and extreme empiricism mingled with a disdain for any underlying evolutionary foundation.[29] In other words, they have been approaching the human mind in a manner that does not and will not produce any unifying explanation for its functioning.

- *Modularity of the Brain.* As our ancestors adapted to evolutionary pressure in eons past, domain-specific mechanisms evolved that became part of the human brain. These modules do not serve general purposes, i.e., they are not used for several intents. Rather they are focused and specific. The human brain has a large number of these domain-specific modules, and the task of EP is to identify them. The massive modularity hypothesis (MMH) states that the human mind is composed almost entirely of these highly specialized cognitive systems as opposed to how previous generations of scientists understood the brain.[30] The brain functions with such seamless efficiency that we are not aware of various modules operating to perform some complicated task. The best evidence for modularity, evolutionists argue, is seen in brain pathology caused by injury or chromosomal abnormality. One example is William's disease, a genetic defect[31] that causes mental retardation but whose victims can

---

29. T. G. Fikes, "Evolutionary Psychology as Computational Theory in the Cognitive Sciences," *Journal of Psychology and Theology* 29 (2001): 349.

30. R. Samuels, "Massively Modular Minds: Evolutionary Psychology and Cognitive Architecture," in *Evolution and the Human Mind: Modularity, Language, and Meta-Cognition,* ed. P. Carruthers and A. Chamberlain (Cambridge: Cambridge University Press, 2000), 16.

31. C. Badcock, *Evolutionary Psychology: A Critical Introduction* (Cambridge: Polity Press, 2000), 251–52.

accomplish some cognitive tasks with great ease while other cognitive skills are greatly impaired.

- *A Universal Human Nature.* Because the human race displays a common descent, we can also posit that a universal human nature exists that characterizes all people, literate or illiterate in developed and undeveloped areas of the planet. Some authors describe this component of EP as species typicality. This feature of EP contrasts with previous and widely held views that did not hold to a universal human nature but instead focused on how the environment and culture created the person by writing on the *tabula rasa* of the mind.
- *Cognitivism.* As we have already mentioned, EP follows in the train of the cognitive revolution that moved the focus of psychological attention from merely exploring human behavior to an investigation of what cognitive functions undergird behavior.
- *Environment of Evolutionary Adaptation (EEA).* The human mind emerged during the Pleistocene era 500,000 years ago on the savannah of East Africa. The human mind, it is alleged, has changed little since then.

The above summary describes what some scholars refer to as narrow evolutionary psychology.[32] Advocates of this narrow form of EP argue that it is one of only three possible causal processes that can account for complex mechanisms known as adaptations. The other two are creationism ("Largely incapable of being verified or disproved by observation or experiment and is not a scientific theory") and seeding theory ("The idea that extraterrestrial organisms visited Earth many years ago and planted the seeds of life").[33] Other evolutionists object and assert that there are many emphases in Darwinian and post-Darwinian theory that can adequately handle observed data and that narrow EP is not the only game in town. Meanwhile, "The narrow approach has generated a series of flourishing research programs which solidify its theoretical basis."[34]

The third evolutionary approach in contemporary American psychology that we will briefly mention is evolutionary developmental psychology (EDP). The focus of this movement is on the developmental processes that

---

32. Scher and Rauscher, "Nature Read in Truth or Flaw," 7.
33. Buss, "Evolutionary Psychology," 2.
34. Scher and Rauscher, "Nature Read in Truth or Flaw," 20.

characterize the growth of human infants and children, as well as change patterns that appear in adolescence and adulthood. Advocates of EDP assert that natural selection has facilitated patterns of behavior and cognition that are now a part of standard development sequences, and that evolution has had a role in shaping these sequences across the life span.[35] This movement, unlike EP, utilizes both domain-specific modules as well as domain-general modules to explain patterns of aggression among preschoolers, sexual segregation in early adolescence, kin recognition, and inbreeding avoidance. Arguments typical of EDP recognize the influence of our biological underpinnings, of plasticity in how development for any given individual proceeds, of phylogenetic continuity in explaining human mental functions, and of the role of the environment in shaping that person.[36]

EDP attempts to identify examples of adaptation in the reconstructed evolutionary history of the species that proved helpful for the original environment but which are detrimental in the contemporary scene. Although other evolutionary movements also seek to highlight this problem, EDP is taking the lead in identifying early adaptations that have become, in essence, maladaptations in current functioning. This approach leads to a very different understanding of what we call psychopathology. EDP scholars express a hopeful attitude that this approach will help "explain present and future behavior, including the amelioration of some 'problem' behaviors (e.g., child abuse, male-on-male violence, rape, reading/math disabilities)."[37]

How are we to evaluate these new and growing movements in American psychology (the remnants of sociobiology, narrow EP, and EDP)? Do they represent the best science available? Is it inevitable that psychology as a discipline will be at increasing odds with Scripture's account of the origin of the human race because of the influence of these evolutionary themes? To answer these questions, we will first examine secular critiques of these evolutionary approaches. If these critiques are effective in deflating the high levels of confidence that some secular scholars currently have in approaches such as EP, these movements will suffer a fate no more glorious than that of sociobiology. Second, we will enumerate the various criticisms of these evo-

---

35. Bjorklund and Smith, "Evolutionary Developmental Psychology: Introduction to the Special Issue," *Journal of Experimental Child Psychiatry*, 196.

36. C. H. Blasi and D. F. Bjorklund, "Evolutionary Devopomental Psychology: A New Tool for Better Understanding Human Ontogeny, *Human Development* 46 (2003): 261.

37. Ibid., 263.

lutionary themes coming from Christian scholars who operate from the base of a theistic worldview.

## Secular Critiques

- *Narrow EP is too narrow.* The most frequent complaint, even from psychologists who are committed evolutionists, is that the major expression of EP cuts itself off from other evolutionary approaches, from the effects of the contemporary environment to shape human cognition and behavior, and from the power of developmental processes on an ontogenetic (not phylogenetic) level.

To the extent that EP and these other approaches represent biological determinism, critics see massive problems. Every evolutionist must make some assertions about the degree of influence and power that our evolutionary inheritance makes on current functioning. If genetics and domain-specific modules in the brain are the primary or sole influence on functioning, the level of determinism is critically high and unacceptable to most scholars, Christian or otherwise. To the degree that evolutionists are willing to include other influences (the environment, developmental process, individual plasticity) in the mix, the levels of determinism become more acceptable and the criticisms become more muted. Any uni-factor determinism, be it biological or environmental, is widely regarded as "hideous" and "nonsense" by most contemporary scientists.[38]

- *Some practitioners make sensationalist and reckless claims.* Science and the media have a love-hate relationship with one another. The media feel compelled to report on new scientific "discoveries," and scientists benefit from the exposure their work gets to the general public. But the American public has repeatedly displayed an almost insatiable appetite for new and glamorous explanations, and the press gladly accommodates them. The result is sometimes embarrassment among members of the responsible scientific community.

Laland and Brown have articulated this critique most effectively as the following quotations demonstrate. "Judging by its media profile and its

---

38. Tudge, *The Impact of the Gene,* 178.

representation in academic and popular science, evolutionary theory would seem to provide the solution to almost every puzzle." "Inevitably [scientists] will fear that inflammatory declarations, careless popularizations, and adaptationist story-telling will produce a backlash against all evolutionary approaches in the social sciences." "A genuine marriage of the biological and social sciences will only emerge when the ratio of sense to nonsense is improved."[39]

- *Scientific rigor is often missing in evolutionary explanations.* EP researchers have set very ambitious goals for themselves. They have argued that a major, if not the major, explanatory goal for understanding human cognition and behavior as we know it is to reconstruct what happened in the human evolutionary process one-half million years ago. We can no longer observe those processes, nor can we be certain that our speculations are more accurate than alternative explanations. Our work, in other words, is nonfalsifiable.

Philip Kitcher asserts that evolutionists pretend to have scientific rigor when, in fact, they have none. He contends that they deserve irreverence, "In short, the Bronx cheer."[40] Almor contends that the scientific rationale for domain-general brain mechanisms is as strong as the rationale for domain-specific mechanisms, although EP advocates rarely admit as much.[41] Sterelny contends that some evolutionary material is "both tentative and gappy."[42] Stanford asserts that the savannah model for the EEA is "a great story" but is "probably fiction."[43] And finally, Steven Rose argues that EP "impoverishes" biology with regard to the processes of evolution, development, and neural formation and makes two major conceptual errors in mis-

39. K. Laland and G. R. Brown, *Sense and Nonsense: Evolutionary Perspectives on Human Behaviour* (Oxford: Oxford University Press, 2002), 1, 318, and 318 respectively.
40. P. Kitcher, *In Mendel's Mirror: Philosophical Reflections on Biology* (Oxford: Oxford University Press, 2003), 352. To be fair we must point out that Kitcher is also harsh on what he calls the born-again creationism of Philip Johnson when he calls it "a sham" (ibid., 377).
41. A. Almor, "Specialized Behavior Without Specialized Modules," in *Evolution and the Psychology of Thinking*, 102.
42. K. Sterelny, *Thought in a Hostile World: The Evolution of Human Cognition* (Malden, Mass.: Blackwell, 2003), 4.
43. C. Stanford, *Significant Others*, 8.

understanding enabling and causal mechanisms and favoring distal over proximate causes of behavior.[44]

- *EP and similar approaches have denigrated women.* Feminists were among the strongest critics of sociobiology, and they are likewise very suspicious of its successor movements that maintain that stereotypical roles and functions for women are hard-wired into the modern brain and that violence and aggression such as occur in rape are natural acts with understandable causes.

Scientists who make such arguments are quick to state that understanding the origin of a human behavioral phenomenon such as rape is not the same thing as condoning it. In fact, evolutionists who argue that rape was at one time a natural act also contend that this understanding will help us decrease the incidence of rape in our contemporary world, where rape is now an unnatural act.[45] Feminists are not convinced. Scholars who studied rape in the 1970s and 1980s and concluded that this act was an act of power quickly reject the notion that rape is reproductive and sexual in nature.[46] "Despite their protestations that they want to help women, the version of evolutionary psychology offered by Thornhill and Palmer is offensive both to women and also to the project of building a culture which rejects rape."[47]

Feminists have earned the right to critique evolutionary theory by participating extensively in the field of animal behavior. While carrying out their scientific observations, female scholars noticed that their observations of both male and female behavior among primates painted quite a different picture of sexual behavior than had been seen for decades through all male eyes. Feminists argue that EP presents a cardboard version of both animal and human females. "It is only slightly kinder to men."[48] While admitting

---

44. S. Rose, "Escaping Evolutionary Psychology," in *Alas, Poor Darwin: Arguments Against Evolutionary Psychology,* ed. H. Rose and S. Rose (New York: Harmony Books, 2000), 299.

45. R. Thornhill and C. T. Palmer, *A Natural History of Rape: Biological Bases of Sexual Coercion* (Cambridge, Mass.: MIT Press, 2000), 198–99.

46. C. B. Travis, "Talking Evolution and Selling Difference," in *Evolution, Gender, and Rape,* ed. C. B. Travis (Cambridge, Mass.: MIT Press, 2003), 3–4.

47. Rose and Rose, *Alas, Poor Darwin,* 3.

48. A. Fausto-Sterling, "Beyond Difference: Feminism and Evolutionary Psychology," in *Alas, Poor Darwin,* 223.

that rape is a significant social problem that warrants strenuous scientific investigation, why focus so much attention on the behavior of a small minority who indulge in atypical behavior, asks deWaal?[49] Not all feminists are ready to abandon evolutionary approaches to psychology,[50] but many evolutionary themes fare poorly in most feminist circles.

## Christian Critiques

- *EP is poorly prepared to explain altruism, free will, and meaning.* Any person seeking to explain human functioning must deal with aspects contributing to the richness and uniqueness of human experience, themes such as those listed here. No one is asking evolutionists to explain spiritual or religious factors; we are just asking them to explain and help account for human factors.

Altruism and its counterpart selfishness have been the focus of many evolutionary analyses. Evolutionists are quick to say that altruism toward one's spouse makes good evolutionary sense since such behavior fosters better reproductive fitness and success. The same explanation makes fairly good sense when applied to siblings or kin. But what about altruism directed toward strangers? The best answer to emerge among evolutionists is that it is in the interest of an individual to be altruistic toward a stranger because of reciprocity (If I scratch your back, you are more likely to scratch mine). But critics, both Christian and non-Christian alike, point out that when one posits self-interest to be at the heart of altruism, you are no longer talking about genuine altruism.[51] A purely genetic-based theory does not explain altruism well.[52] Even many secularists are quick to support this basic criticism of EP. Science has serious limits "in its ability to answer some of

---

49. DeWaal, "Evolutionary Psychology," 189.

50. A. Campbell, *A Mind of Her Own: The Evolutionary Psychology of Women* (Oxford: Oxford University Press, 2002), is but one example.

51. W. Hurlburt and P. Kjalanithi, "Evolutionary Theory and the Emergence of Moral Nature," *Journal of Psychology and Theology* 29 (2001): 332.

52. E. Fehr and U. Fischbacher, "The Nature of Human Altruism," *Nature* 425 (2003): 785–91. See also S. G. Post, L. G. Underwood, J. P. Schloss, and W. B. Hurlburt, eds., *Altruism and Altruistic Love: Science, Philosophy, and Religion in Dialogue* (Oxford: Oxford University Press, 2002).

the most profound questions we are given to ask."[53] These central features of human experience resist a purely naturalistic explanation.[54]

- *EP is incomplete in its analysis of human nature.* Originally evolutionists attempted to explain only the biological nature of humans. Now that it has adopted the goal of also explaining human cognition and behavior with natural selection arguments, it has taken upon itself a monumental task, namely, the explanation of socialization, spirituality, God-awareness, and religious instincts. Simplistic arguments based on adaptation will not suffice.

While recognizing the importance of this criticism, we should also note that a thoughtful analysis of EP will include affirming some of its components that are indeed consonant with biblical faith. Christopher Grace maintains that some of the research conducted by EP scholars will, in the end, lend greater support to intelligent design theory than it will to EP. Also, we can agree with EP scholars in their interest in understanding the past, in their identification of self-centeredness as a key component of human functioning, and in their insistence on a universal human nature.[55] Yet EP struggles to give us adequate or satisfying explanations of moral sensitivity, conscience, aesthetic wonder, creativity, and love.[56]

- *EP poorly accounts for post-Pleistocene millennia.* If the human mind developed to the level we can now observe, how can we explain why this evolvement suddenly stopped and remained fairly unchanged for thousands of subsequent years? Granted, evolution is a slow process; but by definition it continues over time and does not stop.

This critique is not an inherently Christian one, but it has been forcefully advanced by a group of Christian scholars. If Pleistocene evolutionary

---

53. J. Dupre, *Human Nature and the Limits of Science* (Oxford: Oxford University Press, 2001), 4.
54. S. Horst, "Evolutionary Explanation and Consciousness," *Journal of Psychology and Theology* 30 (2002): 41–50.
55. Grace, "The Pleistocene Mind," 297.
56. M. J. Boivin, "Feeling Humans and Social Animals: Theological Considerations for an Evolutionary Account of Human Emotion," *Journal of Psychology and Theology* 29 (2001): 319.

development produced a human brain consisting of many domain-specific modules, how do we account for reading? Countless observations of human reading skills have confirmed that there is as much evidence for a reading module as there is for any other module: reading skills seem to follow a universal pattern, the skills are acquired in roughly the same sequence no matter what language the subject is learning to read, and adults can learn to read as well as children. There does not appear to be a prime window of acquisition facility for reading as there is for language. Each of these observations becomes very relevant when we realize that alphabets appeared only about 6,000 years ago. Even if we were to concede that some alphabets existed 20,000 years ago and have not yet been located, how could a reading module have evolved universally and so recently during a supposed period of evolutionary quiescence?[57]

## Infancy

We have given consideration to beginning-of-life issues in psychology as they deal with the race as a whole. Now we will explore some themes that deal with the origin of the individual, issues that pertain to infancy. We will first look at three issues regarding the infant from the viewpoint of the parents: fertility versus infertility, pregnancy and childbirth, and abortion and the postabortion syndrome. All three of these issues have attracted considerable attention among psychological researchers. Each of the three can present parents with substantial challenges that have powerful psychological implications. For Christian parents, the issues can be even more complex since each of the three can raise important theological questions: Is our infertility related to barrenness as described in Scripture? Why does God allow some pregnancies to end in spontaneous abortion? Does God forgive those who have obtained an abortion?

Second, we will explore beginning-of-life issues from the standpoint of infants themselves. What do we know about prenatal development as it relates to psychological processes?

---

57. E. L Johnson, J. Hetzel, and S. Collins, "Reading by Design: Evolutionary Psychology and the Neurophysiology of Reading," *Journal of Psychology and Theology* 30 (2002): 3–25. Evolutionists concede that humans may have used domain-general modules to learn to read or the human brain may have undergone some sort of late cognitive revolution. See D. S. Wilson, "Evolution, Morality, and Human Potential," in *Evolutionary Psychology*, 67–68.

*Fertility Versus Infertility*

Most people in contemporary society assume that they will be able to have a child when they wish to. And while fertility may be the rule for the majority, estimates are that 10 to 15 percent of couples of reproductive age cannot conceive a child after one year of coitus without the use of contraceptives (a standard definition of infertility).[58] Other estimates push the ratio even higher: one out of every six couples will have some experience with infertility during their marriage.[59] What accounts for this relatively high frequency of infertility problems among modern couples in an age of unprecedented medical success in most all other areas? Some possible causes for this high incidence rate are: damage to the reproductive tract caused by sexually-transmitted infections, environmental toxins, possible damage from contraceptives, and increased age at which women seek to conceive (at the age of thirty-five, women begin a downward journey toward lower probability of pregnancy).[60]

Approximately one half of those who seek medical treatment for their infertility will conceive; the other half will not. In about 50 percent of the cases, the infertility problems rests with the woman; in about 40 percent with the man; and for the remaining 10 percent with both partners.[61] Couples struggling with infertility, whether they eventually conquer it or not, experience a considerable amount of psychological distress as they move through the process. "There is considerable frustration, sadness and a feeling of being out of control when they learn that their plans are not being fulfilled."[62]

---

58. M. B. Rosenthal, "Therapy of Working with the Childless Woman: The Pathos of the Unrealized Dreams, The Psychology of Female Infertility," in *Infertility: A Crossroad of Faith, Medicine, and Technology,* ed. K. W. Wildes (Dordrecht: Kluwer Academic, 1997), 39. We must remember, however, that voluntary childlessness is also a cultural feature of Western societies; not all couples without children are infertile. See F. van Balen and M. C. Inhorn, "Interpreting Infertility: A View from the Social Sciences," in *Infertility Around the Globe: New Thinking on Childlessness, Gender, and Reproductive Technologies,* ed. M. C. Inhorn and F. van Balen (Berkeley: University of California Press, 2002), 6.

59. S. E. R. Kurpius and S. E. Maresh, "Women's Health Issues: A Focus on Infertility, Gynecological Cancer, and Menopause," in *The Emerging Role of Counseling Psychology in Health Care,* ed. S. Roth-Roemer, S. E. R. Kurpius, and C. Carmin (New York: W. W. Norton, 1998), 333.

60. Ibid.

61. Rosenthal, "Therapy of Working with the Childless Woman," 39.

62. Ibid., 40.

Treatment for the infertility is often burdensome, invasive (particularly for the woman), and taxing. In addition, "The rise and fall of emotions that accompany the menstrual cycle intensify for women during infertility treatment. . . . A rollercoaster ride is a common metaphor used by women to describe this hope-loss cycle."[63]

As recently as the mid-1960s, experts felt that about 50 percent of infertility cases had an organic basis and that the other 50 percent had a psychological cause. Because of advancing medical knowledge, most experts now contend that 85 to 90 percent of infertility cases have some organic or biological cause. When the best medical opinion argued that one-half of all infertility cases were caused by some psychological factor or factors, researchers spent a great deal of time searching for this cause or causes. Current research, however, focuses not on the emotional causes of infertility (which turns out to be relevant in only a small percentage of cases) but instead on the psychological effects of infertility.

Therapists who work frequently with couples struggling with infertility report that they too often link their entire sense of identity to their infertile condition. Therapists strive to help both the men and the women involved accept infertility as merely one aspect of who they are. Acceptance is crucial as opposed to resolution. Infertility may never resolve itself; couples can experience its implications throughout their lifetime. Infertility, as well as miscarriage, ectopic pregnancies, fetal death, and stillbirths all can contribute to a sort of "shadow grief" that often "intensifies at anniversaries of conception, due dates, death dates, and holidays."[64] But accepting the condition as part of one's life experience is crucial.[65] Medical science continues to develop new interventions designed to produce conception. Current alternatives include intrauterine insemination, in vitro fertilization, intracytoplasmic sperm injection, gamete intrafallopian transfer, and zygote intrafallopian transfer.[66] And the list continues to expand with each passing year.

---

63. Mikesell, Susan G., "Infertility and Pregnancy Loss: Hypnotic Interventions for Reproductive Challenges," in *Healing from Within: The Use of Hypnosis in Women's Health Care*, ed. L. M. Hornyak and J. P. Green (Washington, D.C.: American Psychological Assoc., 2000), 197.

64. Ibid., 198.

65. L. L. Deveraux and A. J. Hammerman, *Infertility and Identity: New Strategies for Treatment* (San Francisco: Jossey-Bass, 1988), 12–13.

66. Mikesell, "Infertility and Pregnancy Loss," 193.

## Pregnancy and Childbirth

Pregnancy and childbirth are likewise aspects of the life cycle that can be fraught with emotional struggle for some people. The joy of the first trimester is counterbalanced by the oft-present morning sickness; the renewed energy of the second trimester can give the expectant mother time to plan and dream for impending arrival of the child; and the awkwardness of size and weight that characterize the third trimester can often create impatience as well as excitement.[67] Approximately 10 percent of expectant mothers experience some mood disturbance during the nine months of pregnancy. Since many of the symptoms ape the symptoms of pregnancy itself (appetite and sleep disturbance, low energy, etc.), diagnosis is difficult. Not all psychopharmacologic agents for depression are appropriate to use during pregnancy, so treatment of maternal depression during a pregnancy is also difficult.[68]

Childbirth itself is accompanied by a wide range of varied emotions for the parents: fear, joy, pride, exhaustion, excitement, and letdown. As the mother begins to move through a period of readjustment to her new nonpregnant condition, hormonal changes often bring mild to moderate levels of postpartum depression. Press reports of tragic cases of mothers who kill their children have alerted the public to the dangers of untreated and severe postpartum depression. While infanticide by mothers is rare, its occurrence even in small numbers should alert all parties concerned about the possibilities of psychotic illness after childbirth. While mental illness is the cause of many cases of maternal infanticide (either neonaticide, killing a newborn, or filicide, killing a child), scholars have linked other causes to these events as well: spousal revenge, an unwanted child, accidental death, and abuse.[69]

---

67. M. I. Oster and C. P. Sauer, "Hypnotic Methods for Preparing for Childbirth," in *Healing from Within*, 162.

68. R. Nonacs and L. S. Cohen, "Assessment and Treatment of Depression During Pregnancy: An Update," in *Women's Mental Health*, ed. S. G. Kornstein and A. H. Clayton (Philadelphia: W. B. Saunders, 2003), 547–49.

69. C. L. Meyer and M. Oberman, *Mothers Who Kill Their Children* (New York: New York University Press, 2001), 20.

### Abortion and the Postabortion Syndrome

On January 22, 1973, former President Lyndon Baines Johnson died and the United State Supreme Court handed down its famous *Roe v. Wade* decision. The legalization of abortion in all fifty states greatly overshadowed the former president's death, a foretaste of how significant, contentious, controversial, and troublesome this abortion question would become in American life and thought. For the past thirty years pro-choice and pro-life camps have debated, recruited, campaigned, and pilloried each other. The debate has permeated all corners of the academic, political, and religious worlds. And we find little evidence that the furor is diminishing or will quiet down anytime soon. "In the years since the *Roe* decision . . . the political struggle over the role of abortion in U.S. society has fiercely resisted eclipse."[70] At the present time, both the pro-life and the pro-choice sides in the debate continue to be very polarized, and neither side seems willing to seek a compromise.[71]

The abortion clamor has produced some interesting incongruities: evangelical Christians joining with Roman Catholics to advocate pro-life policies; pro-life radicals advocating murder;[72] and scientific organizations taking political sides in the debate and making public policy statements. The American Psychological Association is one such organization, even though the membership of the association contains both pro-life and pro-choice advocates. Psychology's main involvement, however, has been in trying to ascertain through a variety of research strategies how abortion affects people psychologically.

Both pro-choice and pro-life groups have advanced various arguments based on their understanding of the research. As with most all factors associated with the abortion controversy, research sometimes has its pronounced bias, depending on the goals of the researchers who are involved. So it is not too surprising that each side is able to find research findings supportive of its position. A frequent weakness of research projects investigating this area

---

70. R. Solinger, *Beggars and Choosers: How the Politics of Choice Shapes Adoption, Abortion, and Welfare in the United States* (New York: Hill and Wang, 2001), 3,

71. M. Y. Herring, *The Pro-Life/Choice Debate* (Westport, Conn.: Greenwood Press, 2003), 193.

72. P. Baird-Windle and E. J. Bader, *Targets of Hatred: Anti-Abortion Terrorism* (New York: Palmgrave, 2001), 77–82.

is the use of volunteer subjects only and the lack of long-term follow-up studies, especially longer than two years.[73]

A major argument advanced by pro-life groups deals with the risk to the psychological health of the mother when she decides to undergo an abortion. This appeal to risk as a factor that should deter society in general from easily accessible abortion and individuals in particular from making a decision to abort is one that has prompted a great deal of research. In fact, some people active in the movement have given considerable attention to the concept of a postabortion syndrome, a psychological state that represents poor mental health subsequent to an abortion.

In 1992 Speckhard and Rue proposed criteria for just such a syndrome. They based their suggestions on post-traumatic stress disorder (PTSD) as delineated by the current diagnostic manual of the American Psychiatric Association. Among the symptoms Speckhard and Rue suggested for their proposed postabortion syndrome were exposure to a real or perceived trauma, delayed onset of a troubling and anxiety-ridden response to the trauma, and an intrusive and unwanted re-experiencing of the traumatic event. The public has become quite familiar with some of these criteria by learning about PTSD and Vietnam veterans. Clinicians who work with distressed women who have had an abortion have observed some of the same symptoms as reported by veterans who have experienced the trauma of war.

No one disputes that a certain number of women experience a severely negative reaction after obtaining an abortion. Opinions do vary, however, as to how common this reaction is among postabortion women, whether the rate of occurrence justifies a new diagnostic category, and whether the condition is discrete enough from PTSD to warrant a separate diagnostic label.[74] Clinicians who have seen many women with just such a traumatic reaction might conclude that this severely negative reaction is fairly common. But clinicians deal with a skewed sample (persons distressed by the experience), a sample that might not fairly represent the larger population of women who have had an abortion. Most observers who attempt to sample the total number of women who have elected to have an abortion contend

---

73. C. J. C. Maxwell, *Pro-Life Activists in America: Meaning, Motivation, and Direct Action* (Cambridge: Cambridge University Press, 2002).

74. Nothing would prevent a clinician from using PTSD as a diagnosis for a woman experiencing a severe and delayed reaction to a traumatic abortion if she otherwise meets all the criteria for the disorder. See *DSM*-IV, 463–68.

that negative reactions are rare, even though at times they can be severe. Some research suggests that the risk rates for a negative reaction are similar to those of childbirth and that stress levels are often higher before the abortion than after it.[75] According to some researchers, appealing to the psychological risk factor as a deterrent is probably a better political or social strategy than a scientific one.[76]

Women who cope well with abortion report having minimal ambivalence about making the decision to abort, receiving support for their decision to abort from the father and/or other significant persons, and having strongly positive expectations about their ability to cope after the event is over.[77] Women are more likely to have a negative reaction to an abortion if they attend church regularly, belong to a group that opposes the practice of abortion, are young and unmarried without other children, have difficulty making the decision to abort, have low levels of social support around them, and have a low level of confidence in their ability to cope. This final factor is not just correlated with negative outcome; research has also established that it is causally related to negative outcome.[78]

Therapists, clinicians, and pastors who work with women struggling with a personal history of abortion have many psychological treatment options available to them. Depending on the individual involved, the traumatic reaction may be chiefly related to loss, to the violation of norms, to a troubled decision-making style, to learned behaviors, or to poor capacities for dealing with stress.[79]

## Neonatal Development

The most common response of parents when they first see their newborn child is to be filled with wonder. No other event reminds us of God's

---

75. S. Gold-Steinberg and A. J. Stewart, "Psychologies of Abortion: Implications of a Changing Context," in *Abortion Wars: A Half Century of Struggle: 1950–2000*, ed. R. Solinger (Berkeley: University of California Press, 1998), 358.

76. G. H. Wilmoth and M. de Alterius, "Prevalence of Psychological Risks Following Legal Abortion in the U.S.: Limits of the Evidence," *Journal of Social Issues* 48 (2002): 37.

77. Gold-Steinberg and Stewart, "Psychologies of Abortion," 358.

78. N. E. Adler et al., "Psychological Factors in Abortion: A Review," *American Psychologist* 47 (1992): 1200. See also B. Major and C. Cozzarelli, "Psychosocial Predictors of Adjustment to Abortion," *Journal of Social Issues* 48 (1992): 137.

79. W. B. Miller, "An Empirical Study of the Psychological Antecedents and Consequences of Induced Abortion," *Journal of Social Issues* 48 (1992): 81–83.

creative power as well as does the gestation of a child and the ensuing birth of that child. Biblical evidence, as we have seen, points to the time frame of conception as the beginning of life for an individual child. The birth of that child is something of a second beginning, a day we commemorate each year. We can observe that the child's birth displays both discontinuity with prenatal development and continuity with it. The discontinuity stems from the major change that occurs when the child ceases to receive its nourishment and oxygen through the placenta attached to its mother and begins to receive nourishment through its own mouth and oxygen through its own nose and lungs. Research has documented that the continuity between the child's prenatal and postpartum existence is likewise remarkable: the growth the child has been experiencing in the womb simply continues after birth as organs and systems continue to mature.

Maternal behavior while her child is yet unborn has a direct impact on the later intelligence and psychological functioning of that child. We know that a mother's alcohol consumption can have "devastating and long-lasting effects on the exposed individual."[80] The effects range from prenatal death to the devastating fetal alcohol syndrome (FAS) with its craniofacial abnormalities and central nervous system dysfunction to softer effects among children whose symptoms do not quite qualify them for FAS: behavioral and cognitive impairments.[81] The brains of these children are literally malformed.

We can see continuity in the ongoing connection between mother and child after birth. In the womb, the mother undergoes substantial adaptation in her cardiovascular, renal, hematological, respiratory, gastrointestinal, endocrine, and metabolic systems to facilitate the growth and development of her child.[82] After birth she continues to provide nourishment for the infant and care for its ongoing needs. The interaction between fetus and mother is proving to be far more extensive than researchers previously understood. "It is now clear that the signals that initiate labour originate in

---

80. T. M. Roebuck, S. N. Mattson, and E. P. Riley, "Prenatal Exposure to Alcohol: Effects on Brain Structure and Neuropsychological Functioning," in *Alcohol and Alcoholism: Effects on Brain and Development*, ed. J. H. Hannigan, L. P. Sear, N. E. Spear, and C. R. Goodlet (Mahwah, N.J.: Laurence Erlbaum, 1999), 1.

81. Ibid., 1–2.

82. A. D. Bocking, "Maternal Adaptation of Pregnancy," in *Fetal Growth and Development*, ed. R. Harding and A. D. Bocking (Cambridge: Cambridge University Press, 2001), 224.

the fetus. These signals represent the expression of the fetal genome acting through endocrine pathways involving the fetal brain, adrenal gland and placenta as well as mechanical signals acting directly on the myometrium as a result of the growth of the fetus. . . . Inappropriate expressions of these signals or their bypass under pathological conditions, probably makes a major contribution to preterm labour."[83] And the interaction between the fetus and its mother becomes all the more intense after birth.

The psychology of the fetus and the infant is important for us to consider, even if we sometimes invest more energy in trying to understand physiological development. We know that the fetus is very active in the womb, especially in the last half of the pregnancy (an example of behavior). The child practices both the sucking reflex and breathing movements even though no air enters the lungs.[84] The fetus is responsive to sound, pain, temperature changes, and touch; all of the senses except vision are operative in the womb.[85] Learning begins to occur at even greater rates almost immediately after birth. If learning is occurring, we surmise that memory is also functioning; a person cannot learn if memory does not assist in the process. Even though the memory is active for the infant, children and adults do not have the ability to consciously retrieve material stored in that area of the mind (see chap. 8).

Researchers from many disciplines have uncovered many of the secrets of development for both the fetus and the child, but many more secrets remain to be discovered. The human fetus and child are not psychologically inert but are active, acquisitive, and interactive in ways we are only now beginning to understand more fully. Consider the following examples from current research projects:

- *Fetal movement predicts later temperament.* Fetuses move during the last half of gestation on an average of one time per minute during the 10 to 30 percent of the time that they are active. Fetuses who were more active in the womb showed less distress to frustration and restraint at the age of one and more interactions with toys with an experimenter apart from the mother at the age of two than chil-

---

83. S. J. Lye and J. R. G. Challis, "Parturition," in *Fetal Growth and Development*, 241–42.
84. P. G. Hepper, "Prenatal Development," in *Introduction to Infant Development*, ed. A. Slater and M. Lewis (Oxford: Oxford University Press, 2002), 55.
85. Ibid., 51–54.

dren who were less active in the womb. Researchers are currently seeking to find the specific psychological mechanism underlying this connection. But even with unrefined measures of movement in the womb (researchers cannot directly see, touch, or handle the moving infant), fetal movement patterns robustly predict later temperament in a way that "merits notice."[86]

- *The style of infant attention patterns predicts adolescent intelligence.* Researchers have discovered that adolescents whose attention style as an infant was characterized by short looks will score higher on intelligence tests than adolescents whose attention style was characterized by long looks. Researchers remain puzzled about what mechanism could possibly link these two phenomena together. But the fact that a measure of infant attention patterns in the first few months of life "is able to predict intelligence 18 years later is remarkable."[87]

- *Infants prefer Baby Talk (BT) to adult speech.* Parents the world over know that they can stimulate greater response from their baby by using BT than when they talk in adult speech patterns to the baby. Why? Researchers have found that the baby's preference is for the positive affect that accompanies BT rather than for BT itself. When adults speak to babies with regular language accompanied by the same amount of positive affect that usually accompanies BT, the preference disappears.[88]

- *Infants can discern maternal depression.* Research has established that infants react to the depressive symptoms of their mother by preferring smiling stimuli.[89] We cannot say that the infant is trying to make the mother feel better by showing this preference, but we can remind everyone concerned that treating maternal depression is an important health goal since the infant is clearly affected by it.

---

86. J. A. DiPietro et al. "What Does Fetal Movement Predict About Behavior During the First Two Years of Life?" *Developmental Psychobiology* 40 (2002): 359–69.

87. M. Sigman, S. E. Cohen, and L. Beckwith, "Why Does Infant Attention Predict Adolescent Intelligence?" in *Infant Development: The Essential Readings,* ed. D. Muir and A. Slater (Malden, Mass.: Blackwell, 2000), 251.

88. C. T. Best, "Infants' Listening Preferences: Baby Talk or Happy Talk?" *Infancy* 3 (2002): 365.

89. T. Striano, P. A. Brennan, and E. J. Vanman, "Maternal Depressive Symptoms and Six-Month-Old Infants' Sensitivity to Facial Expressions," *Infancy* 3 (2002): 125.

- *The vision of infants is much better than previously thought.* Many of the infant's visual abilities are intact at birth (shape constancy, size constancy). At birth infants appear to have an innately specified representation of faces that allows them to recognize human faces very early in their development. And we now know that "many visual functions approach adult standards 3 or 4 months from birth."[90]

- *Infants help shape their environments.* Observers of human infants have often made the mistake of assuming that the child is a passive responder to the environment around it. A large body of evidence now confirms that the infant is, in fact, actively involved in shaping what that environment is. For example, the cries of an infant are a powerful stimulus for soothing care from the parent. The infant and its environment have reciprocal influence on the other. "Social interaction becomes increasingly mutually regulated, with the infant and parent each adjusting their responses based on the partner's prior behavior."[91]

These examples serve to remind us that while we know a great deal about the beginnings of life for the human infant, much more remains to be discovered in the future.

## END-OF-LIFE ISSUES

Scripture treats human origin and human destiny themes with noticeable evenhandedness. We learn that beginnings are connected to endings, that God's redemptive goals for the human race are connected to His created intent for the race, and that God's intentions for humans at the time of creation were likewise linked to the eventual destiny He envisioned for them. Modern psychology, however, has not been so finely balanced in considering beginning-of-life and end-of-life issues. Death with its many ramifications has received much less attention than the beginning-of-life themes we have just reviewed. Psychology is very much embedded in modern, West-

---

90. A. Slater, "Visual Perception in the Young Infant: Early Organization and Rapid Learning," in *Infant Development,* ed. Muir and Slater, 98–105.

91. K. H. Karraker and P. Coleman, "Infants' Characteristics and Behaviors Help Shape Their Environments," in *Infant Development: Ecological Perspectives,* ed. H. E. Fitzgerald, K. H. Karraker, and T. Lester (New York: Routledge Falmer, 2002), 172.

ern culture, and its benign neglect of death probably just reflects the larger society that gave birth to the discipline.

We will explore how psychology deals with six end-of-life issues: near-death experiences, euthanasia, suicide, the meaning of death itself, counseling for the dying, and grief and loss as important components of human functioning.

## Near-Death Experiences

In spite of our society's general lack of interest in death, stories of near-death experiences (NDE) attract a great deal of attention in both public and academic spheres. Observers of this phenomenon estimate (conservatively) that some eight million people in America have experienced a NDE. The sheer number of occurrences, of course, proves nothing as to the meaning and true nature of the NDE. NDE occurs in approximately 30 percent of all near-death instances.[92] Persons with impressive scholarly credentials have dedicated a great deal of study to the topic and have established the *Journal of Near-Death Studies* and the International Association of Near Death Studies.[93] Biologists, philosophers, psychologists, and theologians have all investigated the phenomenon.[94] Near-death experiences have occurred throughout recorded history and in most all cultures, although experts disagree about whether or not the NDEs are primarily similar across cultures or whether they bear some important distinctions from each other. "The phenomenon is abundantly (not to say excessively) documented and analysed in a vast literature, specialist as well as popular, which has piled up over recent years."[95]

The majority of those who experience NDE are in a health crisis that has taken them close to death's door; a minority has experienced a terrifying trauma just before their NDE occurred. Of those who are physically ill,

---

92. E. E. Valarino, *On the Other Side of Life: Exploring the Phenomenon of the Near-Death Experience* (New York: Plenum, 1997), 2.

93. M. Cox-Chapman, *The Case for Heaven: Near-Death Experiences as Evidence of the Afterlife* (New York: G. P. Putnam, 1995), 2–8.

94. L. W. Bailey and J. Yates, eds., *The Near-Death Experience: A Reader* (New York: Routledge, 1996), 12.

95. C. Cherry, "Are Near-Death Experiences Really Suggestive of Life After Death?" in *Beyond Death: Theological and Philosophical Reflections on Life After Death,* ed. D. Cohn-Sherbok and C. Lewis (New York: St. Martin's Press, 1995), 146.

doctors have declared some but not all of them clinically dead. Those who have passed through such an experience become firm believers in the reality of the experience and generally speak of the event as though it were an example of "hyper-reality."[96]

NDEs generally begin with feelings of peace and quiet, contain a sense of being out of the body (perhaps rising above the operating table or hospital bed), going through a dark tunnel, meeting a Being of Light, experiencing a life review (having your entire life flash by you), having a choice of return- ing or being compelled to return, and experiencing significant change as a result of the NDE.[97] Some observers wonder if the Being of Light often encountered is, in fact, related to satanic deception since Scripture describes Satan as a great deceiver masking in light. Additional evidence for the pos- sibility of satanic deception revolves around the accounts of some people who relate that during their NDE a voice told them that all was well and they should return and continue living as they were doing.

People who offer explanations for these NDEs can be grouped into two categories: those who see the NDE as evidence for life after death and those who see the NDE as the manifestations of a dying brain. Christians might be tempted to view the NDE as experiential confirmation of what the Bible teaches about personal eschatology. But we must be cautious about rushing to such a conclusion since this explanation does not solve all the riddles attached to the NDE experience. Considerable evidence exists in support of the dying brain hypothesis: the brain does emit certain chemicals when death is imminent, chemicals that can produce hallucinatory-like experi- ences, as well as a sense of bright light; the tunnel experience could reflect the physiology of the brain's cortex; and the resulting change in outlook toward life can merely reflect the close encounter with physical death.[98]

## Euthanasia

Christians have expressed grave concerns about various expressions of euthanasia that have appeared in American society recently. Physician-

---

96. K. Ring, *The Omega Project: Near-Death Experiences, UFO Encounters, and Mind at Large* (New York: William Morrow, 1992), 97.

97. J. N. Bremmer, *The Rise and Fall of the Afterlife* (London: Routledge, 2002), 100–101.

98. S. Blackmore, *Dying to Live: Near-Death Experiences* (Buffalo, N.Y.: Prometheus Books, 1993), 261–63.

assisted suicide has gained legal status in at least one state, and considerable pressure exists to extend this practice to other sections of our country. Derek Humphrey's book *Final Exit* has become a widely distributed title that in essence is a manual for how to take your own life.[99]

The two major arguments proponents of euthanasia put forward are autonomy (we all should have the "right" to determine when we die) and suffering (the death process for some terminally ill people involves intolerable levels of physical suffering). Christian apologists can effectively respond to the first: God has not given us the prerogative of determining when our birth or death will occur. Physicians can deal with the second since palliative care and pain management regimens continue to improve with every passing year. Neither autonomy nor suffering form a sufficient basis for violating society's traditional cultural norms that respect the sanctity of life and provide care for those who are ill and suffering. Experience in countries such as the Netherlands indicates that physician-assisted suicide does not necessarily raise the levels of control and power the sick individual has over his or her life but tends instead to raise the power of the physician.[100]

Obtaining informed consent from a terminally ill person is not a simple or easy task. Many, if not all, ill persons are experiencing some levels of depression that can cloud their judgment. Clinicians of all stripes face a great difficulty in verifying the voluntariness of a sick person's consent. How much information is sufficient to allow the dying person to make an informed decision? How valid is a decision made prior to the illness? Who determines competence to make such a major decision?[101]

---

99. In a more recent edition of the book, Humphrey admits that some people who were depressed or mentally ill "misused" his book as an instruction manual for suicide. Although Humphrey expressed regret, he said he could "do nothing about it." (*Final Exit: The Practicalities of Self-deliverance and Assisted Suicide for the Dying* [New York: Random House, 2002], xv.)

100. J. Dupre, *Human Nature and the Limits of Science* (Oxford: Oxford University Press, 2001), 4. See also E. J. Larson and D. W. Amundsen, *A Different Death: Euthanasia and the Christian Tradition* (Downers Grove, Ill.: InterVarsity, 1998), 244–48.

101. S. J. Younger, "Competence to Refuse Life-Sustaining Treatment," in *End of Life Decisions: A Psychosocial Perspective,* ed. M. D. Steinberg and S. J. Younger (Washington, D.C.: American Psychiatric Press, 1998), 19–22.

## Suicide

Even though the Bible does not specifically condemn suicide, Jewish and Christian scholars alike have always understood from the implicit teachings of both Testaments that suicide is morally wrong, sinful, and outside the parameters of God's desire for people. By way of contrast, suicide has merited the close attention of both the academic and the clinical wings of psychology. Suicidology is a specialty within the field characterized by journals, societies, and research groups. Suicide prevention is a standard component in all training programs for mental health workers, and it attracts a considerable amount of government funding because of its cost to society in general.

Approximately 31,000 people die as a result of suicide every year in the United States, making it the ninth leading cause of death in the population at large and the third leading cause of death among adolescents.[102] As surprising as it may be to some people, we also know that children commit suicide even though their deaths are often reported as mere accidents. Experts have suggested that one-third of the U.S. population has experienced thoughts of suicide (suicidal ideation) at least one time during their lifetimes. Emergency rooms at hospitals treat 650,000 cases of suicide attempts each year. Suicidal clients represent the most frequent emergency that counselors and psychotherapists encounter in the course of their work and are the source of "endless disquiet" for mental health workers.[103] Clearly, suicide is a serious societal problem that merits all the attention psychology has directed toward it, if not more.

Many factors contribute to the eventual suicide of a distressed person. Ninety percent of all suicides are connected to psychopathology and/or substance/alcohol abuse.[104] While some would argue that at times suicide is a "rational" decision, others (including most Christians) would maintain that the decision to kill oneself is never fully rational nor is it ever the best alternative facing even the most miserable of people. Biological, psychological, social, and cultural influences all make an impact on the suicidal phenom-

---

102. B. Bongar, *The Suicidal Patient: Clinical and Legal Standards of Care,* 2d ed. (Washington, D.C.: American Psychological Association, 2002), xix–xx; and S. K. Goldsmith, T. C. Pellmar, A. M. Kleinman, and W. E. Bunney, eds., *Reducing Suicide: A National Imperative* (Washington, D.C.: National Academies Press, 2002), 2.
103. Bongar, *The Suicidal Patient,* 3.
104. Goldsmith et al., *Reducing Suicide,* 2.

enon. Hopelessness appears at the core of the suicidal person's affect no matter which diagnostic label best describes the person. The nearly universal presence of hopelessness among suicidal people provides the church and concerned Christians with a powerful point of intervention. Hope is at the heart of the gospel message and can be the most potent gift we can offer those who struggle profoundly with thoughts of suicide.

Clinicians have long observed that many suicides occur just after the depressed person seems to have made a turn for the better. One explanation for this is that once the depression begins to lift, a person has access to more energy to carry out plans previously made. Another explanation may relate to the possibility that depression and suicidality are actually two different conditions that often occur together (comorbidity) but which in fact respond differently to treatment. For example, depression often lifts in response to effective medication regimens, while suicidality does not. Conversely, suicidality appears more responsive to psychotherapy than does depression.[105]

In an effort to improve the assessment and prediction of suicide, scholars have directed a great deal of attention to the identification of proven risk factors. We know that the strongest predictors of a suicide attempt are associated with females under the age of thirty who are unmarried, unemployed, and depressed. The strongest predictive factors for suicide completion are associated with males in their thirties and forties who are unmarried, unemployed, and suffering either from depression or schizophrenia.[106] Factors that lower the risk of suicide include religious affiliation and church attendance, good coping skills, and good problem-solving ability. Assessment requires the clinician to collect relevant demographic information directly from the patient, examine current and historical indicators, screen for risk as to its level and imminence, and implement a treatment intervention that will provide safety for the client.[107] However, in spite of improvements in our ability to detect the level of risk among suicidal persons, "no psychological test, clinical technique, or biological marker is sufficiently sensitive and specific to accurately assess acute prediction of suicide in an individual."[108]

---

105. Ibid.
106. Bongar, *The Suicidal Patient*, 35.
107. Ibid., 83–84.
108. Goldsmith et al., *Reducing Suicide*, 5.

Counselors have access to two helpful interventions: the therapeutic alliance between the counselor and client and a negotiated safety contract. Research tells us that the therapeutic alliance by itself is not as effective in reducing risk as it is when combined with a written and verbal safety contract, and a safety contract without a positive therapeutic alliance is nearly worthless. The safety contract is not a replacement for thorough risk assessment, is not a fail-safe intervention, should be reevaluated at regular intervals, is not useful in emergencies, and should be utilized for the client's best interests and not primarily to lower the counselor's anxiety or sense of risk.[109]

The general public is aware that adolescent suicide has some distinctives of its own. The function of the peer group for an adolescent can both prompt a suicide attempt and lead to copycat behavior once a friend has successfully completed the act. Intervening in school or church settings after a teenager has died because of suicide has become routine, but most experts agree that prevention programs even before someone has died are more effective. Curricula designed to help teenagers deal with thoughts of suicide are now common in most public schools. Research shows that these programs are most successful when they deal with both depression and substance abuse (including alcohol education) and when they involve both students and parents.[110]

Family members and close friends who survive the suicide of a loved one represent an often-neglected population of hurting people. A successful suicide is a violent act committed by a person close to the survivors and is an act that they desperately sought to prevent or would have sought to prevent if they had known about the severity of their loved one's misery. Survivors frequently need professional or lay help in dealing with the shame and guilt they feel and with the silence, distortion, and secrecy that those around them may impose upon their tragic situation.[111]

---

109. R. I. Simon, *Assessing and Managing Suicide Risk: Guidelines for Clinically Based Risk Management* (Washington, D.C.: American Psychiatric Publishing, 2004), 68–75.

110. J. S. Wodarski, L. A. Wodarski, and C. N. Dulmus, *Adolescent Depression and Suicide: A Comprehensive Empirical Intervention for Prevention and Treatment* (Springfield, Ill.: Charles C. Thomas, 2003), 28–37.

111. N. Farberow, "Helping Suicide Survivors," in *Suicide Prevention: Resources for the Millennium,* ed. D. Lester (Philadelphia: Brunner-Routledge, 2001), 190–91.

## The Meaning of Death

The Christian worldview contains at its very heart a fairly specific view of the meaning of death. Christians throughout the world take great comfort in the hope that results from understanding biblical teachings regarding the meaning of death. At times it is difficult for Christians to understand how people without a firm belief in Christian hope can function in life. Paul urged us to put this hope at the center of our lives and not "to grieve like the rest of men, who have no hope" (1 Thess. 4:13).

Secular psychology does not operate according to Christian hope and has not focused extensively on this topic. Three major reasons account for this neglect. First, most observers define the field of psychology as the study of human behavior and/or of human cognition. We know that behavior stops when the person dies, and psychologists who are naturalistic monists (see chap. 5) assume that cognition stops when the brain dies. If mind cannot operate without the brain, how could cognition survive death? Second, the standard means of investigation (surveys, questionnaires, correlational studies, controlled experiments, etc.) are methods that cannot be applied to the study of death. If we can't study the phenomenon with our normal tools of analysis, how can we derive any sense of what death means? Third, psychology is primarily concerned with what occurs between birth and death; what happens after death is, in many ways, beyond the scope of psychology's investigative interests.

In spite of these limitations, some psychologists have sought to investigate the meaning of death. A fundamental problem has been ascertaining just when death occurs. As we have seen with conception, pinpointing the exact moment when death comes to the dying individual has only become more complicated as medical advances tell us more and more about the death process. We know, for example, that electrocardiogram signals continue for several minutes after the heart has stopped beating, that doctors can observe pronounced pupillary responses three hours after the heart has stopped beating, that surgeons can graft skin tissue up to twenty-four hours, bone grafts up to forty-eight hours and arterial grafts up to seventy-two hours after the heart has stopped beating.[112] So when does death occur? When does living tissue become dead tissue? Even though death often appears to

---

112. H. Brennan, *Death: The Great Mystery of Life* (New York: Carroll and Graf, 2002), xiii.

survivors as an event, we can better describe it as a relatively brief process during which life ebbs away as the brain dies, the heart stops, respiration ceases, and the many types of tissue in the body gradually give up life and energy.

A second complication for psychological research into the meaning of death is that individuals construct idiosyncratic attitudes toward death that can make generalizations and population-wide summaries meaningless. "Our individual constructions of death are influenced by our unique experiences within our unique physical, interpersonal, and cultural milieu."[113] Whereas the nearly universal fear of death and Freud's postulated death instinct may affect every person to some degree, other factors impacting the meaning of death are much more personal. We know, for example, that people successfully accept the meaning of death for another person long before they can maturely deal with their own eventual death. The point of time at which these feats of maturation are achieved will vary from person to person.[114]

In spite of these difficulties, psychologists have established several centers to investigate death. The Institute for the Study of the Afterdeath utilizes a major research instrument, Research Grids, to collect data that they can analyze statistically and discursively regarding death and its meaning to individuals.[115] And the Survival Research Foundation "explores for empirical facts which may *suggest* that a human personality or consciousness has survived death"[116] (emphasis in original). A major source of information for both of these groups, as well as for other investigators, however, is data from the non-Christian religions of the world and from paranormal experiences of people. Both sources of data are problematic from a Christian point of view.

## Counseling the Dying

Even though psychology has not proven to be a discipline that can make substantial investment in investigating the meaning of death, the field has

---

113. R. Kastenbaum, *The Psychology of Death,* 2d ed. (New York: Springer, 1992), 83–84.
114. Ibid., 84–88; 138–94.
115. S. Miller, *After Death: Mapping the Journey* (New York: Simon and Schuster, 1997), 201–2.
116. A. Berger, "Death and the Afterlife: New Approaches to an Old Question," in *Beyond Death: Theological and Philosophical Reflections,* 138.

generated a considerable amount of work on counseling the dying person. Administering help and comfort to the dying person, by necessity, will vary from culture to culture. Ironically, many so-called primitive or nondeveloped societies will deal with death more responsibly and in a more mature fashion than we sometimes observe in Western societies. Modern American culture isolates people from the reality of death. Many children grow up to their adult years having never attended a funeral or viewing a corpse. The picture of death that children are exposed to is an artificial, unreal portrayal by the entertainment industry through visual images in the cinema and on television and video.[117] In societies where adults and children are regularly and naturally exposed to death and dying, death is a recognizable and natural part of the rhythms of life.[118] But in societies like contemporary American culture, death for many people can be a shocking event that seems unfair and unnatural.

Counseling the dying is a needed yet difficult enterprise. Dying represents a complex blend of certainty and uncertainty. Death is certain for every living person, even if the timing of that certain death is unknown. The counselor (perhaps a therapist, perhaps a hospice nurse, perhaps a caring volunteer) can serve a very useful purpose in helping the dying person face this certainty of eventual death. People arrive at the dying process through a variety of circumstances. Perhaps it is merely an intuitive sense that life is ebbing away; perhaps a person has received a grave or terminal medical diagnosis; perhaps advancing years and life expectancy tables simply indicate that life is not likely to last a lot longer. Apart from persons who experience sudden and unexpected accidental death, all dying people need to deal directly with this certainty of death. The counselor who is mature and secure enough to talk about death can certainly assist the dying person deal with its certainty.

Dealing with the uncertainty of death is more complicated. People who think they are dying because of their intuitive sense may or may not be correct. Many times a medical diagnosis with its attendant prognosis is absolutely correct. Yet doctors who arrive at a serious or potentially terminal medical diagnosis sometimes have to base their assessment on probabilities

---

117. M. K. Bowers, E. N. Jackson, and J. A. Knight, *Counseling the Dying* (Northvale, N.J.: Jason Aronson Press, 1975), 6.

118. A. Orbach, *Life, Psychotherapy, and Death: The End of Our Exploring* (London: Jessica Kingsely, 1999), 11.

rather than certitudes. ("Most people with this particular type of cancer do not respond to treatment.") Doctors sometimes disagree about diagnoses. The response of individuals to disease varies from person to person. And no one can conclude that passing the age of life expectancy as listed on an insurance mortality schedule means that someone is going to die within the year. The dying process is fraught with uncertainties. The challenge for counselors is to gently challenge the dying person to marshal every ounce of maturity available to deal with the ambiguities of the dying process.

Telling the truth becomes a vital component of dealing with those who are dying. Until recently many doctors shielded patients from the truth by evasion or concealment. Most medical practitioners assumed that if patients were told the truth about the terminal status of their illness, the patients would lose hope and feel sentenced to doom.[119] Now the prevailing opinion among medical personnel is that truth is far easier to deal with than partial truth or deceit and that we can best serve the dying with whom we come in contact by following the moral imperative and our ethical obligation to be truth tellers.

The dying process is also a combination of crisis and loss.[120] Depending on individual circumstances, most people who are dying experience a sense of crisis at some point. Perhaps the initial shock that comes with a dreaded diagnosis or perhaps the realization that a treatment regimen is not having the desired effect will precipitate the crisis. Helpers who have training in dealing with people in crisis or who have good intuitive sense regarding the needs of people in crisis can provide valuable help in these cases. As the dying process progresses, the sense of loss becomes more prominent. In a generic sense, the impending loss of life undergirds all the various losses that the dying person can feel: the loss of health, independence, privacy, relationships, and time. People can respond with three different reactions to either crisis or loss: retreating into a protective mode, regressing to an earlier style of coping, or rising to meet the challenge with maturity and growth.[121]

The counselor's interventions need to be appropriate for the particular phase of dying through which the person is passing. At first, the dying pa-

---

119. E. J. Cassell, "Telling the Truth to the Dying Patient," in *Cancer, Stress, and Death,* ed. J. Tache, H. Selye, and S. B. Day (New York: Plenum Medical, 1979), 124.

120. G. S. Lair, *Counseling the Terminally Ill: Sharing the Journey* (Washington, D.C.: Taylor and Frances, 1996), 11–14.

121. Ibid., 11.

tient is in some sort of life-threatening stage characterized by uncertainty. In the mid-phase, the attending doctors and perhaps the patient begin to realize that the outcome will be terminal, even though no one knows how long the process may last. In the final phase of dying, the patient begins making the final moves to the end. Those who work extensively with the dying have learned to spot the signs of imminent death and can sometimes help family members and others involved be aware of this third and final phase in the process.[122]

People who work with the dying are positioned to greatly benefit from this involvement. "Individuals who have been fortunate enough to share in the death of someone who understood its meaning seem better able to live and grow because of their experience."[123] Dying persons who handle the process well engage in a reassessment of their lives, a reaffirmation of their values, and a reordering of their priorities. When and if the dying person is able to communicate with others about these processes, others stand to benefit greatly. As dying persons learn valuable lessons (that they may not have time to apply), they become teachers of those who survive.[124] Living can become a different experience for the helper who has walked through the dying process with the patient. Working with the dying always confronts helpers and caregivers with their own mortality.

On occasion the dying person will need to and/or want to deal with unfinished business. A counselor might hear a confession *in extremis*. The counselor might have the opportunity to serve as a catalyst for reconciliation or forgiveness as the dying patient navigates the final stages of life.

## Grief and Loss

The name of Elizabeth Kübler-Ross (1926–2004) is as associated with the topic of grief as grief is with loss. Based on her experiences with death in war-torn Europe, Dr. Kübler-Ross wrote and spoke extensively on the subject of grief and loss throughout her long and distinguished career. Her professional work equipped her to handle her own personal crisis when in

---

122. R. Sachs, *Perfect Endings: A Conscious Approach to Dying and Death* (Rochester, Vt.: Healing Arts Press, 1998), 155–61.

123. E. Kübler-Ross, *Death: The Final Stages of Growth* (Englewood Cliffs, N.J.: Prentice-Hall, 1975), 117.

124. E. Kübler-Ross and D. Kessler, *Life Lessons: Two Experts on Death and Dying Teach Us About the Mysteries of Life and Living* (New York: Scribner's, 2000), 223.

1995 she suffered a severe stroke that left her for the "next few years at death's door."[125] Kübler-Ross is best known for her stage theory of the grieving process: denial/isolation, anger, bargaining, depression, and acceptance. These stages have become part of the vocabulary of our age because the concept of a process characterized by stages is easy for the general public to understand. After all, nearly everyone has known of grieving persons who represent each of these five areas.

Scholars working in this field, sometimes called thanatologists, have conducted a substantial amount of research in an attempt to determine whether empirical data verify what Kübler-Ross's stage theory predicts. Most people now agree that the results of this work do not give substantial support to Kübler-Ross's approach. Research has failed to establish a discernible sequence of phases in the grieving process or an end point to the process that could come close to her final stage, acceptance.[126] Perhaps these five "stages" are just experiences that many people have at some point in their grieving process but are not arranged in any invariable order and not all persons experience all five phenomena. Kübler-Ross's theory does not account for other well-known features of grieving such as guilt, undoing, and disorganization.[127] As a result, some experts maintain that the stage theory of grief may now have outlived its usefulness in generating helpful interactions that would assist those who grieve.

Three new approaches have emerged to help fill in this gap.

1.  Many new approaches to grief bear the marks of postmodern thought. Features of these new approaches include a move away from a stage approach, a de-emphasis on the psychoanalytic idea that grieving is a withdrawing of invested energy in the relationship with the deceased person, the addition of cognitive features of grieving to what has primarily been viewed as an affective process, a greater awareness of the impact of culture and subculture on grief, the view that grief is not just a private process but is anchored in the person's interpersonal network, and a focus of posttraumatic growth as a healthy outcome of grief.[128]

---

125. Ibid., 11.
126. R. A. Niemeyer, ed., *Meaning Reconstruction and the Experience of Loss* (Washington, D.C.: American Psychological Association, 2001), 3.
127. J. H. Harvey, *Perspectives on Loss and Trauma: Assaults on the Self* (Thousand Oaks, Calif.: Sage, 2002), 41.
128. Neimeyer, *Meaning Reconstruction and the Experience of Loss,* 3–4.

2. Scholars have made substantial progress in identifying the biological correlates of the grieving process. With regard to the neuroendocrine system, observable changes occur in adrenocortical activity among those who experience intense grief as opposed to those whose grief is in the more normal range. Animal studies have identified changes in brain neurotransmitters emitted during periods of loss and separation. Brain imaging procedures have documented changes in cerebral blood flow during periods of induced sadness. All of these findings (and others) are merely correlates of grief; in other words, nothing is known about how they may be causes or effects, just that they occur in the brains of grief-stricken people.[129]

3. Narrative therapy has made a significant contribution to these new discussions regarding grief and loss. Narrative theories argue that humans are inveterate storytellers. Research has confirmed that the human memory is constructed around scripts, event structures, and story schemas. We build our identity around plot and theme, and story helps us organize what otherwise is "inchoate experience."[130] Grievers need to tell their story, to rearrange the major themes of their lives, and to identify parts of their disrupted narrative that do not cohere or that are confused.

Those engaged with the powerful forces of grief can benefit from realizing their losses are relative to one another and that there is value in ranking the losses. Losses have a cumulative effect, so understanding current loss in the context of other recent losses can likewise make a healing impact. Our clients need to be aware that major loss can produce major change in a positive direction in our lives. Our challenge is to find new patterns of meaning in the sum total of our life in light of the disruption of old meaning patterns caused by the death of our loved one.[131] Since major loss assaults our sense of self, we need to attend to that assault by growing through the experience.[132]

---

129. B. Raphael and M. Dobson, "Bereavement," in *Loss and Trauma: General and Close Relationship Perspectives,* ed. J. H. Harvey and E. D. Miller (Philadelphia: Brunner-Routledge, 2000), 48–49.

130. R. M. Neimeyer and H. M. Lefvitt, "What's Narrative Got to Do with It? Construction and Coherence in Accounts of Loss," in *Loss and Trauma,* 402.

131. G. Hagman, "Beyond Decathexis: Toward a New Psychoanalytic Understanding and Treatment of Mourning," in *Meaning Reconstruction and the Experience of Loss,* 2–4.

132. Harvey, *Perspectives on Loss and Trauma,* 29–32.

Loss comes in a myriad of forms and the resulting grieving process likewise follows many pathways and directions. Three major losses involve the loss of a parent, the loss of a spouse, and the loss of a child. Many have observed that when you lose a parent, you lose a part of your past; when you lose your spouse, you lose a part of your present; and when you lose a child, you lose a part of your future.

- The loss of a parent represents a transferring of responsibility, the passing of a generation, the advent of a new season of life. A parent gave us life, and now death has taken a life away. Interaction is no longer possible. In place of the physical absence, we now have to put in place memories of past experience that can enliven and enrich our current lives. We must learn from the graces, gifts, contributions, and imperfections of our parents so that our lives benefit and are improved thereby. And we must step into the new role that we now have: being a part of the oldest generation in our family network rather than the second oldest.[133]

- Losing a spouse deposits the survivor into the midst of loneliness and isolation. The survivor has to shift from the "we" to the "I." Rituals, anniversaries, and marker events all become painful reminders of the gaping hole left by the deceased spouse. One's world is shattered and has to be reconfigured to account for the loss. The survivor must search for new meanings and directions while maintaining connection to the deceased spouse, even perhaps while establishing a new, replacement relationship.[134]

- The loss of a child triggers a grief that never ends, even though it evolves. In pioneering work studying now childless mothers, researcher Kay Talbot found that some mothers survive the experience while others display chronic mourning that does not relent. Those who did better in handling this almost unspeakable horror were mothers who frequently shared with others their inner struggles, who perceived that family and friends around them were helpful,

---

133. For a moving account of the loss of a parent, see D. S. Davenport, *Singing Mother Home: A Psychologist's Journey Through Anticipatory Grief* (Denton, Tex.: University of North Texas Press, 2002).
134. C. A. Walter, *The Loss of a Life Partner: Narratives of the Bereaved* (New York: Columbia University Press, 2003).

who were not exposed to additional, major losses, who reached out to others for help, who made a conscious decision to survive, and who wrestled with the spiritual implications of their experience with the loss of a child.[135]

---

135. K. Talbot, *What Forever Means After the Death of a Child: Transcending the Trauma, Living with the Loss* (New York: Brunner-Routledge, 2002), 46.

# CHAPTER 3

# ORIGIN *and* DESTINY INTEGRATED

IN ORDER TO ARRIVE AT A complete understanding of the human person, the work of integration is necessary for at least two reasons. First, the truthful and authoritative Word of God is not a manual of all possible truths, as a moment's reflection on disciplines such as astrophysics or endocrinology makes clear. Rather, the Bible contains a set of infallible principles and truths focused on the goal of redemption from which manuals of human learning are produced. The so-called cultural mandate set forth in Genesis 1:28 entrusts to human persons the high task of exploring, researching, codifying, applying, et cetera the worlds of human experience and culture for the glory of God and the good of the creature. Second, all human disciplines, including psychology, are infected with errors. Thus they must be subjected to correction from the revealed principles and truths contained in the Scriptures responsibly interpreted. Our conclusion is that Scripture and psychology together contribute to a fuller understanding of the human person.

The task of integrating ancient truths from Scripture and truths from contemporary scholarship is both a complicated and a rewarding enterprise. The complications stem from the fact that the contexts in which ancient, biblical truths are embedded are in some respects different from contemporary worldviews. This means that scholars pulling material together from Scripture and psychology can experience difficulty in accomplishing the task in a way that respects the original setting of both sets of ideas. The rewards come (1) from observing how the wisdom contained in Scripture can illumine and enrich even the best work of contemporary scholars and (2) from interacting with contemporary ideas and models so as to win a hearing for God's truth in arenas otherwise hostile toward it.

We are convinced that integrative enterprises such as are needed in the study of the human person face a serious danger if they too quickly align with a passing trend or short-lived fad, be it philosophical, theological, or psychological. How valuable would be an integration of biblical faith with transactional analysis (popular in the 1960s and 1970s)? How useful would be a merging of one's theology with systems of Marxian liberation theology or Whiteheadian process thought? Or how authentic would be an uncritical adoption into theology of the main features of postmodern ideology?

We choose, rather, to avoid any form of integration that implies a fusion or merging of short-lived, contemporary approaches to an issue with biblical truth. Such a "hard" form of integration runs the risk of resulting in error or inconsequence. Instead, we prefer to build responsible, working alliances between authoritative Scripture and contemporary systems of human inquiry that seek to fulfill the cultural mandate of Genesis 1:28. This "softer" form of integration between biblical truth and extrabiblical perspectives utilizes the benefits of the integrative task and avoids its downsides. If the working alliance between biblical truth and a contemporary approach to the same topic area proves useful in advancing our understanding, improving our ministry and clinical interventions, or in facilitating fruitful conversations with colleagues, we will have achieved our goals without running the risk of eventual irrelevance.

Our format for discussing the integrative implications of the origin and destiny of humans is first to identify the various Christian certainties that seem tenable in both the theological and the psychological sides of the discussion when they speak to the same issue. That which we designate as "Christian certainties" represents our own carefully measured conclusions; readers may choose to develop for themselves a differently nuanced set of conclusions. We then propose a brief integration of assured theological and psychological perspectives on the anthropological topic under consideration. Finally, we identify selected areas where additional research and investigation appears warranted.

## HUMAN ORIGIN

### Christian Certainties

1. *Scripture speaks with a clear and convincing voice regarding the creation of the human race.* We cannot find a descriptive, scientific account of the creation of humans in the Bible, but we do find a detailed and frequently repeated acknowledgment that a special act of creation by the triune God formed the first human pair.

2. *The Bible's creation accounts assert that God created the body of Adam in a mediated fashion and the life of the body in an immediate fashion.* The Genesis description of creation is more than a literary or metaphoric statement. It directly hints at two components of the unified human person: a material body formed from the dust of the ground and an immaterial, vital force inbreathed by the Creator that later is identified as soul/spirit.

3. *Scripture teaches us that God wisely and lovingly oversees the formation of each human life.* If we considered only the biological evidence, we could miss the revealed fact that God directly involves Himself in the origin of each person in his or her rich complexity.

4. *Human life begins at conception.* The conception process is likely completed within a twenty-four-hour time frame. From that point on, the zygote/embryo/fetus is a proper person, not merely a potential person. Scripture attests this reality both in the case of the incarnate Son of God conceived in Mary's womb and as regards every unborn human.

5. *Evolutionary explanations for the origins of the human race are unsatisfactory.* Evolutionism says that no one took nothing out of nowhere and fashioned everything. We grant that if one makes a dogmatic assertion to the effect that a supernatural God does not exist, then naturalistic, evolutionary processes are probably the best extant explanation for human origins. But the assumption that God does not exist is clearly unwarranted by virtue of claims made in the divinely inspired and factually attested biblical record, as well as by indicators of purpose, values, and order evident in the created world around us.

6. *Modularity explanations for the human mind are inadequate and unproven.* Chomsky's discovery that humans appear to possess a lan-

guage acquisition module in their brains does not require that the entire brain is so constructed, nor does the language acquisition module lend itself to adaptation origins. If anything, Chomsky's work speaks to the presence of an intelligent design in human origins.

7. *The human race is a unity.* Christians agree with evolutionary psychology that all humans possess a common descent and that a universal human nature characterizes all persons irrespective of national origin, ethnicity, and gender.

8. *Evolutionary psychology cannot explain the richness of human life.* The list of documented human features that fall beyond the explanatory power of evolutionary principles is long indeed. Free will, autonomy, creativity, moral responsibility, and religious sensibility are but a few of the markers that differentiate human beings from lower forms of life.

9. *Abortion constitutes the morally culpable act of destroying a human life.* Consider, for example, the following incongruity. Abortions thought to be justified are performed well into the third trimester, but some infants are born at six months or earlier and live perfectly normal lives. Psychologically, the presence or absence of a verifiable postabortion syndrome should not be central to either the pro-life or pro-choice argument. Christians rightly oppose abortion because of the clear moral teachings of the Bible that forbid taking an innocent life.

10. *Life is continuous from prenatal existence through the birth process into postnatal life.* Human birth does provide some discontinuities for the newborn as compared to life in the womb: the baby breathes on its own and receives nourishment through its mouth. But the continuities are even greater: the beating heart, the ongoing development of internal organs, the maturation of the neurological system, and the formation of personality.

## Brief Integration

God in wisdom, love, and power created the first human pair to resemble Himself in significant respects. The origins of both the body and the life of the body (i.e., soul/spirit) directly stem from the original creative acts of God (Gen. 2:7). Clear gaps in the fossil record argue against the naturalistic evolution of human beings from lower forms of life. The human mind with all of its cognitive capacities gives evidence of intelligent design, and evolutionary explanations for the mind that are dependent on adaptation as a mechanism are inadequate to explain the observed data.

God directly oversees the origin of every human life that descended from the first pair. Human life begins at conception—in the twenty-four-hour period following the union of sperm and egg. The zygote/embryo/fetus is a proper, not merely a potential, person. Personhood, moreover, is defined by neither an arbitrary standard of functionality nor a judgment as to social utility. An unborn child known to possess a survivable deformity must be allowed to live and to be treated with dignity and love. Abortion represents both a direct assault on the dignity of the developing child and a violation of God's command not to take an innocent life. Scientific and medical manipulations of the conception process run the substantial risk of interfering with God's authority to bring forth life and His intentions for that particular life.

The divine inbreathing of life into a material body constitutes human beings as unified wholes, and we should study them in that manner. Investigative strategies that consider individual human functions from either a theological or psychological perspective are helpful if they do not interfere with the important given of human wholeness.

## Needed Research

Christians working in the psychological sciences could make a very valuable contribution to the ongoing debate between adaptationists and advocates of intelligent design. Some features of cognition, brain structure, and neurological functioning display characteristics that are better explained by intelligent design than by adaptation—the core process of evolution. Most observers of this important debate agree that if Christians are to make a substantive contribution to it, they must be involved in basic research, in articulating positions of advocacy, and in developing cogent reasoning pertaining to these issues. Urging our children or our students not to pursue careers in basic psychological science is not the way to gain an ongoing hearing in the debate. We must be engaged on this frontier of science in the twenty-first century.

The abortion debate continues in American society with no signs of an immediate solution on the horizon. The classical Christian tradition that opposes the practice of abortion presents a strong case that our current society needs to hear. Philosophers, ethicists, theologians, biblical scholars, and psychologists each have unique contributions to make to the discussion. If Christians do not represent the pro-life position well and articulate it clearly, the default position may soon be the pro-choice alternative.

## HUMAN DESTINY

### Christian Certainties

1. *The timing of each person's death is within the ordaining sphere of God's will and is not a matter of human choice.* Just as God originates life through conception, so God oversees the end of one's life. Christian ethics demands that we comprehend the human death process under this overarching theological truth. Most theologians conclude that suicide which does not arise from organic causes is rooted in a lack of trust in God's ability to meet the deepest human needs and, as a result, does not please Him.

2. *Death is both an event and a process.* Theologically we understand that at the Fall Adam and Eve experienced spiritual death and the beginning of the process that would eventuate in physical death. Even the event of death itself (the taking of a last breath or the cessation of all brain waves or the stopping of a heartbeat) involves some features of process, especially if we consider the ebbing away of life as a feature of physical death.

3. *The existence of an intermediate state as taught in Scripture prevents us from adopting a pure monism as the best model for human life.* We will explore this concept more fully in part 2, but suffice it to say at this point that the Bible clearly portrays the survival of some parts of the person after physical death. Even most articulations of soul sleep require the ongoing existence of the human person.

4. *Near death experiences are interesting, but not compelling, occurrences.* While some Christians view these accounts as proof of the Christian understanding of the afterlife, we must be cautious about using this line of evidence since many complicating factors make it inadvisable.

5. *Psychology is not suited to explore the meaning of death or the reality*

*of the afterlife.* But theologians who carefully expound the authoritative biblical revelation make substantial contributions to the expansion of our understanding of death, the intermediate state, the final judgments, and the eternal destinies of Christian believers as well as unbelievers.

6. *Approaching one's own death well and grieving the loss of others are important tasks for all persons.* Christian convictions assure us that death is not an accidental feature of human life but that death is a certainty for which we must be prepared. Likewise, grieving is a task required of all people, young and old. Psychologists and theologians can form a powerful team of professionals to help understand these processes and effectively communicate our findings to the public.

## Brief Integration

Psychology alone cannot inform normatively about what eventuates following a person's death. Efforts to do so by transpersonal psychologists are unhelpful and potentially harmful to Christian understandings. Moreover, science, technology, and medical advances are all contributing to changing the way modern society views death. Theologians and psychologists face new and unanticipated challenges in relating the established findings of science as well as the teachings of Scripture to this new climate. Models of both spiritual and psychological maturity must include helping people form healthy strategies for facing death, a feature of life that is inevitable for all living persons.

Theologians committed to the truths of Scripture make a significant contribution as they carefully organize the biblical teaching concerning what lies beyond physical death for the individual and for the human race. Both theologians and Christian psychologists can take that material and build models that will inform people how they ought to live their lives in light of the decisive realities that lie ahead. We know that the revealed truths of Scripture regarding God's program for the future (involving resurrection of the body, the final judgments, and the eternal states) are not given to us to satisfy our curiosity but to inform us how to live lives pleasing and honoring to God. Christian theologians and psychologists working in teams can helpfully communicate to persons the truth about the future: namely, that because death is a defeated foe, there is the possibility of new spiritual life in Christ and the prospect of living forever with God in a new world free from pain and dying.

## Needed Research

Both psychologists and theologians can helpfully contribute to models of counseling that help prepare people for death. As more and more options regarding the end of life become technologically possible (e.g., cryonics, artificial life support), Christians must be prepared to apply the teachings of Scripture to these new options. The meaning of death is central to the redemptive story as revealed in Scripture; consequently, the stakes are high regarding how we humans view death.

Finally, the validity of the intermediate state as a component of personal eschatology continues to come under question, even in Christian circles. Have we constructed the doctrine carefully from the teachings of Scripture? We think so. But we also feel that psychologists can help clarify the arguments so as to build an even stronger case for the intermediate state. Working in this area is fraught with difficulty, but the rewards will be great as we find better ways of understanding Scripture's portrayal of what occurs after physical death.

# PART 2

# THE SUBSTANCE *and* IDENTITY *of the* HUMAN PERSON

CHAPTER 4

# SUBSTANCE *and* IDENTITY
# *in* THEOLOGICAL PERSPECTIVE

ISSUES OF THE HUMAN PERSON'S identity, personhood, and relation to the Creator are of fundamental importance in anthropology. Few members of the human family, however, pause to reflect on who they are and the purpose for which they were created. Augustine observed the incongruity that "men go abroad to wonder at the height of the mountains, at the huge waves of the sea, at the long courses of the rivers, at the vast compass of the ocean, at the circular motion of the stars, and they pass by themselves without wondering."[1] In a later era, the German philosopher Immanuel Kant (1724–1804) identified four fundamental questions that must be addressed in the pursuit of knowledge: (1) What can I know? (2) What ought I to do? (3) What may I hope? (4) What is man? The first three questions are answerable only in the light of a biblically informed understanding of the last—the identity and nature of the human person.

## ESSENTIAL COMPOSITION

The Bible, in general, views the human person concretely and existentially—as he or she lives in relation to God, family, other persons, and the wider world. Yet careful examination of the biblical materials

---

1. Quoted in Jill Haak Adels, ed., *The Wisdom of the Saints* (New York: Oxford University Press, 1987), 31.

provides insight into the meaningful issue of the constitution or nature of the human person. Dallas Willard points out that many voices past and present deny that there is any such reality as a human nature. They do so for the reason that personal identity is seen as compromising human freedom. He writes, "If I am a human being, as opposed to, say a brussel sprout or a squirrel, that places a restriction upon what I can do, what I ought to do, or what should be done to me."[2]

The tendency in late modern and postmodern anthropology to reject the essential self, substance dualism (holistic dualism), and the undying soul renders the human person ambiguous and at the mercy of change and decay. In this chapter we will examine what biblical revelation discloses concerning the human person's essential nature. Specifically, we will look at composition, identity, image-bearing qualities, the reality of the soul, and the vexing mind-body problem. We begin with the issue of the human person's essential composition.

## Historical Perspectives

Interpretations concerning the nature or composition of the human person can be arranged under three broad categories: (1) *monism,* with no differentiation of body and soul; (2) *dualism,* which separates the human into constituent physical and spiritual parts; and (3) *trichotomism,* in which the human essence is divided into material body, soul, and spirit.

### Essential Monism

First, *anthropological monists* propose a holistic portrait of human nature. They claim that science has not yet discovered empirical evidence for the existence of the soul, hence there is no reality distinct from the body. The human person, therefore, is said to be a *substance monism.* No differentiation of the person into separable entities or substances, such as body and soul, is admitted. These terms are said to represent different ways of depicting the human person as a whole or from different points of view. Monism is alleged to represent the Semitic perspective, while dualism was introduced by an alien Greek philosophy.

---

2. Dallas Willard, *Renovation of the Heart: Putting on the Character of Christ* (Colorado Springs, Colo.: NavPress, 2002), 28.

In philosophy, *materialism* and *idealism* depend upon anthropological monism. Materialists such as Epicurus (341–270 B.C.), Thomas Hobbs (1588–1679), Ludwig Feuerbach (1804–1872), and Karl Marx (1818–1883) say matter is the sole substance, explaining the human person as an advanced animal in a material body. All mental, aesthetic, and spiritual activities are chemical products of the brain, which secretes thoughts like the liver secretes bile. Marxist dialectical materialism, for example, claims that the evolved material world, of which humans are part, is the only reality. Mind is a product of matter; the human person, therefore, is a lump of thinking matter.

Idealism, at the opposite extreme from materialism, identifies the human person as all mind or spirit. Idealism is variously represented by George Berkeley (1685–1753), G. W. F. Hegel (1770–1831), Vedanta Hinduism, and process philosophy and theology. The churchman and philosopher Berkeley identified reality only within ideas or perceptions. Minds or mental representations are all that exist. Process philosophy, advocated by Alfred North Whitehead (1861–1947), Charles Hartshorne (1897–2000), and John B. Cobb Jr., rejects substance dualism in favor of a one-order vision of the universe. Reality consists of rapidly occurring energy-events, or subatomic energies, that interact with one another to create new syntheses in the creative advance to novelty. There is no enduring "I"; everything consists of drops or moments of experience called *actual occasions.* Soul, spirit, and body are equally and fundamentally moments of experience.

Much of nonevangelical theology subscribes to a monistic view of the human person. Biblical terms such as *spirit, soul, heart,* and *body* are said to be nontechnical, each connoting the whole person. Monists allege that the notion of the human person as a complex, material-immaterial being was introduced into Christianity from the Hellenistic thought-world. The human person must be viewed *en toto* as an indivisible, unitary life. Rudolph Bultmann (1884–1976), the radical New Testament scholar and theologian, claimed that *sōma* (body) in Paul characterizes the person as a whole. "Paul did not dualistically distinguish between man's self (his soul) and his bodily *sōma* as if the latter were an inappropriate shell, a prison, to the former."[3] Bultmann added, "Man does not consist of two parts, much less three; nor

---

3. Rudolf Bultmann, *Theology of the New Testament,* 2 vols. (New York: Charles Scribner's Sons, 1951–55), 1:201.

are *psyche* and *pneuma* special faculties or principles (within the *soma*) of a mortal life higher than his animal life. Rather, man is a living unity."[4]

The avant-garde Anglican theologian John A. T. Robinson (1919–1983) claimed that the Greek antithesis between a mortal body and an immortal soul is foreign to the Hebrew mind. "The parts of the body are thought of, not primarily from the point of view of their difference from, and interrelation with, other parts, but as signifying or stressing different aspects of the whole man in relation to God."[5] G. C. Berkouwer (1903–1996), the Dutch Reformed theologian, rejected substance dualism as a foreign, Greek construct. "Scripture never pictures man as a dualistic or pluralistic being, but that in all the varied experiences, the whole man comes to the fore, in all his guilt and sin, his need and oppression. . . ."[6] As for the doctrine of the intermediate state, which lends support to anthropological dualism, Berkouwer throws up his hands, claiming such to be "God's mystery."[7]

German Protestant theologian Wolfhart Pannenberg, defers to the findings of secular anthropology.

> The distinction between body and soul as two completely different realms of reality can no longer be maintained. Modern anthropology . . . describes man as a unified corporeal creature like the animals. It does not describe him as a creature constructed out of two completely different materials. . . . No animated behavior can be carefully divided between body and soul.[8]

The evangelical theologian Ray S. Anderson similarly writes:

> The human soul is not an immaterial substance encased in a mortal body. The life of the person (soul) emerges simultaneously with the bodily form of human existence. . . . There is no warrant in

---

4. Ibid., 1:209.
5. John A. T. Robinson, *The Body: A Study in Pauline Anthropology* (Chicago: H. Regnery, 1952), 16.
6. G. C. Berkouwer, *Man: The Image of God,* trans. Dirk W. Jellema (Grand Rapids: Eerdmans, 1962), 203.
7. Ibid., 265.
8. Wolfhart Pannenberg, *What Is Man? Contemporary Anthropology in Theological Perspective,* trans. Duane A. Priebe (Philadelphia, Pa.: Fortress, 1970), 47.

Scripture for asserting that human nature bears some immortal, indestructible soul which has a natural capacity to survive death.[9]

"Soul," Anderson claims, "is the subjective life of the body."[10]

Modern psychology increasingly endorses anthropological monism. To its credit, classical psychology recognized the reality of the soul and its faculties as legitimate objects of study. But modern psychology, influenced by naturalistic evolution and brain science, has focused on the functioning of the brain, thus undermining traditional dualistic anthropology. Advocates of this perspective will be discussed in chapter 5 (see pp. 166–78).

One unusual form of this philosophy is found in the interdisciplinary philosophical and psychological study, *Whatever Happened to the Soul? Scientific and Theological Portraits of Human Nature,* published in 1998). The book proposes a form of monism known as *non-reductive physicalism,* as a compatible bridge between science and Christianity. The idea of "physicalism" is that the soul is not an entity separable from the body and that functions traditionally attributed to the substantial soul must be attributed to the brain. Philosopher Murphy rejects existence of a nonphysical soul or mind. The "soul is a functional capacity of a complex physical organism, rather than a separate spiritual essence that somehow inhabits a body."[11] One need not believe in a substantial soul or mind to account for life and consciousness, she argues. Higher human functions such as self-consciousness, thinking, willing, relating to others and God, and religious experiences (dreams, visions, etc.) can be reduced to brain functioning governed by the laws of neurobiology. "The person is a physical organism whose complex functioning, in society and in relation to God, gives rise to 'higher' human capacities such as morality and spirituality."[12]

Advocates of anthropological monism claim that *holism* offers a better model for total person (i.e., emotional, spiritual, and physical) health; it eliminates the felt tension between saving souls and meeting physical needs; and it offers a better paradigm for environmental conservation. "If matter

---

9. Ray S. Anderson, *The New Age of the Soul* (Eugene, Ore.: Wipf and Stock, 2001), 40–41.

10. Ibid., 41.

11. Warren S. Brown, Nancey Murphy, and H. Newton Malony, eds., *Whatever Happened to the Soul? Scientific and Theological Portraits of Human Nature* (Minneapolis, Minn.: Augsburg Fortress, 1998), xiii.

12. Ibid., 25.

and spirit are separate, then we may despise the material dimension, neglect it, abuse it, pollute it."[13]

Monism represents the default view of Western culture. The press recently reported that the head of the deceased Hall of Fame baseball player, Ted Williams, was severed from his body (a procedure called *neuroseparation*) and preserved by an Arizona cryonics company in liquid nitrogen. Family members ordered this procedure, hoping that when technology allows for the cloning of Williams's body, the preserved memory cells in his brain will be reinserted into the body, reconstituting Ted Williams. In this crude example, memory is seen strictly as a function of brain cells without regard for the soul.

### Essential Dichotomy and Functional Holism

*Substance dualism*, also known as dualistic holism or holistic dualism, represents the majority view of the Christian church throughout history. This view states that the person is a bipartite unity of an immaterial, undying soul/spirit and a material, dying body that functions as an integrated whole.

Aristotle laid a secular philosophical foundation for this view. All earthly things, including the human person, consist of two metaphysically distinct elements or principles: form and matter, which together constitute substance. Form organizes matter into an actual entity (a tree, a human being) and gives it purpose and energy. The soul, the primary principle of life, is only the form of the body. From the soul flows every disposition, bodily movement, and action.

John W. Cooper explains, "Soul-form and matter together constitute a single rational-animal substance, a psychophysical unity which as a whole is the proper subject of all human activities. . . . Aristotle's ontology and anthropology represent an ontological holism of two irreducible principles."[14] It follows, according to Aristotle, that the soul does not survive the death of the body.

Some key early Christian writers blended Greek anthropological notions

---

13. Bruce Reichenbach, *Is Man the Phoenix? A Study of Immortality* (Grand Rapids: Christian University Press, 1978), 88.

14. John W. Cooper, *Body, Soul and Life Everlasting: Biblical Anthropology and the Monism-Dualism Debate* (Grand Rapids: Eerdmans, 1989), 50.

with biblical teaching. Athenagoras of Athens, a vigorous defender of the Christian faith, held that the human person is a unity consisting of soul and body. "The whole nature of man in general is composed of an immortal soul and a body which was fitted to it in the creation."[15] Death sunders the unity of soul and body until that unity is repaired in the healing event of the Resurrection. Regarded as the "father of Latin theology," Tertullian held that the human person consists of the union of two substances—body and soul—the former functioning as the servant of the latter. "Without the soul we are nothing; there is not even the name of a human being, only that of a carcass."[16]

Given the intimacy of the union, the human person functions as a harmonious whole. The unity of the person is conditional; at physical death the indestructible soul separates from the body.

Augustine, bishop of Hippo and arguably Christendom's greatest theologian, defined the human person as "a mortal rational animal."[17] As a Christian Platonist, Augustine employed Plato's terms *spirit, soul,* and *body;* but he united immaterial spirit and soul and contrasted them with the material body. The human person thus is a unity of two substances: a rational soul *(anima)* and a material body *(corpus).* The soul is superior to the body, giving life and direction to it. Yet drawing upon a Trinitarian analogy, Augustine stressed the unity of the functioning person who thinks, wills, and feels. The self, however, resides in the soul rather than in the soul-body unity.

The influential Dominican philosopher and theologian Thomas Aquinas judged that the human being is a complex whole composed of a spiritual and a material substance. "It is clear that man is not only a soul, but something composed of soul and body."[18] Thomas followed Aristotle in claiming that soul—a spiritual substance—is the "form" of the whole body. The soul energizes the functions of thinking, willing, loving and relating, but the material body brings awareness of the earthly objects of these operations. Thomas stressed the unity of the human person: the soul needs the various bodily organs to perform its operations. Until recently, Roman Catholic theology closely followed Aquinas's anthropology.

---

15. Athenagoras, *The Resurrection of the Dead* 15 [*ANF,* 2:157].
16. Tertullian, *On the Flesh of Christ* 12 [*ANF,* 3:532].
17. Augustine, *The Teacher* 8.24 [*FOTC,* 59:36]; cf. idem, *The Magnitude of the Soul* 25 [*FOTC,* 2:112–15].
18. Thomas Aquinas, *ST,* 4:12 [pt. 1, q. 75, art. 4].

Martin Luther (1483–1546), the Augustinian friar who launched the Protestant Reformation, was a competent exegete and theologian. He and most subsequent Lutheran theologians favored essential dichotomy. "Man has a twofold nature, a spiritual and a bodily."[19] Luther added, "The soul is of a substance different from that of the body; and yet there is an intimate union and connection, for the soul loves the body very much."[20] The soul may live without the body, but not the body without the soul. Analogous to the Jewish temple with its Holy of Holies, Holy Place, and outer courts, *functionally* the soul is the instrument of reason and emotions, the spirit the faculty for engaging God, and the body the material vessel that not only houses the immaterial self but also executes its manifold functions.

French Reformer, biblical exegete, and theologian John Calvin held that the soul is an incorporeal, undying essence (or substance) breathed by God into a material body. At death the immortal soul departs the corruptible house of clay. "That man consists of a soul and a body ought to be beyond controversy. I understand by the term 'soul' an immortal yet created essence, which is his nobler part."[21] The soul energizes human cognition, volition, emotion, sense of moral obligation, and religious capacity and blends them into a harmonious whole. Reformed theology, following Calvin, overwhelmingly upholds a dichotomous anthropology.

René Descartes (1596–1650), philosopher and mathematician, pursued a dualistic anthropology by means of a rigorous philosophical analysis. Mind or soul is an indivisible, thinking substance *(res cognitans)*, whereas body is a divisible, extended substance. Hope of the afterlife supports this dualistic anthropology. "It is therefore certain that I am truly distinct from my body, and that I can exist without it."[22] Since the human person can exist without the body, the immaterial mind or soul constitutes the person. For Descartes, essential dualism requires functional dualism. Mind and body function independently but interact through the pineal gland in the brain.

A leader of the modern evangelical movement, Carl F. H. Henry (1913–

19. Cited in Hugh Thompson Kerr, ed., *A Compend of Luther's Theology* (Philadelphia, Pa.: Westminster, 1943) 77.

20. Cited in Ewald M. Plass, comp., *What Luther Says* (St. Louis, Mo.: Concordia, 1959), 876.

21. John Calvin, *Institutes of the Christian Religion*, ed. John T. McNeill; trans. Ford Lewis Battles, 2 vols., LCC, vols. 20–21 (Philadelphia, Pa.: Westminster, 1960), 1:184 [1.15.2].

22. René Descartes, *Meditations on First Philosophy* (Indianapolis, Ind.: Hackett, 1979), Meditation 6.49.

2003), claims that, whereas Scripture does not portray a science of psychology in the modern sense, it does present a consistent picture of human nature. "Its emphasis falls on man as a unitary personality of soul and body."[23] The various functions of the soul or spirit unite in the single, psychic life of the person. Robert H. Gundry likewise argues for this view. "The soul *has* a body and the body *has* a soul and man as a whole *is* both, a psychophysical unity—but a unity, not a monad."[24] Cooper, a Reformed philosopher, concludes that the biblical picture of the human person is best described as a "holistic dualism." The ontological distinction between the material body and the immaterial soul/spirit is necessary because only the immaterial continues into the intermediate state. Cooper locates holism in the functional unity of the person. "The biblical view of human nature is both holistic—emphasizing the religious, phenomenological, and functional integration of life—and dualistic—asserting that persons are held in existence without fleshly bodies until the resurrection."[25]

## Essential Trichotomism

Guided by such texts as 1 Thessalonians 5:23 ("spirit, soul and body") and Hebrews 4:12 ("dividing soul and spirit"), a number of church fathers, Eastern in particular, favored trichotomism. The Greek philosopher Plato theorized that the human person consists of a hierarchy of parts, from the lowest to the highest: namely, body (appetites, desires, sensations), spirit (impulse, will), and mind *(nous)*. Plato emphasized the human person's spiritual nature, while depreciating the body as the prison-house of the soul. In this life the spiritual soul uses the body but longs to be liberated from it.

Plato's emphasis on the person's spiritual nature appealed to many early Christians immersed in the Greek intellectual milieu. Christian trichotomists ancient and modern see the human person as a pie cut in three slices, consisting of three discrete parts: (1) *a physical body* (passions); (2) *a rational soul* (reason, emotion, will); and (3) *an immortal spirit* (that relates to God). The human person thus consists of two immaterial substances and one material substance.

---

23. Carl F. Henry, "Man," in *Wycliffe Dictionary of Theology,* ed. Everett F. Harrison, Geoffrey W. Bromiley, and Carl F. Henry (reprint, Peabody, Mass.: Hendrickson, 1999), 341.

24. Robert H. Gundry, *Soma in Biblical Theology* (Grand Rapids: Zondervan, 1987), 121.

25. Cooper, *Body, Soul and Life Everlasting,* 231.

Origen (185–254), the head of the catechetical school in Alexandria was greatly influenced by the allegorical method of interpreting Scripture then in vogue in rabbinical study. Allegorical interpretation led him to see a divinely ordained correspondence between a threefold sense of Scripture (literal/historical, moral, and mystical) and a threefold nature of the human person (body, spirit, and soul).[26] The person's physical nature corresponds to the literal and historical sense of Scripture; his spiritual nature to the spiritual and mystical sense; and his soulish nature to the moral sense of Scripture.

The issue of the composition of the human person rose to the fore in the fourth century when Apollinarius of Laodicea (310–392) was condemned by the First Council of Constantinople in 381. Apollinarius subscribed to Platonic trichotomism and taught that two forms of being cannot exist in true unity, and that being is contained essentially in the spirit, not the soul. Therefore, Christ could not have both divine and human spirits. Apollinarius claimed that at the Incarnation the Logos replaced the human spirit of Jesus. The incarnate Savior possessed a divine spirit and a human body and soul.

It was Apollinarius's Christology, not his trichotomism, that was found heretical, but the two were linked in theological thought, so that trichotomist views of human composition did not experience a revival until the nineteenth century. Henry Alford (1810–1871), an English Bible commentator, upheld trichotomism in his work, *Alford's Greek Testament*. Expounding 1 Thessalonians 5:23, Alford maintained that *pneuma* "is the spirit, the highest and distinctive part of man, the immortal and responsible spirit." *Psychē* "is the lower or animal soul, containing the passions and desires . . . which we have in common with the brutes." *Sōma* is the material body that houses the two immaterial elements.[27] Likewise, soul and spirit in Hebrews 4:12 "denote two separate departments of man's being."[28]

Franz Delitzsch, a German Lutheran exegete and theologian, in his *System of Biblical Psychology* developed an elaborate psychology/anthropology. On the basis of 1 Thessalonians 5:23 and Hebrews 4:12 he averred that soul and spirit represent two distinct immaterial substances. The body is the material frame taken from the earth, the spirit the life center breathed

---

26. Origen, *Homilies on Leviticus* 5.5.3 [*FOTC*, 83:102]
27. Henry Alford, *Alford's Greek Testament*, 4 vols. (reprint, Grand Rapids: Baker, 1980), 3:282.
28. Ibid., 4:84.

into the body, and the soul "the entire inward nature of man."[29] The soul is derived from the essence of the spirit but is distinct from it. "The spirit is the inbreathing of the Godhead, and the soul is the outbreathing of the spirit."[30] He added, "The spirit is the image of the triune Godhead, but the soul is the copy of this image."[31]

Delitzsch unfolded the three functions of the spirit (will, thought, and experience) and the seven powers of the soul: (1) perception; (2) representation; (3) memory; (4) imagination; (5) understanding; (6) desire; and (7) feeling. Spirit is the organ for reception of the divine.

In a note to 1 Thessalonians 5:23, *The Scofield Reference Bible* states that the human person is a trinity of parts, spirit, soul and body. Spirit and soul are distinct in essence and in function. Spirit is the seat of God-consciousness, soul the seat of self-consciousness, and body the seat of world-consciousness.[32] The Scofield notes indicate that the three principal functions of the human person require three distinct substances. Watchman Nee (1903–72) was a popular author and leader of the "Little Flock" movement in China. Influenced by the founder of the Plymouth Brethren, John Nelson Darby (1800–1882), and the holiness movement, Nee favored trichotomism. He insisted that the division of spirit and soul is "an issue of *supreme* importance for it affects tremendously the spiritual life of the believer."[33] Indeed, "to fail to distinguish between spirit and soul is fatal to spiritual maturity."[34] Nee posited the absolute priority of the spirit, claiming that only the spirit, as distinguished from the soul, is created in the image of God, and only it is renewed by the new birth. "New birth is something which happens entirely within the spirit; it has no relation to soul or body."[35] Consequently, functions of the soul such as rational thought, will, and emotions remain fallen and controlled by the flesh. Thus the soul in no way contributes to spiritual growth. Only through the functions of the spirit— conscience, intuition, and communion—does God teach and lead persons

---

29. Franz Delitzsch, *System of Biblical Psychology* (Edinburgh: T. and T. Clark, 1869), 113; cf. 183.

30. Ibid., 118.

31. Ibid., 119.

32. C. I. Scofield, ed., *The Scofield Reference Bible* (New York: Oxford University Press, 1945), 5, 1270.

33. Watchman Nee, *The Spiritual Man,* 3 vols. (New York: Christian Fellowship, 1968), 1:22.

34. Ibid.

35. Ibid., 1:61.

into fellowship with Himself. Nee concluded, "This is the order God still wants: first the spirit, then the soul, and lastly the body."[36]

## Biblical Exposition

Four biblical, anthropological terms are pivotal to an accurate understanding of the nature of the human person. As mentioned earlier (p. 121), much modern opinion regards the terms *soul, spirit, heart,* and *body* as descriptive of the whole person, not any essential part thereof. For example, a leading resource in spiritual formation states, "Confusion in Christianity between the Judaic and Greek understanding of the word *soul* comes largely through a Gnostic and Neoplatonic misinterpretation of the apostle Paul's use of the Greek words *sarx* ('flesh'), *sōma* ('body'), *pneuma* ('spirit'), and *psychē* ('soul')." Paul used these four terms "in similar ways to refer to the self, reflecting a Hebraic rather than a Greek-Hellenistic understanding."[37]

We now proceed to the Bible's principal anthropological terms and what Scripture does say about the essential makeup of the human person.

### Soul

In the Hebrew Old Testament, *nepeš* occurs 755 times. In the general sense it connotes all biological life. With respect to humans, translators see a great many instances where the term refers to something more personal and most often translate *nepeš* as "soul," "life," and by the personal pronoun "I." The King James Version translates *nepeš* as "soul" (428 times), "life" (119 times), "person" (30 times), "heart" (15 times), "mind" (15 times), "creature" (9 times), and "body" (7 times).[38] *Nepeš* bears the following anthropological meanings:

1.  *A living being,* or the whole person (Gen. 2:7; 9:5; Pss. 6:3; 63:1; 104:1; Ezek. 18:4, 20). Use of *nepeš* for the entire person involves a figure of speech known as synecdoche: a word for a part (e.g., soul) signifies the whole (e.g., person).

---

36. Ibid., 1:30.
37. Keith Beasley-Topliffe, ed., *The Upper Room Dictionary of Christian Spiritual Formation* (Nashville: Upper Room Books, 2003), 255.
38. Ralph L. Smith, *Old Testament Theology* (Nashville: Broadman and Holman, 1993), 267.

2. *The life-principle or life-force* that animates the body (Lev. 17:11; 26:16; Ps. 19:7; Isa. 42:5; Jonah 2:7).
3. *The integration of all interior functions,* the seat of the intellect, will, and emotions, particularly in relations with other people. Accordingly, *nepeš* is the seat of the intellect (1 Sam. 2:35; Prov. 2:10), memory (Lam. 3:20), volition (Gen. 23:8), love (Song 3:1–4), desires (Ps. 10:3; Prov. 21:10), emotions (Deut. 28:65; 1 Sam. 1:10; Job 7:11; Pss. 6:3; 42:5, 11), hope (33:20), and religious life (42:1–2; 84:2; 143:6), including worship (25:1; 104:1).

*Nepeš* originates from the divine inbreathing (*rûaḥ*) into the material body (Gen. 2:7) and departs the body at death (Gen. 35:18; 1 Kings 17:21–22). *Nepeš* is customarily translated by *psychē* in the Greek Septuagint version of the Old Testament.

In the New Testament, the Greek *psychē* occurs 110 times. It too is commonly translated "soul," "life," and "I." In its most significant uses *psychē* denotes:

1. *The whole person* (Acts 2:41; Rom. 13:1; 2 Cor. 12:15; 1 Peter 4:19).
2. *The essential being* or seat of *personal identity*—often in relation to God and salvation (Matt. 10:28, 39; Luke 1:46; John 12:25; Heb. 10:39; James 1:21; 1 Peter 1:9).
3. *The inner life* of the body (Acts 20:10; Eph. 6:6). That is, the seat of the intellect (Acts 14:2; Phil. 1:27; Heb. 12:3), volition (Matt. 22:37; Eph. 6:6), emotions (Matt. 26:38; Mark 14:34; John 12:27), and moral and spiritual life (Heb. 6:19; 1 Peter 1:22; 3 John 2).

The *psychē* returns to God at death (Acts 2:27, 31; 1 Peter 1:9; Rev. 20:4). With the Pauline emphasis on the coming of the Holy Spirit, "soul" almost drops out of Paul's vocabulary (*psychē* occurs just thirteen times in the Pauline letters).

## Spirit

The Hebrew *rûaḥ* occurs 378 times in the Old Testament. In a general sense, it is used for the wind (Gen. 8:1; Amos 4:13), physical breath (Job 9:18; Ps. 135:17), the Spirit of God (Pss. 51:11; 106:33; Isa. 42:1), and the life force of subhuman creatures (Gen. 6:17; Eccl. 3:19, 21). The principal anthropological meanings of *rûaḥ* are

1.   *The whole person* (Ps. 31:5; Ezek. 21:7).
2.   *The vital power or life* from God that animates the body (Gen. 2:7; Judg. 15:19; Job 27:3; Isa. 42:5; note the phrase, "God of the spirits of all mankind," Num. 16:22; 27:16).
3.   *The inner life,* seat of the intellect (Gen. 41:8; Ezek. 20:32), spiritual understanding (Job 20:3; 32:8), wisdom (Exod. 28:3), will (Dan. 5:20), emotions (Gen. 26:35; 1 Sam. 1:15; Prov. 15:13; 17:22).
4.   *The openness of the soul to God.* The inner faculty that is orientated to, and responds to, God (Ps. 51:10; Isa. 26:9).

*Rûaḥ* is translated by *pneuma* in the Greek version of the Old Testament. The Hebrew *nᵉšāmâ* occurs twenty-four times in the Old Testament and has the sense of "breath" (eleven times), "spirit" (two times) and "soul" (once). It signifies

1.   *The breath of life* (Gen. 2:7; 1 Kings 17:17; Isa. 2:22), as breathed in by God (Job 33:4; 34:14; Isa. 42:5).
2.   *The human moral faculty* (Prov. 20:27).

In the Greek New Testament, *pneuma* occurs 146 times in Paul's writings alone, signifying

1.   *The person or personal pronoun* (Gal. 6:18; 2 Tim. 4:22; Philem. 25).
2.   *The immaterial life force* that animates the body and departs at death (Matt. 27:50; Acts 7:59; James 2:26; Rev. 11:11).
3.   With the coming of the Holy Spirit, *pneuma* assumes the primary meaning of *the self that interacts with God* and the spiritual realm (Rom. 1:9; 8:16; 1 Cor. 14:14; Rev. 21:10). *Pneuma* thus denotes "the higher, Godward aspect of human nature."[39] *Pneuma* is frequently contrasted with *sarx,* the flesh.

---

39. H. D. McDonald, "Mankind: Doctrine of," in *EDT,* 732.

*Heart*

The Hebrew words for "heart" are *lēb* (598 times) and *lēbāb* (252 times). They often refer to the physical organ (e.g., Ps. 38:10; Jer. 4:19). With respect to the human person *lēb* denotes

1. *The whole person* (Ps. 22:26).
2. *The core of the inner life of the person* (Exod. 7:3, 13; Ps. 9:1; Jer. 17:9).

The heart is "the wellspring of life" (Prov. 4:23). From this center emerges good and evil thoughts (Gen. 6:5; 1 Kings 3:12; 4:29; Job 8:10; 12:3), memory (Ps. 31:12; Isa. 65:17), intentions (Exod. 35:5; 1 Kings 8:17; Dan. 5:20; note Pharaoh hardening his heart in Exod. 7:14, 22; 8:15, 19, 32), love and hate for God (Deut. 6:5; 13:3; Job 1:5), emotions and passions (Deut. 19:6; 28:67; 1 Sam. 1:8; 1 Kings 8:66; for the Hebrews, emotions often centered in the bowels, liver, and kidneys), courage (Ps. 31:24; Dan. 11:25), conscience (1 Sam. 24:5; Job 27:6; Ps. 51:10), spiritual life (1 Sam. 12:24; Ps. 9:1; Joel 2:12), and good and evil actions (Isa. 32:6).

"Heart" signifies "The seal or instrument of human emotional, volitional, and intellectual manifestations."[40] Cooper correctly describes the heart as "the hidden control-center of the whole human being."[41] Outward words and actions infallibly reveal the true character of the heart, or the inner person.

*Lēb* is translated by *kardia* in the Greek Version of the Old Testament.

The Greek New Testament word for "heart" *(kardia)* occurs fifty-two times in Paul's writing alone. *Kardia* bears the following anthropological meanings:

1. *The governing center* of the person or "the innermost sanctuary of an individual's psychical being"[42] (Matt. 18:35; Rom. 6:17; 2 Cor. 5:12).
2. *The seat of intellectual life and memory* (Matt. 9:4; Acts 8:22; 1 Thess. 2:17), volition (Luke 21:14; Rom. 2:5; 1 Cor. 4:5), including love (Matt. 22:37; 2 Cor. 7:3), good and evil desires (Matt. 15:19; Rom. 1:24; 10:1), emotions (John 16:22; Acts 2:26; Phil. 4:7), moral

---

40. Ibid., 731.
41. Cooper, *Body, Soul and Life Everlasting,* 42.
42. McDonald, "Mankind: Doctrine of," 732.

character and conscience (Rom. 2:15; Acts 2:37; 1 Tim. 1:5), and spiritual life (Rom. 10:9–10; Col. 3:16; Heb. 13:9).

"Whereas *nepeš* relates to the whole of a man's individuality, 'heart' is concerned specifically with . . . the *psychical* functions."[43] That is, all vital functions of the soul proceed from the metaphorical heart, the control center or core of the person.

## Mind

Old Testament Hebrew has no specific word for "mind." Several Hebrew words address the human, rational and intellectual functions, including, *nepeš* (Gen. 23:8), *rûaḥ*, (26:35), and especially *lēb* and *lēbāb* (Deut. 29:4; Prov. 18:15).

Several New Testament words signify human cognitive capacity or rational and intellectual functioning, especially for perceiving spiritual realities:

1.  *Nous,* used twenty-four times in the New Testament (Luke 24:45; Eph. 4:17, 23; Rev. 13:18), connotes "mind," "reason," or "understanding." The word conveys the human capacity to think and perceive, particularly in the religious realm. *Noēma* occurs six times (2 Cor. 10:5; Phil. 4:7) signifying "mind" and "thought." The verb *noeō* occurs fourteen times and means to "grasp with the mind" or "perceive."
2.  *Dianoia* occurs thirteen times in the New Testament as the faculty of thought or perception. It is used in the Great Commandment: "Love the Lord your God . . . with all your mind" (Matt. 22:37) and in other texts (Eph. 1:18; Heb. 8:10; 1 John 5:20).
3.  *Phronēma* (four times: Rom. 8:6–7, 27) bears the meaning "way of thinking." The verb *phroneō* means "think; judge."

## Body

Biblical Hebrew has several nontechnical words sometimes translated "body." The following are two of the more common.

---

43. J. A. Wainwright, *God and Man in the Old Testament* (London: SPCK, 1962), 82.

1. *G<sup>e</sup>wîyâ* (body, carcass, dead body) occurs twelve times in the Old Testament. It denotes either a living body (Gen. 47:18; Neh. 9:37) or a dead carcass (1 Sam. 31:10, 12).
2. *Bāśār* (flesh) sometimes denotes the physical body (Exod. 30:32; Lev. 15:16; Num. 8:7).

In the New Testament, *sōma* occurs eighty-one times in Paul alone and describes

1. *The physical body* (Mark 5:29; Rom. 8:11; Gal. 6:17; James 2:16).
2. *The whole person* (Rom. 12:1; Eph. 5:28; Phil. 1:20).
3. *The fallen, carnal nature* (Rom. 6:6; 8:13; Phil. 3:21).

In the Bible, human living in the world and before God always is used with the clear assumption of an embodied experience.

Closely related to *body* in Scripture is *flesh*. *Bāśār* occurs 266 times in the Old Testament. In a general sense, *bāśār* can refer to a blood relative (Gen. 29:14; 2 Sam. 5:1), humankind collectively (Gen. 6:12 13; Job 34:15; Ps. 145:21; Zech. 2:13), and every living thing (Gen. 9:15–17). In the last sense, it highlights the physical affinity between humans and animals. *Bāśār* bears the following anthropological meanings:

1. *The material substance* of the body (Gen. 2:23; 17:14; Job 19:26; see also above under Body).
2. *The whole person* (Lev. 17:11; Pss. 16:9; 63:1; Eccl. 4:5).
3. *The person as weak, dependent, and transitory* (Gen. 6:3; 2 Chron. 32:8; Ps. 78:39; Isa. 40:6). *Bāśār* in the Old Testament, however, does not designate the seat of sin.

In the Septuagint *bāśār* is translated by the Greek word *sarx*. *Sarx* occurs 147 times in Paul alone. Its general meanings include both kinship (Rom. 9:3) and humanity generally (Rom. 3:20; 1 Cor. 1:29). In the instances relating to this study, *sarx* connotes

1. *The human body* (2 Cor. 4:11; 12:7; Phil. 1:22, 24).
2. *Human creatureliness and frailty* (2 Cor. 10:3; 1 Peter 1:24).
3. *Fallen human nature* (Rom. 7:5, 18, 25; 8:3–9, 12–13; 13:14; Gal. 5:16–17, 19, 24).

Theologian Anthony Charles Thistelton summarizes the evidence that "the outlook of the flesh is the outlook orientated towards the self, that which pursues its own ends in self-sufficient independence of God."[44]

From this comparison, it quickly becomes clear that considerable fluidity and overlap of meanings occur among the biblical words best translated "soul," "spirit," "heart," "body," and "flesh." In some instances terms are used interchangeably, referring to the same reality, as the following relations indicate:

- *Soul, heart,* and *flesh* in poetic parallelism refer to the same reality (Pss. 63:1; 84:2).
- *Soul* and *spirit* in parallel refer to the same reality (Job 7:11; Isa. 26:9; Luke 1:46–47).
- *Soul* and *spirit* are used interchangeably (compare John 12:27 with 13:21 and Heb. 12:23 with Rev. 6:9).
- *Soul* and *spirit* are employed as quasi-synonyms (Heb. 4:12). "That the word of God probes the inmost recesses of our spiritual being and brings the subconscious motives to light is what is meant" in this verse.[45]
- *Soul* and *heart* are used as quasi-synonyms (Deut. 6:5; 10:12).
- *Spirit* and *heart* refer to the same reality (Deut. 2:30).
- *Heart* and *flesh* are used as quasi-synonyms (Ps. 73:26).

Clearly, then, the principal anthropological terms in Scripture are not technically precise by modern standards; consequently, a full-orbed psychology cannot be constructed from them.

Biblical usage, however, allows for identifying soul and spirit with the person's inner life, and body with the outward, material vessel. H. D. McDonald concludes, "From different points of view, soul and spirit appear as two aspects of man's inner nature. Spirit denotes life as having its origin in God; and soul denotes life as constituted in man. . . . The *pneuma* is man's nonmaterial nature looking Godward; and *psyche* is the same nature looking earthward and touching the things of sense."[46]

---

44. A. C. Thistelton, "Flesh," in *NIDNTT,* 1:680.

45. F. F. Bruce, *Commentary on the Epistle to the Hebrews,* The New London Commentary on the New Testament (London: Marshall, Morgan and Scott, 1964), 82.

46. H. D. McDonald, *The Christian View of Man* (Westchester, Ill.: Crossway, 1981), 79.

## Theological Development

From our survey of the Bible's major anthropological terms, we draw the following conclusions concerning the constitution of the human person.

*Functionally,* Scripture—particularly the Hebrew Bible—depicts the human person operationally as a unified whole. This accounts for uses of soul, spirit, heart, and body that denote the entire person. It is also true, functionally, that words usually translated "soul" often designate the self who thinks, wills, and feels, words translated "spirit" tend to speak of the self that intuits truths, communes with God, and executes moral judgments, and words translated "body" usually mean the material instrument through which soul/spirit functions.

*Relationally,* the entire person (soul, spirit, heart, body) engages and interacts with other humans, God, and the surrounding world. The material body must not be excluded from such relationships. Dietrich Bonhoeffer (1906–1945) pointed out in *Life Together* that Christians actually *feel* the bodily presence of brothers and sisters in the gathered community. It is also true, relationally, that soul often designates the self in relation to itself and others, spirit the self in relation to God, and body the self in relation to the external, material world.

*Ethically,* no dualism exists in Scripture, as in Platonism and Gnosticism. Platonic-influenced philosophy judges the immaterial soul/spirit to be good and the material body to be evil. Neither is the material body a prison-house from which the soul longs to be freed.

*Essentially,* the human person is a complex unity that includes an outer, material body and an inner, immaterial soul/spirit or heart. As A. W. Tozer (1897–1963) noted, "Deep inside every man there is a private sanctum where dwells the mysterious essence of his being."[47] Often in the Bible unity includes complexity. Common examples are one family, one nation, the triune God, and Jesus Christ as God and man.

What variously has been designated as complex unity, dualistic holism, or holistic dualism is attested by a number of considerations. In Scripture, material and immaterial constituents or substances of the human person are plainly distinguished. A visible, material and temporal body is contrasted with an invisible and immaterial, undying soul/spirit in numerous texts,

---

47. A. W. Tozer, *Man: The Dwelling Place of God* (Harrisburg, Pa.: Christian Publications, 1966), 9.

such as Genesis 2:7; Job 4:19; Ecclesiastes 12:7 (cf. Gen. 3:19); Daniel 7:15 ("I Daniel was grieved in my spirit in the midst of my body" [KJV]—the body is likened to a sheath); Micah 6:7; Matthew 10:28; 26:41; Romans 8:10; 1 Corinthians 7:34; 2 Corinthians 12:2–3; James 2:26; and 3 John 2. Matthew 10:28 reads, "Do not be afraid of those who kill the body but cannot kill the soul. Rather, be afraid of the one who can destroy both soul and body in hell." Soul/spirit and body are substances, each with distinguishing qualities. Philosophically, a quality must inhere in a substance, either material or immaterial/spiritual.

Inner and outer aspects of the human person are distinguished and not reducible to one another. Numerous Scriptures attest this: Zechariah 12:1; Romans 7:22–23; 8:23; 2 Corinthians 5:1–9. See also Ephesians 3:16 and Colossians 2:5. Paul wrote in Romans 2:28–29a, "A man is not a Jew if he is only one outwardly, nor is circumcision merely outward and physical. No, a man is a Jew if he is one inwardly; and circumcision is circumcision of the heart, by the Spirit." Second Corinthians 4:16 reads, "Though outwardly we are wasting away, yet inwardly we are being renewed day by day." Walther Eichrodt (1890–1978) concludes, "The distinction between an inner, spiritual aspect and a physical aspect of human nature . . . is a constituent element of the whole Old Testament view of Man."[48]

The doctrine of redemption establishes a distinction between immaterial and material aspects of the human person. The Christian's material substance (the body) decays, but the immaterial substance (the soul/spirit) is being renewed by the indwelling Spirit. Redemption in this present life involves transformation of the inner self; at the Parousia, when the dead in Christ shall rise, redemption will involve transformation of the outer self, the body. This is plainly indicated in biblical texts such as Romans 8:10, 23 and 2 Corinthians 4:16.

The doctrine of the intermediate state further supports holistic dualism. At death the soul/spirit separates from the body to await the resurrection. The conscious, bodiless existence of the self in the intermediate state is anticipated by such Old Testament texts as Job 19:25; Psalms 16:11; 49:15; and Isaiah 14:9 ("spirits of the departed"). References are far more abundant in the New Testament, relating to the intermediate state: Matthew 17:3; Luke 16:19–31; Acts 7:59–60; 2 Corinthians 5:1–9; Philippians 1:22–24; Hebrews

---

48. Walther Eichrodt, *Theology of the Old Testament*, 2 vols. (Philadelphia, Pa.: Westminster, 1961–67), 2:131.

12:23; 2 Peter 1:13–15; Revelation 6:9–11; and 20:4. In dialogue with the Sadducees, Jesus inferred that Abraham, Isaac, and Jacob, who had died physically long before, were even then alive in heaven (Matt. 22:29–32). Moreover, the Lord said to the criminal crucified at his side, "Today you will be with me in paradise" (Luke 23:43b). With his last breath, the thief's soul/spirit left his body and was carried into God's presence. In 2 Corinthians 5:1–8, Paul acknowledged that at death the believer's immaterial self (soul/spirit) leaves the body to be with Christ. Contemplating the prospect of being "unclothed" as a bodiless spirit, Paul experienced anxiety at a human level. But he concluded that it is far better "to be away from the body and [be] at home with the Lord." Tozer put it this way: "In the time of our departure, the body that He gave us will disintegrate and drop away like a cocoon, for the spirit of man soars away to the presence of God."[49]

The accumulated biblical evidence leads us to dissent from the verdict of anthropological monists, who deny the intermediate state (e.g., "The concept of a disembodied soul is alien to a biblical anthropology, even through the experience of death and resurrection"[50]). The beloved KJV-based internment liturgy expresses soul-body dualism well: "Forasmuch as it hath pleased Almighty God to take out of this world the soul of our deceased brother/sister, we therefore commit his/her body to the ground; earth to earth, ashes to ashes, dust to dust."

Psychiatrist and clergyman Jeffrey Boyd agrees with Augustine that "it is impossible to have a robust and healthy theology in the absence of a doctrine of the soul."[51] The soul/spirit is an immaterial, invisible, personal, living, active, everlasting substance, ego, self that thinks, wills, feels, distinguishes right from wrong, relates to oneself, others, and God, and whose identity endures beyond the grave. Study of the biblical uses of the terms *spirit* and *soul* indicates that either can designate the inner person who thinks, wills, emotes, discriminates between right and wrong, and relates.

The body is the physical, visible, and temporal frame that decays at death. "The matter-energy of the body cannot be reduced to the spirit and its

---

49. A. W. Tozer, *I Call It Heresy* (Harrisburg, Pa.: Christian Publications, 1974), 15.
50. Ray S. Anderson, "Anthropology, Christian," in *The Blackwell Encyclopedia of Modern Christian Thought*, ed. Alister E. McGrath (Cambridge, Mass.: Blackwell, 1995), 7.
51. Jeffrey H. Boyd, "Self-Concept: In Defense of the Word *Soul*," in *Care for the Soul*, ed. Mark R. McMinn and Timothy R. Phillips (Downers Grove, Ill.: InterVarsity, 2001), 107.

energy, for each has a *mutually exclusive set of attributes*. The qualities of the matter-energy of the body include visibility, extension in space, build or figure, weight, color, measurable temperature, tangibility," according to Gordon Lewis and Bruce Demarest. They add, "None of these serve as attributes of spirit (cf. Luke 24:39)."[52]

Old Testament scholar James Barr supports the existence of a substantial soul and our finding of holistic dualism. "Hebrew *nepeš*, 'soul,' is not a unity of body and soul or a totality of personality but rather does on occasion actually mean 'soul' in something like the traditional sense (i.e., something which is immortal, the principle of personal unity, distinct from the body and at death finally separable from it)."[53]

Within the unity of the person, the immaterial soul/spirit resides in the body and acts through the body as its instrument. The soul/spirit conceives a plan, wills it, and directs the body to accomplish its end in the external world. In addition, various faculties of the soul/spirit interact (see chap. 7, pp. 229–30). Moreover, the human soul/spirit and body are mutually conditioning; the soul/spirit acts on the body, and the body acts on the soul/spirit. How this interaction works is not entirely clear. Neither is it clear how God, who is spirit, acts on the material universe. Experience, however, offers numerous examples of psychosomatic interaction. For example, communion with God revives physical energy; chemical imbalances in the brain's neurotransmitters depress the soul/spirit; and a depressed spirit reduces the body's ability to control tissue inflammation. Lewis and Demarest make this observation regarding the composition of the human person:

A person inwardly is like God, an invisible, personal, living, and active spirit, a conscious subject with a sense of presence and a continuing identity. A person outwardly is unlike God as an extended, visible, tangible physical organism. The whole person is a complex unity composed of two distinct entities, soul and body, intimately interacting with one another. Neither of them is the whole person, yet either part can stand figuratively for the whole person. While they are alive the two natures (physical and spiritual) are neither

---

52. Gordon R. Lewis and Bruce Demarest, *Integrative Theology*, 3 vols. (Grand Rapids: Zondervan, 1987–94), 2:148.
53. James Barr, *The Garden of Eden and the Hope of Immortality* (Minneapolis, Minn.: Fortress, 1993), 218 n. 6.

divided nor confused. A whole person has attributes of spirit and attributes of body. Although body and spirit are separate entities ontologically, in this life they are intricately united. For metaphysical purposes . . . a human being is composed of an *interacting dichotomy* of spirit and body.[54]

# The Created Image

One of the most profound themes of the Bible is the human person as creation image of God. Chapter 7 will examine the fallen image and the redemption image. Adam was fashioned from the dust of the earth, yet he and Eve occupy a special place in the cosmos as unique images of God. Furthermore, all Adam's descendants share that honor. The implications of human persons created in the image of God are immense for theology, psychology, ministry, and Christian living. Ramifications of the *imago* embrace issues of human dignity and value, personal and social ethics, relations between the sexes, the solidarity of the human family (*ʾādām* in Genesis 1:27 embraces humankind collectively), and racial justice.

## Historical Perspectives

Theological perspectives concerning the human person as image of God cluster in three principal categories: (1) *the functional*; (2) *the relational*; and (3) *the substantive*.

### Functional Views

Functional interpretations of the *imago Dei* indicate a preference for operational rather than metaphysical categories. They supplant who a person *is* with what a person *does*. According to those who take one of these views, the image is rooted not in the person's makeup or qualities but in the person's office or task. Typically, functional views interpret the *imago* as the human person's exercise of dominion over the created order and lower creatures. As God reigns over all the earth, so the human person rules the material world under God's authority. Proponents point out that God commanded

---

54. Lewis and Demarest, *Integrative Theology*, 2:149–50.

the first couple to exercise dominion (Gen. 1:26–28; cf. Ps. 8:6) and that Adam named and domesticated the animals (Gen. 2:19–20). This view of the image strikes a resonant chord with contemporary environmental and ecological concerns.

Pelagius (c. 355–c. 435), a heretical British monk and founder of the theological impulse that bears his name, asserted the uprightness of humans entering the world. Pelagius identified the *imago* as the power of reason to know truth, free will to choose the good, and dominion to rule over the created order.

Rationalistic Socinians, the sixteenth-century anti-Trinitarian predecessors of Unitarianism, denied original sin and Christ's atoning death on the cross. They stressed human rational powers, good works, and performance of moral and civic duties. According to the Socinian apologetic treatise *The Racovian Catechism* (1605), the image of God "properly imports the authority of man and his dominion over all inferior creatures, which result from the reason and judgment communicated to him."[55]

The Old Testament authority Gerhard von Rad (1901–1971) reflects the nonevangelical preference for function over essence. "The divine likeness is not to be found in the personality of man, in his free Ego, in his dignity or in his free use of moral capacity, etc."[56] The Old Testament focuses, rather, on the human person's tasks as vice-regent of God. According to von Rad,

> In the ancient world a king erected images of himself throughout the empire to establish his authority to rule. The author of Genesis appropriated this ancient sense of *ṣelem* to conclude that man is placed upon earth in God's image as God's sovereign emblem. He is really only God's representative, summoned to maintain and enforce God's claim to dominion over the earth. The decisive thing about man's similarity to God, therefore, is his function in the non-human world.[57]

Another Old Testament scholar, Hans Walter Wolff (1911–1993), similarly avers, "It is precisely in his function as ruler that he is God's image. . . .

55. *The Racovian Catechism* (Lexington, Ky.: ATLA, 1962), 1.2.21, cited in Lewis and Demarest, *Integrative Theology,* 2:128.
56. Gerhard von Rad, "*eikōn,*" in *TDNT,* 2:391.
57. Gerhard von Rad, *Genesis,* Old Testament Library (Philadelphia, Pa.: Westminster, 1961), 60.

He is evidence that God is the Lord of creation; but as God's steward he also executes his rule, fulfilling his task not in arbitrary despotism, but as a responsible agent."[58]

D. J. A. Clines, an evangelical Bible scholar, claims that dominion exercising is not a *consequence* of the person as God's image but is the very *nature* of it. From the stance of anthropological monism, the entire person—not some higher part—is said to constitute the image. "The image is to be understood not so much ontologically as existentially: it comes to expression not in the nature of man so much as in his activity and function. This function is to represent God's lordship in the lower orders of creation."[59] According to theologian Dale Moody (1915–1992), the governing idea of Genesis 1:1–2:4 is God ruling over all creation. The Almighty, however, willed that humans should exercise stewardship under His lordship. "Man's most distinctive quality is the image of God by which he has dominion over all other creatures and the whole of God's creation."[60]

### Relational Views

Influenced by the "I-Thou" personalism of the Jewish philosopher Martin Buber (1878–1965), theologians in this category identify the image in terms of the human person's various relationships. Karl Barth insisted that no *analogy of being* between the Creator and the creature is possible, only an *analogy of relationship*. The human person is *imago Dei* in that he or she has been created to relate with God and with other humans in community. Within the triune Godhead there exists a profound "differentiation and relation of the I and Thou."[61]

In terms of horizontal relationships, the coexistence and cooperation of God Himself is repeated in the relation of man to man.[62] Since the person's creation in God's image is immediately followed by reference to man as "male" and "female" (Gen. 1:27; cf. 5:1–2), Barth judged that the differentiation and relationship of male and female lies at the heart of the *imago*. In one respect he defined the image as the polarity of the sexes, in essence, as

---

58. Hans Walter Wolff, *Anthropology of the Old Testament* (Philadelphia, Pa.: Fortress, 1974), 160–61.
59. D. J. A. Clines, "The Image of God in Man," *Tyndale Bulletin* 19 (1968): 101.
60. Dale Moody, *The Word of Truth* (Grand Rapids: Eerdmans, 1981), 226, cf. 232.
61. Karl Barth, *CD*, 3.1.192.
62. Ibid., 3.1.185.

the "juxtaposition and conjunction of man and man which is that of male and female."[63]

Another advocate of the relational view was Bonhoeffer, who reasoned that the *imago* pertains to the human person's experience of being free for the other. God, the prototype, is free for the human. Analogously, the human being is free through grace to worship God and to relate to other human beings. Bonhoeffer envisaged the male-female relation as paradigmatic. Reflecting on Genesis 1:27, he wrote, "Man is free for man, *Male and female he created them.* Man is not alone, he is in duality, and it is in this dependence on the other that his creatureliness consists."[64]

Moreover, the human person is free to rule over the lower creation, not to be slavishly ruled by it. In sum, "Man's being free for God and the other person and his being-free-from the creature in his dominion over it is the image of God in the first man."[65]

Reformed theologian G. C. Berkouwer claimed that the image is vested not "in various anthropological distinctions such as ego, personality, self-consciousness, and the like,"[66] but at a deeper level—in the human's social relations with other persons and in his dependence upon and relation to God. "Man never appears as an isolated self-contained entity, or in the pure factuality of his weakness or strength or power or riches, but always and exclusively in that relationship which so decisively defines man in the full actuality of his existence."[67]

Paul K. Jewett (1919–1975), an evangelical theologian, likewise defined the *imago* relationally. "To be created in the divine image is to be so endowed that one lives one's life in an ineluctable relationship with God and neighbor." He adds, "The neighbor is that human 'other,' that 'thou,' in relation to whom I know myself as 'I.'"[68] Ray S. Anderson adds, "In the Judeo-Christian tradition the image and likeness of God can be understood as a capacity for relationship with the self, others and God in a knowing way and an openness to a future which provides hope and meaning to life."[69]

---

63. Ibid., 3.1.195.
64. Dietrich Bonhoeffer, *Creation and Temptation* (London: SCM, 1966), 37.
65. Ibid., 39.
66. Berkouwer, *Man*, 87.
67. Ibid., 196.
68. Paul K. Jewett, *Who We Are: Our Dignity as Human* (Grand Rapids: Eerdmans, 1996), 131.
69. Anderson, *New Age of the Soul*, 42.

Stanley Grenz interprets the *imago* not as something that is given, but that which one becomes: "God desires that we be the image of God."[70] Grenz adds, "Ultimately, then, the 'image of God' is a social reality. It refers to humans as beings-in-fellowship."[71]

## Substantive Views

*Substantive views* identify the human person's likeness to God as a psychical or spiritual quality. Early Christian thought, immersed in the Greek intellectual world, tended to interpret the *imago* in terms of intellect or reason.

The apologist Justin Martyr (100–165) defined the image in terms of reason and moral capacity: "In the beginning when God created man, he endowed him with the power of understanding, of choosing the truth, and of doing right."[72]

Irenaeus, bishop of Lyons in Gaul, was the first theologian to treat the *imago* systematically. He drew a distinction in Genesis 1:26 between "image" and "likeness." The image consists of the endowments of a rational mind and free will ("animal man") retained after the Fall; the likeness consists of the supernatural gift of righteousness and holiness ("spiritual man") bestowed by the Spirit. Irenaeus laid the foundation for the medieval distinction between the person's natural endowments (image) and the superadded gift of righteousness (likeness) lost at Eden but restored at baptism.

Gregory of Nyssa (c. 330–c. 395), bishop of Nyssa, identified the *imago* primarily with the intellect. "The form of man was framed to serve as an instrument for the use of reason."[73] He added, "The soul finds its perfection in that which is intellectual and rational."[74]

From texts such as Ephesians 4:23–24 and Colossians 3:9–10, Augustine judged that the *imago* resides in the rational and spiritual soul. In another line of reasoning, he averred that the human made like God—in whom there is no sex—implies that the image resides not in the body but in the

70. Stanley J. Grenz, *Created for Community* (Grand Rapids: Baker, 1988), 215.
71. Ibid., 80.
72. Justin Martyr, *Apology* 1.28 [*ANF*, 1:172].
73. Gregory of Nyssa, *On the Making of Man*, Introduction, 9 [*NPNF*[2], 5:388].
74. Ibid., 15.2 [*NPNF*[2], 5:403].

spirit of the mind.[75] "We must find in the soul of man that image of the Creator which is immutably implanted in its immortality."[76] Again, God "made the mind of man to His own image and likeness; that is where the image of God is—in the mind."[77] By mind, Augustine understood the human person's capacity "to use reason and intelligence to understand and to behold God."[78]

Augustine was no reductive rationalist, however. His Trinitarian analogies (e.g., memory, understanding, and will or love) unfolded the holistic nature of the human person's capacities to know, recollect, choose, and love. These functions of the human soul operate interdependently, analogous to the operations of the three persons of the Trinity.

Thomas Aquinas wedded Aristotelian logic with Augustinian anthropology. Thomas endorsed the patristic and medieval distinction between image (the intellectual nature retained after the Fall) and likeness (conferred righteousness lost in the Fall). Following Augustine, he asserted that the image consists of memory, understanding, and will or love. The likeness is "not merely a natural gift, but a supernatural endowment of grace."[79]

Martin Luther rejected the distinction between image and likeness, which he judged painted too rosy a picture of fallen human ability to please God by good works. Moreover, if the image consists chiefly of natural faculties, the Devil himself would be an image-bearer of God. Rather, the *imago* consists of the human person's original state of purity—the righteousness, holiness, and wisdom with which God endowed Adam, but which were lost at the Fall. "My understanding of the image of God is this: that Adam . . . not only knew God and believed that he was good, but that he also lived a life that was wholly godly; that is, he was without the fear of death or of any other danger, and was content with God's favor," Luther said in his lectures on Genesis.[80]

John Calvin also dismissed the distinction between image and likeness. The proper locus of the image is the soul, although rays thereof shine into the human person's bodily frame. "The primary seat of the divine image is

75. Augustine, *On the Trinity* 12.7 [*NPNF*¹, 3:158–60].

76. Ibid., 14.6 [*NPNF*¹, 3:187].

77. Augustine, *On the Creed* 1 [*FOTC*, 27:290].

78. Augustine, *On the Trinity* 14.4 [*NPNF*¹, 3:186].

79. Thomas Aquinas, *ST*, 4:318 [pt. 1, q. 95, art. 1].

80. Martin Luther, *Lectures on Genesis*, 2 vols., *LW*, 1:62–63.

in the mind and heart, or in the soul and its powers, yet there is no part of man, not even the body itself, in which some sparks do not glow."[81]

That of which the image consists is shown by its restoration through the work of Christ (Eph. 4:23–24; Col. 3:10), who is the perfect image of God, Calvin wrote. Included therein are natural endowments such as knowledge and understanding, free will, sound affections, properly ordered emotions,[82] and supernatural gifts such as "faith, love of God, charity toward neighbor, zeal for holiness and for righteousness."[83]

In sum Calvin expressed the view that, "God's image was visible in the light of the mind, in the uprightness of the heart, and in the soundness of all the parts."[84]

According to Carl F. H. Henry, the terms *image* and *likeness* synonymously connote that the human person uniquely resembles the invisible God. Henry rejects the neo-orthodox notion that the *imago* concerns the relation in which the person stands to God and others. Rather, the created image exists "formally in man's personality (moral responsibility and intelligence) and materially in his knowledge of God and his will for man." "Man is made for personal and endless fellowship with God, involving rational understanding, moral obedience and religious communion."[85]

Old Testament scholar Walther Eichrodt (1890–1978) believes that the likeness of God's image means that personhood is given to humanity as a definitive characteristic: "He has a share in the personhood of God; and as a being capable of self-awareness and of self-determination he is open to the divine address and capable of responsible conduct. This quality of personhood shapes the totality of his psycho-physical existence; it is this which comprises the essentially human, and distinguishes him from all other creatures."[86]

## Biblical Exposition

We turn now to the major biblical texts that relate to the human person as image-bearer of God. Several of these relate to the Old Testament, and especially to the early chapters of Genesis:

81. Calvin, *Institutes of the Christian Religion,* 1:188 [1.15.3].
82. Ibid., 1:189–90, 270–71 [1.15.4; 2.2.12].
83. Ibid., 1:270 [2.2.12].
84. Ibid., 1:189 [1.15.4].
85. Henry, "Man," 340–41.
86. Eichrodt, *Theology of the Old Testament,* 2:126.

- Genesis 1:26: "God said, 'Let us make man in our *image [ṣelem]*, in our *likeness [dᵉmût]*, and let them rule over the fish of the sea and the birds of the air, over the livestock, over all the earth, and over all the creatures that move along the ground.'" *Image (ṣelem*, translated in the LXX by the Greek *eichōn)* literally means "a statue" (Num. 33:52; Dan. 2:32). Metaphorically a *ṣelem* is a a copy or representation (Ps. 73:20).[87] The near synonym, *likeness (dᵉmût*, translated in the Septuagint by the Greek *homoiōsis)* denotes "a resemblance or a similarity."

- *Genesis 1:27:* "So God created man in his own image *[ṣelem]*, in the image of God he created him; male and female he created them." This verse states that men and women were created in God's image and thus the genders were invested equally with personhood and dignity.

- *Genesis 5:1b-2:* "When God created man, he made him in the likeness *[dᵉmût*, translated in the Septuagint by the Greek *eichōn]* of God. He created them male and female; at the time they were created, he blessed them and called them 'man.'"

- *Genesis 5:3:* "When Adam had lived 130 years, he had a son in his own likeness *[dᵉmût]*, in his own image *[ṣelem]*; and he named him Seth." Adam's son resembled him in a manner somehow similar to the human person's resemblance to God.

- *Genesis 9:6:* "Whoever sheds the blood of man, by man shall his blood be shed; for in the image *[ṣelem]* of God has God made man." This text mandates the death penalty for the murder of a human person because he or she is a valued image of God.

"Likeness," then, adds nothing new to the word *image;* their juxtaposition reflects common Hebrew parallelism. The patristic distinction between natural qualities and supernaturally endowed gifts thus is unfounded. According to Victor Hamilton, "The more important word of the two is 'image,' but to avoid the implication that man is a precise copy of God, albeit in miniature, the less specific and more abstract *dᵉmût* ("likeness") was added."[88]

---

87. John E. Hartley, "*ṣelem,*" in *TWOT,* 2:767.
88. Victor P. Hamilton, "*Dᵉmût,*" in *TWOT,* 1:192.

- *Psalm 8:5–8:* "You made him a little lower than the heavenly beings and crowned him with glory and honor. You made him ruler over the works of your hands; you put everything under his feet: all flocks and herds, and the beasts of the field, the birds of the air, and the fish of the sea, all that swim the paths of the seas." Compared with the vast splendor of the cosmos, the finite human being appears microscopically insignificant. Yet as the consummation of God's creation and as its crowning jewel, the human person is the unique object of God's special consideration and care. The human's creation for relationship with God and for rule over the earth invest him with glory and honor.

The New Testament adds considerable specificity to the concept of the *imago Dei*. The apostle Paul sheds light on the nature of the *imago* by unfolding the restoration in Christ of what was ruined by sin. Four texts—Romans 12:2; Colossians 3:10; Ephesians 4:23–24, and James 3:9—highlight the nature of the renovation brought about by Christ's saving work.

- *Romans 12:2a:* "Do not conform any longer to the pattern of this world, but be transformed by the renewing of your mind *[nous]*." *Nous* signifies "mind, the thinking power, reason in its moral quality and activity."[89]
- *Colossians 3:10:* ". . . and have put on the new self, which is being renewed in knowledge *[epignōsis]* in the image of its Creator." What is being renewed in the Christian is knowledge and understanding, the end of which is perfect knowledge of God and reality in the age to come (cf. 1 Cor. 13:12).
- *Ephesians 4:23–24:* ". . . to be made new in the attitude of your minds *[pneumati tou noos];* and to put on the new self, created to be like God in true righteousness *[dikaiosynē]* and holiness *[hosiotēti tēs alētheias,* lit. *'the genuine holiness']*." What the Spirit continually renews is knowledge, righteousness, holiness, and devotion to God.
- *James 3:9:* "With the tongue we praise our Lord and Father, and with it we curse men, who have been made in God's likeness *[homoiōsis]*." James acknowledges that a significant resemblance exists between God and the human person; consequently the one who curses a human being curses God.

---

89. Cleon L. Rogers Jr. and Cleon L. Rogers III, *NLEKGNT,* 339.

## Theological Development

Although Scripture offers no systematic explanation of the *imago Dei,* it does present sufficient information to determine what is signified by this phrase. The human person is not the ultimate image-bearer of God; Jesus Christ is (2 Cor. 4:4; Col. 1:15). By entering our time and space, the Son of God has given visible demonstration of what God is like (John 1:18; 14:9). God's purpose for His twice-born children is that they should "be conformed to the likeness of his Son" (Rom. 8:29). Thus through the new birth and life-long "imitation of Christ" (Thomas à Kempis [c. 1379–1471]), believers are being shaped into the likeness of Christ, the perfect image of God. The fact of the human being's creation in God's likeness is stated in the first page of the Bible; but not until the revelation of God's Son and His redeeming work did the full implications of the human person's resemblance to God become clear.

The human person shares God's communicable attributes (including kindness, mercy, and love) but does not share God's incommunicable attributes (such as self-existence, eternality, and immutability). The human person thus bears resemblance to God only in a secondary sense. Moreover, it must be emphasized that male and female humans are image and likeness of God (Gen. 1:27). Their common creation as *imago Dei* guarantees the personal and spiritual equality of the sexes, while allowing for their complementarity psychologically and functionally. Paul's statement that "the woman is the glory of man" (1 Cor. 11:7) does not negate her creation as God's image. Exposition of the image also affirms that people of all races and ethnic groups are *imago Dei.* All humans, without respect to gender, race, or degree of functioning, are children of God by creation and poten-tially children of God by redemption. This reality directly challenges all forms of ethnocentrism, caste systems, and other subtle and not-so-subtle forms of discrimination. Because the man and the woman are *imago Dei,* murder is strictly forbidden (Gen. 9:6; Exod. 20:13).

In what ways, then, does the human person as created image resemble, reflect, and represent God? The following categories address this issue, as well as the perennial question posed by thinking people: What is man?

*Metaphysically,* the human person is a living, personal, active, indivisible, everlasting, and substantial soul/spirit—"a conscious subject with a sense of presence and a continuing identity."[90] Moreover, in some mysterious

---

90. Lewis and Demarest, *Integrative Theology,* 2:149.

manner the beauty of God shines through the human's corporeal frame to which the soul/spirit is wedded in the unity of the person. The whole human person (soul/spirit and body), not just an aspect thereof, is *imago Dei.*

*Intellectually,* the human person possesses a rational mind, meaning the capacity to know formally and experientially itself (self-consciousness), other persons (other-consciousness), the surrounding environment (world-consciousness), and supremely God Himself (God-consciousness). Intellectual capacities include critical and logical thought, intuition, memory, imagination, language for communicating thoughts, and creativity. Concerning self-knowledge, Augustine wrote: "For we are, and we know that we are, and we love to be and to know that we are."[91]

*Volitionally,* the human person possesses the capacity to propose and choose worthy goals, as well as the strategies by which to achieve these goals. In this sense of personal self-determination in horizontal relations apart from external constraint the will is said to be free.

*Emotionally,* the human person experiences and evokes a wide range of feelings and affections, such as desire, elation, compassion, fear, jealousy, anxiety, anger, hostility, guilt, and shame.

*Morally,* the human person possesses the ability to discern the absolute standards of right and wrong, experience moral obligation or ethical "oughtness," do what is right, evaluate personal behavior, experience objective guilt, and pursue righteousness. Conscience *(syneidēsis)* is that moral faculty of the heart that attests compliance or noncompliance with God's moral law implanted within at creation and codified in the written Scriptures.

*Relationally,* the human person is capable, horizontally, of connecting with and communicating with others, and of feeling love for self (I-self) and other personal subjects (I-thou). He or she possesses the capacity, vertically, to relate with, respond to, and worship God (I-Thou). The human person intrinsically is a religious being, capable of cultivating a theistic spirituality. Moreover, the human person as image is created for sonship (Deut. 14:1; Isa. 1:2; cf. Luke 3:23–38), inasmuch as Scripture likens the relation between Yahweh and the human person to that of a father to his child (cf. Gen. 5:3). Human relational capacity also involves forging trusting communities or solidarities at a collective level.

*Functionally,* the human being serves worthy and beneficial purposes,

---

91. Augustine, *City of God* 11.26 [*FOTC,* 14:228].

including procreation of offspring, subjugation of the earth, the exercise of dominion over the lower creatures, and the utilization of earth's resources for the glory of God and the good of humankind. Under God's sovereign authority, human beings possess delegated authority over the created order (Gen. 1:26, 28; Ps. 8:5–9).

Resembling God in the above respects, the human person is wisely designed to reflect or show forth in the created order the nature and activity of God. The human being, as *imago Dei,* was created to display in material form who God is and what God does. In the words of J. I. Packer, "Image means representative likeness."[92]

Theories of the *imago Dei* often isolate one aspect thereof, whereas our integration brings together several biblical emphases descriptive of the human person's resemblance to God. Plantinga insists, "The image of God may plausibly be said to consist . . . in the whole set of these (and many more) likenesses. . . . The image will thus emerge as a rich, multi-faceted reality, comprising acts, relations, capacities, virtues, dispositions, and even emotions."[93] Within the unity of the person, the above capacities of the human being as *imago* function interdependently, not independently. The one human person, thinks, wills, feels, relates, and acts as an organic whole. The construct of explaining the *imago* under the categories of likeness to God formally and materially (so Emil Brunner and Carl F. H. Henry) is consistent with our more detailed representation.

The locus of the image is the entire person—soul/spirit and body. God, of course, has no body (cf. John 4:24), and the second commandment (Exod. 20:4) explicitly forbids fashioning material images of God. Consider for a moment 1 Corinthians 15:49, which teaches that in the resurrection the Christian will be conformed to the image of the God-man. Since Christ, man's redeemed image, possesses a glorified body, the created image also extends to the body in the unity of the person. Michael Ramsey correctly observed, "Man, when he is raised up with Christ in glory, will be man as God created him to become . . . like unto Christ's perfect manhood."[94]

---

92. J. I. Packer, "Reflected Glory," *Christianity Today,* December 2003, 56.

93. Alvin Plantinga, "Images of God," in *Christian Faith and Practice in the Modern World,* ed. Mark Noll and David Wells (Grand Rapids: Eerdmans, 1988), 52.

94. Michael Ramsey, *The Glory of God* (London: Longmans, Green, 1949), 151. Cf. Philip Edgcumbe Hughes, *The True Image: The Origin and Destiny of Man in Christ* (Grand Rapids: Eerdmans, 1989), 27: "The predestined end . . . is not just a starting again. It is the completion of creation."

In what sense is the human a being invested with personhood? A person may be defined as an "intelligent, self-conscious, self-determined, responsible agent capable of appreciating values, choosing purposes, and sharing them with others in fellowship and action."[95] In theological terms a being is personal because created in the image of a personal God. God as personal is a living, invisible, infinite spirit who knows, wills, feels, and relates with the Son and Holy Spirit and created beings, and who acts. The bedrock of human personality thus is the image of God with which man as male and female is invested. The human is personal, because in the unity of being he or she is *nepeš/psychē, rûaḥ/pneuma, lēb/kardia, bāśār/sōma* with above capacities included therein.

An alternative definition of a personal being might be "a complex agent, a unity of an inner (spiritual) and outer (physical) being with a multiplicity of capacities for developing excellence and ruling the world intellectually, morally, emotionally, volitionally and relationally."[96] Efforts to recover human dignity in a troubled world hinge on a critical revaluation of the human person as *imago Dei*.

Indeed, it is the *imago Dei* that distinguishes a man or woman from the animal kingdom. Similarities exist between human beings and animals. Like humans, animals originated from the dust of the ground and possess an animated body (Gen. 6:17; 7:15, 22). Humans (2:7) and animals (1:20, 24) are referred to as living beings (*nepeš ḥayyâ*). They display physiological similarities (brain, circulatory system, blood), and they are mortal (Eccl. 3:19). Yet the differences between humans and animals are more profound. Scripture describes animals as "brute beasts *[aloga zōa]*, creatures of instinct *[physika]*" (2 Peter 2:12) and "unreasoning animals *[aloga zōa]*" (Jude 10). Animals are living beings but not image-bearers of God and not persons. Thus Adam found a suitable helper, not among the animals, but in Eve (Gen. 2:20–22). Moreover, humans exercise dominion over animals (Ps. 8:6–8) and may take the life of an animal but not another person (Gen. 9:3–6). Consider the following similarities and dissimilarities between human beings and animals:

*Intellectually,* animals lack a rational-spiritual soul. Animals lack the high level of self-consciousness observed in humans, do not research the nature and connection among things, lack the power of imagination, do not employ

---

95. See Lewis and Demarest, *Integrative Theology,* 2:274.
96. Ibid., 2:160.

sophisticated language (although they do communicate), are bound to their particular form of environment,[97] and possess no openness to the future (i.e., do not know the future as future).

*Volitionally,* animals do not intentionally set goals and strategies for achieving said goals. Animals do not redirect their instinctual drives by force of mind and will to the attainment of worthy objectives.

*Emotionally,* animals do experience certain emotions (fear, anger, sadness) but lack the full range of human emotions (joy, regret, *agapē* love).

*Morally,* animals do not discriminate between good and evil, right and wrong. Neither do they experience guilt and shame or bear moral responsibility for their actions.

*Relationally,* animals do not relate to other creatures in the personal "I-thou" manner that humans do. Only of Adam (man) is it written, "But for Adam no suitable helper was found" (Gen. 2:20). Above all, animals do not long for, commune with, pray to, and worship God. Contrary to some popular opinion, animals do not enjoy a destiny beyond this world.

*Functionally,* animals do not create cities, cultures, and civilizations; they do not exercise dominion over the earth as God's vice-regents. Indeed, Adam named and domesticated the animals, not vice-versa (Gen. 2:19–20).

Thus, against evolutionists and some animal rights advocates, there is ample evidence in the study of personhood that the human person is more than a highly developed and intelligent animal. The human person's dignity and distinctiveness vis-à-vis the animal world rests on special creation as image and likeness of God. The breath *(nᵉšāmâ)* breathed into Adam (Gen. 2:7) is used only of human beings, never of animals. Only of the human is it said that he was created "a little lower than the heavenly beings" (*ᵉlōhîm*, Ps. 8:5). In contemplating such distinctions, Blaise Pascal intoned, "Man in the state of his creation . . . is exalted above the whole of nature, made like unto God, and sharing in his divinity."[98]

Only the human person lives in two realms, at the interface of the material and the spiritual worlds. Created from the earth, the human being is the subject of science; created in the image of God, the human being is intelligible only in the light of biblical revelation.

---

97. Pannenberg observes: "Man *has* a world, while each species of animals is *limited to* an environment that is fixed by heredity and that is typical of the species" (*What Is Man?* 4).

98. Blaise Pascal, *Penseés.* Trans. A. J. Krailsheimer (Baltimore: Penguin Books, 1966), 66 (no. 131).

## ORIGIN AND IMMORTALITY OF THE SOUL

## Historical Perspectives

### Preexistence of Souls

Influenced by Plato and later Greek thought, a few Christian theologians viewed the soul as preexisting the person's conception and birth. Plato himself regarded the soul as the immaterial aspect of the human person that most resembles the nature of the gods. Corresponding to innate ideas in the mind are eternal objects in the pretemporal world. From the first moment of consciousness, the mind, or soul, possesses such ideas. These ideas are not born of sense experience and must correspond to something known from a previous existence. Plato subscribed not only to eternal preexistence but also to the transmigration of the soul.

Origen, who was well versed in Greek philosophy, concluded that from the foundation of the world God created, along with the angels, a predetermined number of souls or rational spirits. Through misuse of their freedom, some souls in the heavenly realm rebelled against God and fell from rectitude. The most evil of these souls became demons; others who sinned less grievously God judged by uniting them with material bodies to become humans. Origen regarded the earthly experience of the human soul as one epoch in an endless cycle of rebirths. The Greek father allegedly found support for his preexistence theory in God's choice of Jacob and rejection of Esau before their births (Rom. 9:11–13). Origen's view was condemned at the Second Ecumenical Council of Constantinople (553). The eleventh canon, written against Origen begins, "Let him be anathema who asserts the fabulous pre-existence of the soul and the rash restoration of all things."

Founded by Joseph Smith (1805–44), Mormonism claims that humans were begotten by God the Father in the spirit world as spirit beings. These spirits received physical bodies by natural procreation. As embodied humans beget children in this life, they fulfill their heavenly destiny.

### Creationism

This theory of the soul's origin, influenced by Aristotle's thought, argues that God creates each individual soul directly and instantaneously at its infusion into the body. Creationism posits the dual origin—human and divine—of the human person. Advocates appeal to Scriptures such as Ecclesiastes 12:7, Isaiah 42:5, Zechariah 12:1, and Hebrews 12:9. Supporters of creationism judged that this position was necessary to underscore the distinctiveness of the human person vis-à-vis lower forms of life. The centuries-long controversy regarding the origin of the soul pitted Catholics and Calvinists against Lutherans.

The North African apologist Lactantius (260–320) advanced the first developed case for the soul's creation. A material body, he argued, can beget another material body, but an immaterial soul cannot beget another soul. Rather, God creates *de novo* each individual soul at the moment of conception. "It is evident that life-principles [i.e., souls] are not given by parents, but by one and the same God, the Father of all."[99] Jerome examined at length the three main views. He judged the *traducian* view that "souls are said to be infused through the insemination of the human seed" to be "the vulgar view."[100] Jerome accepted the opinion that God created the soul with the body. "God creates souls daily and infuses them in bodies of individuals as they are born."[101]

Thomas Aquinas rejected the traducian hypothesis as heretical, since he saw the soul as the spiritual form of the body. A spiritual form, he insisted, cannot be procreated from a material substance. The soul was created by God, not separately, but with the body.[102] The heading of volume 2 (titled *God the Origin of Creatures*), chapter 87, to his *Summa Contra Gentiles* condemns any notion that the human soul is transmitted with the male sperm.

Calvin held that God forms the soul of each infant by an *ex nihilo* act of creation:

> If man's soul be from the essence of God through derivation [i.e., procreation], it will follow that God's nature is subject not only to change and passions, but also to ignorance, wicked desires, infirmity, and all manner of vices. Nothing is more inconstant than man. ... Therefore we must take it to be a fact that souls, although the image of God be engraved upon them, are just as much created as

---

99. Lactantius, *The Workmanship of God* 19 [*ANF*, 7:299].

100. Jerome, *Against Rufinus* 2.10 [*FOTC*, 53:116].

101. Ibid., 3.28 [*FOTC*, 53:199].

102. Thomas Aquinas, *ST*, 4:261 [pt. 1, q. 90, art. 4].

angels are. But creation is not inpouring, but the beginning of essence out of nothing. Indeed, if the spirit has been given by God, and in departing from the flesh returns to him (cf. Eccl. 12:7), we must not forthwith say that it was plucked from his substance.[103]

The latest, comprehensive doctrinal standard of Rome, the *Catechism of the Catholic Church,* promotes creationism in these words: "The Church teaches that every spiritual soul is created immediately by God—it is not 'produced' by the parents—and also that it is immortal; it does not perish when it separates from the body at death, and it will be reunited with the body at the final Resurrection."[104]

## Traducianism

*Traducianism* holds that body and soul are transmitted from parents to children by natural procreation. Adam's soul was created immediately by God, as was Eve's; but the soul of every other human is formed through the union of male sperm and the female ovum at conception. Although material and psychical/spiritual aspects of an offspring are received from its biological parents, the process is fully dependant on God (mediate creation). Proponents suggest that this view best accords with the solidarity of the human race and the transmission of Adamic sin to the human family. Moreover, traducianism seems to avoid directly implicating God in the creation of sinful souls.

Traducianism gained wide currency in the Christian West through the writings of Tertullian. Emphasizing humans' body-soul unity, he averred that the entire race propagated through the joining of two seeds: one soulish and one physical. "The soul is a seed placed in man and transmitted by him, that from the beginning there was one seed of the soul, as there was one seed of the flesh, for the whole human race."[105] At the same time and in the same manner, "the soul is implanted in the womb along with the body."[106]

Writing against the preexistence theory, Gregory of Nyssa insisted that since the human person is a unity of body and soul, it must be that body

---

103. Calvin, *Institutes of the Christian Religion,* 1:191 [1.15.5].
104. *Catechism of the Catholic Church* (New York: Image Doubleday, 1995), no. 366.
105. Tertullian, *On the Soul* 36.1 [*ANF,* 3:217].
106. Ibid., 36.2 [*ANF,* 3:217].

and soul were formed via human procreation. "The seminal cause of our constitution is neither a soul without a body, nor a body without a soul, but that, from animated and living bodies, it is generated at the first as a living and animated being."[107]

Augustine wrestled throughout his life with the issue of the soul's origin. In his refutation of Pelagianism, he was attracted to traducianism as offering a more satisfactory explanation of the spread of sin to the human race. Augustine struggled, however, with traducianism's alleged materialistic view of the soul, as well as with creationism's other difficulties. Augustine judged that the question of the soul's origin was beyond the scope of human knowledge. All the biblical texts adduced prove uncertain with regard to the soul's origin.[108] Ultimately, Augustine was concerned with the practical issue of the destiny, not the origin, of the indestructible human soul.

Luther concluded that the propagation of guilt and depravity to the human race is more adequately explained by the traducian theory. "The people who think that the soul comes from one's parents *(ex traduce esse)* seem to hold a view that is nearest to Scripture." Luther added, "When a child is generated, the soul is created together with the body. . . . And although all oppose this view, I believe that the soul is not added to the body from without but is created out of the substance of the seed."[109]

A Lutheran, Delitzsch believed that traducianism is supported by the creation Sabbath if God now rests from all further creating or generative activity. This would seem to include rest from the transmission of Adam's sin to the human race and the incarnation of the Word, which involved a begetting of Christ's entire person (Ps. 2:7). Though a mystery as to how physical procreation can produce a spiritual-psychical nature, the evidence points toward the formation of the human person's entire spiritual-bodily nature by natural generation. "The spirit of the individual comes into existence by an immediate appointment of God . . . just as little as does his body."[110] W. G. T. Shedd (1820–1894), the American Calvinistic theologian, presented in his systematic theology a lengthy defense of traducianism, concluding, "God created two human individuals, one male and the other female, and in them also created the specific psychico-physical nature from

---

107. Gregory of Nyssa, *On the Making of Man* 30.29 [*NPNF*², 5:426].
108. Augustine, *The Soul and its Origin* bk. 1, *passim* [*NPNF*¹, 5:315–30].
109. Cited in Plass, *What Luther Says*, 876.
110. Delitzsch, *System of Biblical Psychology*, 134.

which all the subsequent individuals of the human family were procreated both psychically and physically."[111]

## Biblical Exposition

The question of the human soul's origin informs issues such as the evolution-creation debate. Creationism is said to guard against any idea that the origin of the soul arises from natural processes. But the origin of the soul also influences theological considerations of the nature of the human person and the spread of sin to the race. It has implications in evaluating ethical issues such as abortion. "The discussion concerning the origin of the soul may appear to belong to another age and to have little relevance to contemporary thought. But this is not so," wrote H. D. McDonald. "The strong opposition among Roman Catholics to abortion derives from the Creationist view of the beginning of human life by an immediate creative act of God."[112]

Several Scriptures are said to favor creationism:

- *Genesis 2:7:* "The Lord God formed the man from the dust of the ground and breathed into his nostrils the breath of life, and the man became a living being." God breathed the animating soul/spirit into Adam by a *de novo* act. The creation of the first man's soul, of course, is unique in that Adam had no human ancestors.
- *Ecclesiastes 12:7:* "The dust returns to the ground it came from, and the spirit returns to God who gave it." The donation of the human spirit refers not to the formation of each person but to the creation of the first human person (Gen. 2:7).
- *Isaiah 42:5:* "God the LORD . . . gives breath to [the earth's] people, and life to those who walk on it." In the context of God as Creator of heaven and earth, this verse reaffirms that God is the originator of human life. Note the presence of Hebrew parallelism in this verse.
- *Isaiah 57:16:* "Then the spirit of man would grow faint before me— the breath of man that I have created." The reference is to the vital life force breathed by God into humans (cf. Gen. 2:7).

---

111. William G. T. Shedd, *Dogmatic Theology,* 3 vols. (Grand Rapids: Zondervan, 1953), 2:7.
112. McDonald, *Christian View of Man,* 74.

- *Zechariah 12:1:* "The Lord, who stretches out the heavens, who lays the foundation of the earth, and who forms *[yāṣār]* the spirit of man within him." In context this verse affirms that by virtue of His awesome creative power, God is able to perform what He declares He will do.
- *Hebrews 12:9* contrasts "human fathers"—earthly fathers, who discipline on the human level—and "the Father of our spirits"—God, who exacts discipline at the spiritual level. "God is here confessed as the deepest and unique Origin of all living creatures, as Giver of, and Ruler over, all of life."[113]

These texts identify God as *ultimately* the Creator of human spirits, rather than that He is *immediately* their Creator. The corollary is that the human soul is entirely dependent upon God for continued existence.

Other biblical texts regarding the soul's origin point in the direction of traducianism:

- *Genesis 5:3:* "When Adam had lived 130 years, he had a son in his own likeness, in his own image." The resemblance between a parent and child is not limited to the physical body but extends to the offspring's psychical nature. A child receives from its biological parents not only physical traits but also resemblances that inhere in the soul.
- *John 3:6:* "Flesh gives birth to flesh, but the Spirit gives birth to spirit." *Sarx* here connotes not the material body but the whole of human nature in its fallen condition. Every person inherits from his or her parents a body with animal life and passions. New spiritual life eventuates from the transforming work of the Holy Spirit.
- *Acts 17:26a:* "From one man [God] made every nation of men." The unity of the human family is more adequately explained by the hypothesis that the entire person, not merely the body, is transmitted from one generation to the next.
- *Hebrews 7:10:* "When Melchizedek met Abraham, Levi was still in the body of his ancestor." Arguing for the superiority of Christ's

---

113. Berkouwer, *Man,* 298. Bruce, *Commentary on Hebrews,* 360, adds: "To try to trace metaphysical implications in the phrase is unwarranted."

priesthood to the old Jewish order, the author viewed Levi—both as to his material and his immaterial self—as "in" (we would say, "genetically represented in") his ancestor Abraham. Genesis 46:26 suggests the same principle.

## Theological Development

By an immediate act of inbreathing, God created Adam's soul/spirit. Eve in her entire being was taken from Adam (Gen. 2:22–23); nothing is said about the special creation of her soul. The Scripture texts on the traducian side of the debate favor the theory that all offspring thereafter receive their unified psychico-physical nature by natural generation from their biological parents.

Traducianism better accounts for the unity and solidarity of the human race (Acts 17:26), which is as much psychical and spiritual as physical. Moreover, Scriptures such as Psalm 51:5 ("Surely I have been a sinner from birth, sinful from the time my mother conceived me") seem to link sinfulness with human generation. In addition, traducianism presents a more just rationale for condemnation of the entire human race—each person being in Adam psychically and physically. Scripture is clear that in Adam "all sinned" (Rom. 5:12) and "in Adam all die" (1 Cor. 15:22). Furthermore, the creationist hypothesis would appear to implicate God in the creation of a sinful soul, since every person from conception is sinful and sin resides more in the soul/spirit than in the body. Creationism would seem to violate the biblical teaching that God is so pure that he cannot look approvingly upon sin (Hab. 1:13).

"Creationism places race solidarity in man's bodily existence, whereas Genesis locates it in that deeper reality of human nature in which God's breath of life made man a living soul (Gen. 2:7)."[114] *How* an immaterial soul/spirit can be generated by the union of sperm and ovum remains unclear. But *how*-type questions in the metaphysical realm often are obscure. The traducian theory accords with the psychico-physical interaction we observe across the spectrum of human life, as noted above. Traducianism, then, offers the more cogent theological explanation for the origin of the human soul and the spread of sin to the race with the least number of difficulties.

How should we understand the so-called immortality of the human soul?

---

114. McDonald, *Christian View of Man*, 72.

"God . . . alone is immortal," wrote the apostle Paul (1 Tim. 6:15–16; cf. Rom. 1:23), for He exists from eternity past to eternity future. Biblical teaching concerning the intermediate and the eternal state strongly suggests that God created humans as personal agents with an identity that endures through and beyond the grave. At death the righteous enter paradise to be with Christ, whereas the unrighteous enter hades separated from Christ (Luke 16:19–31). At the Second Advent, the saved receive glorified bodies and dwell in the New Jerusalem, whereas the unsaved are reunited with their bodies and cast into hell (Rev. 20–21).

The term *immortality,* as commonly used, signifies the undying nature of the human soul or self (i.e., *posse non mori*). In this respect the human person possesses a derivative immortality conferred by the immortal God. That said, when applied to humans the word *immortality (athanasia)* in Romans 2:7; 1 Corinthians 15:53–54; and 2 Timothy 1:10 denotes God's eschatological gift of eternal life to believers in the risen Christ. At the resurrection, those who belong to Christ become immune from decay and death and experience perpetuity of life through the reunion of their soul/ spirits with their glorified bodies. Paul's teaching of conferred immortality differs radically from the Platonic notion of the soul's innate immortality and its quest for liberation from the contamination of the body in order to enter the world of eternal ideas.

Informed by St. Paul, we assert the *everlastingness* (having no end) of the human soul rather than its *eternality* (having neither end nor beginning). The radical New Testament teaching was hinted at in the Old Testament wisdom literature: "In the way of righteousness there is life; along that path is immortality" (Prov. 12:28).

# CHAPTER 5

# SUBSTANCE *and* IDENTITY
# *in* PSYCHOLOGICAL PERSPECTIVE

THE BIBLE CONTAINS A VAST amount of material concerning the essential composition and identity of human persons as God designed them to be. In essence these two topics seek to answer the questions: What is the human person? and Who is the human person? We have also seen how Christian scholars have discussed and synthesized these issues throughout the history of the church. We should not be surprised that twentieth-century psychology has also dealt extensively with these two themes. After all, any discipline or inquiry that seeks to study humans must begin that study with an examination of these two foundational issues: Is the human person composed of one substance or two or more substances? And what are the characteristics of people that constitute their essential humanness?

Psychologists and other social scientists who deal with these issues do not, however, organize their investigations around scriptural categories. At one time scholars took their investigative agenda from the pages of the Bible or from the theological categories derived from it, but those days are long gone. Thus we will not find listings in the indexes of psychological volumes for "Image of God" or "soul." Yet we will find psychological material directly related to human characteristics we believe are related to the image-bearing status of humans (spirituality, awareness of God/religion) and to issues related to human features traditionally associated with soul (mind, thinking, memory, etc.).

Psychology has dealt with issues of human substance and identity in four primary ways. We find matters of substance or essential composition spread throughout the discipline in the form of the mind-body problem (MBP). We also find that psychology has wrestled with the identity of humans by asking and attempting to answer three major questions: What is the self/person/persona of a human being? What does it mean to be a male or female human? And what explains the religious/spiritual impulse found everywhere throughout human society? These four issues are related and interlocking. If one assumes a materialist solution to the MBP, then one's understanding of personhood, sexuality, and spirituality are dramatically affected. If one prefers a solution to the MBP that is not reductionistic, then other consequences govern one's understanding of the remaining three identity issues. To look at this interlocking phenomenon from a different perspective, what I conclude about the sexuality of a person and its deeper meaning will affect what I conclude about the self. What I decide is the best psychological explanation for personhood will likewise bear a strong impact on how I view the human religious impulse. And so forth.

In this chapter we will explore how investigators have treated these four matters (essential composition, personhood, sexuality, and spirituality) within twentieth-century psychology. At the conclusion of the chapter, we will present some integrative considerations that hopefully will facilitate readers as they seek to understand how the biblical and theological conclusions of chapter 4 cohere with or do not cohere with the psychological conclusions we will discuss in this chapter.

## ESSENTIAL COMPOSITION

Modern psychology primarily has dealt with the issue of whether humans consist of one or more substances in an indirect manner. More often than not, the issue is implied or assumed rather than explicated by psychological investigators.[1] Philosophy (especially in a specialty called philosophy of mind) has been and continues to be the primary discipline in which discussions of the MBP occur. Well-trained psychologists may receive training in the history and philosophy of psychology, but more often than not these topics receive only cursory attention in psychological training programs. Many psychological investigators would prefer to open up new av-

---

1. Michael Wertheimer, *Fundamental Issues in Psychology* (New York: Holt, Rinehart and Winston, 1972).

enues of inquiry regarding the essential composition of the human rather than risk getting mired down in the intellectual cul-de-sacs that have plagued philosophy for centuries with regard to the MBP.

Psychology and psychiatry have been associated with the study of the mind throughout the twentieth century. Psychiatry emerged as a medical specialty out of the field of neurology, and psychiatrists continue to be certified by a board that regulates both neurology and psychiatry. The history of both psychiatry and neurology has been intertwined for one hundred years, and they are now working toward even greater degrees of synthesis.[2] In recent years a loosely affiliated group of disciplines sometimes called cognitive science (psychology, neuroscience, linguistics, and philosophy) has increasingly converged on the topic of the science of the mind, resulting in a "tightening (of) the link between mind and brain."[3] Any proposed solution to the MBP relates to the issues of will, freedom, and pathology; and all of these topics are of vital interest to psychology.[4] In prior centuries, scientists and philosophers have investigated how the physical relates to the spiritual, but increasingly current debates have explored how the physical relates to the psychological.[5]

Psychology has made contributions to the overall discussion of the MBP in three main areas. First, psychology has directed a massive amount of its investigative energy into understanding cognition, memory, reasoning, concept formation, language, and consciousness, all of which relate to the "mind" side of the MBP. Understanding the mind, according to neurosurgeon William Penfield, is "perhaps the most difficult and most important of all problems."[6] Second, the clinical branches of psychology have demonstrated that psychopathology, developmental deficits, intelligence, and normal and abnormal personality patterns can all have connections to both "mind" and

---

2. L. J. Cozolino, *The Neuroscience of Psychotherapy: Building and Rebuilding the Human Brain* (New York: Norton, 2002), 3.

3. Malcolm Jeeves, *Mind Fields: Reflections on the Science of Mind and Brain* (Grand Rapids: Baker, 1994), xi. See also M. Bunge, *The Mind-Body Problem: A Psycho-biological Approach* (Oxford: Pergamon, 1980), xv; and Jaegwon Kim, *Philosophy of Mind* (Boulder, Colo.: Westview Press, 1996), xii.

4. J. Benjamin, "The Mind-Body Problem in Contemporary Psychiatry," *Journal of Psychiatry and Related Sciences* 2 (1990): 67.

5. H. Feigl, "Some Crucial Issues of Mind-Body Monism," in *Philosophical Aspects of the Mind-Body Problem,* ed. D-Y Cheng (Honolulu: The University Press of Hawaii, 1975).

6. William Penfield, *The Mystery of the Mind: A Critical Study of Consciousness and the Human Brain* (Princeton, N.J.: Princeton University Press, 1975), 85.

"body." In fact, they each seem to be connected to the linkage between mind and body, whatever that may be.[7] And third, psychology has participated with other disciplines in an unprecedented exploration of the human brain, the "body" side of the mind-body equation. Of these three avenues of study, the explosion in knowledge regarding the human brain has had the greatest and most substantial impact on current discussions of the MBP. Before we explore the status of the MBP discussion in contemporary social science, it will be helpful to survey in a brief manner some of what recent science has uncovered about the functioning of the human brain.

## Brain Studies

The relatively small organ known as the human brain represents a vast territory of almost unimaginable complexity that "has been slow to give up its secrets."[8] While we have learned an immense amount of information about the brain, in many ways it continues to represent a frontier with numerous mysteries yet to be untangled. Scientists can study the brain at any of the six main levels of the central nervous system: subcellular, cellular, neural microsystems, neural macrosystems, the organism itself, and how the organism functions within groups.[9] These different levels of investigation require different teams of researchers: physicists work at the subcellular and subatomic levels (exploring such mysterious components as antiparticles, neutrinos, photons, muons, tau, quarks, and gluons[10]), chemists work at the cellular level (seeking to understand how neurotransmitters function according to chemical and electrical laws), biologists work at the neural micro- and macrosystems levels, and psychologists and social psychologists work at the organism and group levels. "Until relatively recently the gap between studies by neuroscientists investigating events occurring at the level of single cells and by psychologists studying processes like attention and thinking was so large that it seemed virtually unbridgeable. . . ."[11] But the gap is closing as more and more evidence accumulates pointing to the necessity of a holistic understanding of brain functioning.

---

7. D. L. Robinson, *Brain, Mind, and Behavior: A New Perspective on Human Nature* (Westport, Conn.: Praeger, 1996), xv.

8. R. Carter, *Mapping the Mind* (Berkeley: University of California Press, 1998), 6.

9. Bunge, *The Mind-Body Problem*, 35.

10. J. W. Elbert, *Are Souls Real?* (Amherst, N.Y.: Prometheus Books, 2000), 127–31.

11. Jeeves, *Mind Fields*, 53.

The brain contains 100 billion cells call neurons.[12] These neurons, supported by other cells known as glial cells, communicate with one another, "together giving rise to the overwhelming richness and complexity of the brain's neural circuits."[13] Each neuron contains a body (soma, containing a nucleus, ribosomes, and Golgi apparatus), dendrites (branching extensions that receive input from other cells), and an axon (the terminals of which give out neurochemical information to other cells across a small gap known as a synapse). The brain contains many types of dendrites related to their location and function in the organ and many types of neurons themselves (Purkinje and pyramidal cells are two examples). The ends of the axons contain small terminals called boutons that number between 10 and 1000 and make contact with the dendrites of up to 1000 different neurons. Some axon branches are quite long, making contact with cells in a different part of the brain whereas other axons communicate only with nearby neurons.

We must stop to marvel at this amazing product of God's creative handiwork. Cramped inside the human skull is a mass of tissue weighing three pounds and containing 100 billion cells. As hard as it is for us to comprehend the immensity of that number, the matter becomes far more complicated when we realize that each of the axons of these 100 billion neuronal cells can contain between 10 and 1000 information output terminals. Based on what he knew about creation, David wrote, "O LORD, our LORD, how majestic is your name in all the earth!" (Ps. 8:1). What would he have written if he could have known about neurons, axons, and dendrites? We can ascribe even greater levels of majesty to God, the Creator of the human brain, based on what we currently know. And our current knowledge is obviously partial and incomplete.

At one time research into brain function concentrated on mapping the topography of the brain to determine which areas controlled which functions (Wernicke's area for meaningful speech and Broca's area for motor speech are just two examples) and on studying hemispheric differences between the two halves of the brain. But these topographic and hemispheric studies have proven to be rudimentary when compared to current understandings of the neural micro- and macrosystems that can now be observed with recent technological advances. The brain is a "living machine operating all the

---

12. M. W. Dubin, *How the Brain Works* (Oxford: Blackwell, 2002), 3.
13. Ibid., 3. Dubin's volume is the source for subsequent information in this paragraph, and it serves as a readable introduction to current brain science.

time."[14] Even in its resting state, the brain hums with activity. A neuron in its resting state has an electric potential of "about -75 mV (millivolts) relative to the potential in the extracellular space."[15] The membrane of the neuron contains ion channels (thousands per square micron) that are either closed or open and that are specialized to allow only one type of chemical to pass through. Potassium (K+) is concentrated inside the cell when it is resting as compared to surrounding spaces, and when the cells fire or become active the chemical concentration quickly changes due to the opening and closing of the membrane's ion channels. And on and on goes the complexity of brain function.

> The firing of a single neuron is not enough to create the twitch of an eyelid in sleep, let alone a conscious impression. It is when one neuron excites its neighbours, and they in turn fire up others, that patterns of activity arise that are complex and integrated enough to create thoughts, feelings, and perceptions. Millions of neurons must fire in unison to produce the most trifling thought. Even when a brain seems to be at its most idle a scan of it shows a kaleidoscope of constantly changing activity. Sometimes when a person undertakes a complex mental task or feels an intense emotion the entire cerebrum lights up.[16]

The amazing gains we have witnessed in understanding the human brain have come as a result, in part, of a steady increase in technological advancements. Neurosurgeons working at the midpoint of the twentieth century solved some of the brain's mysteries by studying the damaged brains of living patients who suffered from epilepsy, stroke, tumors, or other neurological pathologies.[17] Cutting through the corpus callosum of persons suffering from severe forms of epilepsy helped science understand more fully the functioning of the brain's two hemispheres.[18] Electrical stimulation of

---

14. L. W. Swanson, *Brain Architecture: Understanding the Basic Plan* (Oxford: Oxford University Press, 2003), 90.
15. Dubin, *How the Brain Works*, 5.
16. Carter, *Mapping the Mind*, 19.
17. See K. M. Heilman and E. Valenstein, eds., *Clinical Neuropsychology*, 4th ed. (Oxford: Oxford University Press, 2003), for material related to various brain pathologies and which neural systems they affect.
18. Jeeves, *Mind Fields*, 23.

various parts of living brains helped map the brain as to its major functions. Electroencephalograms (EEGs), positron emission tomography (PET scans), magnetic resonance imaging (MRI), functional magnetic resonance imaging (fMRI), and more recently magnetoencephalography (MEG) have all contributed to our ability to "see" the brain at work and to measure its activities in new and very promising ways.[19] Scientists can now "watch" the brain operate at conscious and unconscious levels during activity, during awake resting states, and during the various stages of sleep.[20]

The challenge then for cognitive scientists is to take information known about the brain's functioning at the cellular and subcellular levels and apply it to the higher functions of the mind. If the simplest thought involves the activity of millions of neurons, and if the identical thought activates different cells the second time around, we can see why the task of moving from cellular levels of analysis to larger systems of neural connections involved in thinking and planning is such a monumental task. Based on current understanding regarding brain function, researchers have had to jettison earlier models of brain functioning, such as the brain as a computer or the brain as a passive responder to external stimuli, because they were too simplistic for the data.

Cognitive scientists strive to understand how a host of mind functions relate to brain activity. How can we use our current knowledge of brain neurochemistry best to account for:

- Language, speech (both receptive and expressive), writing
- Thinking, feeling, sensing
- Memory (both short-term and long-term), retrieval, decay
- Learning, change, intelligence
- Consciousness, wakefulness, sleep, altered states of consciousness, awareness, temporality

---

19. Z. L. Lu and L. Kaufman, eds., *Magnetic Source Imaging of the Human Brain* (Mahwah, N.J.: Lawrence Erlbaum Associates, 2003), 36–37; see also V. Walsh and A. Pascual-Leone, *Transcranial Magnetic Stimulation: A Neurochronometrics of Mind* (Cambridge, Mass.: MIT Press, 2003); and A. Pascual-Leone, N. J. Davey, J. Rothwell, E. M. Wasserman, and B. K. Puri, eds., *Handbook of Transcranial Magnetic Stimulation* (London: Arnold, 2002).
20. C. Furst, *Origins of the Mind: Mind-Brain Connections* (Englewood Cliffs, N.J.: Prentice-Hall, 1979), 3–5, 75–93.

- Intention, willing, volition
- Behavior, personality, motivation, perception?[21]

The above list provides quite an agenda for twenty-first century researchers who will continue to extend the boundaries of our knowledge about the human brain.

What valid conclusions can we draw from this very cursory survey of recent brain studies? Some observers are gloomy regarding the future of brain research. "It would be a fatal error to presume that the heuristic toolbox of the neurosciences will be capable of explaining every aspect and meaning of human feeling, thinking, and acting."[22] Yet the brain is "far and away the most complex yet intrinsically interesting object that we know of" even though ". . . in all honesty, no one at this point in time pretends to understand how the brain as a whole works."[23] However, recent brain research has changed the landscape of the MBP forever in one crucial aspect: Any proposed monism or dualism or any combination of the two must deal with the inescapable fact that whatever interaction there may be between brain and mind is intimate, inseparable during life, and interlocking to a degree that could not have been understood as recently as fifty years ago.

## The Demise of Dualism

Never before have debates about the MBP taken place in the context of this vastly larger body of knowledge regarding the mind and the brain. And perhaps this new context is the very reason why we have witnessed a noticeable decline, though not a total disappearance, of dualistic understandings of the MBP. Expanded levels of knowledge about the brain and its physiology and complex functioning seem to have driven dualism, especially substance dualism, into a demise. The Christian lay public, however, continues to use a Thomistic and Cartesian-like dualism to understand the teachings

---

21. See Bunge, *The Mind-Body Problem*, 35ff.; Dubin, *How the Brain Works*, 23–46; D. Gareth Jones, *Our Fragile Brains: A Christian Perspective on Brain Research* (Downers Grove, Ill.: InterVarsity, 1981).
22. Sergio Moravia, *The Enigma of the Mind: The Mind-Body Problem in Contemporary Thought* (Cambridge: Cambridge University Press, 1995), 205.
23. L. W. Swanson, *Brain Architecture*, vii, x.

of Scripture.[24] The body (brain) is animated or enlivened by the part of the self that leaves the body at death and is rejoined to it at the resurrection. Philosophers generally refer to such beliefs as examples of folk psychology, and the vast majority of them have moved away from a Thomistic and Cartesian substance dualism toward either a strong materialism or a softened and modified dualism.

Dualism makes five claims:

1.  There is a mental realm.
2.  The mental realm is fundamental.
3.  There is a physical realm.
4.  The physical realm is fundamental.
5.  The two realms are ontologically separate.[25]

The main objections to dualism center on this fifth component: that the human is composed of two distinct substances that have no ontological similarity to each other. How is it possible, the critics ask, for one kind of substance to interact with and have causal connections with a totally different kind of substance?[26] To people unaccustomed to philosophical reasoning, the objection seems unimposing; but philosophers see it is a nearly insurmountable problem. Merely asserting that the two substances interact in a causal and influential way with each other will not satisfy skeptics. They want dualists to specify the nature of the interaction and to explain how it can occur.[27] In addition, they argue, we have identified more and more of what we formerly understood as examples of mind activity (thinking,

---

24. C. Taliaferro calls such people the "untutored" or "pretechnological primitives" who rely too heavily on commonsense appeal rather than on logic and reason. C. Taliaferro, "Emergentism and Consciousness: Going Beyond Property Dualism," in *Soul, Body, and Survival: Essays on the Metaphysics of Human Persons,* ed. K. Corcoran (Ithaca, N.Y.: Cornell University Press, 2001), 60–61.

25. J. Foster, *The Immaterial Self: A Defense of the Cartesian Dualist Conception of the Mind* (London: Routledge, 1991), 1.

26. Keith Yandell, however, argues that this objection assumes that only like can affect like and that something in space can only be affected by something else that is also in space, assumptions he alleges are unproven. See "A defense of Dualism," *Faith and Philosophy* 12 (1995): 548–66.

27. Warren S. Brown and Malcolm A. Jeeves, "Portraits of Human Nature: Reconciling Neuroscience and Christian Anthropology," *Science and Christian Belief* 11 (1999): 139–40.

reasoning, language, etc.) as having neurocognitive correlates. For example, a thought does not occur solely in the "mind." We know that brain activity accompanies or is associated in some way with every thought.

Philosophers also object to substance dualism because in the centuries in which it was dominant it did not produce a precise model for how the brain and "mind" interact, it excelled at labeling rather than explaining, it did not acknowledge the strong evidence for the molecular and cellular roots of abilities and disorders, and it was otherwise a barren system.[28] Given this depressing and stark assessment of substance dualism by contemporary philosophers, we are somewhat surprised that some dualists continue to exist. Although a minority, they continue to make their voices heard in academic circles.[29]

Does the Christian faith stand to lose intellectual viability if dualism falls? Some philosophers argue that dualism is not essential to Christianity. Eleonore Stump argues that if we use a concept of soul as taught by Aquinas, we do not need a substance dualism to undergird Christian theology.[30] Baker argues that a Christian need not be a dualist and therefore should not be a dualist.[31] Others see dualism as a part of Christianity but not an original part.[32] Most everyone agrees that the early church fathers were heavily influenced by Platonic dualism;[33] scholars disagree, however, regarding the nature and extent of dualism found in the teachings of the New Testament. Yet other scholars readily concede that biblical Christianity and some form of Thomistic or Cartesian dualism go hand in hand. Foster argues that the

---

28. M. Bunge, *The Mind-Body Problem*, 4, 16–21.
29. See S. T. Davis, "Physicalism and Resurrection," in *Soul, Body, and Survival*, 229, 245; J. P. Moreland, "A Defense of a Substance Dualist View of the Soul," in *Christian Perspectives on Being Human*, ed. J. P. Moreland and D. M. Ciocchi (Grand Rapids: Baker, 1993), 55–86; J. Foster, "A Brief Defense of the Cartesian View," in *Soul, Body, and Survival*, 15–29; E. T. Olson, "A Compound of Two Substances," in *Soul, Body, and Survival*, 73–88; W. Penfield, *The Mystery of the Mind*; Karl R. Popper, *Knowledge and the Mind-Body Problem: In Defense of Interaction* (London: Routledge, 1994); and Richard Swinburne, "Dualism Intact," *Faith and Philosophy* 13 (1996), 68–77.
30. Eleonore Stump, "Non-Cartesian Substance Dualism and Materialism with Reductionism," *Faith and Philosophy* 12 (1995): 505.
31. L. R. Baker, "Need a Christian Be a Mind-Body Dualist?" *Faith and Philosophy* 12 (1995): 489.
32. Bunge, *The Mind-Body Problem*, 10–16.
33. Peter van Inwagen, "Dualism and Materialism: Athens and Jerusalem?" *Faith and Philosophy* 12 (1995): 475–88; Furst, *Origins of the Mind*, 910.

case for a Cartesian dualism is strong and that it is closely linked to theism. "In other words, being confident of the strength of the case for the Cartesian view, I see the need for its theistic underpinning as creating a problem for the atheist rather than for the Cartesian."[34] Thus by the end of the twentieth century, dualism was no longer the dominant view in the secular arena regarding the substance of human nature, although it continues to have its share of Christian and theistic advocates.

## Materialism

The form of monism that has taken the scientific world by storm is materialism. At the beginning of the twentieth century, behaviorists dominated American psychology. They dismissed the mind as a nonscientific concept and attempted to explain human nature in behavioral terms only. Their prevalence on the philosophical scene was short-lived as the concept of the mind returned to the discussion table. But when brain science began to explode with new and unexpected discoveries every decade, materialism soon became the predominant force in conceptualizing the substance of human beings.[35]

Materialism is the end result of reductionism, the widespread methodology operative in contemporary science. This methodology proposes that the "higher" levels of science can be best explained by reducing them to the lowest ones. Reductionism "professes that scientific progress consists in the stepwise explanation of the phenomena of the one level in terms of the next lower level. . . ."[36] The sciences thus form an explanatory chain moving from macrolevels (the social sciences) to microlevels (the natural sciences). Political science, social psychology, and sociology study groups of people; psychology studies individuals; biology and chemistry study the cells and groups of cells of these individuals; and physics examines the cell at even more microscopic levels.[37] This methodology places the most complicated of concepts (God) at the top and the simplest at the bottom and considers the

34. J. Foster. "A Brief Defense of the Cartesian View," in *Soul, Body, and Survival*, 29.

35. Bunge, *The Mind-Body Problem*, ix–xv.

36. Maurice K. D. Schouten, "Theism, Dualism, and the Scientific Image of Humanity," *Zygon* 36 (2001): 680.

37. S. Watanabe, "Logic of the Empirical World, with Reference to the Identity Theory and Reductionism," in *Philosophical Aspects of the Mind-Body Problem*, 162–81.

most sublime of explanations to consist of explaining the simplest. Each layer is dependent on or determined by the next lower level.[38] Reductive materialism is both ontologically and epistemologically reductionistic; the psychological ultimately becomes physics.[39]

In this world of multilayered hierarchy or tiers, philosophers take their place as observers and managers of the whole process. The current scientific scene can greatly profit from believers working at all levels in this chain of science and from placing Christian theologians alongside the philosophers to monitor and influence the entire process.

Materialism in its most reductive form considers the human person to consist only of atoms, or neurons, or cells.[40] In many ways, the current emphasis on materialism harkens back to the beginning of the twentieth century when behaviorists advocated a similar reductionism. Materialism "means that we just cannot recognize any reality which cannot be exhaustively described in material or bodily terms."[41] This extreme form of materialism is "essentially incomplete"[42] because it cannot account for sense experience and for the content of the mind. Christians can applaud the scientific progress that a materialist view of science has been able to accomplish. After all, their work in learning more about the intricacies of creation can only, ultimately, bring glory to God. But Christians are also aware that when scientists attempt to utilize an extreme materialism to explain everything about the human person, they are taking great, unsupported leaps of logic across a span of problems that demand a better set of explanations.

If the mind and all of its contents are purely neurochemical events, religion as we understand it is at stake.

> It is easy to see that being able to get your God Experience from a well-placed electrode could—at the very least—undermine the precious status such states are accorded by many religions. How believers will cope with what many might see as a threat to their faith

---

38. Kim, *Philosophy of Mind*, 221–22.

39. Bunge, *The Mind-Body Problem*, 6.

40. For a humanist critique of materialism, see Roger W. Sperry, "Mind, Brain, and Humanist Values," in *New Views on the Nature of Man*, ed. John R. Platt (Chicago: University of Chicago Press, 1965), 71–92.

41. H. D. Lewis, *The Elusive Self* (Philadelphia: Westminster, 1982), 2.

42. B. Ellis, "Physicalism and the Contents of Sense Experience," in *Philosophical Aspects of the Mind-Body Problem*, 64.

is one of many interesting challenges that brain science will throw up in the coming millennium.[43]

If the laws of chemistry, physics, and biology govern all behavior, what becomes of free will, spirituality, and religious sentiments? Some scholars suggest that our new understanding of how the brain functions will erode all of this and more.

> Ironically, the new understanding shows that a supernatural soul lacks the properties needed to support consciousness. This casts doubt on the idea that a soul, by itself, could support meaningful personal immortality. This argument also extends to other spirits, raising a problem for the idea of angels, and even the idea of a personal God.[44]

Most Christians, however, believe that because so many substantial problems exist within the reductive materialism view, its impact on religion will be minimal and short-lived. Only the most ardent scientist is willing to assert that nothing but the material exists in the world and that all apparent "mind" functions are merely expressions of electrochemical brain events.

If we imagine a continuum with substance dualism on one end and reductive materialism on the other, we can find in the current scene a host of alternatives that take their place somewhere between these two extremes. Many of these options are a combination of some monistic and some dualistic themes. Scientists anxious to embrace the implications of recent brain science will deny that their favorite solution to the MBP contains some soft dualism, whereas others will readily admit some of the following systems do contain dualistic implications that nonetheless fall short of full-blown Thomistic or Cartesian substance dualism. The major options are:

---

43. Carter, *Mapping the Mind,* 19. Other views about this issue abound. Bruce R. Reichenbach, "Monism and the Possibility of Life After Death," *Religious Studies* 14 (1978): 34, argues that monism does not rule out life after death. R. Audi, "Theism and the Mind-Body Problem," in *Faith, Freedom, and Rationality: Philosophy of Religion Today,* ed. J. Jordan and D. Howard-Snyder (Lanham, Md.: Rowman and Littlefield, 1996), 159, writes that there are substantial problems inherent in any assertion that the mind equals the brain.

44. Elbert, *Are Souls Real?* 14. See also Schouten, "Theism, Dualism, and the Scientific Image of Humanity," 682.

- Epiphenomenalism (Mind is a bundle of nonmaterial phenomena that emerges from its materialistic base but cannot interact with it. Mental events are effects but not causes of anything.)
- Identity Theory (Perception and consciousness exist but cannot be dissolved into behavior; they are physical processes, not spiritual phenomena, and identical with material processes in the brain.)
- Eliminativism (The existence of the mental is part of folk psychology and needs to be excluded from our consideration.)
- Functionalism (The mind is a function of the brain; all mental properties are input-output relations of the brain.)
- Emergentist Materialism (Mental events are a set of emergent brain functions that appear when an organism becomes appropriately complex, functions that cannot be reduced to neurobiology once they emerge.)[45]
- Interactionism (The mental and the physical interact, a position very close to Descartes's substance dualism.)
- Nonreductive Physicalism (See below.)

While some of these positions may seem hardly discrete from others in the list, they each contain technical features that distinguish them. Limitations of space prevent a detailed discussion of all but the last one listed. We will give it more consideration because of its appearance in many Christian circles as an alleged viable option to the supposedly less desirable alternatives of substance dualism or reductive materialism.

A multidisciplinary group of professors at Fuller Seminary have contributed a great deal to the development of nonreductive physicalism (NRP).[46] Advocates of this position argue that the mind is physiologically embodied and that higher levels of explanation supervene on lower levels to explain behavior. The position bears some similarity to the double as-

---

45. Most introductions to the MBP, including many of the sources cited above, will contain definitions of these various options. See especially D. M. Armstrong, *The Mind-Body Problem: An Opinionated Introduction* (Boulder, Colo.: Westview Press, 1999); and S. Guttenplan, ed., *A Companion to the Philosophy of Mind* (Oxford: Blackwell Reference, 1994).

46. See Nancey Murphy, "Nonreductive Physicalism: Philosophical Issues," in *Whatever Happened to the Soul? Scientific and Theological Portraits of Human Nature*, ed. W. S. Brown, N. Murphy, and H. N. Malony (Minneapolis: Fortress, 1998), 127–48; and Brown and Jeeves, "Portraits of Human Nature," 139–50.

pect monism of earlier centuries and seeks to place a limit on how the reductionistic methodology is applied to the understanding of human functioning. Thus the position also shares an emphasis found in emergentism: Certain human features appear that cannot be reduced to their place of origin. NRP, sometimes also called nonreductive materialism, does contain ontological reductionism, but it seeks to avoid causal reductionism and reductive materialism.

Dr. Murphy affirms that this alternative is a new position in the philosophical world.[47] In philosophy, as in most all other academic arenas, new proposals to old problems emerge in the literature on a periodic basis. Then critics begin to identify inconsistencies or unacceptable consequences of the new proposal that either prompt other philosophers to improve the new proposal or to abandon it altogether for even newer options. As one example of this process, advocates of psychoneural identity theory at one time trumpeted it as "the one (approach) in tune with a worldview adequately informed by the best contemporary science."[48] Yet within only a few years it too fell into disfavor. So we do not yet know how (NRP) will fare over time. Jaegwon Kim, a respected figure in the field of philosophy of mind, is doubtful that the position will survive. He calls NRP a myth, a theory with dim prospects, and an approach that is not inherently stable (i.e., it will naturally drift closer to eliminativism or to a dualism of some sort).[49]

## Conclusion

Questions about the unitary or dualistic nature of humans have fascinated thinkers throughout the ages. We have seen how Scripture deals with this issue and how theologians have systematized that material into theological convictions. Although psychology does not often deal directly with the philosophical issues surrounding monism or dualism, psychologists have actively participated in advancing our knowledge about the brain and the mind. Their research has forever changed the landscape of the mind-body debate. David Olds has given us one example of a synthesizing approach

---

47. Murphy, "Nonreductive Physicalism," 148.
48. Jaegwon Kim, *Supervenience and Mind: Selected Philosophical Essays* (Cambridge: Cambridge University Press, 1993), 266.
49. Ibid., 265, 279, 284.

that pulls together the major clinical theories of the twentieth century and shows how they all can be anchored to a brain-centered psychology.[50] His approach regards "higher" levels of brain dysfunction as fodder for the psychoanalytic approach to treatment, "mid-range" levels of brain disorders to be responsive to other treatments such as behavioral interventions, and the "lower" levels of brain functioning problems to be responsive to neurochemical interventions (medicine).

In general, however, clinicians operate in accordance with dualism. Therapists may give verbal allegiance to monistic materialism, but they tend to deal with their clients as if dualism were true. Clinicians seek to deal with the inner life of a person, to help the person sort out issues and resolve conflicts, and so on. Rarely do therapists conceptualize these features of the inner landscape of a person as anything but immaterial entities.

Although materialism dominates in current discussion of the MBP, researchers have not adequately accounted for the "mental" or the "mind." Sergio Moravia has called for scientists to attend more to a subject to which they can attribute these psychic states and events: the human person.[51] Perhaps we should change the phrasing of the question at hand from "What is the relation between the mind and the brain?" to "What is the relation between the body and the person?" In any event, the identity of the person (the entity that possesses a mind) is just as important an issue as is the problem of the substances that comprise the human. We will now turn to an examination of the identity of the human in recent psychological theory.

## IDENTITY

In the previous chapter we explored how the Bible treats the question of human identity. Scriptural data regarding human identity revolves around the image of God in humans and the soul of the human. Not surprisingly, modern psychology has not focused its quest for understanding human identity on the *imago Dei* or on the soul.[52] Some observers find this ironic:

---

50. David Olds, "Brain-Centered Psychology: A Semiotic Approach," *Psychoanalysis and Contemporary Thought* 13 (1990): 331–63.
51. Moravia, *The Enigma of the Mind*, 251.
52. For an exception to this trend, see Philip Hefner, "Imago Dei: The Possibility and Necessity of the Human Person," in *The Human Person in Science and Theology*, ed. N. H. Gregersen, W. B. Drees, and U. Gorman (Grand Rapids: Eerdmans, 2000), 73–94.

that a discipline named for the soul ("psych"ology) should ignore the very subject for which it was named! But the historical roots of many words including *psychology* bear little resemblance to current understandings.[53] In any event, the discipline as a whole tends to regard matters of the soul and the *imago Dei* as the province of religion rather than social science and hence not worthy of much attention.

Psychology has addressed the issue of human identity primarily through focused attention on the subject of the self and personhood. What is the self? How does an individual develop a sense of self? What is personhood? Attendant to these questions are the topics of gender and religion. Because modern social science considers gender as closely connected to personhood, we will explore recent theories regarding masculinity and femininity in this chapter. We also will explore how psychology has treated the topic of religion because those investigations are the closest that the discipline comes to exploring the *imago Dei* in humans.

## The Self

Nearly every clinical theory of psychology that has emerged in the past century has articulated a fairly detailed view of the self. One difficulty we must face at the outset is the plurality of terms used for this concept: *self, selfhood, person, personhood.* No matter which term we use, we are in reality trying to define and describe the human individual, especially with regard to those features of a person that are not obviously physical. If we describe someone as 26 years old, of medium build, 175 pounds, and 5 feet 9 inches tall, we are certainly referring to some of the features that give this person identity. But psychology in the main has focused on those aspects of identity that cannot be counted on a calendar, seen with the eye, weighed on a scale, or measured with a yardstick. How do we define the person with regard to those features that are more reflective of the inner world, of the psyche, of the personality, and of the emotional life of the individual? Or to speak tautologically, how does psychology view the psychology of an individual?

---

53. See James R. Beck, "Self and Soul: Exploring the Boundaries Between Psychotherapy and Spiritual Formation," *Journal of Psychology and Theology* 31 (2003): 31–32.

## Definitions

- Behavioral schools view the human as having continuity with animals, as learners and responders to reinforcements, and as trainable. The human person, however, has no true freedom or dignity because these concepts are mythical inventions of prior centuries without any scientific basis.[54]
- Cognitive schools view the human as an intelligent thinker whose thoughts produce epiphenomena that we call emotions and values.[55]
- Psychoanalytic schools view the human as a person in turmoil characterized by powerful internal conflicts (Freud), undifferentiated incompleteness (Jung), or misdirected strivings (Adler).[56]
- Humanistic schools view the human as a vast, untapped source of potential that will find appropriate expression if and when the environment and circumstances are conducive.[57]
- Postmodernists in psychology view the individual as possessing numerous selves that are socially constructed.[58]

---

54. B. F. Skinner, *Beyond Freedom and Dignity* (Toronto: Bantam Vintage, 1971). For an excellent Christian rebuttal, see Francis A. Schaeffer, *Back to Freedom and Dignity* (Downers Grove, Ill.: InterVarsity, 1972).
55. Mary Stewart Van Leeuwen, *The Person in Psychology* (Grand Rapids: Eerdmans, 1985), 175.
56. Some current psychoanalytic approaches to the self are described in J. F. Gurewich and M. Tort, eds., *The Subject and the Self: Lacan and American Psychoanalysis* (Northvale, N.J.: Jason Aronson, 1996). For a description of a Kohutian variant on classic psychoanalytic views of the self, see H. Kohut, *Restoration of the Self* (New York: International Universities Press, 1977). For a description of approaches to the self in other quarters of the current psychoanalytic scene, see L. A. Sass, "The Self and Its Vicissitudes in the Psychoanalytic Avant-Garde," in *Constructions of the Self*, ed. G. L. Levine (New Brunswick, N.J.: Rutgers University Press, 1992).
57. See Abraham Maslow, *The Farther Reaches of Human Nature* (New York: Viking Press, 1971).
58. Psychology and related disciplines increasingly emphasize the social dimensions of the self; the circle of these advocates includes but goes beyond postmodern thinkers. See L. E. Cahoon, "Limits of the Social and Relational Self," in *Selves, People, and Persons: What Does It Mean to Be a Self?* ed. L. Rouner (Notre Dame, Ind.: University of Notre Dame Press, 1992); M. E. George, "The American Origins of the Postmodern Self," in *Constructions of the Self*; and A. C. Thiselton, *Interpreting God and the Postmodern Self: On Meaning, Manipulation, and Promise* (Grand Rapids: Eerdmans, 1995).

In summary, Rick Hoyle and his colleagues have given us an overarching definition of the self that seeks to be transtheoretical. "Self is a dynamic psychological system, a tapestry of thoughts, feelings, and motives, that define and direct—even destroy us."[59]

Most Christians would view these various definitional approaches not as wrong but as incomplete. Each one of these approaches to defining the individual person is deficient from a biblical standpoint, as we shall examine further in the integrative comments following this chapter. Their fundamental flaw is that they take one feature of human functioning and assume that it represents the whole or is sufficient to explain the entire range of personhood. By committing this error, these definitions all fall short of the biblical standard, which defines individuals primarily by the fact that they are created in the image of God for the purpose of glorifying God and enjoying Him forever.

## Development of the Self

The particular pattern of development related to the self depends a great deal on the definition of self that one is using.[60] Each school of thought that develops a view of a mature self will also, almost by definition, describe a sequence of steps, phases, or tasks through which the individual passes to achieve that mature status. Behaviorists, for example, often view the infant as a learner waiting to be reinforced for random or purposeful behaviors. As children grow the behavior patterns that emerge become more complex and sophisticated until they reach adulthood. Psychoanalytic theorists organize their view of development around a sequence of psychosexual stages through which every young child passes. Successors to the psychoanalytic tradition have modified their understanding of just what is contained in this process, but they generally develop a schema of stages through which the self develops into maturity. Object relations theorists, for example, focus

---

59. Rick H. Hoyle, Michael H. Kernis, Mark R. Leary, and Mark W. Baldwin, *Selfhood: Identity, Esteem, Regulation* (Boulder, Colo.: Westview Press, 1999), 1. For an overview of current research on the self, see J. G. Snodgrass and R. L. Thompson, eds., *The Self Across Psychology: Self-Recognition, Self-Awareness, and the Self Concept* (New York: New York Academy of Sciences, 1997).

60. See Theodore Lidz, *The Person: His and Her Development Throughout the Life Cycle* (New York: Basic Books, 1976), for a comprehensive look at many twentieth-century developmental theories.

on the earliest years of a child's life even more intently than did Freud. They find the first twenty-four months of a child's life to be crucial in creating the structure on which adult function later occurs.[61] Erik Erikson also developed a unique set of development steps, although his schema spans the entire life span, each step building on previous ones until we complete all of the tasks life demands of us.[62]

These various proposals for the development of the self share a common theme. The route to maturity is fraught with danger. At any stage, defects, errors, faulty learning, poor reinforcement, or unresolved conflicts can occur and can often have long-term consequences. In fact, many views of adult pathology explain the presence of an emotional disorder or a bad trait or an ineffective coping style as related to some psychological transaction along the developmental sequence that went awry. Perhaps the bonding with an adult caregiver was faulty. Perhaps influential people in the young child's life reinforced the wrong set of behaviors. Perhaps one or both parents was emotionally absent or distant or abusive or overly enmeshed with the child. And so forth. Thus one's view of the self, one's view of maturity or normality, and one's view of pathology or dysfunction are all linked with developmental processes.[63]

We can easily forget that these developmental understandings of how the self develops were not always a part of our culture's knowledge base. What now has taken on the semblance of common sense was not always so considered by our ancestors. Twentieth-century psychology has made an important contribution to our society's understanding of the psychological vulnerabilities of infancy and childhood, of the peculiar features of that enigmatic phase of modern life called adolescence, of the importance of parenting and childcare, and of the potential hazards of trauma. We now understand in expanded ways that the processes of moral reasoning for a child are different than they are for an adult. We know that various cogni-

---

61. Harry Guntrip, *Psychoanalytic Theory, Therapy, and the Self* (New York: Basic Books, 1973); James R. Masterson, *The Real Self: A Developmental, Self, and Object Relations Approach* (New York: Brunner Mazel Publishers, 1985); Margaret S. Mahler, Fred Pine, and Anni Bergman, *The Psychological Birth of the Human Infant* (New York: Basic Books, 1975).

62. Erik H. Erikson, *Identity: Youth and Crisis* (New York: W. W. Norton, 1968).

63. For a postmodern account, see David M. Levin, ed., *Pathologies of the Modern Self: Postmodern Studies on Narcissism, Schizophrenia, and Depression* (New York: New York University Press, 1987).

tive skills, such as abstract reasoning, appear sequentially throughout the early years of a person's life. And we know that socialization skills develop over time rather than appearing full-grown in a person's life. We are not suggesting that these approaches to the development of the self were unheard of in prior centuries; but we are suggesting that psychology has documented them to a degree that they now function almost as psychological laws in contrast to being minimally articulated ideas in the past.

Unlike theology, psychology has not devoted a great deal of time attempting to understand the origin of the soul. In the last chapter, we learned that theologians have developed two major theories regarding the origin of the soul, creationist and traducianist perspectives. But if we loosely define the soul as the person or the self, we can find a related theme in modern psychology that deals with the issue.[64] Dr. Stephen Greggo, who teaches at Trinity Evangelical Divinity School, has compared these theological schools with the nature-nurture theme in developmental psychology.[65] Developmental psychology is increasingly committed to the position that the human personality develops through a process that is a complex mixture of genetic factors and environmental experience. For any given individual, the process will be distinct and idiosyncratic. Even identical twins raised in the "same" environment will manifest some individual differences, although we must admit that no identical twin can ever experience exactly the same environmental influences as the other twin experiences. Greggo's conclusion is that:

> The human soul is not the sole product of human reproductive forces or divine action alone. Rather, the origin of the human soul is a creative convergence of nature, nurture, and interactive forces that are operating within both the human and divine, visible and invisible realms. This process is possible only through God's grace as demonstrated in his initial creation and in his ongoing engagement in human affairs.[66]

---

64. Identifying the self with the soul is a fairly common approach among Christian psychologists. See the special issue "Perspectives on the Self/Soul," *Journal of Psychology and Theology* 26 (1998): 3–122. See also Beck, "Self and Soul," 24–36.

65. Stephen P. Greggo, "Soul Origins: How Do the Creationist and Traducianist Perspectives Hold-up to Current Trends in Developmental Psychology?" (presentation at the Evangelical Theological Society annual meeting, 2001, Colorado Springs, Colorado).

66. Ibid., 14.

### Self-Regard

Psychology regards the topic of the self as a broad topic that includes body focus, self-esteem, identity, self-consciousness, embarrassment, shame and guilt, boundaries, and self-concept.[67] Yet the self is as difficult to define for psychologists as it has been for philosophers. Gunderson writes that we must account for why the self seems "so adept at slipping through the meshes of every nomological set of physical explanations which philosophers have been able to imagine science someday bestowing on them."[68] The study of the self is not confined just to psychology; all the humanities and social sciences are interested in the topic.[69]

Almost all investigators into the nature of the human being agree that the ability to be conscious of one's self is a central feature of our humanity. This ability appears to distinguish humans from animals, although some research suggests otherwise. We have thought for a long time that no evidence exists pointing to self-awareness among animals, even though we routinely project such abilities onto our pets. One can say to a particularly obnoxious pet cat, "You sure think highly of yourself, don't you?" But the reality is that the cat is behaving like a cat no matter what human characteristics we might try to imagine as part of the cat's experience.

Research among chimpanzees has uncovered evidence for some level of self-awareness or self-consciousness among these higher primates. The research strategies utilized by animal biologists are interesting. The first step in the research paradigm is to give the animals opportunity to gain experience in the use of mirrors. In the mirror the chimpanzee is able to see the face and other parts of its body not normally seen. Then, when the animal is under anesthesia, researchers apply a brightly colored mark above one eyebrow and at the top of one ear, a mark that when dry will not exude olfactory or tactile sensations for the animal. After recovering from the anesthesia, the animal is again given opportunity to use the mirror. The animals give evidence of noticing the brightly colored mark by increased use of touch in the marked areas. Statistics noting the number and frequency

---

67. Arnold Buss, *Psychological Dimensions of the Self* (Thousand Oaks, Calif.: Sage, 2001), 6–9.
68. K. Gunderson, "Asymmetries and Mind-Body Perplexities," in *Philosophical Aspects of the Mind-Body Problem*, 99.
69. G. Levine, "Constructivism and the Reemergent Self," in *Constructions of the Self*, 1–3.

of these touch behaviors are significantly higher than one would predict with just ambient touch behaviors.[70] This line of research has its critics, who argue that these touching behaviors do not necessarily reveal self-awareness as we understand it among humans and that the experimental results may simply be artifacts of the use of a mirror or of the anesthesia.[71] Scientists admit that we may be unwise to argue for the complete presence or absence of self-recognition in animals or that one self-aware organism has the same level of that capacity as another organism has. Other interesting research seems to establish that the higher primates can even recognize themselves in a distorting mirror (concave and convex).[72] Perhaps some of the higher primates do display a certain level of self-awareness. This finding does not, however, detract from the assertion that self-consciousness is an important and central component of what it means to be human.

One aspect of self-consciousness has to do with self-regard: How do I value or regard myself? One of psychology's best-known emphases has to do with this very issue. The clinical branches of the discipline, most especially "pop" psychology, have espoused healthy self-esteem as an important component of the effective and mature life. Psychology has focused attention on the issue of self-regard in ways that earlier generations never considered. We can all agree that everyone attributes to self a degree of regard ranging on a continuum from self-hatred to self-loathing to self-acceptance to self-love to unadulterated narcissism. The tendency to hate the self or to worship the self is a natural part of sinful living, even though many, if not most, of our ancestors may have given it little attention. Through the centuries Christians and non-Christians alike have disliked or liked themselves, have been humble or proud with respect to their accomplishments, and have been content or discontent with who they are. What is new to this arena is psychology's advocacy of healthy (read high) self-esteem.

The self-esteem movement spread like wildfire through American society in the third quarter of the previous century. The reasons for its prevalence as a theme in the public square during these decades may have to do

70. Gordon G. Gallup et al., "Further Reflections on Self-Recognition in Primates," *Animal Behavior* 50 (1995): 1525–32.

71. C. M. Heyes, "Self-Recognition in Primates: Further Reflections Create a Hall of Mirrors," *Animal Behavior* 50 (1995): 1533–42.

72. Ann Kitchen, Derek Denton, and Linda Brent, "Self-Recognition and Abstraction Abilities in the Common Chimpanzee Studied with Distorting Mirrors," *Proceedings of the National Academy of Science* 93 (1996): 7405–8.

with the fact that the time was ripe for such a cultural emphasis or that the American public was truly dispirited and ready for a more hopeful theme. Whatever reasons historians may someday attach to its phenomenal success, the self-esteem movement produced both good and not-so-good results. Therapeutically, many persons have benefited from learning how to increase their level of self-regard. But given the insatiable human capacity for selfishness and pride and the powerful American quest for unbridled individualism, the self-esteem movement has at the same time produced undesirable results.[73] However, one can find strong indications that the self-esteem movement has lost quite a bit of its steam. Research questioning the automatic and positive benefits of heightened self-esteem is lowering the levels of ardor among its advocates, and the pendulum toward a more balanced emphasis may currently be occurring. Secular author Richard Keshen argues that we must incorporate self-esteem into our understanding of the mature person only when we combine it with reasonableness and with respect for and consideration of others.[74]

For example, research shows that high self-esteem levels occur along with some very undesirable personality traits just as Christian critics have long suggested.

> For some people . . . , to have high self-esteem means that one is very proud of who one is, feels superior to most other people, and is very willing and able to defend against possible threats to one's positive self-view. In other words, people with high self-esteem engage in self-promoting activities.[75]

Thus even secular clinicians are developing nuanced ways of dealing with self-esteem issues in order to avoid producing undesirable outcomes.

---

73. Roy Baumeister in his book *Escaping the Self* (New York: Basic Books, 1991) argues that our undue emphasis on self ironically has fueled escapism, this time for the burden of selfhood. See also James L. Collier, *The Rise of Selfishness in America* (New York: Oxford University Press, 1991); and Michael A. and Lise Wallach, *Psychology's Sanction for Selfishness* (San Francisco: W. H. Freeman and Co., 1983.)

74. Richard Keshen, *Reasonable Self-Esteem* (Montreal: McGill-Queen's University Press, 1996), 3–19, 146–72. For another secular example of this trend, see Philip O. Hwang, *Other-Esteem: Meaningful Life in a Multicultural Society* (Philadelphia: Accelerated Development, 2000).

75. Hoyle, Kernis, Leary, and Baldwin, *Selfhood,* 85.

In addition, the mixed research regarding self-esteem and its contribution to healthy functioning may be due to a lack of definitional clarity regarding self-esteem itself. Researchers are currently suggesting that we will not fully understand the possible contribution of self-esteem to human functioning until we utilize tighter definitions that will distinguish among the various manifestations of self-esteem. For example, self-esteem can be defensive or genuine, explicit or implicit (conscious or nonconscious), contingent or true (dependent on or independent of constant validation), and labile or unstable (self-worth feelings linked to environmental events or feelings of self-worth that are extremely short-lived).[76] We may learn about the genuine impact of various levels of self-esteem on human functioning only when researchers employ more finely tuned and nuanced definitions of this variable in their work.

Critics within the church who question the value of psychology in Christian ministry have focused their most strident criticism against psychology's emphasis on healthy self-esteem.[77] They argue that forwarding positive feelings toward oneself is directly contrary to the teachings of the New Testament. To assess this issue fairly, all interested parties need to ask themselves the following questions.

1. Does self-denial as taught by Jesus require us to hate ourselves? (See Matthew 16:21–28 and parallel passages in Mark 8:31–38 and Luke 9:21–27.)
2. Did Jesus literally require of His disciples that they hate their own lives? (See Luke 14:25–27.)
3. Is God honored when we regard ourselves with loathing and disparagement?

The answer to each of these questions is an unqualified no. A careful interpretation of the texts in question will help us avoid misreading and misapplying the teachings of the New Testament dealing with self-regard.

Although we want to include most of our integrative comments in the section immediately following this chapter, a few comments here are called for. We can all agree that thinking more highly of ourselves than we ought

---

76. Ibid., 88–93.
77. Paul C. Vitz, *Psychology as Religion: The Cult of Self-Worship,* 2d ed. (Grand Rapids: Eerdmans, 1994).

to think is pride and a great sin in the eyes of God. We can all agree that Christians are obligated to be other-centered, not self-centered, and to regard the other as better than themselves. Therefore, we can affirm that thinking more highly of ourselves than God does is pride and thereby sinful. We can affirm that self-denial is self-denial, not self-hatred as some would have us believe. Self-denial is putting Christ first, putting our own personal agendas second, and following Christ even if it means following Him to our deaths. The three self-denial passages in the Gospels come in the context of warnings Jesus was giving His disciples about His upcoming death in Jerusalem. Jesus warned them that they too needed to be prepared to take up a cross and follow him by denying themselves (giving up their own personal agenda for their lives and becoming cross-bearing followers of Jesus).

Terry Cooper has convincingly demonstrated that pride and self-debasement are not discrete categories of human experience. Throughout history arguments have been advanced that one or the other of these two problems is at the heart of human misery and dysfunction. Augustine was an early spokesman for the "primacy of pride" thesis, and many have followed in his train.[78] In more recent times, low self-esteem or some sort of related derogation of the self has been suggested as the root cause of human dysfunction. This assertion, made by many psychological theorists, has typically enraged Christian observers who are accustomed to the Augustinian view and who defend biblical self-denial as a necessary form of self-regard. Cooper demonstrates, however, that some degree of self-doubt and low self-esteem is always involved in pride and prideful states, hidden though they may be. Conversely, pride is never far away from the person who strives to excel in self-denial. Self-debasement and pride exist in human experience, not as separate or distinct sins, but as linked problems with one in ascendancy and one in concurrent obscurity. "One may be dominant, but the other does not lie far behind. Thus, there is unexpected low self-esteem in pride and unexpected pride in low self-esteem."[79]

We must also remember that the text commanding the disciples of Jesus to hate their very own lives also contains the command to hate father and mother. Since the command to hate father and mother directly contradicts other passages commanding us to love and honor our parents (Exod. 20:12;

---

78. Terry D. Cooper, *Sin, Pride, and Self-Acceptance* (Downers Grove, Ill.: InterVarsity, 2003), 164.

79. Ibid., 165.

Eph. 6:2–3), exegetes of the Lukan passage uniformly understand the meaning of hatred toward family to be relative.[80] In other words, disciples must love Jesus with such ardor and intensity that their love for wife, children, mother, and father pales in comparison and seems to be hatred. Readers cannot take the Luke 14:26 command literally any more than we can take the statements of Jesus in Matthew 5:29–30 literally even though some literalists and psychologically disturbed individuals have tried to do so. Paul did not hate the fact that he was a Jew and that he had lived a faultless life as measured by legalistic righteousness; he considered these features of his background as rubbish only by comparison with his love for Christ (Phil. 3:4–9).

We are not left without standards, however, for the degree of self-regard a Christian must forward to the self. The standard is to regard myself as God regards me—no more and no less. What God hates about me, I am to hate (Rom. 12:9). What God loves about me, I am to love (Matt. 6:26). God hates my sin, so must I. God created me in His own image and so loved the world (including me) that He sent His only-begotten Son to die for me. I must acknowledge such wonder and mystery and utilize these truths in monitoring how much regard I forward to myself. If I regard my self more highly than does God, it is sin. Learning how to monitor my own self-regard so that it matches the regard God forwards to me is not an easy task. In fact, it is a lifelong challenge. But when we can engage heartily in this endeavor, God is honored, and we are protected from pride and false humility.[81]

Self-esteem, then, is a useful concept that has been overemphasized but should not be abandoned by researchers or clinicians. The evidence suggests that we should continue the pursuit of understanding how self-esteem contributes positively and negatively to adjustment and that we should engage in this pursuit in a balanced fashion. Healthy and accurate self-esteem is not a cure-all for any human woe, but it is one component of healthy adjustment that we should help people achieve. Helping people distinguish a level of self-regard that pleases God from a self-centered effort at self-enhancement at the expense of relating to others is an ongoing challenge for all practitioners of counseling and ministry.

---

80. Norval Geldenhuys, *Commentary on the Gospel of Luke* (Grand Rapids: Eerdmans, 1966), 398; John Nolland, *Word Biblical Commentary: Luke 9:21–18:34* (Dallas: Word Books, 1993), 762–63.

81. James R. Beck, *Jesus and Personality Theory: Exploring the Five Factor Model* (Downers Grove, Ill.: InterVarsity, 1999), 197–216.

Psychic health, like physical health, is an unquestionable good, and it does not really matter what we call it. But neither form of health guarantees that people, individually or collectively, will do what they should do to remedy injustice, teach children skills that will help them lead productive and happy lives, or end the scourge of racism. Enhanced self-esteem is no more a shortcut to happiness or a better society than a low cholesterol count or well-defined abs. Healthy selves in healthy bodies can put their energies to good purposes or bad ones.[82]

## Gender

Scripture links gender with the identity of the first couple in Genesis 1:27: "So God created man in his own image, in the image of God he created him; male and female he created them." The close linkage in Scripture between human identity and gender is also reflected in contemporary psychology. According to researchers in all of the social sciences, masculinity and femininity represent key components of human identity because they represent core issues anchored both to our genetic makeup and to our functioning throughout the life span.

"It's a boy!" or "It's a girl!" are often the first words attendants in a birthing room will give to the new parents. And if the parents have not known about the child's sex before birth, this information triggers a veritable cascade of expectations, hopes, dreams, wishes, and wants. But the news also signals some restrictions and limitations as well.[83] Gender is an appropriate subject for psychological investigation because we live in a gendered world. In addition to learning more about how the two genders live out their lives with each other in human society, we need to understand how men and women are alike and how they are different.

Psychology received its impetus for exploring the topic of gender from the broader social movements in our society regarding women. The story of how society has treated women over the centuries is not an uplifting one. In the United States freed male slaves received their franchise fifty years

---

82. John P. Hewitt, *The Myth of Self-Esteem: Finding Happiness and Solving Problems in America* (New York: St. Martin's Press, 1998), 142.

83. James R. Doyle, *The Male Experience,* 2d ed. (Dubuque, Iowa: Wm. C. Brown Publishers, 1989), 3.

before women did (The Fifteenth Amendment to the Constitution was proclaimed on March 30, 1870, and the Nineteenth on August 26, 1920). Women have had to face prejudice regarding their intelligence, the stability of their personality, their leadership capability, and a host of other impediments to their full participation in society. The women's liberation movement, a broad-based effort that touched all segments of American society, attempted to address the issues described in the following quote:

> Females rank as a lower caste, generally deprived of wealth, power, and prestige. They are trained psychologically so that direct expression of hostility toward males is often impossible. Excluded from the power structure of major institutions, their opportunities to change the normative structure of the society are very limited.[84]

In the last half of the twentieth century, considerable progress occurred in rectifying inequities that had existed in the past and in raising levels of awareness regarding women's issues in all of the academic disciplines. Feminist scholars in psychology began reexamining existing theory, locating areas where it poorly represented or misrepresented females and offering new models that better explained the data available from both men and women. As soon as feminist researchers revised some of psychology's approaches to women, corresponding investigations into the meanings of masculinity emerged to expand our understanding of maleness. We will briefly explore just two areas in psychology regarding the subject of gender that have greatly changed as a result of these processes: our understanding of the differences between men and women and our enhanced understanding of the psychology of women and men.

In evaluating how psychology has treated the subject of gender, however, we must keep in mind that premodern, modern, and postmodern ideologies lurk quietly behind the stage on which twentieth-century social science has conducted its research. As Christian sociologist Elaine Storkey has eloquently pointed out, each of these ideologies brings with it strengths and weaknesses that have enhanced as well as tarnished interpretations given to obtained data.[85]

---

84. Janet S. Chafetz, *Masculine, Feminine, or Human? An Overview of the Sociology of Gender Roles*, 2d ed. (Itasca, Ill.: F. E. Peacock Publishers, 1978), 236.

85. Elaine Storkey, *Origins of Difference: The Gender Debate Revisited* (Grand Rapids: Baker, 2001).

*Sex and Gender Differences*

Research results showing similarities between men and women rarely get published, just as journalism generally shows preference for printing "bad" news over "good" news. But the topic of differences between men and women has generated much attention. The volume of psychological research into this topic is massive.[86] All parties agree that some of the observed and documented differences between the two sexes are anchored in biology and flow from genetic, hormonal, or other physiological factors. Others of the observed and documented differences between the sexes are socially constructed, due to environmental influences, parenting, learning, and socialization. Controversies rage regarding which of the differences stem from which source and regarding the relative balance between biological and environmental influences on any particular observed difference.[87] Few scholars of any persuasion would argue that all the observed differences are biological in origin or that environmental forces create all of them.

Researchers have utilized several nomenclatures to describe their work, which includes the study of sex-related differences or simply the study of gender.[88] Some contributors to these investigations refer to the differences between men and women that are biological in origin as sex differences and to the differences that are environmental in origin as gender differences; we will observe this nomenclature here in this chapter.[89] Psychological investigators working in the area of sex and gender differences face the daunting task of teasing out the origin of the differences by means of fairly sophisticated research design strategies. When contradictory findings emerge from studies exploring the same area, research teams must devise yet additional studies to refine and clarify the findings. The task is ongoing. The following summary merely represents current findings that are always subject to change as more research emerges.

---

86. When the distinguished psychology professor at the University of Southern California, Dr. Carol Nagy Jacklin, undertook the task of assembling the most relevant pieces of research regarding gender, the enterprise resulted in four large volumes containing a total of nearly two thousand pages. See C. N. Jacklin, ed., *The Psychology of Gender*, 4 vols. (New York: New York University Press, 1992).

87. Anne E. Beall and Robert J. Sternbert, eds., *The Psychology of Gender* (New York: Guilford Press, 1993).

88. Jacklin, *The Psychology of Gender*, 1:xiii.

89. Michael S. Kimmel, *The Gendered Society* (New York: Oxford University Press, 2000), 1–4.

Modern biological science has established that the sex of a fetus is determined at the moment of conception when a sperm carrying an X chromosome fertilizes the ovum producing a girl or a sperm carrying a Y chromosome produces a boy. Although the development of the fetus for both sexes is undifferentiated for the first five to six weeks, differences in intrauterine development soon appear as triggers on the sex chromosomes move the process in a male direction or a female direction.[90] Barring some genetic defect or developmental abnormality, the sex of the newborn is easy to determine. External genitalia accompanied by the corresponding internal organs distinguish boys from girls. At puberty both sexes develop secondary sex differences that further distinguish them. We have a more challenging task, however, to identify the more subtle sex differences between the sexes. Are boys more mathematical than girls? Are boys more analytic and girls more emotional? And if such differences do exist, are they biological and thus fairly fixed and determined, or are they environmental and social and thus more subject to modification if we as a society should so choose?

The following list represents material gathered from several sources according to topic.[91]

- Verbal ability. Many studies have identified an advantage in verbal abilities for women and girls. But "the verbal advantage that was once associated with women is not only small but disappearing."[92]
- Mathematical ability. Men and boys beginning at junior high school age have an advantage, but these differences are not clearly due to innate ability.
- Spatial ability. Men excel at spatial visualization, spatial perception, and mental rotation, but women show an advantage in tasks of perceptual speed and memory for placement of objects. Thus a clear male advantage in spatial ability is less clear than it was in early reports.

---

90. Herant A. Katchadourian, *Biological Aspects of Human Sexuality*, 4th ed. (Fort Worth: Holt, Rinehart and Winston, 1990), 41–43, 140.
91. Linda Brannon, *Gender: Psychological Perspectives* (Boston: Allyn and Bacon, 1996), 104–11, 464–65; Mahzarin R. Benaji, "The Psychology of Gender: A Perspective on Perspectives," in *The Psychology of Gender*, ed. Beall and Sternbert, 251–73.
92. Brannon, *Gender*, 110.

These differences between men and women are relatively small, especially when compared to the range of differences among all men or among all women. Research has shown no differences between men and women in overall levels of intelligence, ability to learn and memorize, creativity, musical ability, and ability to read nonverbal cues in spite of various stereotypes that would suggest such differences. Studies exploring gender differences in more subtle psychological traits and features are numerous but beyond the scope of this brief review.[93]

As to whether these differences are sex differences (due to biology) or gender differences (due to environmental forces), the answers are varied. In general, current thought leans more heavily toward a social constructionist explanation than to a biological one. Brannon argues that if we are to find a biological base for differences in mental abilities, we must first find different structures in the brains of men and women and a link between those structures and the differences we have documented above. Some evidence exists for differences between male and female brains (lateralization, hormonal-influenced brain organization), but the evidence for a link between these brain features and mental abilities is weak.[94] And if, for example, the observed difference between men and women in verbal ability is truly biological in origin, we would expect the difference to remain stable over time. But evidence for the difference continues to shrink in magnitude over recent decades of research, suggesting instead an environmental cause.

Yet we must remember that "the controversy revolves less around known facts than around what we want the facts to be and what we want them to mean."[95] Why should these "facts" regarding differences between men and women be subject to such controversy? The answer relates to the topic of roles. If the differences between men and women are, in fact, sex differences (anchored in biology), then biology to a certain degree becomes destiny and the basis of set roles. But if the differences are more heavily related to environmental influences, then the roles we observe in society are not determined or necessary but are primarily the expression of choices made by

---

93. As one example, see Robert F. Bornstein and Joseph M. Masling, eds., *The Psychodynamics of Gender and Gender Role* (Washington, D.C.: American Psychological Assoc., 2002).

94. Brannon, *Gender*, 107–9.

95. M. Gay Hubbard, *Women: The Misunderstood Majority* (Dallas: Word, 1992), 138–39.

our societies and cultures. This debate echoes through the halls of secular institutions and up and down the pews of churches.[96]

## The Psychology of Men and Women

In the first half of the twentieth century, scholars became aware that the work of Sigmund Freud had assumed that masculinity was the norm and femininity was a deviation from that norm. Karen Horney, a member of the third generation of psychoanalysts, began to expose systematically the male bias of Freudian theory and to articulate a psychoanalytic approach to women that was not androcentric.[97] Freud's patriarchal bias had led him to frequently pair femininity with passivity, to question the objectivity of women, and to virtually ignore their early (prephallic) development.[98] "Freud's generalizations concerning girls and women do injustice to both his psychoanalytic method and his clinical findings."[99]

As more and more women entered the field of psychology and began to look at how the major theories of development and personality had been constructed, they found that most approaches were based on male patterns. Researchers had predominantly utilized sampling techniques with only males as subjects and assumed that the findings also applied to women. Certain aspects of psychology thus turned out to be psychologies of males. Investigators soon opened up lines of investigation into all aspects of the field

---

96. For material regarding how the debate expresses itself in the evangelical world, see James R. Beck and Craig L. Blomberg, eds., *Two Views on Women in Ministry* (Grand Rapids: Zondervan, 2001); Anne Carr and Mary Stewart Van Leeuwen, eds., *Religion, Feminism, and the Family* (Louisville, Ky.: Westminster John Knox, 1996); Stephen B. Clark, *Man and Woman in Christ* (Ann Arbor, Mich.: Servant Books, 1980); Kaye Cook and Lance Lee, *Man and Woman Alone and Together: Gender Roles, Identity, and Intimacy in a Changing Culture* (Wheaton, Ill.: Bridgepoint Books); Rebecca M Groothuis, *Good News for Women* (Grand Rapids: Baker, 1996); John Piper and Wayne Grudem, eds., *Recovering Biblical Manhood and Womanhood* (Wheaton, Ill.: Crossway Books, 1991); and Mary Stewart Van Leeuwen, *After Eden: Facing the Challenge of Gender Reconciliation* (Grand Rapids: Eerdmans, 1993).

97. For a collection of her papers, see Karen Horney, *Feminine Psychology* (New York: W. W. Norton, 1967).

98. Roy Schafer, "Problems in Freud's Psychology of Women," in *Female Psychology: Contemporary Psychoanalytic Views,* ed. Harold P. Blum (New York: International Universities Press, 1977), 331–60.

99. Ibid., 359. (This judgment comes from within the psychoanalytic movement and is shared by most all observers.)

with the result that theories are now more carefully nuanced with regard to how males and females operate psychologically. Subtle differences emerged between the psychology of men and women in areas of the sense of self, the role of empathy, effective psychotherapy interventions, power, anger, aggression, and the self-in-relation.[100] Two scholars have made particularly important contributions to this new understanding of women: Carol Gilligan and Mary Belenkey. Dr. Belenkey and her colleagues explored women's ways of knowing and processing information, skills that undergird styles of interacting with the world and people. She documented passive, received, subjective, procedural, and constructed ways of knowing.[101] Dr. Gilligan found that a complete understanding of the psychological understanding of women required careful attention to intimacy and issues of generativity.

> In view of the evidence that women perceive and construe social reality differently from men and that these differences center around experiences of attachment and separation, life transitions that invariably engage these experiences can be expected to involve women in a distinctive way.[102]

The emphasis on women's studies in psychology has triggered new interest in studying men and masculinity in a more focused manner. The men's movement, however, has primarily been a social movement among largely white, middle class, and college educated men who have expressed the need for help in adjusting to the new expressions of femininity and female participation in society that have characterized the last half of the twentieth century.[103]

---

100. Judith V. Jordan et al., *Women's Growth in Connection: Writings from the Stone Center* (New York: Guilford, 1991).

101. Mary Belenkey, Blythe Clinchy, Nancy Goldberger, and Jill Tavile, *Women's Ways of Knowing* (New York: Basic Books, 1997).

102. Carol Gilligan, *In a Different Voice: Psychological Theory and Women's Development* (Cambridge, Mass.: Harvard University Press, 1982), 171.

103. Michael Shiffman, "The Men's Movement: An Exploratory Empirical Investigation," in *Changing Men: New Directions in Research on Men and Masculinity,* ed. Michael S. Kimmel (Newbury Park, N.J.: Sage, 1987).

## Religion

The entire domain of scriptural studies and the theological disciplines concerns itself with religion. But as we have seen in the last chapter, the scriptural theme that relates most closely to the religious or spiritual identity of the human person is the concept of the image of God. In some magnificent and ineradicable way, every human bears as part of his or her identity the stamp of God's likeness. All humans are image bearers. The field of psychology, however, has not largely been committed to the idea of the reality of a supernatural God who is the Creator of the human race. Psychology does not entail atheism or agnosticism (witness the active participation of Christians in the field), but many in the field do not profess a belief in God or believe that such a profession of faith is relevant to their work.

Defining religion is a matter of some controversy among social scientists. Many definitions focus on belief as a core component of the phenomenon. But since belief cannot be observed but only self-reported, it does not satisfy those scientists who want a more easily studied factor. We all know that self-reports are subject to deliberate deception or self-delusion. Belief does not always correlate well with behavior, and reports of belief are subject to intense levels of social conformity. Perhaps the idea of the supernatural should be at the heart of any definition that attempts to explain the religions of the world. The involvement of ideas and convictions regarding the supernatural is indeed present in most religious systems. But again, scientists are restless with a definitional concept that they cannot measure. "Because supernatural things or powers cannot be identified, correlations involving them cannot be demonstrated; something supernatural cannot be shown to be correlated with any observable event."[104] In an effort to provide a definition that will facilitate social science research, Steadman and Palmer suggest that religion is the "communicated acceptance of a supernatural claim, a claim that cannot be shown to be true by the senses (of the observer)."[105] Crafting a definition such as this one for the purposes of efficient research protocols often leaves us with a hollow, incomplete description of the phenomenon. Surely that is the case in this instance. Religion is

---

104. Lyle B. Steadman and Craig T. Palmer, "Religion as an Identifiable Traditional Behavior Subject to Natural Selection," *Journal of Social and Evolutionary Systems* 18 (1995): 152.
105. Ibid., 157.

a rich mixture of allegiances and beliefs that take the individual beyond self to important relationships with a stronger being for the purpose of living a safer, more satisfying life.

Psychology is more likely to study how humans create God in their image, than how God created humans in his own image. Many secular theorists conceive of God as a creation of human projections. "It is by no means certain whether we are made in the image of God, as Christians proclaim, or whether it is out of our need to believe that we may have created God in our own image."[106] To understand how this theme plays out in the discipline, we will explore the theories of religion of four of the major figures in twentieth-century psychology (Freud, Jung, Allport, and Fromm), the work of researchers in the specialty of the psychology of religion, and recent work exploring the possible genetic basis of religion.

## The Pioneers on Religion

Sigmund Freud has earned his reputation as an unrelenting critic of belief in a supernatural religion. He did not practice Judaism, the faith of his ancestors. He was exposed to Roman Catholicism as a child in his native Czechoslovakia, but the evidence that this brief exposure had a strong impact on him is weak.[107] Freud wrote about religion in various papers from 1907–1926, but in the spring of 1927 he began work on his first book on the subject.[108] *The Future of an Illusion* was the first in a series of books written in the last twelve years of his life dealing with civilization and religion and how one can utilize psychoanalytic principles to explain them.

Freud developed his explanation for the naturalistic origin of religion by beginning with the primitive human's fear of nature. By humanizing natural forces (storms, lightning, thunder, etc.) and regarding them as father figures (gods), our ancestors behaved in a manner identical to that of every human infant (infants are terrorized by their helplessness and are fearful of their fathers). The infancy of the human race thus bears similarity to the

---

106. In true agnostic tradition, Patrick Casement poses the question but ultimately says that it cannot be answered in "In Whose Image?" in *Beyond Belief: Psychotherapy and Religion,* ed. Samuel M. Stein (London: Karnac Books, 1999), 20.

107. Although Paul C. Vitz argues in *Sigmund Freud's Christian Unconscious* (New York: Guilford Press, 1988) that Freud had a Christian unconscious structure to his personality against which he struggled throughout his career.

108. Sigmund Freud, *The Future of an Illusion* (Garden City, N.Y.: Anchor Books, 1964), ix–x.

infancy of every person. Later our ancestors reduced the numbers of their gods to one and added loving and kind features to the terrorizing traits of God. Humans have deeply ambivalent feelings about God: we fear God and we fear (hold in awe) God. Thus religion is a human creation designed to help us deal with our terrors and fears. Once we mature, we no longer need to have religion soothe our infantile wishes and illusions. According to Freud religion is an illusion, an obsessional neurosis that civilization will one day outgrow, although Freud reserved the right to be wrong.[109]

> I will moderate my zeal and admit the possibility that I, too, am chasing an illusion. Perhaps the effect of the religious prohibition of thought may not be so bad as I suppose; perhaps it will turn out that human nature remains the same even if education is not abused in order to subject people to religion. I do not know. . . ."[110]

Carl Jung's attitudes were remarkably proreligious, especially when compared to the dark views of Freud regarding religion.[111] Jung was the son of a pastor in the Swiss Reformed Church. For Jung, religion, including Christianity, shared common ground with spirits, demons, laws, and ideals that humans found to be "powerful, dangerous or helpful enough to be taken into careful consideration, or grand, beautiful and meaningful enough to be devoutly adored and loved."[112] He supported the religious practices of his patients if it "works for" them as a defense.[113] Religion for Jung was a source of great richness and symbolic treasures, although there is little evidence that he believed in a supernatural God who was separate from the world but active in it.

Gordon W. Allport, a psychology professor at Harvard, was an active Christian layman who had a lifelong interest in religion. "All the great religions of the world supply, for those who can subscribe to their arguments and affirmations, a world-conception that has logical simplicity and serene

---

109. Ibid., 49, 70–71.
110. Ibid., 79.
111. See Wallace B. Clift, *Jung and Christianity: The Challenge of Reconciliation* (New York: Crossroad, 1985); and Murray Stein, *Jung's Treatment of Christianity: The Psychotherapy of a Religious Tradition* (Wilmette, Ill.: Chiron, 1985).
112. Carl Jung, *Psychology and Religion* (New Haven, Conn.: Yale University Press, 1938), 5.
113. Ibid., 55.

majesty."[114] He could not agree that religion represented prelogical think-ing; if so, how do we account for "the development of logic, mathematics, and scientific method" that religious institutions have fostered over the cen-turies?[115] Religion is not an escape from reality for its adherents. The roots of religious interest vary from individual to individual. "A man's religion is the audacious bid he makes to bind himself to creation and to the Creator. It is his ultimate attempt to enlarge and to complete his own personality by finding the supreme context in which he rightly belongs."[116]

Erich Fromm, a neo-Freudian, existential psychoanalyst, was convinced that every person has a religious need, that is to say, a need for an orienting frame and for something or someone to revere.[117] In both authoritarian and humanistic religious systems, the character of God is a projection from the human. Psychoanalysis is one method of helping the patient regain what he or she has given away to God, parts of the self from which the individual has become detached.[118]

## Current Approaches to Religion

This brief overview of the attitudes toward religion held by some of the pioneers of modern psychology and psychotherapy illustrates that religion has not been a neglected topic in the discipline. Each theorist has given religion a different twist, and none of these twists compares exactly with biblical faith. As a specialty within psychology, the psychology of religion has taken up the task begun by these and other founders of the discipline to understand more fully how religion functions in human experience.

We often describe our age as secular, but the persistent findings of poll-sters and researchers alike is that religion still plays a very central role in American society. "Historical scholarship indicates that religious institu-tional membership as a percent of our population has increased linearly from 1776 to the 1990s, except for a brief period during the Civil War."[119] The majority of Americans continue to believe in the existence of God, in

---

114. Gordon W. Allport, *The Individual and His Religion: A Psychological Interpretation* (New York: Macmillan, 1950), 19.

115. Ibid., 22.

116. Ibid., 161.

117. Erich Fromm, *Psychoanalysis and Religion* (New York: Bantam, 1950), 25.

118. Ibid., 49, 85.

119. Bernard Spilka, "The Future of Religion" (unpublished manuscript), 6.

life after death, and in heaven.[120] And while church membership and a stated belief in God, life after death, and heaven may not to many people be satisfactory proof of genuine Christianity, these facts are remarkable given the overall tone and tenor of contemporary society. Many clinicians and scholars in psychology now concede that an all-out attempt to destroy religion despite its adherence to supernatural and transcendent themes is unjustified, given two demonstrable facts: religion often serves as a constructive organizing force in one's life, providing hope and comfort; and religion is and has been an effective purveyor of moral principles that are necessary for societal health.[121]

Psychologists of religion also study how religion expresses itself over the life span, how religious persons deal with doubt and death, the phenomenon of conversion, mysticism, prayer, worship, and the demographics and personality patterns of religious people.[122] An emerging area of research seeks to determine whether a genetic basis exists for religion. Evidence from twin studies suggests that genetic factors do seem to influence religious expression among people but that the effect is probably not direct but indirect through the interaction of other psychological factors that do have direct genetic underpinnings: need for meaning (pertinence), need for control, and need for sociality.[123]

Evolutionary psychologists have displayed a surprising amount of interest in the topic of religion. Normally we view evolutionists as antireligious or at least inimical to religion as a constructive component of the human experience. Recently, however, evolutionists have reconstructed what they believe is a defensible account of how religion evolved among humans. Evolutionary psychologists see religion as an inborn feature of the human brain.

---

120. Ibid., 10–11.
121. Robert A. Hinde, *Why Gods Persist: A Scientific Approach to Religion* (London: Routledge, 1999), 233–44.
122. An early classic in the field is Walter H. Clark, *The Psychology of Religion: An Introduction to Religious Experience and Behavior* (New York: Macmillan, 1958). For more recent works, see C. Daniel Batson, Patricia Schoenrade, and W. Larry Ventis, *Religion and the Individual* (New York: Oxford University Press, 1993); Robert Crawford, *What Is Religion?* (London: Routledge, 2002); and Bernard Spilka, Ralph W. Hood, Bruce Hunsberger, and Richard Gorsuch, *The Psychology of Religion: An Empirical Approach*, 3d ed. (New York: Guilford Press, 2003).
123. Bernard Spilka and Kevin L. Ladd, "The Psychobiology of God: Evolution and Genetics" (paper presented at the Convention of the Society for Scientific Study of Religion, Salt Lake City, Utah, November 2002).

They cite three lines of evidence in support of this assertion. First, religion appears to be a valid part of human societies all around the world. This cross-cultural validity is universal to human culture. Second, the vigor of faith persists even in hostile environments such as the state-supported atheism of the Soviet Union or the skeptical scientism of the twentieth century in the West. Religion is a force "which exceeds most other leanings."[124] Third, the amount of resources and energy allocated to religion indicates to evolutionists that the factor is important and central. Genes that thus push people in a sensible direction, such as happens with religion, will increase because they have adaptive advantage.

Several brain arrangements (see chap. 2 for a discussion of modular brain models) evolved to facilitate the development of religion. The necessary modules for the development of religion are: "Submission to a higher power, the creation of thought constructs and adhering to the belief in them whether or not they can be substantiated, the redirections of love and devotion towards abstract beings, as well as socializing based on spiritual aspects such as in connection with rituals."[125] Once these brain components had evolved by means of adaptation processes, the stage was set for the emergence of the religions of the world.

So should religion be abandoned? No, say the evolutionists. Grinde urges people to go with their nature. If religion is part of the brain's system that has evolved over the centuries, we live best when we live in harmony with that internal reality. Be religious, says Grinde, "yet I would choose my god carefully."[126] Surely his advice qualifies as one of the most ironic twists to emerge from the field of evolutionary biology.

---

124. Bjorn Grinde, "The Biology of Religion: A Darwinian Gospel," *Journal of Social and Evolutionary Systems* 21 (1998): 20.
125. Ibid., 23.
126. Ibid., 26.

# CHAPTER 6

# SUBSTANCE *and* IDENTITY INTEGRATED

IN THE INTEGRATION OF theological and psychological material related to the question of what comprises the human being, some truths are firmly established.

## SUBSTANCE

### Christian Certainties

1. *A pure materialism with regard to human nature is incompatible with authoritative biblical revelation.* Reductive materialism reduces all components of the human person to atoms and molecules, an approach that accounts for only one-half of the process described in Genesis 2:7. Numerous biblical texts cited in chapter 4 identify an immaterial substance. So, for example, as he was being stoned to death, Stephen prayed, "Lord Jesus, receive my spirit" (Acts 7:59). Similarly, Jesus uttered these words as he was dying; "Father into your hands I commit my spirit" (Luke 23:46).

2. *We best account for biblical data by positing that humans have both material and immaterial natures.* Even though these categories may not fit precisely with units of analysis common among philosophers and psychologists, they most closely cohere with the teachings of Scripture on the subject.

3.  *The "mind" of the Mind-Body Problem (MBP) seems to fit most closely with what Scripture describes as the soul/spirit/mind.* Scripture uses these constitutional terms in a fluid manner, and so must we. They are not precise, scientifically defined words in the Bible, but together they comprise what contemporary scholarship calls the mind.

4.  *The material and immaterial (brain and mind, if you will) of the human being causally interact with each other.* Some philosophical solutions to the MBP affirm that only the brain can causally interact with the mind, but the data of Scripture and modern psychology have established that both causally affect each other.

5.  *The mind and brain are intimately connected in living persons; we have no experience with one acting alone without the other.* Science tells us that every thought is accompanied by brain activity, and conscious or unconscious experience seems to accompany every brain event.

6.  *The intermediate state is an important and relevant doctrine for this debate.* Some advocates of nonreductive physicalism (NRP) seem more concerned about accounting for brain science than accounting for personal eschatology (the state and destiny of the human being after death). The doctrine that a believer at death enters the presence of the Lord (2 Cor. 5:8), although supported by only a few texts, is important nonetheless because it speaks to the substantial composition of the human being.[1] We must not lightly dismiss this data of biblical revelation.

7.  *The fact that we have no experience with the mind acting apart from the brain does not mean that the mind (the immaterial reality) could not function apart from the brain (the material reality) after death.* We have no personal experience with this eventuality, but the fact that we have not observed the immaterial functioning in this manner does not mean that it does not occur. Granted, having to take some issues by faith may not be intellectually satisfying to many interested parties, but at times allegiance to Scripture's teaching requires such a commitment of us.

---

1. James R. Beck, "Questioning the Intermediate State: A Case Study in Integrative Conflict," *Journal of Psychology and Christianity* 10 (1991): 24–35; and David G. Myers, "Are We Body and Soul: A Response to James Beck," *Journal of Psychology and Christianity* 10 (1991): 36–38.

## Brief Integration

The substance dualism position articulated over the centuries represents the majority position of competent and responsible Christian scholars. The thesis of holistic dualism continues to offer the best solution to the MBP in light of revealed truths contained in Scripture. The findings of modern brain science do not require that Christians abandon their understanding of how the mind (soul/spirit/person/immaterial reality) is related to the body (brain/material reality). The findings of brain science do, however, give us useful information about how the mind and brain relate to one another in living persons. Christians must abandon their conception of a mind operating by itself in a living person. The operation of the mind always includes the operation and activity of the brain and vice versa. It is only when physical death, an eventuality caused by the advent of sin into the world (Gen. 2:17; 3:19), rudely destroys the created unity of the person and temporarily separates the immaterial from the material that the mind operates apart from the brain. At the resurrection, this unnatural existence of the immaterial existing apart from the material will be rectified.

We can appreciate the careful work conducted by the team at Fuller Seminary that has introduced nonreductive physicalism (NRP) to the theological world. However, their system fails to satisfy the demands of all the certainties we have listed above when it fails to account well for the fact that Scripture distinguishes the material and immaterial constituents of human nature, that the Bible distinguishes between the inner and the outer aspects of humans, that the doctrine of redemption deals with both immaterial and material aspects of humans, and that reality of the intermediate state is clearly taught in Scripture (see chap. 1). We prefer the proposals advanced by J. P. Moreland and John W. Cooper to this problem.[2] As apologist Douglas Groothuis writes, "(Jesus) drew a distinction between two aspects of the person, which are interrelated but not identical or reducible to one another."[3] So also did the apostle Paul in his teachings on the subject. An integration of current psychological findings with our best

---

2. John W. Cooper, *Body, Soul and Life Everlasting: Biblical Anthropology and the Monism-Dualism Debate* (Grand Rapids: Eerdmans, 1989); and J. P. Moreland and Scott Rae, *Body and Soul: Human Nature and the Crisis in Ethics* (Downers Grove, Ill.: InterVarsity, 2000).

3. Douglas Groothuis, *On Jesus* (Belmont, Calif.: Thomson Wadsworth, 2003), 41.

understanding of scriptural truth will require us to develop some type of dualistic understanding that allows both mind and brain the levels of functioning we have described in the above list of certainties.

We are convinced that the development of solutions to the MBP requires the participation of scholars from many disciplines: theology, psychology, philosophy, and other social sciences. Most philosophers will no doubt continue to struggle with substance dualism as a viable position. We understand that substance dualism is not without its own set of philosophical problems, but we are more content leaving these issues unsolved than we are disregarding the data of Scripture that requires a separate sphere of operation for the material and the immaterial in living humans. When making a theological judgment, we must accept the hypothesis that coheres with the greatest body of biblical and extrabiblical data with the least number of difficulties.

## Needed Research

The search for a completely satisfying solution to the MBP, although futile to date, should be a quest that attracts bright minds with a philosophical bent. Christians need to be engaged in this process so that the church can benefit from integrations that take seriously the teachings of Scripture and the findings of science, which is a challenging intellectual task indeed. Brain science has not produced data that would destroy the foundations of our faith. If anything, brain science has provided us yet additional information into some of the secrets of creation that prompts us to stand in even greater awe before our Creator. But short of finding some yet-to-be-discovered solution to the MBP that solves all the philosophical and intellectual questions attendant to the issue, we need to hold the truths of Scripture and the findings of science together in the best integration possible. Surely this integration will contain mysteries and unresolved tensions, but such are to be expected when delving into metaphysical and spiritual issues.

## IDENTITY

If we can feel comfortable with a brain-mind dualism, we are ready to move to the more central subject of who we are as human beings. Scripture offers some further certainties about human identity.

## Christian Certainties

1. *The self is a holistic concept that encompasses both the physical and the nonphysical, the material and the immaterial.* The church has striven diligently during the past two millennia to steer a clear course between two heretical extremes: (1) that the immaterial is more valued and important to God than the material or (2) that the material is more important and valued to God than the immaterial. The data of Scripture and of psychological science providentially prove congruent on this point: the person is a whole.

2. *The exact term we use to signify the human being (self, person, or soul) is not crucial to the integrative task.* We appreciate the fine work of Jeffrey Boyd, who has called the mental health profession to account for abandoning the term *soul* in favor of more recent terminology such as *person* or *self.* Boyd is correct is asserting that the change of terms signifies a departure from the historic Judeo-Christian understanding of the human being. But we are convinced that Christian theologians and psychologists can appropriately and usefully utilize *self* or *person* as the designated term for the human being as long as the meanings infused into the term are holistic and reflective of scriptural teachings regarding image-bearing features of humans.

3. *This whole person, both material and immaterial, is the object of God's redemptive work and is the subject of eschatological hope.* Psychology has introduced a considerable degree of richness to our understanding of the human *psyche.* This material neither contradicts nor undermines the data concerning the human person that is depicted in the pages of Scripture.

4. *A central feature of the human person is the image of God each person bears.* The image, intrinsic to human nature, distinguishes men and women from other living beings. We favor an omnibus, or multiplex, definition of this image: humans (created to reflect God's nature and works) are spiritual, rational, volitional, emotional, moral, and relational beings. This image appears in every person, redeemed or unredeemed, is the basis on which God forwards love and concern to all persons, and is the datum on which we are to forward dignity and respect for all individuals.

5. *God revealed his nature to us; we did not create God's nature out of our*

*wishes and projections.* A naturalistic understanding of the origin of religion and of God is thoroughly unsatisfying. It may be the best explanation for the investigator who has ruled out any possibility for theism before even launching the debate; but for those who allow the possibility of a theistic understanding of the universe, the description of God's nature given to humans by revelation is eminently possible, factually accurate, and existentially satisfying.

6.  *Humans do form psychological images of God, images that may be distorted by developmental flaws.* This psychological fact does nothing to undermine biblical faith, but it does greatly inform ministry and spiritual formation as we seek to encourage one another to greater degrees of maturity in Christ.

7.  *Sex (biological) differences between men and women bear the stamp of God's creative work; socially constructed (gender) differences may or may not reflect God's purposes for the human race.* We continue to face challenges in sorting out sex and gender differences. Our task is to exegete Scripture carefully when it speaks to the matter of gender and to utilize these teachings as a guide to psychological findings regarding the meanings of gender.

8.  *The Christian's challenge to mature in Christ and to conform to his image is intertwined with the Christian's status as an image-bearer, a holistic self, and a gendered creature.* Any integration of factors related to human identity must take into account God's design for our sanctification and for our development as his disciples in kingdom mission.

## Brief Integration

Theological anthropologies of the future will be stronger, more cohesive, and more helpful when they include all the data of Scripture regarding human identity as well as well-established data emerging from the psychological sciences regarding the self, gender, and the religious impulse. The psychological self is clearly more complex than previously imagined. Human personality, including motivation, is an arena of human functioning that psychology has been able more fully to illuminate and explain. When we combine these findings with scriptural teaching about poor personality functioning (the works of the flesh, Gal. 5:16–21) and God's intended functioning for His children (the fruit of the Spirit, Gal. 5:22–26), we gain an enriched understanding of human identity.

Our integration of material regarding human identity must always attend to a dual purpose. We must first articulate human identity with its created intent and with its sinful expressions. Second, we must explain how salvation restores that created intent for humans. In other words, we cannot be satisfied with merely explaining the psychology of the believer (a Christian psychology). We must also define what it means to be human apart from redemption. An integrated approach will spell out human identity as taught in Scripture and as enhanced by psychological science in a manner that identifies the human condition before the entry of sin into human experience, the human condition as tarnished and affected by sin, and the human condition as experienced by those who are redeemed by the blood of the Lamb.

## Needed Research

Psychologists and theologians can profitably investigate further the nature of the image of God. Clearly, the image is related to some of or all of the psychological functions we have investigated here. But we still do not have a satisfying integration of how the image reflects intelligent design, God's nature, sin's impact, and psychological process.

Christian scholarship must continue to focus on how the psychological self meshes with scriptural teaching regarding the human person. How do the definitions of self as advanced by the major schools of psychology relate to Scripture? How can we incorporate these varied approaches in such a way as to correspond correctly with what the Bible says about human identity? How can we understand new findings regarding the psychology of men and women in light of what the Bible teaches us about roles? And how can we utilize new approaches to God-concepts that psychology presents to us in a way that enhances our approach to ministry and spiritual formation? As always, the challenge is to exegete Scripture carefully and to locate material in psychology that is reliable, replicated, and responsible as we bring these materials together in our constructive integrative task.

# THE FUNCTION *and* BEHAVIOR *of the* HUMAN PERSON

# CHAPTER 7

# FUNCTION *and* BEHAVIOR *in* THEOLOGICAL PERSPECTIVE

PART 2 EXPLORED THE ESSENTIAL nature and composition of the human person as unique image and representation of God. We concluded that the human being is a complex unity of an immaterial and undying soul/spirit and a material body. In part 3 we consider from biblical and psychological perspectives the wide range of human capacities and functioning resulting from their privileged creation in God's likeness. Human relational capacity and functioning will be treated in part 4. The task at hand explores potential human capacities and functioning as created, the impairment that ensued due to the fall of the race in sin, and the possibility of restored capacities and functioning by virtue of redemption in Christ.

## HUMAN FUNCTIONING AS CREATED

Human beings reflect but a pale representation of God's original intention for them as the highest and noblest of His creatures. From the creative hand of God, Adam and Eve were endowed with a range of untarnished capacities that enabled them perfectly to fulfill the divine Artisan's purpose for their lives, as well as to achieve maximal, personal fulfillment. Mind, volition, emotions, conscience, and behaviors—finely attuned to the life and will of the Creator—were capable of extraordinary achievements. It is, of course, the whole person who thinks, wills, feels, relates, and acts morally and spiritually. But for the purpose of analysis, we proceed to examine the capacities and functioning of human image-bearers in the pristine condition in which they were created.

## Historical Perspectives

Theologians and philosophers through the centuries have emphasized as dominant particular capacities and functions of the human person.

### Emphasis on Intellect and Reason

Leading Greek philosophers judged that the primary human faculty is *nous*, the capacity for thinking and reasoning. Plato divided the human soul *(psychē)* into three parts: (1) the rational *(logistikon);* (2) the spirited *(thymikon);* and (3) the appetitive *(epithymetikon).* Reason is the principal aspect of the soul that governs the desires, emotions, and passions, enabling the soul to attain excellence and rise upward. Defining the human person as an *animal rationale,* Aristotle postulated a threefold hierarchy of life-forms. Plants possess a nutritive faculty, animals also a sensitive faculty, and humans also a spiritual faculty capable of reasoning. Through reason, the highest of the human faculties, humans realize the good life.

Many early church fathers emphasized the human person's intellectual capacity. The second-century apologist Athenagoras of Athens wrote of the human person, "whose nature involves the possession of mind and who partakes of rational judgments."[1] Gregory of Nyssa similarly stressed the intellectual faculty, that "the form of man was framed to serve as an instrument for the use of reason."[2] He added, "The soul finds its perfection in that which is intellectual and rational."[3] Following Aristotle, Thomas Aquinas viewed the human person as a rational animal capable of considerable knowledge. Thomas posited a hierarchy of life-forms consisting of vegetable soul (growth, nutrition, reproduction), animal soul (locomotion, exterior and interior senses, and sensory appetite), and rational soul (passive intellect, active intellect, and will). In the absolute sense, intellect is the highest and governing power of the soul, moving the will and all the other powers according to its understanding of what is good.[4]

---

1. Athenagoras, *The Resurrection of the Dead* 12 [*ANF,* 2:155].
2. Gregory of Nyssa, *On the Making of Man* 9 [*NPNF²,* 5:395].
3. Ibid., 15.2 [*NPNF²,* 5:403].
4. Thomas Aquinas, *ST,* 4:139–44 [pt. 1, q. 82, arts. 3–4].

René Descartes, the father of modern philosophy and a mind-body dualist, rejected medieval authoritarianism in favor of the reasoning human subject *(res cogitans)*. His famous first principle of philosophy, "I think, therefore I am," confirmed the centrality of the mind and reason. Humanness, Descartes argued, exists as a thinking substance independent of sense experience. Descartes brought all truth claims under the purview of *a priori* concepts and deductive reason.

Persuaded that humankind had come of age intellectually, philosophers of the eighteenth-century were abandoning revelation and dogma in favor of reason. Some defined revelation as "exalted reason" and claimed that all persons who live according to the light of reason are "Christians." The British empiricist John Locke (1632–1704), who paved the way for deism, claimed that reason adjudicates the claims made by revelation. "Reason must be our last judge and guide in everything."[5] Locke argued that "humans are rational beings for whom knowledge is the means to achieve earthly happiness."[6] Deists such as John Toland (1670–1722) and Matthew Tindal (1655–1733) stressed the role of autonomous reason in identifying the tenets of the universal religion embedded in the structure of nature. According to Tindal, "I cannot have any faith that will not bear the test of reason."[7] European rationalists, such as Hermann Reimarus (1694–1768), Gotthold Ephraim Lessing (1729–1781), and Johann Semler (1725–1791), insisted that humans secure truth and forge their futures through reason alone.

Protestant Scholasticism in the post-Reformation era extolled reason for the purposes of developing the science of dogmatics and defending the faith. On the basis of supernatural revelation, many Reformed theologians, such as Francis Turretin (1623–1687), Charles Hodge, and B. B. Warfield (1851–1921), stressed the rational mind's competence to identify truth and expose error. The evangelical rationalist Gordon Clark (1902–1985) states that every book of the Bible presents the human person as a rational, thinking being. With respect to John 1:9, Clark claims, that "the Logos or rationality of God . . . can be seen as having created man with the light of logic as the

---

5. John Locke, *An Essay Concerning Human Understanding* (New York: New American Library, 1974), 432.

6. Robert Anchor, *The Enlightenment Tradition* (Berkeley, Calif.: University of California Press, 1967), 59.

7. Matthew Tindal, cited in Edward G. Waring, *Deism and Natural Religion* (New York: F. Ungar, 1967), 150.

distinctive human characteristic."[8] Many in this tradition, in reaction to charismatic and experiential theologies, insist on the primacy of reason. Truth clearly presented to the mind itself is judged sufficient to transform the life. Reformed theologian Howard Rice comments, "Persons in the Reformed tradition need to be careful of trusting the mind too much. Too often we have made an idol of rationality. . . . The emotions cannot be left aside when we approach God."[9]

### Emphasis on the Will

Various impulses in philosophy and theology stressed human volitional capacity and functioning. Medieval voluntarists (from the Latin, *voluntas*, "will"), such as Anselm of Canterbury (1034–1109), William of Ockham (1285–1347), and Duns Scotus (1266–1308), claimed that, for humans as well as for God, the will rules the intellect. Duns Scotus argued that love—an act of the will—is the greatest of the virtues. Hence liberty, or free will, is the supreme human capacity and value. All moral activity is directed by the human will.

While not an irrationalist, Blaise Pascal nevertheless upheld proud reason's inability adequately to fathom ultimate questions of God and human destiny. Thus, "It is the heart that feels God, not reason: that is what faith is. God felt by the heart, not by reason."[10] Pascal's famous "wager" encouraged a decision of the will in favor of God, which risks little if God does not exist but promises much—even an eternity of life and happiness—if God does exist. Inviting decision, Pascal enjoined the interlocutor, You must make a choice: Which option will you choose? Whom will you worship? Pascal's "will inclined him to wager on the problematical but infinitely momentous alternative of faith."[11] The Swiss thinker Jean Jacque Rousseau (1712–1778) insisted that the will directs the mind and orders the passions. "The ability to make choices, to will one's aims distinguishes man from the animals . . ."[12]

---

8. Gordon Clark, *The Biblical Doctrine of Man* (Jefferson, Md.: The Trinity Foundation, 1984), 18–19.

9. Howard L. Rice, *Reformed Spirituality* (Louisville, Ky.: Westminster John Knox, 1991), 56.

10. Blaise Pascal, *Pensées,* trans. Honor Levi (Oxford: Oxford University Press, 1995), 157 [no. 680].

11. Tsanoff Radoslav, "Evil, Problem of," in *Dictionary of the History of Ideas*, ed. Philip P. Wiener, 5 vols. (New York: Charles Scribner's Sons, 1973–74), 2:168.

12. Judith N. Shklar, "General Will," in *Dictionary of the History of Ideas,* 2:276.

Rousseau adds, "A man with a will . . . wills what is necessary for his own felicity, and does nothing except what he wills. That is freedom."[13]

Theological existentialism holds that human authenticity is achieved by courageous decision making and consequent action. Opposing Enlightenment and idealist rationalism, Søren Kierkegaard (1813–1855) postulated the paradoxical nature of Christian faith. The fact that the infinite God has come as a finite man to dwell with finite beings is scandalous to human reason. Human fulfillment is achieved not by reason, logic, or science but as one withdraws from the crowd and makes an individually willed "leap of faith." Not the ability to think, but decision and responsibility for one's choices are of utmost importance.

The supreme example of the costly faith-decision is Abraham's willingness to sacrifice his son Isaac in obedience to God's command. According to the Scottish existential theologian John Macquarie, the authentic self (not a substantial soul) is actualized through the process of intentional decision making and commitment. "The self is not given ready-made but has to be made in the course of existence. . . . What is given at the outset is not a fixed entity but a potentiality for becoming a self."[14] Other factors that actualize personhood include openness to others, self-giving love, and capacity for letting others be.

### Emphasis on Emotions and Feelings

Romanticism, a movement that prevailed from 1780 to 1840, opposed the Enlightenment ideal of analytical but barren reason, believing that the latter destroyed the aesthetic and spiritual aspects of life. Modern romantics find "man's uniqueness and divinity not in his reason but in the impulsive and emotional life which bridges the gulf between body and spirit."[15] German literary figures such as Johann Wolfgang von Goethe (1749–1832) and Friedrich von Schiller (1759–1805) and British literary personalities such as William Blake (1757–1827), William Wordsworth (1770–1850), and Samuel Taylor Coleridge (1772–1834) contributed to the romantic impulse in religion. Romantic philosophers and theologians insisted that humans engage invisible realities, not formally by reason, but experientially by acute

---

13. Ibid., 2:277.
14. John Macquarie, *Principles of Christian Theology* (New York: Scribner, 1977), 76.
15. W. M. Horton, *Christian Theology* (New York: Harper and Brothers, 1958), 160.

awareness, feeling, and aesthetic sensibility. Romanticism in literature, philosophy, and theology was individualistic and tended toward pantheism.

The leading theologian in the romantic tradition, Friedrich Schleiermacher (1768–1834), judged that intuition and feeling, rather than objective belief or moral action, constitute the locus of religion and the foundation of theology. "Piety . . . is, considered purely in itself, neither a knowing nor a doing, but a modification of feeling, or of immediate self-consciousness."[16] Feeling is prereflective or prior to conscious thought. "True religion," Schleiermacher insisted, "is sense and taste for the Infinite."[17] By means of the religious consciousness, or what is felt, humans are capable of engaging the Infinite or All. The human being experientially is a *homo religiosus*. Fairly can it be said that "Schleiermacher diverts the emphasis from rationalistic doctrinal assertions to individual feeling or experience."[18]

Some twentieth-century charismatic groups embrace the romantic spirit by emphasizing as normative intense feelings, emotional states of enthusiasm, and heightened religious fervor. Their weakness is that, in practice, elevated emotional states tend to take precedence over objective truths mediated to the mind through the Scriptures.

### Emphasis on Moral Capacity

Immanuel Kant initially was influenced by rationalism, but after engaging David Hume's (1711–1766) observations on causality, he abandoned this emphasis. Kant affirmed that the human mind can know the empirical world as it is structured by the categories of the human mind, but he denied cognitive knowledge of the noumenal or supernatural realm. Practical reason (the sense of moral obligation), however, engages the universal and unconditional moral law that testifies to the human conscience. Kant is well known for the saying, "Two things fill the mind with ever increasing wonder and awe . . . the starry heavens above me and the moral law within me."[19] The universally binding moral command Kant called the "categorical imperative." Thus in place of the Cartesian "I think," Kant postulated the ethi-

---

16. Friedrich Schleiermacher, *The Christian Faith* (Edinburgh: T. and T. Clark, 1928), 5.
17. Friedrich Schleiermacher, *On Religion: Speeches to Its Cultured Despisers* (New York: Harper and Row, 1958), 39.
18. J. H. Elias, "Romanticism," in *NDT,* 598.
19. Immanuel Kant, *The Critique of Practical Reason,* in *Great Books of the Western World,* ed. Mortimer T. Adler, 60 vols. (Chicago: Encyclopedia Britannica, 1990), 39:360.

cal "I ought." Kant "considered the fulfillment of the moral law to be man's only serious task, a task which defines and brings into being human nature proper."[20] From the indisputable moral law follow the postulates of human freedom, the immortality of the soul, and the existence of God.

Kant's transcendental idealism reduced religion to a system of ethical rules and moral conduct. Christ symbolized the highest moral perfection, and the church brings about the kingdom of God on earth through encouraging the performance of duty.

The neo-Kantian theologian Albrecht Ritschl (1822–1889) influenced development of nineteenth-century classical theological liberalism. Ritschl claimed that religion must be practical and ethical, not theoretical or metaphysical. Ritschl's theology stressed the human moral sense and conscience. Humans, he insisted, must obey the voice of God within as the moral law, mediated to the heart by the conscience. As persons cultivate ethical virtues and practice dutiful action, the kingdom of God on earth is realized—the kingdom being the fellowship of persons living morally according to the law of love embedded in Jesus' teachings. Twentieth-century liberal theology was also highly ethical in nature, stressing humanity's power of moral discrimination and the inauguration of the kingdom of God on earth by ethical action. Walter Rauschenbusch (1861–1918), who contrasted human "ethical and spiritual nature" with "animal nature," averred that "the moral demands within us are the highest and ought to rule."[21]

## The Integration of All Human Capacities and Functions via the Heart

God at creation gave to the human soul a mind that is enabled by reason and "capable of knowledge and of receiving instruction, fit to understand what is true and to love what is good,"[22] insisted Augustine. Reason *(ratio)* is the power by which the soul acquires knowledge of temporal, changing things *(scientia),* and understanding *(intellectus)* is the power by which the soul immediately intuits eternal, changeless principles *(sapientia).* Free will represents another power of the soul—the will being directed by a weight

---

20. Anchor, *The Enlightenment Tradition,* 114.
21. Walter Rauschenbusch, *The Righteousness of the Kingdom* (Nashville: Abingdon, 1968), 134.
22. Augustine, *"City of God"* 22.24 [*NPNF*¹, 2:502].

that is one's dominant love.[23] Augustine also posited the reality of human emotions and passions, especially the fundamental desire, joy, fear, and sorrow.

Moral conscience, which distinguishes between good and evil, represents yet another power. Augustine upheld the interrelation of all the soul's capacities and functions that image the harmonious functioning of the Trinity. "We *will* to know and love. We *love* to know and will. And we *know* what we will and love."[24] All the soul's powers direct the actions of the body.

Martin Luther's Genesis commentary states that within the unity of the person is a "most beautiful" and "most excellent" harmony, as intellect drives memory, will, desires, emotions, moral discrimination, and dominion.[25] John Calvin attested the wide range of human powers, including reason, understanding, will, emotion or affections, and conscience.[26] Contrary to the subtle classification schemes of ancient philosophers, Calvin judged that all of the soul's capacities can be included within the understanding and the will. "No power can be found in the soul that does not duly have reference to one or the other of these members. And in this way we include sense under understanding."[27]

Within the human soul or self, according to Dallas Willard, are six basic aspects of (1) thought (ideas, images, memories, beliefs), (2) feeling (sensation, desire, emotion), (3) choice (intentions, decisions, character), (4) body, (5) social context, and (6) soul.[28] The human mind consists of thoughts and feelings. "Every human being thinks (has a thought life), feels, chooses, interacts with his or her body and its social context, and . . . integrates all the foregoing as parts of one life. These are the essential factors in a human being, and nothing essential to human life falls outside of them."[29] The basic human capacities and functions, according to Willard, are interdepen-

23. Augustine, *On the Trinity* 11.7.12 [*NPNF*[1], 3:151].

24. Gordon R. Lewis and Bruce Demarest, *Integrative Theology*, 3 vols. (Grand Rapids: Zondervan, 1987–94), 2:150.

25. Cited in Hugh Thompson Kerr, ed., *A Compend of Luther's Theology* (Philadelphia: Westminster, 1963), 81.

26. John Calvin, *Institutes of the Christian Religion*, ed. John T. McNeill, trans. Ford Lewis Batles, 2 vols., LCC, vols. 20–21 (Philadelphia: Westminister Press, 1960), 1:186–90, 192–96 [1.15.3–4, 6–8].

27. Ibid., 1:195 [1.15.7]

28. Dallas Willard, *Renovation of the Heart: Putting on the Character of Christ* (Colorado Springs, Colo.: NavPress, 2002), 30–38.

29. Ibid., 31.

dent, mutually conditioning, and nonseparable. For example, "To choose, one must have some object or concept before the mind and some feeling for or against it. There is no choice that does not involve both thought and feeling. On the other hand, what we feel and think is . . . to a very large degree a matter of choice in competent adult persons."[30]

Furthermore, said Willard, "Our actions *always* arise out of the *interplay* of the universal factors in human life: spirit, mind, body, social context, and soul. Action never comes from the movement of the will alone."[31]

## Biblical and Theological Development

Scripture's anthropological focus is on human beings' relationship to the living God as Creator and Redeemer. Human capacities, however, are not overlooked in the biblical revelation.

### Intellect: Reason, Perception, Memory, Imagination

"Reason is the capacity to interpret the infinite flow of sensations so that we comprehend ('perceive,' as psychologists would say) the world as intelligible."[32] The principal *objects* of human knowing are as follows. Humans know themselves, inner and outer reality, in the sense of being authentically *self-conscious* ("I-self"). Paul wrote, "For who among men knows the thoughts of a man except the man's spirit within him?" (1 Cor. 2:11; cf. Ps. 4:4). Humans also know other persons in the sense of being genuinely *others-conscious* ("I-thou"). This kind of knowledge is gained through visible signs such as words, facial gestures, and body language. Moreover, humans know the external, material world by sensation, memory, and experience and so become *world-conscious* ("I-it"). Humans organize knowledge of the external world into sciences such as geology and astronomy. They organize what is known about events into world history and biography. Supremely, human persons were created to know God and to become devotedly God-conscious (I-Thou). Through general revelation, humans know God's existence, character (Rom. 1:19–21; Ps. 19:1–6), and moral

---

30. Ibid., 34.
31. Ibid., 39. Emphasis in original.
32. Paul K. Jewett, *Who We Are: Our Dignity as Human* (Grand Rapids: Eerdmans, 1996), 66.

demands (Rom. 2:14–15). Through special revelation—the person of Jesus Christ (John 14:8–9) and the Scriptures (2 Tim. 3:16; 2 Peter 1:19–21)—humans can know God's laws and the plan of salvation. Knowing God is a rational, not an irrational, activity (1 Cor. 14:14–15, 19).

The *content* of human knowledge assumes several forms. Thoughts are ideas recalled to the mind. Willard defines thoughts as *"all the ways in which we are conscious of things.* That includes our memories, perceptions, and beliefs."[33] Ideas are conceptions formed in the mind as a result of cognitive apprehension. Christian thinkers have developed enduring ideas that have shaped history. The apostle Paul, for example, acquired by revelation the idea that the fullness of the Godhead indwells Jesus Christ bodily (Col. 1:19). Images are concrete, sensuous, and feeling-laden representations drawn by analogy from material objects. Scripture is laced with sensory-rich symbols and images. These portray God as a rock (Ps. 62:2) and a fortress (Ps. 46:11), Christ as a shepherd (1 Peter 5:4) and a vine (John 15:1), and the church as a bride (Rev. 19:7), a temple (1 Cor. 3:16–17), and a flock (Ps. 95:7).

*Knowledge (gnōsis)* is apprehension of facts by observation, experimentation, or experience. After observing Jesus' suffering and death, the Roman centurion acknowledged that Jesus must have had a special relationship with God (Mark 15:39). "Knowledge is the raw material out of which the finest of all machines, the mind, creates its amazing world."[34] Scripture's primary focus is upon the redemptive knowledge of God through Jesus Christ (Phil. 3:8; 2 Peter 3:18). Understanding (Heb. *bîn, śēkel, tᵉbûnâ;* Gk. *synesis, dianoia*) unites intellect with moral and spiritual insights. It involves the perception of spiritual realities together with the application of such knowledge through sound choices (Ps. 14:2). In Scripture, understanding is closely linked with wisdom (Deut. 4:6; Prov. 10:23; James 3:13).

Thus the apostle Paul prayed that the Colossian Christians might be filled "with the knowledge of [God's] will through all spiritual wisdom and understanding" (Col. 1:9b). *Wisdom* (Heb. *ḥokmâ;* Gk. *sophia*), mentioned some three hundred times in the Old Testament alone, involves the application of knowledge into constructive action and virtuous living. The ultimate aspect of wisdom is reverence for God. "The fear of the Lord—that is wisdom" (Job 28:28a).

---

33. Willard, *Renovation of the Heart,* 96.
34. A. W. Tozer, *The Quotable Tozer,* comp. Harry Verploegh (Camp Hill, Pa.: Christian Publications, 1994), 129.

The *methods* by which humans acquire knowledge are *induction, deduction, abduction, and rational intuition. Induction,* reasoning from observed particulars to a general conclusion, is found in Paul's development of an argument for election from the experience of Israel (Rom. 9–11). *Deduction,* reasoning from universals to particulars, is reflected in confessions of faith (e.g., the Westminster Confession of Faith). *Abduction,* testing hypotheses to confirm or invalidate, is reflected in John the Baptist's question to Jesus whether he was the Messiah or someone else (Matt. 11:2–6).

*Rational intuition* involves direct perception of universal truths implanted in the human heart by general revelation. The objects of rational intuition include the existence of God, the laws of logic, and the distinction between right and wrong (Rom. 1:21, 28, 32). In Acts 24:25 Paul spoke with Felix about "righteousness, self-control and the judgment to come"—matters about which the pagan ruler had instinctive knowledge. Rational intuition is distinguished from mystical intuition, wherein one seeks to know by direct apprehension the minds of God and others. Watchman Nee claimed that through intuition the human spirit directly knows God's mind and receives divine guidance.[35] All intuitions, however, must be tested against Scripture via critical reasoning.

*Memory* or the verb *remember* (Heb. *zākar;* Gk. *mimnēskomai*) involves recollection of things past (cf. Ps. 143:5). Scripture enjoins remembrance of God's person (Ps. 63:6), laws (Num. 15:39–40), and saving acts (Ps. 77:11). The memory-stream of thoughts and actions shape the soul's character.

*Imagination,* the faculty by which humans envision possibilities, involves forming mental images of what is not immediately present to the senses and applying them innovatively to life. The task of the human imagination is not to create reality (which is impossible) but to open the soul to neglected dimensions of reality. Calvin lauded human imagination: "Manifold indeed is the nimbleness of the soul with which it . . . pictures to itself whatever it pleases. Manifold also is the skill with which it devises things incredible, and which is the mother of so many marvelous devices. These are unfailing signs of divinity in man."[36]

Given the frequent biblical juxtapositions of mind and heart (Matt. 22:37; Heb. 8:10; 10:16), *mind* (Gk. *dianoia*) is a more comprehensive reality than

---

35. Watchman Nee, *The Spiritual Man,* 3 vols. (New York: Christian Fellowship, 1968), 2:82, 84.
36. Calvin, *Institutes of the Christian Religion,* 1:57 [1.5.5].

intellectual capacity alone. Mind, relates Paul Jewett, "does not refer exclusively to 'reason' or 'understanding,' but to all that is indicated by self-consciousness; hence it overlaps in meaning with what has traditionally been called 'soul' or 'spirit' in theology."[37]

The reliability of human knowing is rooted in the rationality of God and the ordered and coherent nature of the cosmos. Jesus Christ—the Logos of God—is the source and ground of human rationality. The Logos ("word" or "reason") is "the true light that gives light to every man" (John 1:9). Through the Logos all things were brought into being (Col. 1:16), and in Him all things—including human rationality—subsist (Col. 1:17; Heb. 1:3).

### Volition: Intention, Decision, Determination to Love

Volition is the capacity for self-determination or the freedom to be who I am. "The freedom to determine myself as a subject is the basis of my responsibility to myself, to my neighbor, and ultimately to my God."[38] Volition also includes the capacity to choose goals and to select the strategies to achieve said goals. In these respects the will properly may be designated "the 'CEO' of the self."[39]

In the Old Testament, will originates from the human spirit *(rûaḥ)* or heart *(lēb)* and is indicated by the verb *bāḥar*, to "choose." The proverb succinctly states the will's function: "In his heart a man plans his course" (Prov. 16:9). At the very beginning of human history, God set before Adam and Eve in Eden the choice either to obey His will and live under His authority or to assert their own wills (Gen. 2:16–17). Humans are wise when they choose God's revealed will (cf. Isa. 1:19–20)—when they determine to obey, love, and serve the Creator. In the New Testament, volition is indicated by the verbs *boulomai* and *thelō*. The office of the will is "to choose and follow what the understanding pronounces good, but to reject and flee what it disapproves."[40] Willard adds, "Life must be organized by the will if it is to be organized at all. It can only be pulled together 'from the inside.' That is the function of the will or heart: to organize our life as a whole, and, indeed to organize it around God."[41]

---

37. Jewett, *Who We Are*, 9 n. 11.
38. Ibid., 62.
39. Willard, *Renovation of the Heart*, 153.
40. Calvin, *Institutes of the Christian Religion*, 1:194 [1.15.7].
41. Willard, *Renovation of the Heart*, 35.

The will, however, does not function in a vacuum or act independently. Intellect, desires, longings, and emotions present to the will matters for consideration. Our wills may be moved by wholesome or by evil motives, desires, and longings. Moreover, in order to choose, one must possess some feeling for the direction in which one wishes to go.

Love fundamentally is a volitional response. Whereas the French philosopher Jean-Paul Sartre (1905–1980) claimed that love is one person's freedom eating up another's freedom,[42] New Testament *agapē* is the settled purpose of the will that involves the whole person in seeking the well-being of another. *Agapē* is the love that claims and gives independent of the worth of the other person. The near synonym to love—"benevolence"—means "willing well." As Franz Delitzsch put it, "true love is good-will itself."[43] That love is a volitional determination is attested by the fact that God commands human beings to love as He loves us (1 John 4:7–8, 11–12, 16–21).

God created the human will in a state of freedom. In the *general sense,* freedom of will involves the ability to make choices and to act consistent with one's nature, independent of external constraint. Free will in this sense involves the ability to do what one desires to do (1 Cor. 7:37). Liberty does not involve the ability to choose or act contrary to one's nature. That humans are unable to run a two-minute mile, for example, does not imply that they are not free. In the *theological sense,* freedom involves the power of self-determination *and* the power of contrary choice in the moral and spiritual realms. Humans were created free in general and theological respects. Humans' most valuable freedom is "the divine freedom described by Augustine of wanting to do what we ought because we love God and take delight in Him."[44] Because they are created with free will, humans are responsible to God for their decisions and actions. God said to Israel, "I have set before you life and death, blessings and curses. Now choose life" (Deut. 30:19).

Significantly, God can move the human will without violating freedom (Ezra 1:5; Jer. 51:11; Phil. 2:12–13). The position whereby God and humans act in synergy to produce an outcome is known as *compatibilism* or *soft determinism.* One of many biblical examples of this is the hardening of the pharaoh's heart (cf. Exod. 9:12; 10:20 with Exod. 8:15; 9:34).

---

42. Cited by Jean Vanier, *Becoming Human* (New York: Paulist, 1998), 42.
43. Franz Delitzsch, *A System of Biblical Psychology* (Edinburgh: T. and T. Clark, 1869), 244. Willard, *Renovation of the Heart,* 131, describes love as the "will to good."
44. Lewis and Demarest, *Integrative Theology,* 2:158–59.

## Emotions

Humans possess the capacity to experience emotions, feelings, affections, and bodily sensations. Emotion is a state of the soul (e.g., joy, fear, anger) oriented outward toward an object beyond the self. An emotion need not always be felt, and its feeling may be inaccurate. Passion refers to intense emotion and mood to an aggregate of emotions, usually of longer duration. Feeling, on the other hand, is oriented inward, "always of the self-as-in-a-given-state"[45] (e.g., embarrassment, sadness, guilt). Akin to emotions, affections represent "set inclinations of heart with a feeling tone."[46] Sensation is a state of awareness that arises from the body (e.g., hunger, dizziness). Human emotions, feelings, and affections are closely associated with what we know and will, how we relate, and how we act in the moral realm. Human image-bearers are capable of a wide range of emotions, such as desire, joy, compassion, jealousy, pride, anger, disgust, guilt, and shame.

*Desire* represents an emotionally laden longing of the soul that motivates choices and actions. The Bible places considerable emphasis on the desires and longings of the human heart, the worthiest object being God. So the psalmist ruminates, "Whom have I in heaven but you? And being with you, I desire nothing on earth" (Ps. 73:25). Other objects of desire include God's will (Ps. 40:5–8), a spouse or lover (Song 7:10), and unspecified issues of life (Ps. 145:16; Prov. 10:24). Awe, or reverential fear, represents the heart's response to God's majesty, holiness, and power (Isa. 29:23; Mal. 2:5; Acts 2:43). Persons also can be in awe of the magnificence of the creation and of extraordinary human accomplishments.

*Joy* is the emotion of gladness or delight associated with an abundance of good things, both material (Acts 14:17) and spiritual (1 Chron. 15:25; 2 Chron. 30:21–25). Regardless of one's outward circumstances, walking with integrity and serving others delights the heart. The word *joy* occurs some fifty-five times in Israel's hymnbook, the Psalms. Humans find joy in God Himself (Pss. 16:11; 43:4), God's Word (Ps. 19:8), God-given victories (Esther 8:16–17), and the birth of a child (Luke 1:58).

*Compassion* (literally a "suffering with another") represents the profound

---

45. Robert C. Roberts, *Emotions: An Essay in Aid of Moral Psychology* (Cambridge: Cambridge University Press, 2003), 323.
46. J. I. Packer, *A Quest for Godliness: The Puritan Vision of the Christian Life* (Wheaton, Ill.: Crossway, 1990), 66.

emotion of concern for persons in need, usually accompanied by actions undertaken to relieve the distress.

A healthy *jealousy* is the righteous desire to claim and possess what is rightfully one's own (Prov. 6:34; Song 8:6).

*Pride* is the satisfying feeling of one's inherent worth.

Righteous *anger* is the emotion of indignation directed against injustice, betrayal, or other evil (Exod. 32:19; 1 Sam. 20:34). Extreme anger involves a heated rush of fury or rage. Scripture warns against allowing justifiable anger to become an occasion for sin (Ps. 4:4). In his ministry Jesus demonstrated the emotion of righteous anger (Mark 3:5; John 2:15–16).

*Disgust* is the emotion of loathing caused by what is offensive or reprehensible (Gen. 27:46; Ezek. 23:17, 18, 22, 28).

*Guilt* is the feeling that we have violated a binding moral law, and *shame* is the capacity to feel unworthy as a result of having committed a dishonorable act. In the positive sense, shame is a signal that we are not what we ought to be. "A healthy sense of shame is perhaps the surest sign of our divine origin and our human dignity."[47]

Since humans were created by God to experience a wide range of emotions and feelings, we must not suppress feelings, as Stoic philosophers urged, nor eliminate desires, as Buddhism demands. Humans find fulfillment as God-created emotions are properly expressed and negative emotions controlled. As William P. Wilson remarked, "Only in Christianity is man's emotional life given such a place of prominence."[48]

## Moral Capacity: Conscience

God created humans to live in a condition of moral rectitude. The "Preacher" put it simply: "God made mankind upright" (Eccl. 7:29a). There the descriptor *yāšār* means "disposed to faithfulness and obedience." With a clear soul, humans possess the moral capacity to know the difference between good and evil (Gen. 3:5, 22). Later Solomon prayed for the ability to "distinguish between right and wrong" (1 Kings 3:9). Conscience is the faculty of moral evaluation that dialogues between human thoughts and

---

47. Lewis B. Smedes, *Shame and Grace: Healing the Shame We Don't Deserve* (San Francisco, Calif.: HarperSanFrancisco, 1993), 32.
48. W. P. Wilson, "Emotion," in *Baker Encyclopedia of Psychology and Counseling,* ed. David G. Benner and P. C. Hill, 2d ed. (Grand Rapids: Baker, 1999), 358.

actions and God's law implanted on the heart (Rom. 2:14–15) and revealed in Scripture (Ps. 19:7–12). Conscience attests a person's compliance or noncompliance with the moral law with consequent approval or disapproval and hence blessing or punishment. Because they are morally constituted, humans are responsible to God for their thoughts, words, and deeds.

The Old Testament has no word that can be translated "conscience"; its operations are represented as a function of the heart. Thus Job testified, "My heart does not reproach my days" (Job 27:6). Proverbs 20:27 represents conscience as a lamp that illumines the human person's moral core. "The lamp of the LORD searches the spirit of a man; it searches out his innermost being." The New Testament word often translated conscience (*syneidēsis*, literally "co-knowing"), occurs thirty-two times. Referring to his sorrow and anguish vis-à-vis Jewish unbelief, Paul wrote, "I am not lying, my conscience confirms it in the Holy Spirit" (Rom. 9:1). Defending his apostolic ministry, Paul declared, "By setting forth the truth plainly we commend ourselves to every man's conscience in the sight of God" (2 Cor. 4:2; cf. 5:11).

Thus the human person as created is morally discerning. The faculty of conscience produces guilt and shame for failure to fulfill God's law and a sense of peace and well-being for compliance. God holds persons accountable for acting on moral principles guided by the dictates of their consciences. Through this inner moral compass, humans become their own judges. "A conscience at harmony with his Creator's will is the true pulse beat of his humanity."[49]

### Bodily Actions, Behavior, and Dominion Exercising

Within the unity of the human person, the physical body functions harmoniously with the mind, volition, emotions, desires, and moral sense. Because it is created by God, the body (contrary to Greek Platonism) is good and to be valued. Humans were fashioned to engage in meaningful, creative work, which provides for material necessities and enhances dignity and satisfaction. Clerics, monks, and nuns engage in no more meaningful work than do God-fearing housewives and clerks. Work includes the God-ordained task of tending the earth and administering its affairs (Gen. 1:26,

---

49. Philip Edgcumbe Hughes, *The True Image: The Origin and Destiny of Man in Christ* (Grand Rapids: Eerdmans, 1989), 60.

28; 2:19–20; Ps. 8:5–8). The Old Testament describes many creative endeavors, such as the development of language (Gen. 2:20), farming (2:15; 3:23; 4:2; 9:20), domestication of animals (4:2), and playing musical instruments (4:21). People create by establishing cities (4:17), constructing buildings, (11:3–4), governing subjects (1 Kings 3:9), writing literature (4:32), and developing science and technology (1 Kings 4:33; Job 28:1–10). The development of structured human civilization is a creative enterprise. In order to fulfill the cultural mandate, humans must apply intellect, imagination, memory, and aesthetic sense to technology, manufacturing, medicine, the humanities, and the fine arts.

Human labor represents a calling and provision of God rooted in the Creation, not the Fall. Scripture depicts work as part of the fabric of a good life and as a gift (Eccl. 3:13; 5:18–19). Two extremes, however, must be avoided. Laziness leads to poverty (Prov. 6:9–11; Eccl. 10:18), and overwork can be addictive. To avoid the latter God ordained the Sabbath day of rest (Exod. 31:12–17), patterned after His own rest following six days of creative activity (Gen. 2:2–3). The goal for which we humans must strive is reasonable diligence (Prov. 10:4; 21:5), to which God adds His blessing (Ps. 127:1–2).

## The Nexus of Human Functioning

Various capacities of the human soul are inextricably interrelated. Within the unity of the person, there occurs the complex interplay of intellect, volition, emotion, desire, moral sense, bodily actions, and behaviors. The mind informs the will (choices), and the will shapes the mind (John 7:17). The will energizes emotions (as in love), and emotions reinforce the will. Emotions generate energy that impels behaviors, and behaviors shape emotions. Behaviors impact the mind, and the mind directs behaviors. Feelings direct behaviors, and behaviors shape feelings. One's moral sense or conscience guides behaviors, and behaviors have an impact on conscience and shape moral character. And so the interactions multiply.

The terms *soul*, *spirit*, and *heart* (see chap. 4, pp. 130–34) take in these dynamic interactions. The one human person thinks, wills, feels, senses obligation, relates, and acts. Steve Shores sums up this interaction of faculties:

> God designed us to be integrated, whole beings, with emotion, mind, imagination, will, and body working together in complete harmony.

Otherwise, why would he command us to love him with all our heart, soul, mind, and strength (Deut. 6:5; Mark 12:30)? Inner unity, not fragmentation, is our heritage. Wholeness is our birthright, not an internal chaos where one capacity competes with the others for domination.[50]

## HUMAN FUNCTIONING UNDER SIN

### Historical Perspectives

Those who have accepted the historicity of the fall of Adam have struggled to understand what happened to the inner man when the first man sinned. A number of views have been suggested.

#### Functioning Unimpaired by Sin

According to the tradition that humans are mostly unspoiled by Adam's sin, his actions affected only himself. Humans are still born into the world with faculties intact, including a natural freedom of will, or the ability to do what is right without divine assistance.

Faced with the obvious fact of human wrongdoing, evolutionary scientism claims that humans have had insufficient time to tame the beast within. Humanistic educators wistfully imagine that persons will behave humanely when they gain sufficient knowledge. Geneticists allege that humans act irresponsibly because of defective genes. Sociologists blame violent behavior on faulty social environments.

Denying original sin, the British monk Pelagius insisted that Adam's descendants are born free from depravity. Humans are able to perform God's requirements without recourse to empowering grace. Pelagius reasoned that if persons were incapable of obeying God's commands, they could not be punished for failing to do so. Pelagians have believed that some persons, such as Abel and John the Baptist, lived sinless lives. Others sin by following negative examples. Pelagianism's full-blown optimism regarding human nature was condemned at the councils of Carthage (418) and Ephesus (431).

Unitarians insist that infants are born into the world morally upright or at worst morally neutral. That helpless infants should enter the world in-

---

50. Steve Shores, *Minding Your Emotions* (Colorado Springs, Colo.: NavPress, 2002), 79

clined to evil and subject to punishment is considered repugnant to the notion of a benevolent God. According to Harvard divinity professor Henry Ware (1764–1845), "Man is by nature . . . innocent and pure; free from all moral corruption. . . . He has natural affections, all of them originally good, but liable by a wrong direction to be the occasion of error and sin."[51] Unitarians typically define sin as antisocial behavior.

Many have decided with humanist Corliss Lamont that God is an illusion and the fall of the human race into sin a myth. "Modern medicine," Lamont said, "has demonstrated that many undesirable human traits which used to be ascribed to original sin or bad character are actually attributable to glandular insufficiencies or deep-seated emotional frustrations."[52] Human beings, he alleges, can achieve their destinies. "Humanism, having its ultimate faith in man, believes that human beings possess the power or potentiality of solving their own problems, through reliance primarily upon reason and scientific method applied with courage and vision."[53]

Lamont insisted that moral freedom is necessary for moral responsibility. He said that humanism "believes that human beings, while conditioned by the past, possess genuine freedom of creative choices and actions, and are, within certain objective limits, the masters of their own destiny."[54]

*Humanist Manifesto III* (2003) disavows the existence of God while affirming human autonomy, omnicompetence, and freedom. The document states, "Humanism is a progressive philosophy of life that, without supernaturalism, affirms our ability and responsibility to lead ethical lives of personal fulfillment that aspire to the greater good of humanity."[55] It adds, "The responsibility for our lives and the kind of world in which we live is ours and ours alone."

## Functioning Weakened by Sin

A little less optimistic are those who go so far as to say that human beings are born spiritually weak. But that doesn't mean they are unable to help themselves, but only that they need some divine assistance. Reacting against

---

51. Cited by H. Shelton Smith, *Changing Conceptions of Original Sin* (New York: Scribner, 1955), 245.
52. Corliss Lamont, *The Philosophy of Humanism* (New York: Frederick Ungar, 1982), 233.
53. Ibid., 13.
54. Ibid.
55. *Humanist Manifesto III*, http://www.americanhumanist.org/3 (accessed June 15, 2004).

Augustine's teaching, Semi-Pelagian theologians such as John Cassian (360–435), Vincent of Lerins (d. c. 450), Hilary of Arles (d. 449), and Faustus of Riez (c. 405–c. 490) admitted that Adam's descendants inherit a tendency to sin. As persons actualize their weakened human natures and commit discrete sins, they become morally accountable. Semi-Pelagianism was condemned at the Council of Orange (529).

John Cassian rejected the positions of both Pelagius and Augustine on sin and grace. He believed that humans are afflicted with only a tendency to evil and envisioned God's grace as but assistance to natural human capacities. "When [God] notices good will making an appearance in us, he at once enlightens and encourages it ands spurs it on to salvation, giving increase to what he himself planted and saw arise from our own efforts."[56] Cassian posited a libertine view of the human will: "There always remains in the human being a free will that can either neglect or love the grace of God."[57]

As noted (pp. 145–46), Roman Catholic anthropology distinguishes between "image" (human natural qualities) and "likeness" (righteousness and holiness). Due to the Fall the likeness was lost, but the image remains unscathed except for "concupiscence." Catholic theology thus takes a rather optimistic view of human powers. Such things as thinking, willing, and feeling are weakened by sin, not radically corrupted. The Council of Trent (1545–63) claimed that Adam's sin "injured" the human race. For example, "If anyone saith that, since Adam's sin, the free-will of man is lost and extinguished; . . . let him be anathema."[58] The recent *Catechism of the Catholic Church* maintains that human nature is "weakened" and "wounded."[59] "Original sin," according to *Catechism*, "is a depravation of original holiness and justice, but human nature has not been totally corrupted: it is wounded in the natural powers proper to it; subject to ignorance, suffering, and the dominion of death; and inclined to sin—an inclination to evil that is called 'concupiscence.'"[60]

---

56. John Cassian, *The Conferences,* ACW (New York: Paulist, 1997), 474 [13.8.4]. Cf. ibid., 478 [13.11.5]: "For when God sees us turning in order to will what is good, he comes to us, directs us, and strengthens us. . . ."

57. Ibid., 480 [13.12.8].

58. *The Canons and Decrees of Trent,* session VI, canon 5, in *The Creeds of Christendom,* ed. Philip Schaff, 3 vols. (Grand Rapids: Baker, 1977), 2:111.

59. *Catechism of the Catholic Church* (New York: Doubleday, 1995), 115, 117 [nos. 407, 417, 418].

60. Ibid., 114 [no. 405].

Arminian theologians believe that prevenient grace that flows from Christ's Cross nullifies the effects of depravity. Thus, human powers crippled by sin are restored. John Wesley (1703–1791) generally followed Reformation teaching that Adam's sin passed down to the entire human race, although he is not clear as to how he believed this occurred. Yet Wesley asserted that from the Cross there flows to all human beings prevenient grace that restores in measure human functioning. This grace—"free for ALL as well as in ALL"[61]—renews the mind and will, such that humans are able to work out their salvation.

Thus "there is no man that is in a state of mere nature; there is no man, unless he has quenched the Spirit, that is wholly void of the grace of God. . . . Every one has some measure of that light, some faint glimmering ray, which, sooner or later, more or less, enlightens every man that cometh into the world."[62] Concerning this grace, Wesley adds, "Something of this is found in every human heart, passing sentence concerning good and evil, not only in all Christians, but in all Mahometans, [*sic*] all pagans, yea, the vilest of savages."

Charles Finney (1792–1875) rejected the notion that Adam's descendants are born with a sinful nature. Depravity is not a radical corruption of natural human faculties as a deprivation thereof. Finney linked freedom of will with moral responsibility: "Moral obligation implies moral agency and moral agency implies freedom of will. A just command always implies an ability to obey it."[63]

Finney rejected Wesley's notion of "gracious ability," judging that it implied human inability, which would undercut human responsibility. Indeed, Finney affirmed that sinners are capable apart from supernatural new birth of changing the dispositions of their hearts and reforming their lives.

### Functioning Crippled by Sin

Others believe that the effect of sin was disabling or death to all ability. Adam and Eve's disobedience brought upon themselves and their

---

61. John Wesley, "Free Grace," in *The Works of John Wesley*, 3d ed., 14 vols. (Grand Rapids: Baker, reprint, 1978), 7:374.
62. Cited in Robert W. Burtner and Robert E. Chiles, eds., *A Compend of Wesley's Theology* (Nashville: Abingdon, 1954), 148–49.
63. J. W. Jepson, ed., *A Digest of Finney's Systematic Theology* (Lyons, Ore.: J. W. Jepson, 1970), 58.

descendants guilt, depravity, and the sentence of condemnation. By virtue of original sin, natural faculties of mind, will, emotions, moral sense, and so on are seriously corrupted. Righteousness and holiness are altogether lost. Because the unsaved live in bondage to sin, divine illumination and special grace are required to obey the gospel.

Augustine judged that Adam's self-sufficiency and pride brought upon him and all his descendants guilt, depravity (corruption of nature and evil dispositions), and liability for eternal punishment. The corrupt tree (Adam and Eve) brings forth corrupt fruit (humanity). The fallen mind is blind to spiritual truths, the will is hostile to God,[64] emotions are disordered, conscience is defiled, behavior is corrupted, and the body decays. The unsaved supplant love for eternal things (the city of God) with a desire *(libido)* for passing, temporal things (the city of this world). Augustine insisted that sinners' resemblance to God has been distorted but not obliterated. "God's image has not been so completely erased in the soul of man by the stain of earthly affections as to have left remaining there not even the merest lineaments of it."[65]

Martin Luther likewise posited the pervasive depravity of the unregenerate human heart. By virtue of Adam's rebellion, the human race is corrupted, judicially guilty, and liable to condemnation. Righteousness and holiness have been altogether lost, whereas the natural faculties of intellect, will, and emotions are diseased. In *On the Bondage of the Will* (and other writings), Luther affirmed that the human will is bound by sin in the spiritual realm. "Godward, or in things that pertain to salvation or damnation, he has no 'free-will,' but is a captive, slave, and servant, either to the will of God, or to the will of Satan."

More comprehensively, Luther insisted, "All our faculties are leprous, indeed, dull and utterly dead."[66] Common grace enables unbelievers to perform acts of civil righteousness; but God's saving grace empowers the mind and will to receive the gift of eternal life.

According to John Calvin, depravity is total in that it defiles every aspect of

---

64. Augustine stressed that the will is bound (not free) apart from grace: "A man's free-will, indeed, avails for nothing, except to sin, if he knows not the way of truth" (Augustine, *On the Spirit and the Letter* 5 [*NPNF*[1], 5:84–85]). "The fact is that the human will does not achieve grace through freedom, but rather freedom through grace. . . ." (Augustine, *Admonition and Grace* 8 [*FOTC*, 2:265–66]).

65. Augustine, *On the Spirit and the Letter* 48 [*NPNF*[1], 5:103].

66. Martin Luther, *Lectures on Genesis,* 2 vols., *LW,* 1:66.

human nature and functioning. "The whole man is overwhelmed—as by a deluge—from head to foot, so that no part is immune from sin."[67] The sinner's natural capacities are distorted and corrupted. According to Calvin, "man's mind, because of its dullness, cannot hold to the right path, but wanders through various errors and stumbles repeatedly, as if it were groping in darkness."[68] Moreover, "the will . . . was so bound to wicked desires that it cannot strive after the right."[69] By God's common grace the unregenerate are capable of many noble intellectual and artistic achievements. The powers of faith, love for God, and holiness, however, are completely lost in the unregenerate. "Our own insight . . . is utterly blind and stupid in divine matters."[70] The *imago Dei* is deeply tarnished, with only remnants surviving.

Article X of The Thirty-Nine Articles of the Church of England (1579) reads:

> The condition of man after the fall of Adam is such, that he cannot turn and prepare himself, by his own natural strength and good works, to faith; and calling upon God. Wherefore we have no power to do good works pleasant and acceptable to God, without the grace of God by Christ preventing us, that we may have a good will, and working with us, when we have that good will.

The Westminster Confession of Faith (1647), chapter 6.2, states concerning the sin of Adam and Eve: "They fell from their original righteousness and fellowship with God, and so became dead in sin and completely polluted in all their faculties and parts of body and soul." Chapter 6.4 affirms that "from this original corruption, whereby we are utterly indisposed, disabled, and made opposite to all good, and wholly inclined to all evil, do proceed all actual transgressions."

## Biblical and Theological Development

### Historic Fall of Adam and Eve

Adam and Eve were real time-space persons, and the Genesis record of their rebellion is historically factual—no less so than the account of the

---

67. Calvin, *Institutes of the Christian Religion,* 1:253 [2.1.9].
68. Ibid., 1:271 [2.2.12].
69. Ibid.
70. Ibid., 1:278 [2.2.19].

origins of the earth, vegetation, fish, and animal life likewise recorded in Genesis 1:1, 11–12, 20–22, 24–25. God placed the first pair in a paradise with provision for their every need. As a test of Adam and Eve's willingness to live under the Creator's lordship, God placed in the midst of the garden the "tree of the knowledge of good and evil" (Gen. 2:9), the fruit of which He forbade them to eat (v. 17). Satan in the form of a serpent seduced the couple to disobey the Lord of life by eating the forbidden fruit. The record of Adam and Eve's unbelief and elevation of self-will accounts for the origin of moral evil in the human race. Jesus (John 8:44) and Paul (1 Tim. 2:14) certified as historical fact that the human race fell into sin.

### Effects of the Fall on the First Pair

By choosing self-autonomy, Adam and Eve lost integrity. As lawbreakers they experienced *objective guilt*, symbolized by the shame of nakedness (Gen. 3:7) and reflected in the fear of God's wrath (v. 10).[71] The first pair also experienced *estrangement from*, or loss of fellowship with, God (vv. 8–10). Instead of enjoying blissful communion with their Creator, Adam and Eve fled from His presence. The first couple also experienced *depravity*, a sinful heart or the pervasive inclination to sin, evidenced by their evasive answers to God's questioning (vv. 11–13).

The effects of the Fall on the woman were pain-filled births and unfulfilling competition with men (v. 16). The results of the Fall upon the man were strenuous labor in a sin-cursed environment (vv. 17–19). The man and the woman would experience *physical death* (v. 19), symbolized by banishment from the garden lest they eat of the tree of life and live forever (vv. 22–24).

### The Spread of Sin

Adam and Eve's sinfulness passed to their offspring. Cain, their eldest son, hated and then murdered his brother, Abel (Gen. 4:8). Seth, the third son, experienced death, the stated penalty of sin (Gen. 5:8). Early in humankind's history we read, "The LORD saw how great man's wickedness on the earth had become, and that every inclination of the thoughts of his

---

71. Delitzsch, *System of Biblical Psychology,* 162: "Looking upon their nakedness, they are seized with shame; and perceiving God's nearness they are seized with fear."

heart was only evil all the time" (Gen. 6:5). Again, "the earth was corrupt in God's sight and was full of violence" (v. 11; cf. 8:21). The biblical record testifies to human tyranny, brutality, corruption, sexual perversions, and superstition. The book of Job describes "man, who is vile and corrupt, who drinks up evil like water" (Job 15:16). The psalmist affirms that none understand and seek after God (Ps. 14:2-3). According to the Teacher, "There is not a righteous man on earth who does what is right and never sins" (Eccl. 7:20).

Pauper, prince, and professor all suffer the scourges of sin. The history book and the daily newspaper tell the grim tale of human corruption reflected in drug trafficking, Internet pornography, domestic violence, and white-collar crimes. We are horrified to read accounts of Nazi, Russian, and Cambodian exterminations of millions, through the 1994 Rwandan genocide, in which a million innocents were slaughtered.

The Old Testament teaches that all persons are born with a perverted nature. After his sins of adultery and murder, David confessed, "Surely I have been a sinner from birth, sinful from the time my mother conceived me" (Ps. 51:5; cf. 58:3).

The book of 2 Esdras reflects Jewish thought between the Testaments: "O Adam, what have you done? For though it was you who sinned, the fall was not yours alone, but ours also who are your descendants" (2 Esdras 7:48; cf. Sirach 25:24).

In the New Testament, Paul argues that Adam's disobedience brought guilt and condemnation (liability for punishment) upon the entire human race: "The many died by the trespass of the one man" (Rom. 5:15). "By the trespass of the one man, death reigned through that one man" (v. 17). "The result of one trespass was condemnation for all men" (v. 18). "Through the disobedience of the one man the many were made sinners" (v. 19). In his first letter to the Corinthians, Paul added, "Death came through a man" (1 Cor. 15:21) and "in Adam all die" (v. 22). Original sin refers to the depravity and guilt humankind incurs through its connection with Adam. Discrete sins occur as humans actualize their fallen natures in the form of unrighteous thoughts, words, and deeds.

Theologians have proffered explanations as to how Adam's sin affected every person born into the world. The *covenantal,* or *federal headship, view* states that Adam legally represented all humanity, much as a president acts on behalf of the nation's citizens. In what Reformed scholars designate the "covenant of works" established between God and Adam, Adam's guilt and penalty were imputed to the human race he represented. The *seminal*, or *natural headship, view* states that the first pair transmitted to their offspring a fallen nature through procreation (cf. John 3:6), a view that takes seriously the realistic solidarity of the human race (Gen. 3:20; Acts 17:26). Scripture does not explicitly address this question, but a combination of the two views may account for the biblical data. As humanity's legal head, Adam represented the entire human family. As humanity's biological head, the entire human race was in Adam in undistributed form and so received from him a corrupted nature.

## Sin's Effects on Adam and Eve's Unredeemed Descendants

The Bible realistically portrays human functioning as diminished by the effects of sin. All humans possess fallen natures with impaired abilities to know, love, and serve God. Scripture paints a vivid mural of human functioning following the Fall.

**Intellectually, on the Mind.** Sin distorts human rational processes, particularly in the spiritual realm. In matters relating to the kingdom, the sinful mind is afflicted with darkness, being blind to truths about God and His redemptive purposes. Isaiah wrote, "The ox knows his master, the donkey his owner's manger, but Israel does not know, my people do not understand" (Isa. 1:3; cf. Ps. 92:6). Concerning the Gentile world, Paul wrote, "For although they knew God, they neither glorified him as God nor gave thanks to him, but their thinking became futile and their foolish hearts were darkened. Although they claimed to be wise, they became fools" (Rom. 1:21–22). Spiritual realities appear to unregenerate minds (lacking the Holy Spirit) as foolish and absurd. "The man without the Spirit does not *accept* [*dechomai*, "receive," "welcome"] the things that come from the Spirit of God, for they are *foolishness* [*mōria*] to him, and he cannot understand them, because they are spiritually discerned" (1 Cor. 2:14). See also Ephesians 4:17–18; Colossians 2:18; 1 Timothy 6:4–5; Titus 1:15; and Jude 10.

Paul attributes sinners' blindness to the Evil One: "The god of this age has blinded the minds of unbelievers, so that they cannot see the light of the gospel of the glory of Christ, who is the image of God" (2 Cor. 4:4). The Bible recognizes a "wisdom," so-called, vaunted by the unsaved (1 Cor. 1:17,

19, 21–22, 25), but such wisdom is "earthly, unspiritual, of the devil" (James 3:15). Scripture testifies, in the words of Gordon Lewis and Bruce Demarest, that "human mental efforts in the direction of spiritual experience and religion are plagued by error and resist the clear evidence of truth."[72]

**Volitionally, on the Will.** Post-Fall human wills are inclined to sinful motives, decisions, and choices. Unregenerate persons use their volitional powers to pursue selfish goals and devise sinful intentions rather than choosing for God and His purposes. Zedekiah, the last king of Judah, "rebelled against King Nebuchadnezzar. . . . He became stiff-necked and hardened his heart and would not turn to the LORD, the God of Israel" (2 Chron. 36:13). The psalmist warned, "Today, if you hear his voice, do not harden your hearts as you did at Meribah, as you did that day at Massah in the desert, where your fathers tested and tried me" (Ps. 95:7-8). Non-Christians boast of their freedom, but G. C. Berkouwer pronounces the judgment that "the call for freedom, which can be heard in all ages . . . is nothing but the lust for lawlessness."[73] Psalm 2:3 and 2 Peter 2:19 add further testimony to this truth.

The unconverted, moreover, suffer misdirected loves. The unsaved typically love self (2 Tim. 3:2), the world system (1 John 2:15), evil (1 Cor. 13:6; 2 Peter 2:15), wickedness (2 Peter 2:15), money (1 Tim. 6:10; 2 Tim. 3:2; Heb. 13:5), and pleasure (2 Tim. 3:4). Misdirected love readily morphs into enmity. The sinful mind is hostile to the Lord (Rom. 8:7) because the true God challenges its false gods. Scripture teaches that the world "hates" Jesus and the Father (John 15:18, 24–25), as well as God's people (John 17:14). The judgment stands that, when brought face-to-face with the righteous God and His demands, fallen humans become insolent and rebel.

Much discussion focuses on the issue of the freedom or bondage of the will in the unconverted. Since persons choose according to their natures, unregenerate people lack the motivation as well as the ability to honor God. Scripture depicts the will of the unsaved as held captive by the sin principle (Rom. 6:6, 16, 20), the "law of sin" (Rom. 7:25), the sinful nature (2 Peter 2:19), sundry lusts and passions (Titus 3:3), sinful practices (John 8:34), and evil powers (2 Tim. 2:26). Paul describes the unregenerate as spiritually lifeless, or "dead in . . . transgressions and sins" (Eph. 2:1; cf. Col. 2:13).

---

72. Lewis and Demarest, *Integrative Theology,* 2:213.
73. G. C. Berkouwer, *Man: The Image of God,* trans. Dirk W. Jellema (Grand Rapids: Eerdmans, 1962), 330.

Through persistent sinning, the unconverted lose the freedom of will with which they were endowed at the first. "The evil deeds of a wicked man ensnare him; the cords of his sin hold him fast" (Prov. 5:22). Furthermore, "Their deeds do not permit them to return to their God" (Hos. 5:4). Although volitionally impotent spiritually, the unregenerate nevertheless bear responsibility for their sinful intentions. The compatibilism of a bound will and personal responsibility is illustrated by a severely intoxicated person who is incapable of driving his car safely but who nevertheless is responsible before the law for causing an accident while trying to drive under the influence of alcohol.

Christian theology following Augustine has defined the nature of freedom in four states:

1. Before the Fall, Adam and Eve possessed the power of self-determination *and* contrary choice (i.e., to honor or dishonor God).
2. After the Fall, the unregenerate possess the power of self-determination but have lost the power of contrary choice in the spiritual realm.
3. In the regenerate state the saved, endowed with an old nature and a new nature, possess the power of self-determination *and* the power of contrary choice morally and spiritually (i.e., they can choose to walk after the flesh or according to the Spirit).
4. In the glorified state, confirmed in righteousness, the redeemed will *not* have the power of contrary choice in the sense of having the ability to sin. Calvin stated, "Simply to will is of man; to will ill, of a corrupt nature; to will well, of grace."[74] We must not glibly profess "freedom of the will" but define precisely what it means and how it applies in the various human, spiritual states.

**Emotionally, on Desires, Feelings, and Affections.** Sin causes a disordering of the human desires, emotions, affections, and feelings. The apostle Paul wrote, "All of us also lived among them [i.e., the disobedient] at one time, gratifying the cravings (*epithymia* can refer to a strong desire or lust[75]) of our sinful nature and following its desires and thoughts" (Eph. 2:3; cf. 1 John 2:16). Within the human heart there lurks "evil desire" by which one

---

74. Calvin, *Institutes of the Christian Religion,* 1:295 [2.3.5].
75. Cleon L. Rogers Jr. and Cleon L. Rogers III, *NLEKGNT,* 571.

"is dragged away and enticed" (James 1:14). Similarly, "when we were controlled by the sinful nature, the sinful passions (*pathēma*, "passion, strong physical desires"[76]) aroused by the law were at work in our bodies, so that we bore fruit for death" (Rom. 7:5). James teaches that the source of all quarrels and conflicts are the "desires that battle within" (James 4:1). Even twice-born Christians are assailed by "sinful desires, which war against [the] soul" (1 Peter 2:11). Every human emotion becomes corrupted when it falls under sin's power. Consider the following:

Sinful *pride* (Prov. 16:18), the inordinate feeling of one's importance, is the antithesis of humility and love. The unredeemed person is a little Nebuchadnezzar, whose "heart became arrogant and hardened with pride" (Dan. 5:20).

*Envy* (*phthonos*)—the proverbial "green-eyed monster"—is the strong emotion of wanting what another person possesses. James writes, "The spirit [God] caused to live in us tends toward envy" (4:5). The Scripture repeatedly inveighs against the sin of envy (Job 5:2; Rom. 1:29; Gal. 5:21; Titus 3:3; James 3:14). The tenth commandment prohibits the related emotion of *covetousness* (Exod. 20:17), which is described as a root of all sorts of evil (1 Tim. 6:10). Greed represents a heightened form of covetousness (1 Cor. 5:10–11; Eph. 5:5; Col. 3:5). *Jealousy* (The Heb. verb *qānāʾ* literally means "to become red or flushed.") is the desire born out of covetousness to possess what is not rightfully one's own (Prov. 27:4; Rom. 13:13; 1 Cor. 3:3).

*Hatred* (Prov. 10:12) involves the intense emotion of hostility toward another person. Paul writes, "At one time we . . . lived in malice and envy, being hated and hating one another" (Titus 3:3).

*Lust* is wrongly directed desire or appetite (Col. 3:5; 1 Peter 4:3), including misdirected sexual desire (Rom. 1:27). Lust results in pollution of soul and body, which in turn leads to crimes against others.

Some passions related to the Fall are not sins, but they can relate to sinful emotions. *Fear* as fright (Ps. 55:5; Rom. 8:15; Heb. 2:15) fills the heart with terror. Unsaved hearts are stubbornly haunted by the fear of death (Heb. 2:15). Unhealthy fear diminishes functioning and growth to maturity. *Anxiety* is the restless distress the soul feels in a threatening world when disconnected from God (Prov. 12:25; Isa. 57:20–21). *Emptiness* (Isa. 32:6; Luke 1:53; 1 Peter 1:18) is the feeling that one's life is destitute of significance.

---

76. Ibid., 328.

*Sorrow* connotes grief, sadness, or regret caused by misfortune or loss (Ps. 6:7; Jer. 20:18). *Despondency* and despair represent feelings of hopelessness and gloom. Wistfully the psalmist writes, "Why are you downcast, O my soul? Why so disturbed within me? (Ps. 42:5; cf. v. 11; Ps. 43:5; 2 Cor. 7:6).

*Resentment* is the emotion of displeasure directed toward another who threatens or inflicts injury (Job 5:2; 36:13).

Sinful *anger* (Prov. 27:4; 2 Cor. 12:20; James 1:20)—kindled by fear, pride, or jealousy—is the strong emotion of hostility accompanied by the impulse to cause harm to another. Sinful anger incites further evils such as strife (Prov. 30:33) and dissension (Prov. 29:22). Rage is a form of vehement anger. When Shadrach, Meshach, and Abednego refused to worship Nebuchadnezzar's golden image, the king was "furious with rage" (Dan. 3:13). Paul identifies "fits of rage" as an effect of the sinful nature (Gal. 5:20; cf. Col. 3:8). Often rage is impelled by a fragile or wounded ego.

Subjective guilt represents the feeling of having violated a universal moral standard (1 Cor. 8:7; 1 John 3:20). Unhealthy or undeserved shame (2 Sam. 19:3; Ps. 44:15) is the feeling of unworthiness and self-contempt by virtue of what others have done to us (e.g., rape or other forms of violence) or what has been projected upon us (e.g., the sense of unworthiness for being poor, black, or undereducated).

Sinful desires and feelings constitute powerful triggers for destructive actions. James writes, "Each one is tempted when, by his own evil desire, he is dragged away and enticed. Then, after desire has conceived, it gives birth to sin; and sin, when it is full-grown, gives birth to death" (James 1:14–15). Let us recognize the potential for ill in distorted emotions and feelings, for feelings often are the targets of Satan's assaults.

**Morally, on the Ethical Life.** Objectively, sin forfeits righteousness and incurs guilt before God (Ps. 32:5; Jer. 2:22; John 16:8). Subjectively, sin is experienced as a guilty conscience (Heb. 10:22) that weighs down and distances the soul from God. Luther rightly observed that "the Holy Spirit cannot live in a man who is guilty of gross sins of any kind against conscience."[77] Because he had sinfully taken a census of Israel, "David was conscience-stricken after he had counted the fighting men, and he said to the LORD, 'I have sinned greatly in what I have done'" (2 Sam. 24:10). After Judas had

---

77. Cited in Ewald M. Plass, comp., *What Luther Says* (St. Louis, Mo.: Concordia, 1986), 335.

betrayed Jesus and witnessed the Lord's unjust fate, "He was seized with remorse . . ." (Matt. 27:3). The fruit of an accusing conscience is inner restlessness (Isa. 57:20–21), self-hatred (Ezek. 20:43), psychosomatic symptoms (Ps. 38:5–10), a troubling sense of disease (Ps. 32:3–4), and in extreme instances suicide (so Judas). "'There is no peace,' says the LORD, 'for the wicked'" (Isa. 48:22).

When repeatedly violated, conscience ceases to serve as an accurate monitor of moral obligation. As sin becomes deeply ingrained, conscience becomes "weak" and "defiled" (1 Cor. 8:7), "corrupted" (Titus 1:15), and "seared" (1 Tim. 4:2), resulting in loss of moral discrimination and sensitivity (Eph. 4:19). In such a state, evil is perceived as good, and good is perceived as evil (Isa. 5:20). What is impure is thought to be pure, and what is pure is thought to be impure (cf. Titus 1:15). The sinful violation of conscience has serious consequences; lacking a moral compass, faith becomes shipwrecked (1 Tim. 1:19).

**On Personal Functioning, Behavior, and Dominion.** Under sin the body becomes the vehicle through which distorted thoughts, desires, emotions, and appetites are lived out. The physical body itself is not sinful but is the instrument through which the soul's fallen faculties exert their negative effects. The Bible candidly chronicles the behaviors of the sinful nature. Paul writes concerning the Gentile world, "They have given themselves over to sensuality so as to indulge in every kind of impurity, with a continual lust for more" (Eph. 4:19). Prior to conversion we "were foolish, disobedient, deceived and enslaved by all kinds of passions and pleasures. We lived in malice and envy, being hated and hating one another" (Titus 3:3). The Bible describes unregenerate persons as producing corrupt and deceitful speech (1 Peter 3:10), drunkenness and carousing (1 Peter 4:3), acts of violence (Rom. 3:15), thievery (Mark 7:21), adultery (Mark 7:21), fornication (Rom. 1:24), murder (Exod. 2:12), and social oppression (Ezek. 22:7; Amos 5:12; Mic. 7:2–3). Those who repress the light of the knowledge of God, according to St. Paul, "become filled with every kind of wickedness, evil, greed and depravity. They are full of envy, murder, strife, deceit and malice. They are gossips, slanderers, God-haters, insolent, arrogant and boastful; they invent ways of doing evil; they disobey their parents; they are senseless, faithless, heartless, ruthless" (Rom. 1:29–31).

Concerning the cultural mandate, humans have fallen short in the task of exercising dominion. Instead of discharging responsible stewardship, humans have depleted natural resources, eliminated many fish and animal species, polluted air, ground, and water, diminished the ozone layer, and destroyed rain forests. One need not be a rabid environmentalist to grieve the careless exploitation of God's good creation. In just a few generations we will have expended earth's known petroleum deposits. In the United States, 6 percent of the world's population consumes 25 percent of the world's natural resources and 35 percent of the petroleum produced worldwide. Beyond the ecological sphere, human civilization is inflicted with exponential population growth, a massive AIDS crisis, endemic poverty, and widespread starvation. Brilliant developments in the technological arena have been perverted into weapons designed to destroy lives on a massive scale. We humans have abused the God-given charge to serve the needs of others. "Our best attempts to fulfill the cultural mandate tend to be tainted with unworthy motives," Lewis and Demarest write. "Our best efforts in religion, philosophy, the sciences, the fine arts, personal religion, or social reform fail to please the Most High."[78]

**Sinful Human Nature and the *Imago Dei*.** The theological term *depravity* asserts the evil nature of the human heart. The book of Job speaks of "man, who is vile and corrupt, who drinks up evil like water!" (Job 15:16). Through Jeremiah the Lord declares, "The heart is deceitful [Heb. *ʿāqōb*, "crooked"] above all things and beyond cure [Heb. *ʾānûš*, "sick"]. Who can understand it?" (Jer. 17:9; cf. Isa. 1:4). The compassionate Jesus diagnosed the human heart as pervasively evil (Matt. 7:11). Inveighing against the teachers of the law and the Pharisees, He said, "On the outside you appear to people as righteous but on the inside you are full of hypocrisy and wickedness" (Matt. 23:28). The apostle Paul stated that from the "earthly nature" flow "sexual immorality, impurity, lust, evil desires and greed" (Col. 3:5). See also Philippians 2:15 and Titus 1:15. Paul upheld human depravity in the word *sarx*, translated in the NIV as "sinful nature" (e.g., Rom. 7:5, 18, 25; 8:3–5; 1 Cor. 5:5; Gal. 5:13) or "sinful mind" (Rom. 8:7). Peter wrote about false prophets and teachers who promise "freedom, while they themselves are slaves of depravity" (Gk. *phthora*, "corruption," 2 Peter 2:19). Peter's words confirm the judgment that by repetitive acts of sin the unregenerate find themselves "controlled by the sinful nature" (Rom. 8:8–9) or indentured to sin (cf. Prov. 5:22; John 8:34; Rom. 6:6, 16–17, 20). J. Barton Payne

---

78. Lewis and Demarest, *Integrative Theology*, 2:211–12.

puts it that depravity means that "man's nature . . . drives him to sin like the compulsion of an animal in heat (Jer. 2:24–25)."[79] It implies that the root of evil in the world politically, economically, and socially is sited in each of us, not fundamentally in the environment, institutions, or lack of education. The observation of Pascal is still true that for those separated from Christ, "there is only vice, wretchedness, error, darkness, death, despair."[80]

Whereas some theologians speak of "total depravity," the term *holistic depravity* is more accurate. Total depravity suggests that unregenerate persons are as evil as they could possibly be, whereas holistic depravity indicates that no human capacity has escaped sin's pollution. According to Lewis and Demarest, "the mind is not exempt, as some rationalists imagine. The conscience is not exempt, as some moralists think. The emotions are not exempt, as some romanticists might wish. And the will is not exempt from the taint of sin, as some activists might hope."[81] Apart from God's grace, sinners are incapable of altering their dispositions (Job 14:4; Jer. 13:23; John 6:44, 65). Given the remnants of the old nature, even Christians struggle to act as they know they ought (Rom. 7:18–20).

The evidence leads to the conclusion that the *imago Dei* in sinners is deformed and degraded but not destroyed. Unregenerate human beings possess a tarnished Godlikeness. Genesis 9:5–6 forbids murder for the reason that a fatal attack on an image-bearer constitutes an attack on God Himself (James 3:9). Although humans at times act like unreasoning beasts (2 Peter 2:12), God's common grace produces in unbelievers a measure of goodness, so that they are not as evil as they could possibly be. Because they are sinful and guilty, unregenerate persons beyond the age of accountability are lost (Luke 19:10) and subject to divine judgment (Nah. 1:3; John 3:18; Rom. 5:18). Unbelievers need to repent (Matt. 3:2; 4:17; Acts 2:38) and receive new spiritual life from Christ, the Savior of the world.

## Human Functioning Renewed in Christ

By personally appropriating the new life Christ offers, humans experience a renewal of their capacities and functioning. The apostle Paul writes,

---

79. J. Barton Payne, *The Theology of The Older Testament* (Grand Rapids: Zondervan, 1962), 210.
80. Pascal, *Pensées*, 10 [no. 35].
81. Lewis and Demarest, *Integrative Theology,* 2:211.

"Though outwardly we are wasting away, yet inwardly we are being renewed [*anakainoō*] day by day" (2 Cor. 4:16). Renewal, or transformation of the person, involves the quickening and empowerment of all faculties by the sanctifying and empowering Spirit.

## Renewal of the Intellect

New life in Christ renews human cognitive functioning. Paul teaches that spiritual transformation begins with renewal of the mind (Rom. 12:2), that is, being "made new in the attitude of your minds" (Eph. 4:23) and being "renewed in knowledge" (Col. 3:10). The indwelling Spirit enables Christians to occupy their minds with what is "true," "noble," "right," "pure," "lovely," and "admirable" (Phil. 4:8). The renewed mind possesses not only enhanced knowledge of God's Word and will but also greater understanding and wisdom. So Paul desires that the Colossian Christians "may have the full riches of complete understanding, in order that they may know the mystery of God, namely, Christ" (Col. 2:2; cf. 2 Tim. 2:7). Similarly, the apostle prays that Christians may increase in wisdom: "I keep asking that the God of our Lord Jesus Christ, the glorious Father, may give you the Spirit of wisdom and revelation, so that you may know him better" (Eph. 1:17; cf. James 3:13–18). James describes the qualities of godly wisdom as "first of all pure; then peace-loving, considerate, submissive, full of mercy and good fruit, impartial and sincere" (James 3:17).

Christians are summoned to cultivate the mind of Christ (1 Cor. 2:16; Phil. 2:5)—a mind controlled by the Spirit (Rom. 8:6) so that all thoughts, ideas, images, and memories are brought under the Savior's control. The contents of the sanctified mind will be congruous with the contents of Christ's mind while on earth. The power of holy ideas cannot be overestimated. Paul's idea of God's forgiving grace challenged the entire Jewish legal system, and Luther's idea of justification by faith launched the Reformation.

Mental images also play a prominent role in spiritual and emotional maturation: "The single most important thing in our mind is our idea of God and the associated images."[82] The image of God as a loving Father, the Son as compassionate shepherd, and the Holy Spirit as a purifying fire nur-

---

82. Willard, *Renovation of the Heart*, 100.

ture the soul. Christians likewise should store in their minds edifying memories that include answers to prayer, acts of deliverance, and occasions of divine guidance.

Spiritual disciplines thus play an important role in renewing human functioning. Spiritual disciplines are activities of mind and body, regularly undertaken, that train the life in wholeness and holiness. Just as consistent physical training is needed to cultivate a healthy body, so faithful discipline is required to nurture human faculties and capacities. It has been said that actions regularly undertaken form a habit, which in turn forms character, which shapes one's destiny. Transformation of the intellect is facilitated by the disciplines of study and meditation. Study of Scripture and the spiritual classics fill the mind with the truth that makes new and sets free. Meditation on the Bible, spiritual writings, God's creation, and saving events in history[83] integrate the cognitive head with the affective heart and augment wisdom and understanding.

## Renewal of the Will

The fallen human will, like a wild horse, needs taming. Persons become self-controlled as they submit to Christ's control and allow him to order their priorities. "It is only by the binding of his will to the divine will that man enters into and enjoys true freedom."[84] Humans realize the elusive goal of volitional freedom only as they are free in and for God (Gal. 5:1). Liberty of will is a gift of God's grace, for David prayed, "Restore to me the joy of your salvation and grant me a willing spirit, to sustain me" (Ps. 51:12). Directed by the Spirit, human thoughts, words, and actions emerge according to a godly, inner necessity. In such a state, the outflow of God's grace from our lives "will be spontaneous and not forced" (Philem. 14).

Volitionally renewed believers are persons of good will, for the proverb states, "Goodwill is found among the upright" (Prov. 14:9). Christians bring forth God-honoring intentions and goals consistent with their new nature, and they choose kingdom strategies (Phil. 3:12–14) for achieving these goals. Under God the renewed will becomes competent to order other human faculties, such as thoughts, desires, emotions, and appetites. Christians

---

83. See Richard J. Foster, *Celebration of Discipline* (San Francisco, Calif.: Harper and Row, 1988), 29–32.
84. Hughes, *True Image*, 146.

experience struggles between the flesh and the Spirit, but they need be mastered by nothing other than Christ, who has set us free. So Paul wrote, "I will not be mastered by anything" (1 Cor. 6:12).

Liberated Christians pursue the path of others-directed, giving love rather than self-directed, getting love. Renewed believers make up their minds to love God (Matt. 22:37), His commands (Ps. 119:47–48, 113, 127), brothers and sisters in Christ (John 13:34; 1 Thess. 4:9), and even enemies who oppose them (Matt. 5:43–44). This ethic of love, or *ordo amoris* (Augustine), is attainable, for Jesus commanded obedience to the two "greatest" commandments to love God and others (Matt. 22:37–39). The apostles repeatedly enjoined love on the part of the liberated. Thus, "Love must be sincere" (Rom. 12:9). "I pray that you [might be] rooted and established in love" (Eph. 3:17). "Above all, love each other deeply, because love covers over a multitude of sins" (1 Peter 4:8; cf. 2 Peter 1:7). Love is measured not by the feelings it evokes but by the sacrifices it makes for others (John 15:13). Love's mandate is stated in 1 Corinthians 13:1–3, and the compelling characteristics thereof are delineated in verses 4–8a. Without love all our abilities, gifts, and works amount to nothing. In his small book *Purity of Heart Is to Will One Thing*,[85] Søren Kierkegaard insisted that the person who wills one thing only—for example, love—with singleness of purpose wills the Good, which is God Himself.

Submission and prayer are spiritual disciplines that retrain the will in a godly direction. Through submission we surrender selfishly chosen goals and strategies to God. Thomas à Kempis urged Christians to pray, "Lord, Your best only, Your will solely; give what you will, how much you will, when You will."[86] The extent to which humans submit to God is the extent to which He brings His grace to bear. We err when we regard prayer simply as lifting our list of requests to the heavenly Provider. Prayer conceived more broadly as conversation and communion with the Lover of our souls progressively brings the erring human will into joyful alignment with the divine will.

---

85. Søren Kierkegaard, *Purity of Heart Is to Will One Thing*, trans. Douglas V. Steere (New York: Harper and Row, 1948).

86. Thomas à Kempis, *The Imitation of Christ*, ed. and paraphrased Donald E. Demarey (Grand Rapids: Baker, 1982), 150–51.

## Renewal of the Emotions

The carnal desires and emotions we have described, whether envy or hatred, must be mortified. Paul says to put to death "whatever belongs to your earthly nature: sexual immorality, impurity, lust, evil desires and greed, which is idolatry" (Col. 3:5); "you must rid yourselves of all such things as these: anger, rage, malice." (v. 8); "Those who belong to Christ Jesus have crucified the sinful nature with its passions and desires" (Gal. 5:24). Our task as Christians "is to recognize the reality of our feelings and agree with the Lord to abandon those that are destructive and that lead us into doing or being what we know to be wrong."[87] Healthy desires and emotions must be embraced and expressed. Believers' supreme desire is for God Himself as told by the deeply yearning psalmist: "Whom have I in heaven but you? And earth has nothing I desire besides you" (Ps. 73:25).

Renewed hearts desire God's laws (Ps. 119:20), aspire to do His will (Ps. 40:8), hunger to live uprightly (Rom. 7:18; Heb. 13:18), and long to be with Christ in heaven (Phil. 1:23). Like Jesus, Christians rejoice at a wedding, feel compassion for the sick, grieve over the erring, and weep over the dying. Renewed human emotions, like those of our Lord, should be rich, appropriate, and controlled.

Although the core of love is a decision of the will, feelings of attachment and affection accompany the choice to give oneself for the good of others. Compassion *(oiktirmos)* can be regarded as felt love in action. Following the example of Jesus, compassion is that deep heart-feeling that moves one to relieve those in distress. Having experienced firsthand Christ's love and grace, Christians feel deeply and compassionately (Eph. 4:32; 1 Peter 3:8).

Because anger can be a destructive emotion, "wise men turn away anger" (Prov. 29:8). Because of its great potential for damaging others, destroying relationships, and grieving the Spirit, Paul commands believers, "Get rid of all bitterness, rage and anger" (Eph. 4:31a; cf. Col. 3:8). Christians, of course, become angry about injustice and oppression, especially when the poor and helpless are victimized. But God's people must not allow anger to rule their hearts and give Satan a foothold (Eph. 4:27). As the psalmist puts it, "In your anger do not sin" (Ps. 4:4a). Fear as fright is overcome by taking refuge in God (Ps. 27:1) and being bathed in the warmth of His love (1 John 4:18).

---

87. Willard, *Renovation of the Heart,* 137.

Favorable outward circumstances can make one happy, but joy—the fruit of salvation (Rom. 14:17; Gal. 5:22)—is a deep inner reality not dependent upon circumstance. Joy thrills the hearts of those who know Jesus as Savior and Lord (John 15:11; 1 Peter 1:8). On life's challenging journey, Christians find joy in God's Word (Ps. 19:8), promises (Ps. 119:162), deliverances (Isa. 35:10), and answers to prayer (John 16:24). Christians remain joyful amidst suffering and persecution (Acts 13:52; 2 Cor. 7:4; James 1:2), demonstrating that joy is a gift that works from the inside out. "The joy of the LORD is your strength" (Neh. 8:10).

Christians experience the emotion of sorrow (*lypē*) as sadness or remorse over the misfortunes of others. Agonizing over the lost condition of his Jewish friends in the flesh, Paul testified, "I have great sorrow and unceasing anguish in my heart" (Rom. 9:2). Through conviction of sins, the Corinthian Christians experienced "godly sorrow" that led to repentance and amended behavior (2 Cor. 7:8–11). Feelings accompanying objective guilt are overcome by confessing faults and receiving God's forgiveness (Ps. 32:5). Unhealthy shame is healed by believing that we are valued, loved, and accepted through the grace of Christ. Believers transcend shame by realizing that God, the sovereign Judge, regards us as fully accepted in Christ and adopted members of His family (Rom. 8:15; 1 John 3:1).

Humans experience emotional healing and wholeness through a personal relationship with the living God and through loving, trust relationships with other persons. Spiritual and emotional maturity are inseparable. Christians attain spiritual maturity as they experience healing and integration of their emotional worlds, and vice versa.

Worship, contemplation, and journaling are ways through which we renew the inner life. Acknowledging God's excelling worth in Spirit-directed worship releases deep longings and emotions. According to A. W. Tozer, "Worship means to feel in the heart."[88] Contemplation—the wordless discipline of focusing by faith on God's character and deeds—is classically known as "the prayer of the heart." Richard Baxter (1615–1691) notes that contemplation "opens the door between the head and the heart" and "presents to the affections those things that are most important."[89] Journaling is

---

88. A. W. Tozer, *The Quotable Tozer II*, comp. Harry Verploegh (Camp Hill, Pa.: Christian Publications, 1997), 196.

89. Richard Baxter, *The Saints' Everlasting Rest* (New York: American Tract Society, 1758), 429–30.

a fruitful, contemplative exercise by which we record reflections on God's Word and insights into God's ways, as well as our deepest spiritual aspirations. On the journal's pages one pours out before the Lord whatever emotions arise from the heart. The Psalms, which can be regarded as a collection of inspired journal entries, reflect the full range of human emotions: awe, joy, fear, loneliness, anger, and confusion.

## Renewal of the Moral Life

New spiritual life through Christ washes away uncleanness and guilt. Christians then launch the lifelong process of sanctification that involves the pursuit of wholeness and holiness. God expressly summons Christians to a life of moral soundness and integrity. Thus God said through Moses and Aaron, "I am the LORD your God; consecrate yourselves and be holy, because I am holy" (Lev. 11:44; cf. 19:2; 1 Peter 1:15–16). The apostle Paul summarized the Old Testament moral mandate when he wrote, "It is God's will that you should be holy. . . . For God did not call us to be impure, but to live a holy life" (1 Thess. 4:3, 7). Renewal of the moral life involves growing in ethical likeness to the living God (Lev. 19:2; 1 Peter 1:15–16).

In moral character believers are called to be "blameless" (Pss. 15:2; 101:2), "upright" (Titus 2:12), and "righteous" (Ps. 33:1). The goal of the moral life is to be "perfect" (Gk. *teleios,* Matt. 5:48), which is not a matter of sinless perfection but of soundness, wholeness, and spiritual maturity (see 1 Cor. 2:6; Eph. 4:13; Phil. 3:15). The best of biblical saints committed sins of omission and commission, as do we (James 3:2; 1 John 1:8, 10). That godly believers were not altogether free of sin is seen in the lives of Job (Job 1:1; 14:16–17), David (Pss. 32:1–2, 5; 51:1–5), Isaiah (Isa. 6:5); Peter (Luke 5:8), and Paul (Rom. 7:14–24). Paul described the Corinthian Christians as "sanctified in Christ Jesus" (1 Cor. 1:2), even though they showed themselves to be defiled in holy living. Luther stated that Christians are *"simil justus et peccator"*—at one and the same time judicially righteous and empirically sinful.

Moral progress toward holiness requires renouncing sinful lusts (1 Thess. 4:3–5) and controlling bodily appetites through the sanctifying Spirit (1 Cor. 6:13, 15). Paul described this process as mortification of the old nature, a dying to sin, and a putting off of the "old self" (Eph. 4:22; Col. 3:9). In addition, ethical progress requires a putting on of the new nature, or the "new self" (Eph. 4:24; Col. 3:10). Only as we actively pursue holiness can we please God and worship Him in unclouded communion (Pss. 15; 24:3–4; Matt. 5:8; Heb.12:14). Realistically the Christian life involves a struggle—often intense—with the old nature (Rom. 7:15, 18–23; Gal. 5:17) and the forces of evil.

As for the soul's moral barometer, Hebrews states, "The blood of Christ . . . cleanse[s] our consciences from acts that lead to death, so that we may serve the living God!" (Heb. 9:14). Christians who renounce sin and pursue holiness gain a clear sense of moral discrimination expressed by the terms *good conscience* (Acts 23:1; 1 Tim. 1:19; 1 Peter 3:21) and *clear conscience* (1 Tim. 3:9; 2 Tim. 1:3; 1 Peter 3:16). Note Paul's holy aspiration in the moral realm: "I strive always to keep my conscience clear before God and man" (Acts 24:16). The fruit of a "pure heart" (1 Tim. 1:5) is a conscience at peace with God and oneself.

Fasting and confession facilitate renewal of the moral life. Abstaining from food or other pleasures for a season silences the demands of the flesh, allowing Christians to commune more singularly with God. During a fast, unruly emotions such as pride and greed often surface, inviting remediation. Searching our hearts under the guidance of the Spirit, agreeing with God about our faults, and repenting of them are steps toward moral transformation. Christians confess their sins privately to God (1 John 1:9) and publicly to brothers and sisters in Christ (James 5:16).

## Renewal of Functioning, Behavior, and Dominion

Persons who are being renewed inwardly and privately are called to live transformed lives outwardly and publicly. They do not offer the members of their bodies as tools of unrighteousness but as instruments of righteousness to God (Rom. 6:13, 19). The glorious reality is that the Christian's body is the temple of the Holy Spirit (1 Cor. 6:19). The retraining of our embodied responses occurs as we "put to death the misdeeds of the body" (Rom. 8:13) and practice righteous deeds. As James puts it, "Who is wise and understanding among you? Let him show it by his good life, by deeds done in the humility that comes from wisdom" (James 3:13).

Rather than beholding evil, the eye will remain focused on Jesus and the needy world (Heb. 12:2).

Rather than spreading lies, the tongue will speak the truth (Eph. 4:25), bless (1 Cor. 4:12), and encourage (Heb. 3:13).

Rather than engaging in wicked schemes, the hands will be lifted in praise to God (Ps. 134:2; 1 Tim. 2:8) and extended to others to help.

Rather than walking in the ways of wickedness, the path taken will be obedient to God's law (Ps. 119:1). These righteous actions clarify Paul's aspiration that "Christ will be exalted in my body" (Phil. 1:20). Observe that the power that flows from the Cross can bring healing to the body (James 5:15–16) as God wills, for the verb *sōzō*, "save," embraces spiritual and physical healing.

The heavens belong to God, but the earth He has entrusted to humans to explore, harness, and use wisely (Ps. 115:16). Humans who profess allegiance to the Creator and Redeemer will glorify Him as responsible viceregents and wise stewards of His gifts. Christians will exercise disciplined stewardship of earth's resources to the praise of God and for the good of the human community.

Since all of the capacities of the soul influence and move the body, each of the disciplines we have mentioned helps train the body in righteousness. The physical discipline Christians pursue is not a radical, ascetical denial of the body but a mortification of its sinful passions and behaviors.

## Renewal of the Image

The new birth initiates the lifelong process of revitalizing the *imago Dei* spoiled by sin. As the Holy Spirit breathes new life into the soul, believers in Christ receive new dispositions, aspirations, affections, and moral qualities. Paul designates this spiritually renewed state as the "new self" (Eph. 4:24; Col. 3:10), and Peter as participation in "the divine nature" (2 Peter 1:4). The Spirit's renewing breath revitalizes every God-created capacity and functioning— intellect, will, desires, emotions, conscience, conduct, and (see chap. 4, pp. 133–47) relational capacities. "Regeneration does not add to, or subtract from, the number of man's intellectual, emotional or voluntary faculties," observed Augustus Strong. Rather "regeneration is the giving of a new direction or tendency to powers of affection which man possessed before."[90]

Regeneration and lifelong sanctification renew believers into the likeness of Jesus Christ, the true image of God (2 Cor. 4:4; Col. 1:15). Christ is the ideal man (John 19:5), the second Adam (1 Cor. 15:45), and the prototype and head of the new humanity God is bringing into being. The goal of

---

90. Augustus H. Strong, *Systematic Theology* (Philadelphia: Judson Press, 1907), 823.

human existence, established by the Father from the beginning, is conformity to the character and conduct of His Son. According to God's gracious plan, believers have been "predestined to be conformed to the likeness of his Son" (Rom. 8:29). Again, "we, who with unveiled faces all reflect the Lord's glory, are being transformed (*metamorphoō*) into his likeness with ever-increasing glory" (2 Cor. 3:18; cf. Gal. 4:19). Complete conformity to Christ will be realized at the Second Coming, when believers will be clothed with spiritual bodies. In that great day "we shall be like him, for we shall see him as he is" (1 John 3:2; cf. 1 Cor. 15:49).

# CHAPTER 8

# FUNCTION *and* BEHAVIOR *in* PSYCHOLOGICAL PERSPECTIVE

BOTH SCRIPTURE AND contemporary psychology have a great deal to say about human function and behavior. We have explored how these two domains view the origin and destiny of people and their composition and identity. Now we will survey what psychology has learned about how the human organism functions. Our survey will seek to answer three central questions: How does the human person get prepared to be a fully functioning adult (life span development)? What are those adult functions (cognitive and behavioral activities)? And how are people alike yet different from others in the execution of these functions (personality)? As with the other parts, we will discuss some of the many integrative issues these questions raise in the integrative summary that follows this chapter.

## THE DEVELOPMENT OF FUNCTION AND BEHAVIOR

Little compares with the thrill of watching your newborn child develop and change on an almost daily basis. At times the changes appear in such rapid-fire succession that proud parents have to record dates and events in a baby book in order to remember all that is happening in the life of the baby. The changes we can observe are continuations of the patterns of development that were occurring in the womb. And most often these marker events occur in the same sequence and at about the same age as predicted in the baby manuals! Developmental psychology seeks to understand the mechanisms that guide human development in such predictable fashion. This specialty within the field of psychology is broad in scope since it seeks to investigate development at many levels over the entire life span (birth to death). Change never ceases to occur with humans, even though the rates of change may vary and the results of change range from growth to decay.

## Variations in Development

Ideas about human development constantly change both in academic circles and in the general public. If we compare how we treat young children in our day with how our ancestors in colonial America (1620–1770) handled their children, we can observe substantial variation. Midwives in the American colonies immediately placed a newborn infant on their laps to shape the head and straighten arms and legs. When all four limbs were as straight as the midwife could make them, the baby was placed in swaddling clothes that kept the baby's arms straight against the torso and the legs as straight as could be. They wrapped the child so that the head was also supported. "There was no risk to the weak little neck, since, no matter how the child was carried, it would remain fully supported within its rigid wrappings."[1] Parents worked hard at keeping the child's legs straight as much as possible to prepare it for the day it could start walking. Children were not allowed to crawl; many people feared that if children crawled, they might never learn to walk. To help prevent crawling, long petticoats were worn by both boys and girls. Parents also worked hard to make sure the child walked as early as possible since it was regarded as bad luck for a child to talk before he or she walked.[2] These child rearing practices seem as strange to us as they seemed normal to our ancestors. Ideas about development do indeed change over time.

Ideas about development not only vary across time, but they also show variation across cultures. Cross-cultural human developmentalists look for both similarities and differences among the many societies of the world regarding child rearing practices, features of adolescence, adult maturity, and so forth. For example, a key component of childhood involves the de-

---

1. K. Calvert, "Patterns of Childrearing in America," in *Beyond the Century of the Child: Cultural History and Developmental Psychology*, ed. W. Koops and M. Zuckerman (Philadelphia: University of Pennsylvania Press, 2003), 64.
2. Ibid., 64–66.

velopment of socialization skills. Among the Semai people of central Malaya, timidity is a preferred childhood trait, and any expression of anger from their children is quietly discouraged. By way of contrast, the Waorani of Amazonian Ecuador rear their children in the opposite manner. Even though these two people groups are similar in their level of technological development and live in similar geographies, one group raises their children to preserve the culture's peaceful lifestyle and the other raises their children to participate in one of the most violent societies in the world.[3]

A major feature of adolescence for females is menarche, or the first menstruation. Researchers compared three groups of Samoans to determine how they experienced menarche. One group lived on an isolated island with very little Western influence, the second group lived in a part of Samoa that was rapidly changing to Western styles, and the third group lived in the state of Hawaii. Results indicated that pain and discomfort associated with menarche increased significantly with the more exposure the young girls had to Western influence.[4] Examples of this type of cultural variance abound. It is important for Christians to realize that the societies in which the authors of Scripture lived are removed from modern Western life by both historical eras and cultural boundaries. "Being human involves constraints and possibilities stemming from long histories of human practices. At the same time, each generation continues to revise and adapt its human cultural and biological heritage in the face of current circumstances."[5]

Next, we will explore a sampler of topics that relate to the three main stages of human development: childhood, adolescence, and adulthood.

## Childhood

The developmental tasks of childhood include language acquisition and the development of social interaction skills. Trying to understand play and its role in facilitating language and sociality has fascinated researchers for decades. Play comes in many forms (constructive, pretend, sociodramatic, rough-and-tumble, and motor activity play). How does play contribute to

---

3. H. W. Gardiner and C. Kozmitzki, *Lives Across Cultures,* 2d ed. (Boston: Allyn and Bacon, 2002), 66.

4. Ibid., 97–98.

5. B. Rogoff, *The Cultural Nature of Human Development* (Oxford: Oxford University Press, 2003), 3.

the child's maturation, and why does it appear to be so essential for the child's growth? Defining play is perhaps the most difficult part in the process of understanding it. Most observers of children argue that play is activity that has no apparent immediate purpose; activity that occurs in a context that is familiar, safe, and relatively stress-free for the child; and activity that leads to immediate consequences or behaviors following the play (cooperation and friendliness as examples).[6] Play is an outgrowth of exploration, an activity that dominates the behavior of children in the first nine months of life. From nine to eighteen months, exploration and play occur in roughly equal proportion. For the rest of childhood, play predominates. Pretend play is perhaps the most fascinating form of childhood play. It generally occupies 12 to 15 percent of a child's play time.[7]

What is the function of play? Some have suggested that children practice in play certain skills that will later be of use to them. For example, taking different roles in play may build the foundation for later being able to do that very thing as an adult. Or play could help the child learn dominance, cooperation, negotiation, or specific social skills such as reciprocity and emotional regulation. Play is important for children; hence it is somewhat alarming that "the pressures of modern society are, in some cases, minimizing the role of play in children's lives."[8] Cutting out recess time in schools to give teachers more instructional time may be an unwise and developmentally risky strategy.

## Adolescence

We are very familiar with the social features of adolescence. Parents face numerous unforeseen challenges as their children pass through the teen years. Peer influence is clearly a factor in making this phase of life a challenge for both children and those who care for and work with them. Our current understanding of adolescence, however, is strongly grounded in the biological underpinnings of this period of great change. Other than pregnancy, puberty is perhaps the most dramatic change that occurs over the

---

6. A. D. Pellegrini and P. Smith, "Development of Play," in *Handbook of Developmental Psychology*, ed. J. Valsiner and K. J. Connolly (Thousand Oaks, Calif.: Sage, 2003), 277–78.

7. Ibid., 278–81.

8. Ibid., 287.

entire life span.[9] Puberty is the onset of adult reproductive capacity. It appears in girls earlier than in boys. It begins when the hypothalamus gland in the brain wakes up from a long period of inactivity (extending back to infancy) and begins to pump into a feedback loop a small peptide hormone that produces dramatic changes. The hypothalamic hormone in turn triggers the pituitary gland, which produces two hormones designed to activate the gonads. This three-part endocrine axis accounts for most all of the changes we observe as children reach the age of puberty. The secondary sex characteristics that appear during puberty are effects of these hormonal causes.

What causes the hypothalamus to suddenly become active after a long period of dormancy? Experts agree that this process is not well understood. Is it primarily a built-in schedule that activates itself when the child reaches a certain age? Or is it triggered by some somatic feature of the child such as physical size or bone structure? Perhaps advances in medical science will understand this process more fully in the future. We seem to know a little more about the end of the puberty phase than we do about the beginning. Most features of puberty stop when the teenager reaches adult height.[10]

## Adulthood

Erik Erikson is often credited with expanding the time line of development to include the adult years and not just childhood and adolescence. Since his pioneering work, researchers have explored many features of the adult experience that change with the passing of time. Developmentalists seek to understand how cognitive functions change over time and what role they play in the aging process, among other things. One of the most interesting areas for investigation pertaining to the adult years involves wisdom, a topic also of great interest to Christians. Developmental psychologists see wisdom as a social and interactive feature of adult life. When persons face daunting challenges, they seek solutions to these problems from those who have solved them in the past. The training and education of youth is another social prompt that evokes response from wise people.[11] Wisdom is

---

9. P. T. Ellison, "Puberty," in *Human Growth and Development,* ed. N. Cameron (New York: Academic Press, 2002), 65.
10. Ibid., 77.
11. U. M. Staudinger and I. Werner, "Wisdom: Its Social Nature and Lifespan Development," in *Handbook of Developmental Psychology,* 585–87.

a personality feature that requires high levels of integrative capacity coupled with abilities to deal with abstract and complex material. "In conjunction with the conceptualization of wisdom as expertise, receiving as well as providing mentorship seems to play a crucial role in the accumulation of wisdom-related knowledge and judgment."[12] (Could this imply that Christians can incorporate the wisdom of Scripture only when they are willing to submit to its mentorship over their lives?) Few people seem willing to describe themselves as wise, but many people claim to be able to identify this trait in others. In the future, researchers hope to determine just which features of personality foster the development of wisdom in the life of an adult. Both the Bible and current developmental researchers seem to view wisdom as a central characteristic of maturity and a desired end-state for the developmental process among adults.

## Research Innovations

Although we have made considerable progress in understanding human development patterns, critics of the field say that the time has come to adopt some research innovations that will expand the boundaries of our knowledge even more. The "problems of psychological development are too complex for traditional verbal theories of development."[13] With the advent of powerful computers, scientists can build models that can replicate certain human actions. The computer simply does what humans could do but with much greater efficiency, accuracy, and power. Scientists interested in human development (especially those with a physics background) are developing neural network models that embody many of the features of human brain structure. The models include input units, hidden mediating units, and output units. When a psychological model is reduced to digitized form that allows for simulation of the phenomena one is trying to understand, scientists can quickly see various weaknesses in the proposed theory: contradictions, inadequate description, and other weaknesses. Scientists have used models such as this in many other fields to advance theory building as well as to improve our understanding of very complex phenomena.[14] The

---

12. Ibid., 593.
13. T. R. Shultz, *Computational Developmental Psychology* (Cambridge, Mass.: MIT Press, 2003), 1.
14. Ibid., 2–18.

expectation of those who build computer models is that our verbal theories will be better grounded in empirical data and that we will substantially improve our ability to explain the human developmental process. "Modeling will never replace conventional verbal theories and empirical psychological research, but the role of modeling . . . will continue to grow in a complementary fashion with these other approaches."[15]

Computer modeling is only one of many quantitative methods that loom on the horizon. The developmental specialty within psychology is on the brink of significant conceptual breakthroughs. The challenge of representing process, which by definition is at the heart of developmental theory, involves introducing methods that yield rigorous results and testability. "Empirically testable representations" will greatly enhance the power of developmental psychology to understand human function and behavior.[16]

## THE COMPONENTS OF FUNCTION AND BEHAVIOR

In the following section, we will be following an organizational scheme that evolutionary psychologists describe as the standard social science model. We have seen how evolutionists prefer to examine the numerous modules comprising the human brain (mind) rather than general-purpose abilities such as intelligence or motivation. However, their evolutionary view of the brain (mind) is not compelling or otherwise proven. The scope of human functioning is so vast and varied that we can comprehend its operation only by looking at the various general-purpose abilities that comprise it and that have been extensively studied by psychological researchers for over a century and a half. We also must realize that many of these components (consciousness, intelligence, motivation) are inferred theoretical constructs. Science frequently utilizes inferred states to help explain unobservable phenomena.[17] But the fact that they are inferred in no way detracts from their usefulness as categories or from their existence in reality.

We also must remember two important caveats. First, the following list of components of human functioning does not represent discrete brain

---

15. Ibid., 270.
16. J. R. Nesselroade and P. C. M. Molenaar, "Quantitative Models for Developmental Process," in *Handbook of Developmental Psychology*, 635.
17. B. J. Baars, "Treating Consciousness as a Variable: The Fading Taboo," in *Essential Sources in the Scientific Study of Consciousness*, ed. B. J. Baars, W. P. Banks, and J. B. Newman (Cambridge, Mass.: MIT Press, 2003), 4.

categories but instead is a set of overlapping and interacting domains. For example, consciousness (awareness) does not occur by itself. It is accompanied by a dynamic emotional response that can be seen in subcortical structures without which no awareness could occur.[18] Second, because we cannot directly observe these important and real components of human functioning, we must use metaphoric language to describe them. For example, we can describe someone's consciousness as "clouded," their intellect as "broad," their cognition as capable of "grappling" with complex issues, and so forth.[19]

In general, the following six areas comprise the "mind" as commonly understood by laypersons. The one exception might be behavior, but behavior is strongly anchored in antecedent functions of various "mind" operations. These six areas also have strong links to the "body" since they are anchored in biological and neurological functions. Thus we should not speak of the mind as opposed to the body or the body as opposed to the mind. Instead, they are interacting features of the human person.

Each side of this interacting equation has great impact on the other. We can easily comprehend how the health and well-being of the body greatly affects the mind, and the reverse is equally true. For example, we know that the mind greatly influences health. The use of psychological interventions in medicine could cut healthcare costs by up to 20 percent, "but the interventions are only rarely used."[20] A veritable revolution has occurred regarding how we conceptualize health and illness. In the future, medicine will view the belief system of the patient as a critical component of treatment. "This new approach to health says loudly and clearly that the causes, development, and outcomes of an illness are determined by the interaction of psychological, social, and cultural factors with biochemistry and physiology."[21] Medicine will no longer consider physical illness as related only to the body, given massive sets of data that confirm the impact of the mind on physical health. The mind is powerful indeed.

We can explore each of the following components of human functioning by describing its ideal or healthy state, its pathological states, and corrective measures or therapy that can or cannot be applied. In some instances

---

18. R. D. Ellis and N. Newton, eds., *The Caldron of Consciousness: Motivation, Affect, and Self-Organization* (Amsterdam: John Benjamin, 2000), x.

19. Ibid., 6.

20. Oakley Ray, "How the Mind Hurts and Heals the Body," *American Psychologist* 59 (2004): 29.

21. Ibid.

we will spend more time on the latter two than in other cases. The components of human functioning that we will examine are consciousness, cognition, intelligence, motivation, behavior, and emotion. Because each of these topics represents a broad swath of academic interest, we can only be brief with each one.

## Consciousness

Investigators of all stripes have been interested in the topic of consciousness since the time of the ancient Greeks until now—with one exception: twentieth-century psychology. Both the Russian Pavlov and the American J. B. Watson disparaged attempts to understand what occurred inside the organism. In an effort to link their work with the natural sciences, they banned all investigation into such things as introspection, attention, mental imagery, dreaming, and hypnosis. The subjective features of human functioning and all phenomena that were not directly observable were taboo. This approach, in the view of most scholars today, was "fatally flawed" as a guiding principle for human psychology.[22] All attempts to understand the complex and rich totality of human nature that do not deal with the unobservable are doomed to produce an incomplete account of human functioning. Even though "consciousness has become fashionable again," a few behaviorists who now call themselves neobehaviorists object.[23] They claim that the public domain of brain physiology and the public domain of observable whole-organism behavior are suitable subjects for investigation by the public science of psychology; but the private world of inner states and consciousness should only be studied without resorting to "mentalistic presumptions."[24]

From a layperson's perspective, consciousness is simply awareness. I can think, and I can at the same time be aware of my thoughts. Because I possess consciousness, I can be aware of the world around me with its sights, sounds, smells, and touch. We take these wonderful features of life for granted most of the time; and some would argue that if we take consciousness apart and examine it scientifically, we ruin it. Adam Zeman illustrates this contrast

---

22. G. Sommerhoff, *Understanding Consciousness: Its Function and Brain Processes* (Thousand Oaks, Calif.: Sage, 2000), 2.
23. J. Staddon, *The New Behaviorism: Mind, Mechanism, and Society* (Philadelphia: Psychology Press, 2001), 159.
24. Ibid., 176.

well with two descriptions of the same scene. The first is his conscious experience of sitting in a chair, and the second is a scientific description of the same event.

1.  "While I write I can just make out the steady patter of the rain on the lawn. A grey light slants through the window. There is a fire rumbling in the grate, scenting the air with wood smoke. My chair is hard, and when my attention wanders from my work, I feel the pressure of my elbows on its arms, . . ."
2.  "A variety of forms of energy impinge upon an organism. Invisible particles vibrate in the air, setting up a resonance in a membrane coiled, like a shell, within the ear. Once they have passed safely through the cornea and lens, quanta of radiation are absorbed by another sensitive membrane, in its eye."[25]

Obviously the first approach is preferable. Yet if we are to understand as best we can how humans function, the formal and objective language of science is also needed.

Psychologists sometimes view consciousness as a broad term encompassing such domains as motivation and emotion.[26] Here we are using the term to represent awareness, a domain roughly equivalent to wakefulness. If we imagine a continuum starting with the lowest level of arousal and ending with the highest level of arousal, we could include coma, sleep, daydreaming, wakefulness, and hyperarousal along that continuum. Consciousness mainly involves the latter two, although some degree of consciousness seems to pertain to all of these arousal states (even though we normally describe a coma as an unconscious state).[27] Another way of looking at consciousness is to envision it as an executive control system. When brain scientists were using computer imagery to describe brain functioning, they often called consciousness the operating system of the brain.[28] Readers will remember that such a mechanism comes very close to what the word "soul" means in Scripture (see chap. 4).

25. A. Zeman, *Consciousness: A User's Guide* (New Haven, Conn.: Yale University Press, 2002), 1, 2.
26. Ellis and Newton, *The Caldron of Consciousness*, ix.
27. G. William Farthing, *The Psychology of Consciousness* (Englewood Cliffs, N.J.: Prentice Hall, 1992), 8.
28. Ibid., 8

This conscious awareness encompasses awareness of self as an entity, awareness of our thoughts and feelings, and awareness of one's surroundings.[29] As such it is foundational to an understanding of how the brain works and how all the other components of human functioning operate. Thus we can conceptualize consciousness as the most basic network of cognition at the base of intelligence.[30] This basic awareness includes perception, which includes basic visual processing, color vision, visual space perception, object perception, sense of movement, attention, basic auditory processes, and so forth.[31] Of course, the brain contains not only consciousness mechanisms but also nonconscious mental processes such as stored memory, automatic processes, irretrievable memory, and so forth.[32]

Consciousness also includes body sensations, memories, imaginary capacity, and inner speech. It is selective; research verifies that we can only do a few things at once. Most knowledge is nonconscious; remembering brings it from "storage" into consciousness. Consciousness is awareness with comprehension. It is always relating events to each other and is never passive but active in interpreting input. Consciousness has content along with comprehension. There is no such thing as an empty mind or pure consciousness.[33]

All healthy, living humans are "richly conscious of our world and of ourselves," and "this consciousness depends upon events in the brain."[34] To describe the activity of consciousness is to simultaneously refer to brain activity. One does not occur without the other. Whereas dualism has always considered these two activities to be separate, modern psychology views consciousness as reducible to brain events (see chap. 5). Again we are forced to ask ourselves whether consciousness as we are aware of it could be separate from the brain. If it is, we have no experience of it in this life. The frustration of attempting to understand the connection between this feature of mind and the human brain is, of course, not a new frustration. "These facts raise questions which have refused to surrender completely to many centuries of philosophical attack."[35]

---

29. Sommerhoff, *Understanding Consciousness,* 1–2.
30. M. Estep, *A Theory of Immediate Awareness: Self-Organization and Adaptation in Natural Intelligence* (Dordrecht: Kluwer Academic, 2003), 279.
31. E. B. Goldstein, ed., *Blackwell Handbook of Perception* (Malden, Mass.: Blackwell, 2001).
32. Farthing, *The Psychology of Consciousness,* 12.
33. Ibid., 7.
34. Zeman, *Consciousness,* 303.
35. Ibid.

If we define normal consciousness as wakefulness, we immediately can recognize that levels of consciousness vary throughout the twenty-four-hour day since we are not awake all of the time. There are many altered states of consciousness: sleep with its dream states, hypnosis, meditative states, drug-induced highs or comas, daydreaming, and comas caused by brain injury lesions. These altered states vary in the level of consciousness that characterizes them. For example, while sleeping most people are aware of noise in the home that is normal and that does not merit investigation; but if a sound of the same volume that is out of the ordinary occurs, they wake up instantly in a state of some alarm. Or a sleeping mother with a newborn in the house will sleep through street noise but will instantly awaken if she hears the cry of her baby. In some unconscious way, the mother has set her consciousness apparatus to screen out normal noise and respond instantly to the needs of her child. The "cure" for these altered states can be simply waking up, ending the administration of the legal or illegal drug causing the change, or surgery to remove the tumor. Of course, when a coma is part of a terminal illness, doctors may not have access to a cure.

Finally, many people have wondered just where consciousness resides in the brain. Descartes made this question famous by speculating that the mind (consciousness) was located in the pineal gland. He selected this feature of brain anatomy because the gland was the highest visible and unitary brain structure under the two hemispheres of the brain. Based on evidence gathered from brain imaging and physical stimulation of various parts of the brain, the scientific answer is: Consciousness is a "widely distributed network that extends over the frontal, anterior, cingulated, and parietal cortices including, of course, their associated thalamic nuclei," and it acts as a "connected whole."[36] In other words, consciousness is not a place in the brain but a set of interconnected brain functions found throughout the organ.

## Cognition

The term *cognition,* like *consciousness,* is sometimes used to describe the entire field of study associated with the mind (as in cognitive science). Here we are using the word in a much narrower sense to refer to thinking. How do we think? What do we know about the process that leads us to solve

---

36. Sommerhoff, *Understanding Consciousness,* 154.

problems, understand concepts, and create ideas with our minds? Even though we may restrict our investigation to this narrower sense, the topic is vast in size since thinking includes concept formation and organization, decision making, problem solving, reasoning, and word meaning.[37] Thinking per se is interconnected with several other brain functions. For example, we cannot solve a problem without utilizing from our memory various strategies we have learned from solving similar problems in the past. And we cannot retrieve memories of earlier problem-solving achievements without the use of language. The interconnections among these functions are even more complicated: We cannot learn language without utilizing our memory function and so forth. These interdependencies remind us that the brain functions as a whole, even though for the purposes of analysis it is helpful to examine the various components of brain function.

The human memory is both fascinating and mysterious. Memory allows us to learn from experience and to retain learning. With the advent of computers, many people suggested that the human brain must operate like computers operate. After all, both take in information, store it, and later retrieve it. More recently, however, the computer analogy has lost currency. We now know that the brain retrieves information in bits and pieces and reconstructs them into a unified memory unlike the operations of a computer. Apparently we do not store material by address as does a computer, and the computer model does not allow for errors that are an inevitable part of the human memory system (either because of encoding errors or because of retrieval problems).[38]

The memory process involves three steps: encoding, storage, and retrieval. When memory works well, all three phases are operating with efficiency. When memory does not work well and forgetting occurs, a problem may have occurred with the original encoding of the material or with the retrieval system. People can learn how to improve both their encoding and retrieval strategies. Most everyone has experienced the "tip of the tongue" phenomenon, a frustration that increases with age. I may know that I know the capital of Wisconsin, but I may not be able to say the word. I may know that it contains three syllables and starts with an *M*, but no matter how hard

37. W. Bechtel and G. Graham, eds., *A Companion to Cognitive Science* (Malden, Mass.: Blackwell, 1998), xiii.
38. S. Y. Auyang, *Mind in Everyday Life and Cognitive Science* (Cambridge, Mass.: MIT Press, 2000), 284–95.

I try, I cannot retrieve the information completely. Perhaps I will verbalize "Milwaukee" but with the sense that this name is not exactly correct. Usually the correct name, Madison, will occur to me later when I am not trying so hard to retrieve it. This glimpse into both how we store and retrieve memories gives us some clue as to how the memory operates.[39]

We can categorize the various types of memory in a number of ways. The most familiar strategy is to distinguish short-term memory from long-term memory. Sensory memory (which we could consider a part of awareness as discussed above) produces a very brief persistence of stimuli that lasts for a few milliseconds. From there, the image or word or sound moves into short-term memory (STM) for storage lasting about twenty seconds. We must do something to move that material into long-term memory (LTM), or it will fade and disappear. We can retain material in STM for a longer period of time by forming "trains of thought." LTM can retain information for years and seems to have no limits on its capacity; STM, however, can hold a maximum of about four "chunks" of information before it can take in no more.[40]

Another way of categorizing the various types of memory is to speak of working memory versus stored memory. When I am in conversation with another person, I need to remember how his sentence began as well as how it ended in order to discern its meaning. And I need to remember how the conversation began so that I can organize a reasonable response. Or if I am reading a paragraph in a book, I need to keep in working memory the beginning lines in order to decipher the ending lines. If I am reading a long novel, I am able to follow the plot by remembering some things that I have previously stored in LTM coupled with much more recent material that I have in my working memory.

Some material that we store in LTM is declarative in nature (facts, events embedded in their context, concepts) and other material is procedural or nondeclarative (habitual knowledge such as walking, riding a bicycle, tying shoelaces). Material in the latter category is difficult to verbalize and is acquired slowly with much practice. [41] We know from brain imaging and from assessment of brain damage that we store various kinds of nondeclarative

39. R. T. Kellogg, *Cognitive Psychology,* 2d ed. (Thousand Oaks, Calif.: Sage, 2003), 164–68.

40. Ibid., 119–20.

41. H. L. Roediger and L. M. Goff, "Memory," in *A Companion to Cognitive Science,* 250.

memory in different parts of the brain. Researchers do not understand why this occurs.[42] Encoding effectiveness is enhanced when we attach meaning to the material going into storage and by qualities inherent in the material we are storing (vividness, distinctiveness). Retrieval is effective when we use the same cues to retrieve that we used to encode and when we utilize the original context of material we are trying to locate.[43]

All people apparently have amnesia for their months of infancy. Perhaps the infant doesn't have requisite skills for encoding material and thus little is ever put into long-term memory; perhaps the infant did encode material that entered LTM, but adult retrieval cues and strategies are unable to access the material. We do not know precisely how to explain infantile amnesia.[44]

How do we solve problems? Although we are not always aware of the specific methods we utilize to tackle any given problem, we normally see a problem as possessing a goal state (the solution we would like to achieve) and an initial state (our current understanding of the givens of a problem). The distance between these two poles is what we must mentally navigate if we are to solve the problem successfully. The entire field (including the initial state, the goal state, and the "territory" between the two) is often called the "problem space."[45] Problem solvers work through this problem space using either an algorithm or a heuristic.

An algorithm is a rule that always produces a solution. At first glance the algorithm appears to be the very best approach, especially if the outcome is always a solution! One example of an algorithm is an exhaustive or systematic search through all possible solutions until the correct one is found. "An algorithm for solving anagrams is to try every possible letter in every possible position until the word solution appears."[46] This exhaustive algorithm works well with a three-letter anagram but very inefficiently with a sixteen-letter anagram. Trial and error is another type of algorithm that theoretically will always yield a solution but without very much efficiency.

A heuristic is a more selective search for a solution by identifying those aspects of the problem that are more likely to hold a clue to the solution.

42. Kellogg, *Cognitive Psychology,* 151.
43. Roediger and Goff, "Memory," 254–57.
44. Kellogg, *Cognitive Psychology,* 119.
45. Ibid., 339.
46. Ibid., 368.

The heuristic approach has no guarantee of success. We may choose to work backward by listing the conditions that would have to be true in order for the goal state to be true. Or we may choose to work forward by identifying what we should do first to move from our current understanding of the problem. Complex problems require the heuristic approach. We are quite familiar with this methodology because we often read about medical investigators who follow a hunch to discover a cure or a drug that arrests a disease. Again, when we engage in everyday problem solving, we are most often quite unaware of whether we are using an algorithm or a heuristic to solve it. But these processes are going on internally nonetheless.[47]

Despite recent progress in untwisting the knotty problem of human thought, the mechanism of thinking remains mysterious. We know it occurs in the brain and consists of thousands of neurons communicating with each other with electro-chemical signals across the tiny gaps that exist between the brain cells. Human thought is fairly easily defined as "how people mentally represent and think about information."[48] But the thinking process itself almost defies imagination. As a reader moves through the material on this page, many different processes could be happening almost simultaneously. Consider some of the possibilities: "This material is very hard to follow." "I'm not very interested in this topic." "I sure would like to learn more about this problem." Or something totally unrelated such as, "I sure am hungry." So while we are visually taking in the words on a page, our thinking processes can be deducing the meaning of the words, making judgments about the value or veracity of that meaning, and either remembering or quickly forgetting what we have just read.

How can all of this occur through the mechanism of electrical signals crossing synaptic gaps? The problem continues to attract the attention of cognitive psychologists and brain specialists throughout the world. The volume of research exploring the human thought process is enormous. Perhaps advances in brain science that will occur in the twenty-first century will dramatically increase our understanding of thought; perhaps the thinking process itself will remain a secret of the creation known only to God.

---

47. R. J. Sternberg and T. Ben-Zeev, *Complex Cognition: The Psychology of Human Thought* (New York: Oxford University Press, 2001), 144–51.
48. Ibid., 1.

## Intelligence

Many people view intelligence as a function that separates humans from the animal kingdom. Animals, of course, possess intelligence, and they vary in levels of intelligence. We view some as sly (foxes), clever (raccoons), smart (dolphins), or dull (sheep). But are these expressions of intelligence on a par with human intelligence? Scholars suggest that human intelligence is unique in three ways: the use of tools, the use of language, and the ability to form mental concepts at high levels of abstraction.[49] In each of these areas, animal biologists have demonstrated that the higher primates, especially chimpanzees and orangutans, can exhibit intelligence in all three of these areas. But the extent of their accomplishments, even in very enriched and attentive environments, is significantly limited. For example, at best a chimpanzee can use language at the level of a thirty-month-old human. But this achievement compares very poorly to the full complement of human language once the abilities of grammar usage become operative at about three years of age among human children.[50] Higher primates do utilize tools such as inserting a stick into a termite hill and then eating the termites that cling to it. But is the stick tool comparable to a Boeing 747, a tool humans use for transportation? Trefil argues that it isn't. Some differences "in degree become differences in kind."[51] It is true that chimpanzees and orangutans can show evidence of self-awareness, but again this example of abstracting mental ability is very limited and isolated compared to the wide range of abstracting abilities that most humans possess.

The intelligence of humans is unique. We have been able to construct large-scale lakes and reservoirs that actually slow down the rotation of the earth.[52] We can transmit nongenetic information from one generation to the next via spoken and written language. We have sent men to the moon and brought them back again. We have sent machines to Mars that can send back pictures of the lonely planet. Animals do not build skyscrapers, write novels, compose symphonies, document the human genome, launch satellites, or build cell phones that use those satellites. But humans do.

---

49. J. Trefil, *Are We Unique? A Scientist Explores the Unparalleled Intelligence of the Human Mind* (New York: John Wiley and Sons, 1997), 37.
50. Ibid., 60.
51. Ibid., 38.
52. Ibid., 2.

Intelligence is a feature of human functioning that everyone understands but no one can define. The definitional problems attached to human intelligence have persisted for more than a century despite enormous efforts to conquer the problem. The first basic problem that we face in defining intelligence is whether intelligence is one thing or a combination of many things (molar vs. modular). Most researchers currently working in this field view human intelligence as a composite of abilities rather than as a single ability.

If human intelligence is a composite, then how are its various components organized? Most theoretical reconstructions use a hierarchical approach to show the levels and interrelationships of intelligence factors as suggested by research outcomes. At the top of the chart is $g$, or general intelligence. In spite of its placement at the top, $g$ is an underlying factor that is positively correlated with all of the more specific components of intelligence. (It may be easier for some people to visualize $g$ at the bottom of the chart.) At the opposite side of the chart are fifty to sixty narrower intellectual abilities that are called first-order factors. Examples of these narrow abilities include general sequential reasoning, speed of reasoning, lexical knowledge, listening ability, memory span, visual memory, spatial scanning, general sound discrimination, memory for sound patterns, creativity, word fluency, numerical facility, semantic processing speed, and many other abilities. Tests of intelligence measure some or all of these narrow abilities. An IQ score is often a summary of many scores on these abilities. The limitation of a single intelligence quotient is that it gives us no information about the various strong or weak areas obscured by the composite score.

These fifty to sixty narrow abilities fall fairly naturally into eight to ten summary categories called second-order factors. These broad factors fall between $g$ and the first-order abilities. Examples of these summary categories composing intelligence are fluid intelligence, crystallized intelligence, general memory and learning, broad visual perception, broad auditory perception, broad retrieval ability, broad cognitive speediness, and processing speed.[53]

What is $g$? This italicized symbol for general intelligence is widely used

---

53. I. J. Deary, *Looking Down on Human Intelligence: From Psychometrics to the Brain* (New York: Oxford University Press, 2000), 15. See also J. B. Carroll, "The Higher-Stratum Structure of Cognitive Abilities: Current Evidence Supports $g$ and About Ten Broad Factors," in *The Scientific Study of General Intelligence: Tribute to Arthur R. Jensen*, ed. H. Nyborg (Boston: Pergamon, 2003), 5–6.

because the term *intelligence* is so fraught with difficulty and controversial issues. *G* is not a thing but a test result. All the broad factors of intelligence, as well as the narrow abilities, are positively correlated with *g*. As the broad factors and the narrow abilities rise, so does *g*; and as these scores fall, so does *g*. In statistical language, "The first unrotated principal component accounts for a large proportion of the variance in mental test batteries given to samples of the population."[54] Arthur Jensen, perhaps the best-known researcher into human intelligence, writes, "The *g* factor has become firmly established as a major psychological construct. Further psychometric and factor analytic work is unlikely either to disconfirm . . . *g* or to add anything essentially new to our understanding."[55]

Some work has started on constructing a view of intelligence that is purely biological. The neural efficiency model examines such brain features as responsivity to external stimuli, rates of metabolism for cerebral glucose, and the velocity of nerve conduction. Proponents of this view argue that with improved technology we should be able to measure what we now know as intelligence with purely neurological monitoring. The attractiveness of such an approach is that it could prove genuinely culture-free, a problem that has plagued other models. But the model has not yet generated consistent research results, so the jury is still out on the viability of this effort.[56]

A model that seems even more satisfactory than the hierarchical approach is the triarchic theory of intelligence advanced by Sternberg. Sternberg includes internal abilities as represented by the hierarchical model. These internal information-processing skills we call intelligence are adaptive with respect to the environment. But Sternberg argues that intelligence is more than just adaptation. We need a model of successful intelligence that represents the "ability to achieve success in life given one's personal standards, within one's sociocultural context."[57] The triarchic model seeks to account for the ability to capitalize on one's experience in solving problems, as well

---

54. Deary, *Looking Down on Human Intelligence,* 8.
55. A. R. Jensen, *The g Factor: The Science of Mental Ability* (Westport, Conn.: Praeger, 1998), 578.
56. J. E. Davidson and C. L. Downing, "Contemporary Models of Intelligence," in *Handbook of Intelligence,* ed. R. J. Sternberg (Cambridge: Cambridge University Press, 2000), 34–36.
57. R. J. Sternberg, "Beyond *g:* The Theory of Successful Intelligence," in *The General Factor of Intelligence: How General Is It?* ed. R. J. Sternberg and E. L. Grigorenko (Mahwah, N.J.: Lawrence Erlbaum, 2002), 448.

as the ability to create an optimal match between one's internal skills and one's environment.[58] Sternberg's successful intelligence includes analytical intelligence (roughly the equivalent of the hierarchical factors described above), creative intelligence, and practical intelligence.

Given all the difficulties of studying intelligence, someone might ask, "Why bother?" The principal answer is that a measure of intelligence has great utility. It is a successful predictor of school performance, work achievement, and ability to contribute to society.[59] In fact, the original effort to devise a simple test that could provide a measure of intelligence came from the United States military, which needed an effective means of identifying people who might make good officers.

Genes account for about 50 percent of intelligence. In more precise language, genetic influence explains 50 percent of the variation in intelligence among people. This estimate is "highly stable across twin versus adoption studies, across diverse populations, and across different measures of intelligence."[60] The 50 percent estimate, however, is a collapsed score. If we look at heritability estimates by age group, we see some interesting variation: When we study children, the power of genes to explain intelligence scores is 40 percent; when we study young adults, its power rises to 60 percent; the figure for older adults is 80 percent; and for the old-old it lowers again to 60 percent.[61] In simpler terms, if we study only older adults and measure their intelligence level, 80 percent of their performance is due to the genes they have inherited from their parents! In each case, the environment (both shared and nonshared) explains most of the balance of the variation (i.e., environmental influences explain 60 percent of childhood intelligence, 40 percent of young adult intelligence, 20 percent of older adult intelligence, and 40 percent of old-old adult intelligence).

The environment is an important contributor to the development of intelligence in children. The goals and values that parents have for their children, the strategies these parents utilize to help their children achieve these goals, and the parenting style that creates an emotional climate in the home all contribute to the environment that is so influential in intellectual devel-

---

58. Davidson and Downing, "Contemporary Models of Intelligence," 41.
59. Deary, *Looking Down on Human Intelligence,* 19.
60. S. A. Petrill, "The Case for General Intelligence: A Behavioral Genetic Perspective," in *Family Environment and Intellectual Functioning,* ed. E. L. Grigorenko and R. J. Sternberg (Mahwah, N.J.: Lawrence Erlbaum Assocs., 2001), 282.
61. Ibid., 284.

opment. Research has documented that the authoritative (not authoritarian) parenting style is positively correlated with high academic achievement and that neglectful parenting is positively correlated with low achievement in school.[62] Parental monitoring of their children is especially important in the emergence of intelligence.

Culture likewise makes a great impact on the development of intelligence. In some settings, high value is placed on nonacademic and practical skills that most measures of intelligence do not recognize. Evidence exists that suggests that some features of culturally influenced intelligence are better measured by dynamic rather than static assessment procedures.

> When cultural context is taken into account, (a) individuals are better recognized for and are better able to make use of their talents, (b) schools teach and assess children better, and (c) society utilizes rather than wastes the talents of its members.[63]

What if a child is mentally retarded? The most frequently used diagnostic procedure for mental retardation uses scores from IQ tests to describe the various levels of retardation (55–69, mild; 40–54, moderate; 25–39, severe; below 25, profound). Extensive study of the phenomenon of retardation provides evidence for both the *g* factor and for the specific factors of intelligence.[64] Approximately 50 percent of retardation cases are attributable to some organic cause, and the remaining 50 percent have an unknown cause. Epidemiologists have identified 795 different causes of organic mental retardation.[65]

The savant syndrome is a well-known phenomenon that gives us a window into some of the mysteries of intellectual functioning. Savants demonstrate "exceptional skills within relatively narrowly defined areas but whose general intellectual functioning is nevertheless markedly sub-average."[66] The syndrome

---

62. L. Okagaki, "Parental Beliefs, Parenting Style, and Children's Intellectual Development," in *Family Environment and Intellectual Functioning,* 142–61.

63. Robert J. Sternberg, "Culture and Intelligence," *American Psychologist* 59 (2004): 338.

64. R. M. Hodapp and E. Zigler, "Intellectual Development and Mental Retardation—Some Continuing Controversies," in *The Development of Intelligence,* ed. M. Anderson (Philadelphia: Psychology Press, 1999), 305.

65. Ibid., 299.

66. T. Nettelbeck, "Savant Syndrome—Rhyme Without Reason," in *The Development of Intelligence,* 247.

occurs in only 1 percent of the mentally disabled population, mostly among males. Ten percent of persons with autism display some savant characteristics, but not all savants are autistic. The exceptional abilities that savants display reflect a relatively narrow range of abilities: music, arithmetic, advanced mathematics (identifying prime numbers, calendrical calculations), artistic ability, mechanical dexterity, fine sensory discrimination, memory for trivia over a broad range of topics, or linguistic ability.[67] A savant may display one or several of these abilities. "That savant skills cluster within such a small range of activities demonstrates that these skills are not random occurrences."[68] The exceptional talents of a savant are not necessarily comparable to high achievement in the same area by a brilliant person. For example, when a savant is musically gifted, the quality of performance is somewhat mechanical, wooden, and lacking in emotive creativity.

Data coming from the study of savants seems to support both the $g$ factor of intelligence and the special abilities approach, both of which are included in the hierarchical model. Recently, scholars have speculated that savant accomplishments may be due to the fact that they have a very different type of long-term memory than do others with low levels of $g$. This may indicate that some features of LTM are independent of $g$ and not necessarily impaired when levels of $g$ are low.[69]

## Motivation

Every system of psychology (personality, psychotherapy, development, and so forth) must take some position regarding the nature of human motivation. Motivation connects cognition with behavior; and without it, the human organism remains inactive, relatively unresponsive, and disconnected from the tasks of life. "Motivation energizes and leads to action."[70] Motivation also serves to foster a synergy between thought and action because all three functions are intertwined and interrelated.[71]

---

67. Ibid., 253.
68. Ibid.
69. Ibid., 269.
70. E. D. Ferguson, *Motivation: A Biosocial and Cognitive Integration of Motivation and Emotion* (New York: Oxford University Press, 2000), 1
71. E. T. Higgins and A. W. Kruglenski, eds., *Motivational Science: Social and Personality Perspectives* (Philadelphia: Psychology Press, 2000), 2.

Over the years, investigations into the phenomenon of motivation have taken a variety of pathways. Behaviorists have seen motivations as approach-avoidance behaviors that are learned and reinforced. "We will repeat behaviours which we find pleasant and which meet our needs, we will stop behaviours which produce no response, and we will actually avoid unpleasant activities."[72] Biologically-based systems have emphasized the instincts and/or drives that seem to be related to motivation. Others have focused on wants or needs. Every psychology student is familiar with Abraham Maslow's hierarchy of needs (physiological, safety, social esteem, growth, and self-actualization). Some research supports the hierarchy, but most approaches now avoid the sequential approach that Maslow's work represents. McClelland focused on achievement, power, and affiliation as three basic motivations that undergird most human behavior.[73]

Much of the academic research on motivation occurs in the field of organizational psychology. Researchers in this specialty are interested in learning how to motivate people in work settings in ways that foster teamwork, personal growth, and corporate health. Studies explore the relative merits of external incentives versus intrinsic motivation. Money is, of course, a strong external motivator. In most work settings, only a few can actually earn as much money as they want; so money by itself is an inadequate motivator. "Money by itself is likely to produce self-serving behavior and skin-deep organizational commitment rather than the type of institution-building behavior that is characteristic of organizations like the Marines. . . ."[74]

Christians working in the mental health field have also been vitally interested in the topic of motivation. Scripture portrays the God-fearing and God-pleasing life as one in which the internal motivational system conforms to revealed standards and in which motivations are Christlike. The apostle Paul was remarkably candid about the motivations that energized his ministry to the churches of the first-century world. Studying Pauline motivations and the motivations of others in Scripture is a fruitful enterprise since it can unlock some of the secrets of faithful service to God.[75]

---

72. C. Hodson, *Psychology and Work* (New York: Taylor and Francis, 2001), 24.
73. Ibid., 25–27.
74. J. R. Katzenbach, *Why Pride Matters More Than Money: The Power of the World's Greatest Motivational Force* (New York: Crown Business, 2003), 1.
75. J. R. Beck, *The Psychology of Paul* (Grand Rapids: Kregel, 2002), 133–58, 256–58.

Robert Emmons at the University of California, Davis has developed a model that views motivation as a complex system of personal strivings. Some strivings reflect ultimate concerns, the type of dynamics that occur in spirituality and religious behavior. Emmons builds his model on the assumption that the human person is a goal-seeking organism. Theologically we would refer to this basic characteristic as teleological. Examples of personal-striving statements that typically begin with the words, "I typically strive to . . ." are:

- ". . . find that special someone."
- ". . . demonstrate my love to my children each day."
- ". . . win at all sports."
- ". . . make life easier for my parents."
- ". . . do something spontaneously, once a week."[76]

Conflict among the goals must be resolved if the person wishes to avoid an assault on the sense of well-being. Persons interested in spiritual themes form a set of ultimate concerns. "The ultimate is beyond which nothing else exists or is possible. . . . Ultimate concerns, then, are that above which no other concerns exist—it is literally at the end of the striving line."[77] "We are embarking on a significant period in the scientific study of spirituality. . . . The goals approach to spirituality shows that we need not compromise scientific rigor and precision in order to make progress in understanding what people find valuable, purposeful, and meaningful."[78]

## Behavior

Of all the topics we are exploring in this chapter, behavior is likely the easiest to comprehend. Behavior occurs when the human organism acts or does something. Cognitive theorists view behavior as the end product of a fairly long and complex chain of internal events that precede it. But even though we all "know" what behavior is, researchers have had a frustrating time defining it adequately. Their frustration illustrates the fairly common

---

76. R. A. Emmons, *The Psychology of Ultimate Concerns: Motivation and Spirituality in Personality* (New York: Guilford Press, 1999), 27.
77. Ibid., 95.
78. Ibid., 178–79.

experience we all have when we start exploring what appears to be a very self-evident concept. The more extensively we look into the matter, the more complicated it becomes.

Behavior that is of interest to psychological researchers displays three foundational characteristics: it must be observable, interpersonally comparable, and measurable.[79] An example of such a behavior would be how much time a college freshman spends on studying for an English 101 final exam. We can watch the student study (although we would not be able to determine how studiously he or she was engaged in the task), we could compare that amount of time to the time spent by others in the same class, and we could easily measure the time. However, we would face various problems looking at this behavior. Studying for an exam, for example, is a cluster of other discrete behaviors: reading, reviewing, understanding, memorizing, rehearsing, and so forth. So when our results were all tabulated, we might know some things about the behavioral cluster but very few things about important individual behaviors within the cluster. In frustration, some behaviorists have defined a behavior as nothing more than what behavioral measures measure![80]

The study of behavior dominated American psychology for much of the twentieth century. Many university psychology departments focused on animal behavior, rat training, pigeon performance, and reinforcement schedules. Undergraduate students often wondered what it all had to do with human functioning, but convinced behaviorists assured them that it all fit together and made perfect sense. The cognitive revolution that we have referred to previously in this volume dethroned behaviorism as the dominant force in psychological research so that now behaviorism is in a state of demise.

B. F. Skinner is the name we most frequently associate with behaviorism. His distinguished career spanned much of the twentieth century, and he well deserves the name of "Mr. Behaviorism." In 1975, a survey of college students found that Skinner was the best-known scientist of all time.[81] And his fame continues. Skinner was a determined investigator of animal

---

79. W. R. Uttal, *The War Between Mentalism and Behaviorism: On the Accessibility of Mental Processes* (Mahwah, N.J.: Laurence Erlbaum, 2000), 165.

80. Ibid.

81. L. D. Smith, "Situating B. F. Skinner and Behaviorism in American Culture," in *B. F. Skinner and Behaviorism in American Culture,* ed. L. D. Smith and W. R. Woodward (Bethlehem, Pa.: Lehigh University Press, 1996), 294.

behavior and how it related to human behavior. Later in his career he expanded his findings into a broad social agenda (based on his philosophy of science known as radical behaviorism) that pleased some and alienated many. Christians generally reacted negatively to Skinner's attempts to explain all of culture as reflective of his stimulus-response-reinforcement triad. Some remnants of Skinner's behavioral social engineering have survived the demise of behaviorism (such as token economies in institutional settings), but people now regard most of his social ideas as misguided utopian schemes that are insufficient to deal with the complexities of human social activity.

Skinner followed in the train of behaviorists who came before him. He believed in Pavlovian conditioning (also known as classical or respondent conditioning) and habituation (the decline of reflexive responses in light of repeated stimuli) although he rarely studied either one.[82] Skinner was convinced that all behavior could be explained in terms of reinforcement, discrimination, and extinction. He conducted most of his work with rats and pigeons in an era when animal rights activists were not quite so prominent in our society. Because evolution posited continuity between the animal kingdom and humans, his concentration on animal studies made perfect sense to him. Christians also observe some continuity between animals and humans, although the amount of that continuity is subject to debate. Skinner's main research focus was on operant conditioning: how a subject operates on the environment. Cognition and language were simply additional examples of behavior and were suitable for investigation as long as the analysis confined itself to his famous stimulus-response-reinforcement triad.[83]

What led to the downfall of behaviorism? Advances in technology opened up many new avenues of investigation for brain studies. Behaviorism had always demurred from engaging in a study of what was inside the "black box." But when measurable and revealing studies began to unlock more of the secrets of brain function, science inevitably moved toward that domain. In the words of a famous behaviorist, the cognitive revolution allowed psychology to do what comes naturally: study mental events.[84] Extensive criticism had also exposed many philosophical and logical errors inherent in

---

82. W. O'Donohue and K. E. Ferguson, *The Psychology of B. F. Skinner* (Thousand Oaks, Calif.: Sage, 2001), 99.

83. Ibid., 106–21.

84. Staddon, *The New Behaviorism,* 125.

behaviorism, weaknesses that contributed to its downfall. Skinner's sweeping application of behavioral principles to social and cultural agendas led many to believe that a new approach was needed. When behaviorism moved from fragmentary knowledge of stimulus-response mechanics to sweeping recommendations about social policy, "its weak philosophy and grandiose claims made (it) a soft target."[85]

Once psychology began to study "mentalist concepts" such as personal awareness, experience, perceptions, cognitive decision making, emotions, feelings, consensual acceptance of existence of each person's mind, and so forth, the rigid restriction of behaviorism to study only behavior gave way to a flood of cognitive studies.[86] To the bewildered behaviorists who were left high and dry by the cognitive revolution, psychology seemed to become a balkanized field of study "willing to embrace almost anything" and "a vacant lot, overgrown and chaotic."[87]

Somewhat surprisingly some behaviorists have acknowledged that religion and religious ideas contribute to the public's unease with pure behaviorism. Uttal sees a theological theme in the work of the founders of behaviorism, "a surrogate for the dualistic notion of a separate kind of reality for the mind. The ideas of soul, free will, ego, self, and consciousness are all tied together as Skinner made clear."[88] The collective past of these ideas, religious and otherwise, is extensive and to give them up or at least consider them as illegitimate targets for scientific inquiry requires courage. Behaviorists realize that almost all people living on earth use some of these mental concepts as part of their daily living. "It is undeniable that such a powerful social and intellectual force has had a significant impact on our scientific outlook—particularly in psychology."[89] In fact, Uttal admits that some sort of dualism that includes a mind or soul as one component may be a logical necessity for any organism that is able to reflect in a complex way on its own existence.[90] Behaviorists, both past and current, recognize many of the domains of human experience that are of such great interest to other researchers, but they maintain that nothing but behavior warrants investigation because only it can be observed and measured. Behaviorists express

---

85. Ibid., 179.
86. Uttal, *The War Between Mentalism and Behaviorism*, 64.
87. Staddon, *The New Behaviorism*, 1.
88. Uttal, *The War Between Mentalism and Behaviorism*, 59.
89. Ibid., 60.
90. Ibid.

chagrin that science would devote attention to "mentalisms," aspects of human experience that they claim are neither accessible nor analyzable.

Behaviorists have not gone away. Many cogent expositors of orthodox behavioral ideas have proposed that the time has come for a revived behaviorism, a neobehaviorism. Mentalism and behaviorism are "the two great contending approaches that have divided and destablilized as well as energized scientific psychology, in particular, for the last 120 years."[91] Neobehaviorists see this great contention as an ongoing battle. Their main argument for a revival of and recommitment to behavioral approaches is that working with observable and measurable phenomena such as behavior is the only way to conduct rigorous science; anything less will simply yield muddied results.

Neobehaviorists are the first to acknowledge the reality of the subjective, inner world of human mental life. To deny this would be to ignore the obvious. And neobehaviorists are quick to admit that any number of these internal processes of the mind underlie the observable behavior that they vigorously study. But they maintain that it is impossible to analyze the antecedents of actions that we can observe. "All responses (or behaviors) are measures of the totality of the experience or awareness of the behaving organism and are the resultant of a combination of many different stimulus, organism, and response variables as well as the past experience and . . . the genetic heritage of the individual. The combination is irretrievably tangled, . . . and little if anything can be done to disentangle the combination."[92] On that pessimistic note, neobehaviorists renew their call to stick with the observation and analysis of behavior only.

Psychologists can utilize behaviorism as a guiding scientific philosophy at several levels.

- *Eliminative behaviorism* asserts that as behaviorism advances, various mentalistic concepts will fade away as prescientific beliefs.
- *Methodological behaviorism* emphasizes that mentalistic concepts are private and thus beyond the scope of scientific enquiry.
- *Logical behaviorism* translates mentalistic concepts into publicly observable conditions so that they can be observed and measured.

---

91. Ibid., 1.
92. Ibid., 5.

- *Operational behaviorism* treats mentalistic concepts as expressions of the operations used to measure the concept.
- *Analytic behaviorism* refers to "behavior and dispositions which serve as the criteria for the application of mental terms."[93]

These various expressions of behaviorism vary in degree as well as approach to the data the scientist is examining.

Neobehaviorism will be somewhat distinct from the forms of it we have observed previously. Staddon proposes that the new behaviorism will have to shore up its philosophical base, will have to account in better ways for purposeful or teleological behavior, and will have to go at least one step beyond what is observable in order to accomplish its agenda.[94] Staddon convincingly argues that we must use some degree of internal state to understand even the simplest of animal behavioral patterns. "If we cannot even fathom the neural basis for the behavior of a 302-neuron nematode worm, what on earth are we doing speculating on consciousness and brain-behavior relations in human beings?"[95] A major challenge for scientists attempting to resuscitate the behavioral paradigm so that it can again be a major force in psychological science is to plan their new identity so that it can function in the postmodern world that now dominates most scientific discourse.[96]

## Emotion

Emotion plays a central role in human functioning. "To live is to experience pleasure or displeasure, happiness, or sadness, anger or fear or contentment."[97] It not only gives life great richness, but it also helps determine how well a person will navigate through life. The ability to monitor one's own emotions, understand the emotions of others, control emotions at the proper time, and express emotions in an appropriate and timely way all contribute to the effectiveness of any given individual in social and community life. In addition, emotional dysfunction is at the heart of many

---

93. Ibid., 23–24.
94. Staddon, *The New Behaviorism*, 1, 137, 151.
95. Ibid., 180–81.
96. L. D. Smith, "Situating B. F. Skinner and Behaviorism in American Culture," 305.
97. L. Berkowitz, *Causes and Consequences of Feelings* (Cambridge: Cambridge University Press, 2000), 1.

psychopathologies. Existence without emotion would be like a world without color or life without music. The relatively positive part emotion plays in current social science is not historically new. The claim is frequently but incorrectly made that prior to the modern age emotion was only viewed negatively, as an involuntary and irrational expression of bodily function.[98]

*Emotion* is a relatively recent word in English. This modern category encompasses semantic territory previously denoted by such terms as *affections, passions, appetites, temperament,* and *sentiments.* Dixon argues that these semantic changes also represent a secularization of the treatment of human affect as we have moved from interest in the passions to the emotions.[99] The study of emotion in psychology revolves around several related terms: *mood, feeling, affect,* and *emotion.* The one term that tends to have a fairly stable range of meanings across researchers is *mood,* understood to be a chronic or fairly long-lasting emotional state. Any of the other three terms can serve as an umbrella concept encompassing all the others. For the purposes of this section, we are using the word *emotion* as that umbrella term to describe this domain of psychological interest.

Definitions for emotion are many and varied among researchers. Emotions occur when "we perceive positive or negative significant changes in our personal situation."[100] Emotion thus is a personal response (bodily and psychological) to cognitive input (perception and its implied meaning). Generally, one's definition of emotion links the concept to other categories and thus becomes a sort of mini-theory that the author espouses regarding the nature of emotion.[101] The various components of a definition of emotion give the researcher variables to explore and investigate. A good definition should include reference to its biological base, its affective quality, its relationship to cognition, and its ability to lead to behavior. Current psychological understanding regarding emotion views each of these four components as crucial. Emotion is connected to brain activity, in some cases to locality and in other cases to neurochemical activity. It is affective in nature; that is, it consists of feelings that vary in valence and intensity. And emo-

---

98. T. Dixon, *From Passions to Emotions: The Creation of a Secular Psychological Category* (Cambridge: Cambridge University Press, 2003), 3.

99. Ibid., 1–25.

100. A. Ben-Ze'ev, *The Subtlety of Emotions* (Cambridge, Mass.: MIT Press, 2000), 13.

101. R. Plutchik, *Emotions and Life: Perspectives from Psychology, Biology, and Evolution* (Washington, D.C.: American Psychological Association Press, 2003), 22.

tion is linked to behavior in that it often precedes, accompanies, or follows human action.

Studying emotion is challenging because of all these complexities. Some aspects of emotion are measurable and observable by others. Other aspects of emotion are entirely private. People can hide or disguise feelings for social reasons, and existing prejudice among some researchers assumes that self-reflection reports regarding emotional states and reactions are unreliable. Perhaps we can see this difficulty in the assessment of emotions best in the lie detector test mechanisms used in law enforcement. Examiners who pay close attention to physiological and facial emotional indicators can do fairly accurate work, but no such test is always correct.

Facial expressions accompany emotion. Facial muscles in the forehead, eyelids, neck, lips, jaw, mouth, cheeks, and nose can all contribute to various emotional expressions. Frown muscles, sometimes called corrugations, control the area between the eyebrows and can change smooth skin into a corrugated furrow with the greatest of ease. Up to forty different anatomical units on the face can move into various configurations, many of which have universal recognizability.[102] Researchers realized in the 1970s that the study of facial expressions as they relate to emotion held great promise for cross-cultural work since the research would not require the use of language, a major hurdle in most cross-cultural efforts. Soon evidence pointed to six universally recognized facial expressions of affect for anger, disgust, fear, happiness, sadness, and surprise. Whenever and wherever people experienced these emotions, the resulting facial expression was the same the world over. Moreover, people from every culture uniformly recognized the emotion by reading the corresponding facial expression. Cultures did vary, however, with regard to display rules (when and where it is appropriate to allow your facial expression to be seen by others).[103] An even more fascinating discovery demonstrates the strong connection between the muscle configurations attached to a given facial expression and the underlying emotion being expressed by the face. "We now know that the bodily sensations produced by making the muscular movements characteristic of a particular emotional state can give rise to the feelings that are typically experienced in that state."[104]

---

102. D. Matsumoto, "Culture and Emotion," in *The Handbook of Culture and Psychology*, ed. D. Matsumoto (Oxford: Oxford University Press, 2001), 173.

103. Ibid.

104. Berkowitz, *Causes and Consequences of Feelings*, 2.

The cross-cultural uniformity of facial expression of certain emotional states leads to the possibility that the expressional pattern of emotion is, to some extent, hard-wired into the brain. In other words, perhaps the patterns have a neurological base that is somehow inherited rather than learned. To test for the possibility more extensively, researchers have carefully examined babies born blind. The congenital blindness of these infants obviously would prevent them from learning how to form facial expressions based on visual imitation. They observed the blind babies in a presumed state of fear (loss of balance), sadness (separation from caregiver), and joy (interaction with caregiver) and found strong evidence that the blind babies formed the very same facial expression respectively for all six of the universal patterns discovered in cross-cultural work.[105]

The cross-cultural study of facial expression, the confirmation of those findings among blind children, as well as other lines of research all point to a few basic emotions that appear to be primary in nature, perhaps analogous to primary colors. As surprising as it might seem, the myriad of colors our eyes are capable of discerning are combinations of the presence or absence of these 3 primary colors. Perhaps human emotions are organized in a similar fashion. Widespread agreement now exists regarding at least 4 primary emotions: anger, fear, joy, and sadness. A fair amount of agreement exists regarding 3 other basic emotions: disgust, surprise, and shame.[106] These current estimates regarding the number of basic emotions vary some from estimates made in previous centuries by the great thinkers of history: Descartes (41), Hobbes (46), Spinoza (48), Hume (20), and McCosh (100+). The estimates of Aquinas (4–11) are closer to current theory. Augustine's argument that all of them are derivatives or departures from love is likewise close.[107] At a secondary level we can identify scores of emotions that represent blends and mixes of these 4 to 7 primary states.

Another feature that distinguishes the primary emotions from the secondary emotions is brain activity. The primary emotions engage the subcortical levels of the brain, whereas many of the secondary emotions (sometimes called higher cognitive emotions) such as love, guilt, embarrassment, pride, envy, and jealousy involve more of the neocortex.[108] More

---

105. Plutchik, *Emotions and Life*, 165–67.
106. Ibid., 22.
107. Dixon, *From Passions to Emotions*, 18.
108. D. Evans, *Emotion: The Science of Sentiment* (Oxford: Oxford University Press, 2001), 29.

cultural variability exists among these secondary emotions than among the primary states. Some scholars have suggested that we could order the secondary emotions into some sort of hierarchy. Original factor analytic work seemed to indicate that there were six to twelve clusters of emotions. But further inspection of the underlying statistics revealed that these clusters were not independent but varied instead on valence and arousal.[109] So it seems better to arrange the primary emotions in a circumplex model.

Imagine two equal-length lines intersecting at the center of each other at a ninety-degree angle. The two lines would form four quadrants of equal size. We could connect the ends of each line by drawing a circle around the endpoints. On the vertical axis we can designate the top point as "high arousal" and the low point as "low arousal." On the horizontal axis we could designate the endpoint to our left as "displeasure" and the endpoint to our right as "pleasure." Emotions of medium to high arousal will appear in the top half of the circle, medium to low in the bottom half. Emotions with negative tone will appear in the left half and positive in the right half. Now we can plot the basic emotions. Because fear is a negative high arousal emotion, it will appear in the upper left-hand quadrant; because joy is high arousal coupled with positive valence, it will appear in the upper right-hand quadrant, and so forth.[110] The advantage of a circumplex presentation of the various emotions is that the model shows that even the basic emotions are combinations of valence and arousal without discrete boundaries and that various emotions, even sometimes the primary emotions, can blend into one another.

Emotion bears an important relationship to cognition. However, a long-standing controversy in psychology revolves around the exact nature of this relationship between cognition and affect. Which causes the other? Or which precedes the other in some important way? Lazarus developed a cognitive theory of emotion that posited beliefs as major antecedents of emotion.[111] Indeed, beliefs often do serve this purpose. But the opposite is also true: emotions and affective states can serve as antecedents for belief systems. The causal dynamic appears to be bidirectional, not unidirectional. This

---

109. Berkowitz, *Causes and Consequences of Feelings*, 13. See also Lisa Feldman and James A. Russell, "The Structure of Current Affect: Controversies and Emerging Consensus," *Current Directions in Psychological Science* 8 (1999): 10–14.

110. Berkowitz, *Causes and Consequences of Feelings*, 13–16.

111. N. H. Frijda, A. S. R. Manstead, and S. Bem, *Emotions and Beliefs: How Feelings Influence Thoughts* (New York: Cambridge University Press, 2000), 1.

same bidirectionality applies to beliefs and emotions associated with relationships as the biblical data presented in the previous chapter has shown.[112]

Emotions and cognition relate to each other in other ways as well. We
cannot envision a cognitive transaction of logic that is totally devoid of any
affective component, nor can we imagine an emotion that contains absolutely no cognitive structure or form. Robert B. Zajonc, the principal spokes-
person for the minority who argue that emotion and cognition are
independent systems, cites two lines of evidence for their independence.
First, the affective system is often the first to be activated by a stimulus.
Sometimes this activation occurs at a subconscious level; therefore, it does
not always include cognition. Second, the brain structures related to cognition and emotion are anatomically distinct.[113]

For most experts, however, emotion and cognition are not separate,
noninteracting spheres of human experience but overlapping systems that
even Zajonc admits "interact constantly in everyday life."[114] "Affect can be
considered a primary and separate response system only if cognition is
defined as excluding early attentional and interpretational processes that
are inevitably involved in stimulus identification before any response is
possible."[115]

The English language contains far more words for emotions with a negative connotation than for emotions that are positive in nature.[116] We can
imagine several explanations for this phenomenon. Perhaps there are more
negative than positive emotions, hence the need for more negative words.
Perhaps negative emotions are more differentiated or discrete, thus requiring more words. Perhaps we are more aware of negative emotions than the
positive ones. Or perhaps the positive emotions resist reduction to verbal
description. We do know that we ruminate about negative emotions about
five times as long as we think about positive emotions.[117] Perhaps this im-
balance is yet another feature of our fallen state.

---

112. M. S. Clark and I. Brissette, "Relationship Beliefs and Emotion: Reciprocal Effects," in
     *Emotions and Beliefs*, 213.
113. R. B. Zajonc, "Feeling and Thinking: Closing the Debate over the Independence of
     Affect," in *Feeling and Thinking: The Role of Affect in Social Cognition*, ed. J. P. Forgas
     (Cambridge: Cambridge University Press, 2000), 44.
114. Ibid.
115. J. P. Forgas, "The Role of Affect in Social Cognition," in *Feeling and Thinking*, 5.
116. Ben-Ze'ev, *The Subtlety of Emotions*, 99.
117. Ibid.

We have already seen how the basic emotions activate parts of the brain distinct from those areas activated by the higher cognitive emotions. When a person suffers from a focal brain lesion, doctors often see emotional changes. Lesions in the left hemisphere are associated with depression and in the right hemisphere with indifference. The observed depression in stroke patients is therefore not totally associated with being ill since patients with right hemisphere strokes are more indifferent than depressed.[118]

Prior to the 1980s, investigations into brain networks associated with emotion focused on the limbic system. More recently, researchers have explored one component of the limbic system, the amygdala, as the major brain area of emotional functioning. This tiny segment of the brain is itself complex. "It is generally believed that there are a least a dozen different nuclei, and that each has several subdivisions, each with its own set of unique connections."[119] The physiology of emotions, however, involves more than just brain pathways. In order for us to understand the complete emotional response in humans, we need to include a study of somatic responses and related neuroendocrine, immune, and autonomic systems and the neuropeptides that integrate these systems.[120] "Clearly, the physiology of emotion has been with us for as long as psychologists have been grappling with the nature of emotion. Somehow, it has been obvious from the start that bodily and hence neurophysiological reactions are involved in some basic way."[121]

The concept of emotional intelligence (EI) has grabbed the attention of the general public as well as scholars who produce materials for the public to read. Taking cues from the familiar concept of intelligence quotients, proponents of emotional intelligence have made the intriguing assertion that a parallel set of emotion skills appears to help or hinder people in their capacity to live life and that this "intelligence" is comprised of several skills, including "the ability to perceive and express emotion accurately and adaptively, the ability to understand emotion and emotional knowledge,

---

118. H. Kirshner, *Behavioral Neurology: Practical Science of Mind and Brain* (Boston: Butterworth Heinemann, 2002), 361–62.

119. J. E. LeDoux and E. A. Phelps, "Emotional Networks in the Brain," in *Handbook of Emotions*, ed. M. Lewis and J. M. Haviland-Jones, 2d ed. (New York: Guilford Press, 2004), 158.

120. J. T. Cacioppo, G. G. Bernston, J. T. Larsen, J. M. Poehlmann, and T. A. Ito, "The Psychophysiology of Emotion," in *Handbook of Emotions*, 187.

121. K. T. Strongman, *The Psychology of Emotion: From Everyday Life to Theory*, 5th ed. (Chichester, West Sussex: Wiley, 2003), 72.

the ability to use feelings to facilitate thought, and the ability to regulate emotions in oneself and in others."[122] Regarding EI, "Those people who are self-aware and sensitive to others manage their affairs with wisdom and grace, even in adverse circumstances. On the other hand, those who are 'emotionally illiterate' blunder their way through lives marked by misunderstandings, frustrations, and failed relationships."[123]

Evaluations of the EI concept among psychological scientists are somewhat mixed. Those who see it as a helpful means of organizing our knowledge about emotion cite its ability to serve as a framework for exploring the intelligent and rational aspects of emotion and as a guide to help identify deficits in the range of skills people need for effective living. We also learn more about the precise function of emotions with better granularity. We know, for example, that positive emotions (in spite of their pleasantness) often lead to shortcuts in thinking style and that negative emotions (in spite of their unpleasantness) can lead to more deliberate thinking styles.[124] Those who are more skeptical of EI, however, argue that it is not likely a new discovery but merely a new presentation of findings. "EI has discovered not some new continent, but what may be a rather minor province of already charted territory."[125]

## THE ORGANIZATION OF FUNCTION AND BEHAVIOR: PERSONALITY

We began this chapter by exploring how the six various aspects of human function and behavior we have identified develop and unfold. We conclude by looking at how patterns of human function and behavior are organized into recognizable patterns that characterize each one of us: our personality. Our exploration of the human person is enriched by looking at the parts as well as the whole. We know ourselves primarily as whole persons rather than as parts of persons, and the larger viewpoint fits well with how Scripture views the individual.

---

122. P. Salovey and D. A. Pizarro, "The Value of Emotional Intelligence," in *Models of Intelligence: International Perspectives,* ed. R. J. Sternberg, J. Lautrey, and T. I. Lubert (Washington, D.C.: American Psychological Assoc., 2002), 263.

123. G. Matthews, M. Zeidner, and R. D. Roberts, *Emotional Intelligence: Science and Myth* (Cambridge, Mass.: MIT Press, 2002), 3.

124. Salovey and Pizarro, "The Value of Emotional Intelligence," 268.

125. Matthews, Zeidner, and Roberts, *Emotional Intelligence,* 545.

## Personality Theory in General

Personality theory attempts to identify the ways in which any given individual is distinct from other people in some respects yet similar to other people in other respects. These characteristic patterns of interaction with people and the environment persist over time and are the primary reason we can return to a fortieth-year college reunion and relate to former classmates in ways very similar to how we interacted decades earlier. Personality theory also attempts to address issues of origin. Am I born with my personality, or do I learn it as I am growing up? Does my personality reflect the part of my inner world that is unconscious, or is it primarily interactive with the world and people around me?

Two main streams of research tradition feed into this branch of psychological investigation. First, psychodynamic theories, beginning with Freud and then moving down through several generations of his successors, have been vitally concerned with identifying the psychological dynamics that energize human personality with all its many variations. Many of these psychodynamic theorists began their work by carefully observing individual people who displayed neuroses (Freud), psychoses (Jung), or normal mental health (Adler). These observers were also interested in various age groups, including children (Freud) and infants (object relations theorists). Those who are familiar with the scientific method recognize that careful observation is a legitimate and widely used way of beginning the process of theory building. Indeed, these observations led to inferences of internal states, processes, or structures that produced the patterns that external observers could document. These inferences became the building blocks of theoretical approaches to the study of personality that we know today as psychoanalytic, neopsychoanalytic, life span, cognitive, and limited-domain theories. Each theory tends to emphasize the internal process that seems most determinative of personality while not denying that other processes do exist within the human. For example, psychodynamic theories tend to view internal conflict or unresolved issues as the primary source of psychic energy, even though these very same theorists would quickly recognize cognition as important. Cognitive theorists tend to view inner cognition processes as the strongest determiners of behavior and personality, even though they readily acknowledge other components in the inner world of the person.

The other approach to personality theory comes not from clinical sources but from research methodologies and empirical strategies.[126] Behavioral personality theories and the social learning approach have both sought to anchor their assertions about human personality functioning in empirical data. However, the strongest of these empirical approaches has been trait theory. Beginning in the 1930s with the work of Gordon Allport at Harvard, researchers have developed trait approaches to personality through the analysis of language, with its extensive verbal descriptions of human characteristics, and through the use of self-report instruments and questionnaires. Although these investigators made some assumptions as they developed their taxonomies of human traits, they used fewer assumptions than did behaviorists or social learning experimenters. The trait approach simply attempted to document the universe of human characteristics and to understand how these characteristics are typically organized.

## Five-Factor Model

The five-factor model (FFM) is now dominant among trait approaches. The major FFM assessment tool in current use is the NEO Personality Inventory, Revised (NEO-PI-R).[127] A useful definition of traits is "enduring tendencies to think, feel, and behave in consistent ways."[128] A vast body of empirical data has been gathered, a body of evidence that exhaustively describes human traits as they appear among persons belonging to the various cultures of the world. This universe of traits invariably reflects five factors, no matter which language or cultural group is investigated. The five factors, sometimes called the big five, are: openness to experience, conscientiousness, extraversion, agreeableness, and neuroticism. Results obtained by all other surveys of personality (such as the MMPI, the Myer-Briggs Temperament Inventory, the Adjective Checklist, or the 16PF) are either complete or partial representations of these five factors. They do not uncover areas of the personality that are not accounted for within the area described by the FFM. A principal advantage of the FFM is that individuals

---

126. D. P. Schultz and S. E. Schultz, *Theories of Personality,* 7th ed. (Belmont, Calif.: Wadsworth, 2001), 7.

127. R. L. Piedmont, *The Revised NEO Personality Inventory: Clinical and Research Applications* (New York: Plenum Press, 1998).

128. J. Allik and R. R. McCrae, "A Five-Factor Theory Perspective," in *The Five-Factor Model of Personality Across Cultures,* ed. R. R. McCrae and J. Allik (New York: Kluwer Academic, 2002), 304.

can describe themselves or be described by others using ordinary language questionnaires that yield descriptive results at an abstract level.[129] In addition, test takers not only recognize but also accept the results they obtain on measures of the FFM.[130] Recent work suggests that the five factors themselves may be characterized by *alpha* (agreeableness, conscientiousness, and reverse neuroticism), an underlying factor representing social desirability, and by *beta* (extraversion and openness), an underlying factor reflective of personal growth.[131] Should the *alpha* and *beta* suggestions gain widespread acceptance, the process of integrating the FFM with other personality theories will become much easier.

The FFM has considerable utility. Scores on measures of the five factors can predict job performance, job satisfaction, and mature religious and spiritual interests.[132] The five factors can discriminate among the ten personality disorders listed in the current *Diagnostic and Statistical Manual (DSM)* of the American Psychiatric Association. In fact, there are good prospects that the FFM will serve a useful purpose in providing a new organizational format for the personality disorders whose diagnostic criteria are currently overlapping and redundant in the DSM system.[133]

The FFM now has the status of a reference model. In other words, research in personality theory needs to connect itself to the FFM so that scholars can understand its relationship to what is currently known about personality configuration. Of the five factors, extraversion and neuroticism have been the most frequently studied human personality traits; the other

129. B. deRaad and M. Perugini, "Big Five Factor Assessment: An Introduction," in *Big Five Assessment,* ed. B. deRaad and M. Perugini (Seattle: Hogrefe and Huber, 2002), 2.

130. P. Andersen and H. Nordvik, "Possible Barnum Effect in the Five Factor Model: Do Respondents Accept Random NEO Personality Inventory-Revised Scores as Their Actual Trait Profile?" *Psychological Reports* 90 (2002): 543.

131. deRaad and Perugini, "Big Five Assessment," 4.

132. T. A. Judge, D. Heller, and M. K. Mount, "Five-Factor Model of Personality and Job Satisfaction: A Meta-Analysis," *Journal of Applied Psychology* 87 (2002): 530–41; V. Saroglow, "Religion and the Five Factors of Personality: A Meta-Analytic Review," *Personality and Individual Differences* 32 (2002): 20–21. See also J. R. Beck, *Jesus and Personality Theory: Exploring the Five Factor Model* (Downers Grove, Ill.: InterVarsity, 1999), for an extended discussion of how the FFM relates to biblical teachings.

133. P. T. Costa and T. A. Widiger, eds., *Personality Disorders and the Five Factor Model of Personality,* 2d ed. (Washington, D.C.: American Psychological Assoc., 2002); T. J. Trull, T. A. Widiger, D. R. Lynam, and P. T. Costa, "Borderline Personality Disorders from the Perspective of General Personality Functioning," *Journal of Abnormal Psychology* 112 (2003): 193–202.

three are more recent.[134] Personality as described in adulthood by this trait approach is remarkably stable. Thus the predictions of William James (that adult character is set like plaster) and Sigmund Freud (that early life experiences form a very stable adult personality) seem to have stronger empirical support than those theories that predict substantial personality change during adulthood (Jung and Erikson). The "predominant stability" of adult personality, however, does not mean that adults do not change. It simply documents that basic character (trait) patterns do not change a great deal.[135]

Two features of the FFM add to our hunch that all future personality theories will have to incorporate these five robust trait factors into their explanations of human personality. First, the FFM has remarkable cross-cultural durability. Too many of the twentieth century's great personality theories primarily reflect Western and/or developed mentalities; they have proved far less powerful in Eastern and nondeveloped settings. But when the NEO-PI-R is translated by native speakers into other languages, people describe themselves in ways that yield the same five broad personality factors. Intercultural scores will vary somewhat from country to country, and intracultural scores indicate considerable individual profile distinction. But the basic pattern of personality factors appears whether the language group being investigated is Indo-European, Uralic, Dravidian, Altaic, Malayo-Polynesian, Sino-Tibetan, or Bantu. Research on all five continents of the planet continues to uncover the five factors, even when researchers control the data analysis for various response sets that vary from individualistic to collectivistic societies.[136]

Many documented intercultural differences in scores do not conform to popular stereotypes that are attached to climate and geography, although we do know that personality patterns found in proximate societies are similar. This similarity is likely due to the confounded effects of shared gene pools, physical environments, and culture.[137] The societies with greater distance from the equator show more extraversion and less conscientiousness, re-

---

134. deRaad and Perugini, "Big Five Assessment," 6.

135. R. R. McCrae and P. T. Costa, *Personality in Adulthood*, 2d ed. (New York: Guilford Press, 2003), 5.

136. J. Allik and R. R. McCrae, "Toward a Geography of Personality Traits: Patterns of Profiles Across 36 Cultures," *Journal of Cross-Cultural Psychology* 35 (2004): 15; and R. R. McCrae, "NEO-PI-R Data from 36 Cultures: Further Intercultural Comparisons," *The Five-Factor Model of Personality Across Cultures*, 115.

137. Allik and McCrae, "Toward a Geography of Personality Traits," 14.

sults that are in some ways counterintuitive; but climate in itself is a poor determiner of personality style.[138] All these data and more point to the intriguing suggestion that we may be on the brink of establishing a universal personality pattern that varies from society to society, is relatively independent of cultural systems including educational practice and religious and moral systems, and is more similar among societies than we ever thought before.[139]

The second feature of the FFM that merits serious attention is the multiple indications that these personality factors have a strong genetic base. While it has been relatively easy for us to adjust to genetic data showing how the various physical characteristics of our children are combinations of the genetic heritage we parents have passed along to them, it is more difficult for us to envision that their personalities are likewise heavily influenced by genetic determiners. We have assumed for decades that the principal shaping force for the kind child, and the quiet child, and the energetic child, and the loving child is the parenting style we have used with them. Environmental influences, including parenting style, is influential; but consistent data from research projects worldwide insist that genetic influence on the personalities of our children is approximately four times more powerful than is our parenting. Some theorists have suggested that this deep and powerful genetic influence accounts for why adult personality is remarkably stable over time; the environment makes a milder impact on deeply embedded features of our psyche than it does on more superficial features.

The comprehensiveness, cross-cultural generalizability, genetic basis, and strong empirical foundation of the FFM have brought it close to lawful status in the psychology of personality. Yet one still finds considerable resistance among advocates of other personality approaches and especially among clinicians who have worked for years with another understanding of personality to accept the trait approach as relevant for their work. The

---

138. Ibid., 15–23.

139. Quantitative cross-cultural comparisons are problematic for many reasons, and researchers must be very cautious in making pronouncements about "national personalities" until more of the research problems have been conquered. See Y. H. Poortinga, F. J. R. Van De Vijer, and D. A. Van Hemert, "Cross-Cultural Equivalence of the Big Five: A Tentative Interpretation of the Evidence," in *The Five-Factor Model of Personality Across Cultures,* 281. See also J-P Rolland, "The Cross-Cultural Generalizability of the Five-Factor Model of Personality, in *The Five-Factor Model of Personality Across Cultures,* 9–10.

most frequent criticism of theories based on traits is that these traits are surface features of the personality representing powerful, unseen dynamics. "The traits themselves are only surface indicators of underlying processes and themes."[140] Indeed, most clinicians have difficulty seeing how traits could be foundational, given years of training and experience that seem to point in the opposite direction. However, the view that traits are surface features of personality does not account for the facts: How could surface features produced by individual dynamics have a strong genetic base? How could similar trait patterns emerge in culture after culture? How could the same five factors repeatedly occur in research findings if they are not somehow hard-wired into the human psyche?

To account for the foundational nature of traits, personality theories must use them as a starting point and then explain the various dynamics of personality functioning (motivation, roles, attitudes, emotional maturity, self-concept, moral development, and so forth) in light of these traits. A well-established trait theory such as the FFM has the potential for turning personality theories upside down. McCrae and Costa have begun to suggest the outlines of just such a revision, namely the five-factor theory (FFT). Obviously, the FFM is incomplete by itself in that it does not account for how "behavior is organized, both moment by moment and over the sweep of a lifetime."[141] A complete personality theory must deal with the well-known ego functions such as the personality's executive operation, conflict resolution, social skills, and interaction with the environment. The FFT accounts for the basic traits of an individual with its heavy biological and genetic influence and posits that the individual's characteristics arise out of the basic tendencies represented by the big five factors. These characteristic adaptations include the self-concept, personal strivings (motivations), and attitudes. Over the length of a lifetime, these characteristic adaptations form the objective biography of the individual that includes memory, experience, learning, and personal history.[142] As work continues on the development of this personality theory (FFT), we will gain a better understanding of how traits relate to the other classic theories of personality that have appeared throughout the twentieth century.

---

140. R. Hogan, "A Socioanalytic Perspective on the Five-Factor Model," in *The Five-Factor Model of Personality*, ed. J. S. Wiggins (New York: Guilford Press, 1996), 178.

141. McCrae and Costa, *Personality in Adulthood*, 162.

142. Allik and McCrae, "A Five-Factor Theory Perspective," 304–6.

CHAPTER 9

# FUNCTION *and* BEHAVIOR INTEGRATED

IN PART 1 AND PART 2, our topic material has fallen neatly into pairs: origin and destiny, substance and identity. In part 3, our material on function and behavior consists of a more integrated whole, so our integrative considerations will reflect this unity. Again we will identify certainties emerging from both the theological and the psychological sides of our inquiry, suggest a possible integration of those certainties, and highlight some issues that warrant further study and work.

## CHRISTIAN CERTAINTIES

1. *Both theology and psychology focus a great deal of attention on the many and varied aspects of human function and behavior.* In some respects this attention from both disciplines reveals a higher degree of overlapping interest than we have seen in the prior two sections. The functioning and behavior of the human person before the Fall, after the Fall, under the impact of redemption, and in the glorified state are at the heart of the biblical message. Consequently, theologies over the centuries have described this domain in considerable detail. Likewise, psychology expresses great interest in what the human person does and how the human functions.

2. *The theological and psychological literatures use slightly different terminology with different nuances for some of the features of human functioning.* For example: Scripture speaks of thinking and

psychology of cognition; the Bible addresses the will, and psychology deals with motivation; Scripture describes desires and emotions, while psychology studies emotion, which includes feelings. Both disciplines, however, address human behavior. Consciousness and intelligence receive more attention in the psychological field than in Scripture.

3.  *Sin has made a deep and pervasive impact on human functioning and behavior.* The Bible describes the newly created human persons, including their capacity to function, as "very good," but not "very good" once sin affected all components of human functioning. The Bible gives us some information about the created state and a great deal of information about the fallen and redeemed states of human persons. Psychology knows nothing of pre-Fall human functioning and only describes humans in their fallen state, although secular psychologists do not acknowledge the Fall of the human race into sin. Nor can psychology fully understand what human functioning can be like in the redeemed state.

4.  *The Bible also asserts that sin has corrupted many "non-spiritual" components of human functioning.* The Fall affects more than just the spiritual nature of humans. All the components of the functions we have examined in this section (consciousness, intelligence, cognition, motivation, emotion, and behavior) display some features of sin's corrupting influence. The general result of this corruption is not that humans apart from God cannot display high levels of intelligence or clear thinking; but the fallen mind does not clearly perceive spiritual realities and the fallen will is distracted from God and kingdom realities.

5.  *Each fallen human being continues to bear the image of God.* As we have previously seen, a central feature of God's creation of the human race centers on the image God stamped on the first pair of humans, an image of God that has passed on to all their descendants. When sin entered human experience, the image did not disappear but was tarnished.

6.  *Consciousness is one of the building blocks of human functioning.* Consciousness is basic to all human functioning. Scripture assumes its reality, and psychology seeks to understand it. Consciousness is subject to illness, injury, and substance toxicity. Consciousness is likely

the humming of the brain that constantly occurs in the living human and that undergirds all brain activity. We can quiet our consciousness, but we cannot empty it as some religious leaders urge their followers to do.

7. *Cognition relates to a broad band of human functions including thinking, reasoning, and problem solving.* Sin has made an impact in this sphere of human functioning and behavior. We do not fully understand sin's impact, however, since we do not have access to models of sin-free cognition. Adam and Eve were sin-free thinkers before the Fall, but we have limited information in Scripture about what their cognitive styles looked like. Jesus was sin-free as well, but His style of cognition is blended with His deity and thus does not give us an exactly parallel view of human, sin-free cognition.

8. *Intelligence is an important component of human functioning that is not evenly distributed throughout the human race.* Because levels of intelligence are related to genetic inheritance, the human gene pool apparently contains factors that yield different capacities in different situations. Sin has impacted the human gene pool, and perhaps this uneven distribution is one example of this corruption. Intelligence is a human gift or skill granted by God that humans may use to give God glory or to serve selfish purposes.

9. *Sin takes its greatest toll on human motivation (volition, will).* Many of the Bible's descriptions regarding the depraved nature of unredeemed persons relate to their corrupted wills. Salvation likewise has a great positive impact on human motivation. The content of human motivation is a major factor in determining whether or not an expressed human function pleases or displeases God. Psychology is vitally concerned with human motivation since this sphere relates closely to the change process.

10. *Emotions represent an important component of human functioning and one that corresponds in part to emotional aspects of God's nature.* Sin likewise makes a substantial impact on the emotional sphere of human functioning. Sanctification, the work of the indwelling Holy Spirit, produces great change in the emotional life of a believer. Emotions are affected by the other features of mental life (consciousness, will, cognition) and affect the other features of mental life (will, cognition, and so forth).

11.  *Both theology and psychology view behavior as an observable end prod-uct of internal processes.* God holds people responsible for their be-havior. Behavior is not fixed but can change. Behavior in the life of a believer can reflect either the sinful nature or the new nature im-parted by salvation.

## BRIEF INTEGRATION

Theology provides us with a wealth of information about the spiritual status of the various components of human functioning. Psychology con-tinues its efforts to understand more of the mechanisms governing these functions. Coupled with advances in biological science, neuroscience, and medicine, our understanding is more complete than ever; yet it is quite incomplete at the same time. Every advance in our understanding of how these features of the mind and brain operate adds more complexity to the picture. One cannot know if future investigations of this ever-increasing complexity will eventually lead to simplicity or not. Some observers won-der if the mysteries of the mind and brain will remain mysteries known only to God or if the mind and brain will yield more of their secrets to investigators in the future.

The Bible appears not to address certain issues involved in human func-tioning such as consciousness or intelligence. Yet it provides an ample amount of information about other components of human functioning such as motivation, behavior, emotion, and cognition. Psychology is best able to contribute information about how these functions are anchored in genetics, how they develop within the life span, and the mechanics undergirding them. Theology is best able to help us understand the spiri-tual implications of these functions, how sin impacts them, and how re-demption and later glorification significantly change them.

## FUTURE RESEARCH

Various psychological theories have addressed the topic of conscience. Additional work could provide helpful information, though, as to how con-science functions in a metatheoretical way and how its operation within the sphere of human functioning relates to the data about the conscience that we find in Scripture.

Scripture reveals to us that human nature is substantially corrupted by the reality of sin. Can we understand more completely, however, in what ways this corruption is expressed and in what ways the image of God in humans continues to find expression? We cannot say theologically or psychologically that humans are as evil as evil can be, nor can we say that unredeemed persons are as good as good can be. How do we describe human depravity in a scripturally faithful way while still allowing for psychological functions that work well?

Both theology and psychology clearly have a part to play in these ongoing discussions.

# PART 4

# HUMAN RELATIONSHIPS
## *and* COMMUNITY

# CHAPTER 10

# RELATIONSHIPS *and* COMMUNITY *in* THEOLOGICAL PERSPECTIVE

THIS VOLUME HAS DEALT WITH the nature, capacities, and behaviors of human persons *as individuals* within the larger human family. Part 4 concerns human beings *communally* in the full range of interpersonal and interobject relations. Humanity in relationship and in community has been discussed by philosophers, theologians, psychologists, and sociologists, and it is of considerable relevance in the contemporary postmodern environment.

## HUMAN RELATIONSHIPS AS CREATED

Chapter 7 explored intellect, volition, emotion, moral sense, and the human exercise of dominion. This leaves one principal capacity of created humanity to consider—*relationality*. Before exploring these theories, an overall definition would be helpful. Gordon R. Lewis and Bruce Demarest define relationships as "connections between things, persons, or ideas."[1] From beginning to end, the Bible depicts persons as individuals created for relationship and designed to be part of a community.

---

1. Gordon R. Lewis and Bruce Demarest, *Integrative Theology*, 3 vols. (Grand Rapids: Zondervan, 1987-94), 2:163. According to Walter Brugger and Kenneth Baker, *Philosophical Dictionary* (Spokane, Wash.: Gonzaga University Press, 1974), 343, "A relation is the habitude or reference of one thing to another."

## Historical Perspectives

From ancient times, philosophers and theologians have proposed two practical theories of human relationality, the theory of external relations and the theory of internal relations.

### Theory of External Relations

The classical view of the person is rooted in *the theory of external relations,* which states that relationships are only external to the person, so they do not affect personhood in an essential way. Relations with persons and objects are *accidens* and do not define the identity of the individuals or the other objects with which there is connection.

Applied to theological anthropology, the theory of external relations holds that the identity and nature of a person are independent of that person's relation to another person or persons. The human person has been understood as an undying and immaterial soul/spirit in a material body with intellectual, volitional, emotional, moral, and relational capacities for acting upon the surrounding world (see part 2). The classical external view identifies personhood with an identity and nature that endures through all of life's changing relations.

Pre-Socratic Greek philosophy focused on a person's unchanging substance (that which exists in itself) and changing accidents (attributes of a substance). Aristotle likewise distinguished between the unchanging substance *(ousia; substantia)* of a thing and its variable accidents *(accidens),* including relations. Relations, Aristotle believed, are not inherent in the substance of a thing. The philosopher divided the human soul into vegetable, animal, and rational "souls," and spoke of powers inherent in each. In this view, the individual is an authentic person prior to entering into relationships.

Augustine assuredly assumed this classical substance ontology: "Man is a rational substance composed of soul and body."[2] The soul, moreover, is "a certain kind of substance, sharing in reason, fitted to rule the body."[3] The

---

2. Augustine, *On the Trinity* 15.7.11 [*NPNF*¹, 3:204]. Augustine explicitly refers to the human person's "substance" and "accidents" in *On the Trinity* 5.5.6 [*NPNF*¹, 3:89] and elsewhere.

3. Augustine, *On the Magnitude of the Soul* 13.22 [*FOTC*, 4:83]; cf. idem, *Letter* 166.11 [*FOTC*, 30:16].

*imago Dei,* Augustine affirmed, reflects the Trinity; but the image of the Trinity lies in the mind, not in relationships, that is, in "mind and the knowledge wherewith the mind knows itself, and the love wherewith it loves itself."[4]

Also guided by Aristotelian philosophy, Thomas Aquinas distinguished between a person's immaterial-material substance and its accidents: "Man is composed of a spiritual and corporeal substance."[5] The human soul is divided into a rational soul with cognitive powers, an animal soul of sensations, and a vegetable soul of growth, and movement as an organism. Relations are not essential to a thing, for person signifies a relation subsisting in a nature.[6]

According to John Calvin, the human soul/spirit is "an incorporeal substance"[7] and "an immortal yet created essence."[8] The principal part of the human person is the soul, distinguished from the body but dwelling within it as in a house: "Unless the soul were something essential, separate from the body, Scripture would not teach that we dwell in houses of clay (Job 4:19) and at death leave the tabernacle of the flesh, putting off what is corruptible."[9] Calvin posits "the three cognitive faculties of the soul" ("understanding, reason, and fantasy") and "the three appetitive faculties" ("will," "anger," and "desire") that impel the person in action.[10]

Calvin mentions other human capacities, including memory, conscience, and affections. The two principal faculties of the soul, however, are the understanding and will. The several human faculties "clearly show that there lies hidden in man something separate from the body."[11] Thus Calvin held to an essential ontology and a faculty psychology. *Essential ontology* regards the components of the human being as consisting of things that are different and ontologically separate in their essences or essential makeup. *Faculty psychology* conceives of the human mind as consisting of separate powers or faculties that work much like muscles that can be strengthened through

---

4. Augustine, *On the Trinity* 15.6.10 [*NPNF*[1], 3:204].

5. Peter Kreeft, *A Summa of the Summa* (San Francisco, Calif.: Ignatius Press, 1990), 243.

6. Thomas Aquinas, *ST,* 2:34–37 [pt. 1, q. 29, art. 4].

7. John Calvin, *Institutes of the Christian Religion,* ed. John T. McNeill, trans. Ford Lewis Battles, 2 vols., LCC, vols. 20–21 (Philadelphia: Westminster, 1960), 1:192 [1.15.6].

8. Ibid., 1:184 [1.15.2].

9. Ibid., 1:185 [1.15.2].

10. Ibid., 1:193 [1.15.6].

11. Ibid., 1:185 [1.15.2].

use. It was the most widely accepted concept of learning in the nineteenth century. In book 1, chapter 15 of *Institutes of the Christian Religion* (1559 edition), Calvin refers to "(human) nature" in a substantial sense half a dozen times.

Millard J. Erickson argues that a relational ontology is fundamentally flawed. Advocates such as Karl Barth and Emil Brunner are "led astray by their wholeheartedly antisubstantialist presuppositions, which we have suggested stemmed from existentialism."[12] Existentialism deprecates essences or substances and values "experience which is present when a relationship is active."[13] Claims Erickson, "The image is something in the very nature of man, in the way in which he was made. It refers to something man *is* rather than something he *has* or *does*."[14]

The human person's ability to enter into relationships with others represents the *application* of his or her powers of personality (intelligence, will, and emotions). Erickson argues that while not constitutive of human personhood, authentic relationships contribute significantly to the purpose for which we were made: "Man is most fully man when he is active in these relationships . . . , for then he is fulfilling his *telos*, God's purpose for him."[15]

On philosophical and biblical grounds, Gordon R. Lewis argues for *classical substance ontology* and *faculty psychology*:

> The essence of anything, simply put, equals its being (substance) plus its attributes. Since Kant's skepticism of knowing anything in itself or in its essence, many philosophers and theologians have limited their general ways of speaking to the phenomena of Jewish or Christian religious experience. Abandoning categories of essence, substance, and attribute, they have thought exclusively in terms of Person-to-person encounters.[16]

A *reductive, relational ontology* fails because "a person's essential attributes and capacities inhere in something."[17] What a person *is*, is not merely *that* a person relates; rather, that a person *relates* expresses fundamentally what a

---

12. Millard J. Erickson, *Christian Theology* (Grand Rapids: Baker, 1984), 511.
13. Ibid., 508.
14. Ibid., 513.
15. Ibid., 514.
16. Gordon R. Lewis, "God, Attributes of," in *EDT*, 492.
17. Lewis and Demarest, *Integrative Theology*, 2:143.

person *is*. Expressed otherwise, the value of relationships can be affirmed only when the identity of the persons that relate is postulated. "Real person-to-person relationships are possible because of the ontological reality of persons as spiritual and physical beings."[18]

## Theory of Internal Relations

Certain recent voices in philosophy and theology reject the classical substantialist-psychological model of the human person in favor of the late-modern-postmodern *socio-relational model* rooted in a metaphysic of becoming. This "turn to relationality" is grounded in the philosophical *theory of internal relations,* which holds that the identity and nature of the individual depends on the relation it sustains to other persons and things. The relation, therefore, is essential (not accidental) to the identity of both the individual and the things in relational context. In theological anthropology, this is called *reductive relationalism,* which holds that the identity and nature of a person depends on the relation it sustains to another person or persons. Thus a child, a man, or a woman is not constituted a person until engaged in authentic relations with another person or persons.

The social behaviorist George Herbert Mead (1863–1932) contributed to the turn to relationality. Affirming that "the self can only exist in relation to other selves," the University of Chicago scholar suggested that we discover who we are only in the context of authentic relationships.[19] The German philosopher Martin Buber (1878–1965) differentiated between *I-Thou* and *I-it* relations. An *I-it* relation involves observation, experiencing, and manipulation of things (including persons) as objects. An *I-Thou* relation requires mutual encounter and submission of one person to another.

Buber asserts that the human *I* does not exist independently of other person(s) it encounters and addresses. Expressed otherwise, *I* and *Thou* in relation constitute personhood. "Through the *Thou* a man becomes *I*."[20] Buber holds that, "a person can become an 'I' only when the object with which one has to do is seen as a 'Thou' rather than an impersonal 'it.'"[21]

---

18. Ibid., 2:159.

19. George Herbert Mead, *Mind, Self, and Society* (Chicago: University of Chicago Press, 1934), 164.

20. Martin Buber, *I and Thou,* trans. Ronald Gregor Smith (Edinburgh: T. and T. Clark, 1937), 28; cf. 4.

21. S. R. Obitts, "Buber, Martin," in *EDT,* 191, commenting on Buber's position.

Buber's relational perspectives significantly influenced neo-orthodox theology.

The father of neo-orthodox theology, Barth, began his massive *Church Dogmatics* with a study of the doctrine of the Trinity. From this basis Barth claims that the relationality constitutive of human being corresponds to relationality within the triune God. The similarity between the triune God and humans consists in the fact that both experience *I-Thou* confrontation and encounter. Humans experience *I-Thou* confrontation vertically with God and horizontally with other humans. "Man can and will always be man before God and among his fellows only as he is man in relationship to woman and woman in relationship to man. And as he is one or the other he *is* man. . . . It is this and nothing else that makes him man."[22]

Barth's relational ontology is clear. "Humanity is the determination of our being in encounter with the other man."[23] Again, "Man is in fact fellow-human. He is in fact the encounter of I and Thou."[24] Simply put, "In its basic form humanity is fellow-humanity."[25]

The Scottish philosopher of religion John Macmurray (1891–1976) advocates the theory of social personalism, which regards the personal unit as "You and I." Triumphantly he claims, "We can now rid ourselves effectively of the ghost of the old faculty psychology which still haunts our philosophies."[26] Macmurray sums up his position, "The idea of an isolated self is self-contradictory. Any agent is necessarily in relation to the Other. Apart from this relation he does not exist. . . . Persons, therefore, are constituted by their mutual relation to one another. 'I' exist only as one element in the complex 'You and I.'"[27]

Aligning himself with open theism and aspects of process theism and relational philosophy, Clark Pinnock claims, "There has been a shift from substantialist to relational categories in modern times . . . nowadays dynamic relational categories are more fundamental than substantialist categories.[28] Pinnock judges that the relational fellowship among the Trinity's persons constitutes a pattern for human relationships. Postulating that God's na-

---

22. Karl Barth, *CD*, 3.1.186.
23. Ibid., 3.2.248.
24. Ibid., 3.2.285.
25. Ibid.
26. John Macmurray, *Persons in Relation* (London: Faber and Faber, 1961), 33.
27. Ibid., 24; cf. 17, 28, 61, 73–75.
28. Clark Pinnock, *The Most Moved Mover* (Grand Rapids: Baker, 2001), 120.

ture changes as it enters into changing relationships, Pinnock concludes that human nature also changes through the relationships it sustains. Pinnock's metaphysic of becoming and relating yields the following conclusion: "The essence of a thing now depends on its relationship with other things. Everything is related to everything else. The network of relationships is more basic than substantial individuals."[29]

Stanley Grenz (1950-2005) likewise opposes the classical model of the individually-focused and substantialist human person in favor of the socially constructed self. Grenz claims that "person" is a relational concept, meaning that "'person' has more to do with relationality than with substantiality and that the term stands closer to the idea of communion or community than to the conception of the individual in isolation or abstracted from communal embeddedness."[30] He adds, "Ultimately the 'self' arises in relationships, and personal identity formation is ultimately a communal task."[31] Grenz finds in a social understanding of the Trinity the model for "a thoroughgoing social-personalist reconception of the self. . . ."[32] Thus "The doctrine of the Trinity does not propose that God is three persons who have relations, but three subsistent relations that are in fact persons."[33] Grenz expands on this communal line of reasoning by asserting that "the contemporary rebirth of Trinitarian theology describes the relational self not merely as person-in-relation but as the ecclesial self, the new humanity in communion with the triune God."[34]

F. LeRon Shults, a Bethel Seminary theologian, rejects substance dualism and faculty psychology as obsolete. He proposes a reconstruction of anthropology, which affirms at its heart that "being is essentially relational,"[35] or that "the relations of things are essential to their being things."[36] Seeking "a more holistic, community-orientated understanding of humanity,"[37] Shults concurs with much late modern and postmodern thought that we

---

29. Ibid., 121.
30. Stanley J. Grenz, *The Social God and the Relational Self* (Louisville, Ky.: Westminster John Knox, 2001), 4.
31. Ibid., 19.
32. Ibid., 14.
33. Ibid., 50–51.
34. Ibid., 312; cf. 331.
35. F. LeRon Shults, *Reforming Theological Anthropology: After the Philosophical Turn to Relationality* (Grand Rapids: Eerdmans, 2003), 181.
36. Ibid., 32 n. 50.
37. Ibid., 165.

must move beyond "the focus on substances and abstract faculties to explore more holistic and dynamic models of human nature."[38] Central to this relational ontology is his belief that "the self [is] always and already immersed in the dynamic processes of knowing and being known in community."[39]

## Biblical and Theological Development

### Ontology and Relationality

Relations are emotionally laden connections between persons, things, or ideas. When discussing relations we must posit the reality of personal agents or objects that relate. Apart from distinct persons or things involved, relations amount to nothing. Discourse about relationships is meaningful only when the identity of the subjects that relate is posited; otherwise we are left with a reductive relationalism that tends toward monism.[40] To the question, What is real vis-à-vis man? the great majority of Christian philosophers, theologians, and the church's creeds have postulated essence or substance as foundational, qualified by properties (e.g., immateriality), capacities or potential (e.g., rationality), and relations (e.g., connectedness).[41]

We have stated that persons are soul/spirits intimately united to a body with intellectual, volitional, emotional, moral, and relational *capacities* for engaging internal and external worlds. Relationality is no less a capacity of the human person than intellect, volition, emotion, or moral sense. Moreover, a fetus, a newborn infant, or an individual in solitary confinement is a human person with the capacity for relationships, even if the person is not actively engaged in relations with other persons. Although the humanity God intended is most fully realized as humans mature through significant relationships, the identity and value of the relating persons must be pre-

---

38. Ibid., 174.
39. Ibid., 181.
40. Gordon R. Lewis writes, "The commitment to internal relations leads one down a steep road to monism, fusing the changing identities of Creator and creature. Arguing from internal relations, philosopher Francis Bradley's *Appearance and Reality* (1893) concluded that since the relations are internal in the direction of both terms, everything is involved in everything else. Everything is . . . in process of becoming an aspect of an unknowable total he called 'the Absolute'" (Gordon R. Lewis, "Pinnock and Inerrancy," www.etsjets.org, "Past Presidents' Comments" [accessed November 5, 2004]).
41. See, for example, J. P. Moreland and William Lane Craig, *Philosophical Foundations for a Christian Worldview* (Downers Grove, Ill.: InterVarsity, 2003), 173, 184, 204, 215–17.

served. An authentic understanding of human persons, therefore, is not a matter of either the classical ontology or postmodern relationality but of both. The fact is that the classical model of the human person, judiciously stated, can do justice to the values of relationality and community.[42]

The metaphorical heart (Heb. *lēb*; Gk. *kardia*) is the seat of relational capacity and engagement. When persons relate, they connect with another in their total created selves. In relationships, the biblical heart of one person engages the biblical heart of another person in a shared experience of understanding, empathy, and satisfaction. Relationships can be good or bad, superficial or substantial, transitory or enduring. Characteristics of a good relationship include "warmth, loving, caring, acceptance, responsiveness, empathy, genuineness, attentiveness, concern, support, [and] understanding."[43] Furthermore, "We feel 'related' when we feel at one with another (person or object) in some heartfelt way."[44] Typically, humans experience relationships as the ebb and flow of closeness and distance. As we explore the relations humans sustain, we follow the order proposed by Henri Nouwen in his book *Reaching Out:* relations with oneself, with others, and with God.[45]

## Horizontally: Relate Authentically to One's Own Self

The human person as created not only recognizes himself as a distinct self or "I" but also engages or relates to himself. Early in the Hebrew history, God commanded His people, "Love your neighbor as yourself" (Lev. 19:18). Relationship with oneself is requisite to loving oneself. Human beings relate to themselves with regard or disdain, gentleness or sternness, pleasure or displeasure. In the Psalter we often read of the psalmists relating to themselves in moments of satisfying or distressing self-reflection. Thus David ruminates, "My heart has heard you say, 'Come and talk with me.' And my heart responds, 'LORD, I am coming.'" (Ps. 27:8 NLT). Similarly, Paul in Romans 7 enters into an intense dialogue with himself concerning motives

---

42. We refer the reader to chapter 4 and discussions of the human person's "Essential Composition" and "The Created Image."
43. Helen Harris Perlman, *Relationship: The Heart of Helping People* (Chicago: University of Chicago Press, 1979), 23.
44. Ibid.
45. Henri Nouwen, *Reaching Out: The Three Movements of the Spiritual Life* (New York: Image Books, 1975).

and behaviors vis-à-vis God's law (vv. 14–25). Thomas à Kempis concluded, "An humble knowledge of thyself is a surer way to God than a deep search after learning."[46] John Calvin, moreover, forwarded the notion of double knowledge: knowledge of oneself and knowledge of God being inextricably related. "No one can look upon himself without immediately turning his thoughts to the contemplation of God, in whom he 'lives and moves' (Acts 17:28)."[47] Although formed to relate to themselves and reflect on their existence, humans never completely fathom the mystery of their personhood.

### Horizontally: Relate Compassionately with Other Persons

Humans are social beings created for interdependence in the form of relationships with other human beings. In relating intimately with other humans, persons find identity, purpose, and fulfillment. The church father Lactantius wrote, "We image God in his inner oneness by our *capacity* to become one with another who is separate and different from us" (emphasis added).[48] By virtue of creation by the relational God, the well-known saying of John Donne (1572–1631) holds true: "No man is an island, entire of itself. Any man's death diminishes me, because I am involved in mankind." We proceed now to consider the range of interpersonal relationships.

**Relationality with One's Spouse.** The following Old Testament Scriptures demonstrate that the covenant of marriage is the first human relationship God created, as well as the foundation of a well-ordered and healthy society.

- Genesis 1:27–28: "So God created man *[ʾādām]* in his own image, in the image of God he created him; male *[zākār]* and female *[nᵉqēbâ]* he created them. God blessed them and said to them, 'Be fruitful and increase in number.'" Whereas Adam and Eve are first designated "man," thus stressing their unity, the words for "male" and "female" (cf. Gen. 5:2; Num. 5:3) that follow emphasize the sexual distinction that undergirds the marital relation. Note God's command that the first couple beget children to populate the earth.

---

46. Thomas à Kempis, cited in Les and Leslie Parrott, *Relationships* (Grand Rapids: Zondervan, 1998), 33.
47. Calvin, *Institutes of the Christian Religion,* 1:35 [1.1.1].
48. Lactantius, *The Divine Institutes* 6.10 [*ANF,* 7:172–74].

- Genesis 2:18: "The LORD God said, 'It is not good for the man to be alone. I will make a helper [ʿēzer, "helper; companion"] suitable for him.'" According to the second creation account, everything God created was "good" or "very good" excepting Adam, who was a solitary. Adam and Eve together constitute what Barbara Bowie calls the "bedrock and essential fabric of human existence, established by God in creation."[49]

- Genesis 2:20b: "But for Adam no suitable helper was found." Among the many animals God created, Adam identified no adequate life companion. Lower, inanimate life forms could not satisfy Adam's relational needs. The male needed a complementary female partner of equal dignity for relationship and procreation of offspring to have maximum fulfillment.

- Genesis 2:21–22 describes the creation of Eve from one of Adam's ribs. She would be the man's companion. "There may be some sexual significance in the rib from the lower part of the body, and from their becoming 'one flesh,'" wrote Dale Moody, "but the primary relation was social, not sexual."[50]

- Genesis 2:23: "'At last,' Adam exclaimed, 'She is part of my own flesh and bone!'" (NLT). This verse registers Adam's cry of delight when he saw Eve—the complementary human companion and relational friend God wisely created for the enjoyment of life together.

- Genesis 2:24: "For this reason a man will leave his father and mother and be united to his wife, and they will become one flesh." Quoted by Jesus in Mark 10:7–8, this verse prescribes that in marriage a man leaves his birth parents and becomes one with his wife in a loving, monogamous relationship. Note that God's command, not economic necessity or social utility, constitutes the basis for marriage.

- Genesis 2:25: "The man and his wife were both naked, and they felt no shame." This verse highlights the personal freedom and absence of shame Adam and Eve experienced together in their state of moral innocence before sin clouded communion with God and with one another.

49. Barbara E. Bowie, *Biblical Foundations of Spirituality* (Lanham, Md.: Rowman and Littlefield, 2003), 39.

50. Dale Moody, *Word of Truth* (Grand Rapids: Eerdmans, 1981), 214.

The first two chapters of Genesis, then, teach that the creation of "man" was not complete until male and female were brought together in an intimate, relational union. Marriage, as a divine institution of faithfulness and intimate union between two people of the opposite sex, is rooted in the order of creation.[51] Of great importance for today's debates, God established marriage as the lifelong union and partnership of a man and a woman as the foundation of the nuclear family and for the begetting of children.

Moreover, marriage is a covenant relation that involves two parties with promises solemnly made to each other before God (Prov. 2:16–17; Mal. 2:10, 14). The marital relation, especially, creates a context in which God's grace is shared among the partners. Monogamous marriage involves exclusively shared ideals, emotional bonding, and committed love. Marriage thrives in an environment of mutual submission, trust, pursuing the welfare of the other, and seeking forgiveness for wrongs committed. The Old Testament celebrates the shared love of Isaac and Rebecca (Gen. 24:67; 26:8), Jacob and Rachel (Gen. 29:18–21), and David and Michal (1 Sam. 18:20). In both Testaments the marriage relation is presented as the normative arrangement for two people of the opposite sex who commit to spending their lives together. In the Old Testament, failure to marry and bear children was regarded as a reproach. The New Testament sets forth a higher obligation: A person's commitment to Christ and the kingdom supersedes the marital relation. Christians are free to choose singleness out of devotion to Christ and His call to discipleship (Matt. 19:12; 1 Cor. 7:7). The Old Testament forbids God's people from marrying pagans (Deut. 7:1–4), and the New Testament prohibits marriage to unbelievers (1 Cor. 7:39; 2 Cor. 6:14).

Sex within marriage represents God's gracious gift (see also 1 Cor. 7:3–5). Rather than muting sexual relations between husband and wife, the Bible celebrates the joys of marital love. The Old Testament recognizes the goodness of erotic love at the heart of the marital relation (Prov. 5:15–20; Eccl. 9:7–9), particularly in the Song of Songs (e.g., 2:16; 4:10–16; 8:1–6), which should be read literally, not metaphorically. The Creator intended intercourse as the highest expression of love between husband and wife and the celebration of the gift of life together. A healthy marriage bed (Heb. 13:4) contributes to emotional and spiritual wholeness of the covenanted partners. A secondary purpose of marriage is the procreation of offspring (Gen.

---

51. Th. C. Vriezen, *An Outline of Old Testament Theology* (Wageningen: H. Veenman, 1958), 217: "God Himself had intended married life and had the family in view at the Creation."

1:28). Scripture depicts children as God's gifts for the blessing of parents and the formation of a family (Ps. 127:3).

Guided by the ascetic impulse and influenced by Neoplatonic dualism and Gnosticism, some churchmen from the second century on devalued married life in favor of celibacy. From the Council of Elvira in 306, rules began to restrict marriage of "holy" men and restrict sexual relations as deflecting the soul from Christ. Augustine described those who married and had children as "weaker brethren" and persons who refrained from marriage as "those who live at a higher level."[52] Jerome enjoined the faithful to "cut down the wood of marriage with the axe of virginity."[53] Peter Lombard believed that "a too passionate desire for one's own wife . . . was really adultery."[54]

Old Testament priests married, however (Lev. 21:13), as did New Testament apostles. Primary leaders among the sixteenth-century Protestant Reformation upheld the God-ordained institution of marriage for laity and clergy alike. Martin Luther insisted that celibacy is contrary to nature and reserved for those few people with the gift of chastity. Aside from the stresses on celibacy for holiness and sexual relations only for procreation in the Roman Church, most Christians throughout history have endorsed Paul's view that the loving, committed relation of husband and wife is an earthly parable of the mysterious relation between Christ and his church (Eph. 5:22–33).

**Relationality within the Family Unit.** Hebrew social relationships were structured in pyramidal fashion as a family, clan, tribe, and nation. In Joshua's time the Lord said to Israel, "Present yourselves tribe by tribe. The tribe that the LORD takes shall come forward clan by clan; the clan that the LORD takes shall come forward family by family; and the family that the LORD takes shall come forward man by man" (Josh. 7:14). The Bible portrays the family as the dynamic nexus of personal relationships between father, mother, children, and extended relations. Children born of the marital union were regarded as a sign of God's favor (Ps. 127:3). In Hebrew culture the extended family (the "father's house," 2 Sam. 3:29) was the basic unit of spiritual nurture, moral preparation, and vocational training.

---

52. Augustine, *The City of God* 1.9 [*NPNF*¹, 2:6].
53. Jerome, *Letter* 2.2, cited in Paul K. Jewett, *Who We Are: Our Dignity as Human* (Grand Rapids: Eerdmans, 1996), 218.
54. Peter Lombard, cited in Jewett, *Who We Are*, 213.

Although the Old Testament family structure was patriarchal, the dignity of women was protected (Deut. 21:10–14; 24:1–5). The New Testament reflects a radical change in the relation, stressing mutual submission, love, and respect between wives and husbands (Eph. 5:21–22, 33; 1 Peter 3:7). The family structure remains normative today, although the roles members play change with the unfolding of God's kingdom purposes.

**Relationality Among a Wider Circle of People.** Unlike modern Western societies that suffer from an unhealthy individualism, a strong community solidarity existed in Judaism. Three or four generations often lived in proximity to, and related closely with, one another. The clan (*mišpāhâ*, Lev. 25:49; Josh. 7:17) in Israel consisted of some twenty family units led by a council of elders. The family and the clan provided members the solidarity of belonging, safety, and nurture. The tribe (*šēbet, matteh*, Josh. 7:16) was an association of clans in a particular area led by a tribal leader, as exists today in such countries as Afghanistan. Tribes of Israel came together to form a nation. Israel, which was constituted a nation (*gôy*; Exod. 19:5–6) at Sinai, was a political solidarity whose members were united by blood ties and common loyalty to Yahweh. Whereas the notion of corporate personality proposed by H. Wheeler Robinson in *People of the Book* is overstated due to its quasi-mystical connections, individual Israelites often were viewed collectively, and the life of the community frequently was concentrated in a single person (cf. Achan's sin in Josh. 7). Given the reality of national solidarity, future generations often reap the consequences of the present generation's virtues and vices (2 Kings 5:27).

The neighbor (*rēaᶜ*) in Israel embraced a wide range of persons, from a close friend to a casual acquaintance. Whatever the relationship, love of neighbor was enjoined. Among the many laws God gave Israel, one fundamental statute reflects the Creator's intention for persons: "Love your neighbor as yourself" (Lev. 19:18)—neighbor being sufficiently inclusive to embrace the stranger and the alien (Lev. 19:33–34; Deut. 10:19). Jesus endorsed this fundamental command of love (Matt. 5:43; 19:19; 22:39). When a Jewish scholar asked the Lord, "Who is my neighbor?" (Luke 10:29), Jesus responded with the parable of the good Samaritan, which affirms that the neighbor is anyone whose need I am able to meet. Justice is another major social obligation that God commanded (Jer. 22:13, 16; Amos 5:24; Mic. 6:8).

Human beings, then, were created to enter into a wide range of relationships. We are born as persons to connect, affiliate, and relate with other humans in a spirit of mercy and love. Humans clarify their identity, experience growth, and find fulfillment in the web of loving relationships. The ancient Jewish rabbi Hillel posed the following crucial questions: "If I am not for myself, who will be for me? But if I am for myself alone, what am I?"[55] The reality is that healthy relationship with others is requisite for relationship with God. "Face to face with our fellowman, in the ordinary ways of daily life, we are face to face with God."[56]

Humans were created to live as a community of persons in relation. Robert Bellah explains the core ideas of *community* as "a group of people who are socially interdependent, who participate together in discussion and decision making, and who share certain *practices* . . . that both define the community and are nurtured by it."[57] In community we listen to each other's stories and receive love and acceptance. A person lacking relationships is consigned to the misery of loneliness. Aristotle wrote, "The individual, when isolated, is not self-sufficing, and therefore he is like a part in relation to the whole. But whoever is unable to live in society, or who has no need of it because he is sufficient for himself, must be either a beast or a god."[58]

The Old Testament scholar Derek Kidner observes that the human person "will not live until he loves, giving himself away to another on his own level."[59] Life's purpose is found not in disengaged solitude but in the friendship and support of other persons. History is replete with examples of lives ruined by forfeiture of healthy relationships. The brilliant Dutch artist Vincent Van Gogh (1853–1890) withdrew from all associations except with his brother Theo. He was reluctant to entrust himself to others and refused others' counsel and support. In time Van Gogh became severely depressed. Disappointed with God, he abandoned the Christian faith and pursued painting with obsessive madness. In due course Van Gogh took his life with a bullet.

Ecclesiastes 4:9–12 highlights the fundamental human need for

---

55. Rabbi Hillel, quoted in Perlman, *Relationship*, 211.

56. H. Wheeler Robinson, *The Christian Doctrine of Man* (Edinburgh: T. and T. Clark, 1926), 344.

57. Robert N. Bellah, ed., *Habits of the Heart: Individualism and Commitment in American Life* (Berkeley, Calif.: University of California Press, 1985), 333.

58. Aristotle, *Politics,* ed. Mortimer J. Adler, trans. Benjamin Jowett, Great Books of the Western World, 2d ed. (Chicago: Encyclopedia Britannica, 1990), 8:439.

59. Derek Kidner, *Genesis,* Tyndale Old Testament Commentaries (London: Tyndale Press, 1967), 65.

companionship, with perhaps a faint allusion to humans' relational need for God (represented by the third strand).

> Two are better than one,
>     because they have a good return for their work:
> If one falls down,
>     his friend can help him up.
> But pity the man who falls
>     and has no one to help him up!
> Also, if two lie down together, they will keep warm.
>     But how can one keep warm alone?
> Though one may be overpowered,
>     two can defend themselves.
> A cord of three strands is not quickly broken.

### Horizontally: Relate to the Inanimate and Lower Animate World

Our definition of relationship, presented above, includes engagements with lower forms of life and material objects. Relationships at these levels "occur when emotion has been called forth in the person by its memory associations or by its moving (emotive) aesthetic qualities."[60]

Shaped from the materials of the ground and sharing earth with lower creatures, humans are capable of engaging and enjoying subhuman species and the physical environment. Observe that Adam gave suitable names to his animal companions (Gen. 2:19–20). Prior to the Fall, Adam and Eve lived in harmony with their inanimate environment and its subhuman inhabitants. Later Noah and his family shared the ark with male and female representatives of every living species (Gen. 6:19–20). According to Psalm 8, humans were made to reflect on and engage bodies that fill the heavens, animals that roam the earth, birds that grace the air, and fish that swim the seas. As recorded in Psalm 104 (a nature psalm), humans encounter clouds, mountains, springs of water, trees, birds, beasts of the forest—all of which reflect the Creator's glory (v. 31). The Bible—especially the Old Testament—extols the reality of human life in the material world. The physical body is the medium through which we humans relate to our environment.

---

60. Perlman, *Relationship*, 26.

## Vertically: Relate Lovingly with God

Humans in Scripture are described largely, though not exclusively, in terms of their relation with God. G. C. Berkouwer refers to "the essential and unique characteristic of man and man's nature—the relation to God."[61] Human beings are the noblest of God's creation, made for the purpose of fellowship with their Creator. Being relationally fulfilled in the Trinitarian life, God was not compelled to create finite beings with whom to have concourse. But in wisdom and love, He chose to fashion human beings with whom to relate on intimate terms. God took the first step to create the divine-human relationship when He said, "Let us make man in our image" (Gen. 1:26). By virtue of their creation in God's image, humans are capable of relating to the relational God. "The fact that man is person from Person explains his ability to interact as person to Person," observes Philip Edgcumbe Hughes.[62]

God designed humans to respond and reciprocate to His love by joining in fellowship with Himself. The Creator's intention was that human persons would commune with, worship, and love the relational God. This is the human person's calling, fulfillment, and destiny. Human hearts are relentlessly restless until they rest in the relational God. In terms of relationship with God, the individual does not dissolve into the community. Although in a general sense a community (e.g., Israel, the church) relates to God, ultimately relationship occurs between an individual and the Almighty. Thus God called Abram (Gen. 12:1), who obeyed, communed, and worshiped his Lord (vv. 7–8). The prophet Jeremiah said, "You understand, O LORD; remember me and care for me. . . . I sat alone because your hand was on me" (Jer. 15:15, 17).

In Eden prior to the Fall, Adam and Eve enjoyed ravishing, unbroken communion with their Creator (Gen. 3:8). No suspicion, fear, or jealousy marred their concourse with the divine Lover. The presence of the transcendent One was not occluded by the fog of self-interest or other sins. Adam and Eve were friends with God, who shared with them His counsels and plans. Later in history, Enoch walked with God for three hundred years

---

61. G. C. Berkouwer, *Man: The Image of God,* trans. Dirk W. Jellema (Grand Rapids: Eerdmans, 1962), 34.
62. Philip Edgcumbe Hughes, *The True Image: The Origin and Destiny of Man in Christ* (Grand Rapids: Eerdmans, 1989), 5.

(Gen. 5:22, 24). To walk with God, as Enoch did, is to reverence and serve the Creator. Given the intimacy of relationship, Enoch was elevated into God's presence without experiencing death. Noah, similarly, fulfilled his destiny by walking with God (Gen. 6:9). From his communion with God, rooted in obedience, Abraham is denoted as God's "friend" (2 Chron. 20:7; Jas. 2:23). Because of their shared life together, Jesus characterized the eleven disciples as his "friends" (John 15:14–15). The prophet Micah sums up humans' relational duties before God: "What does the LORD require of you? To act justly and to love mercy and to walk humbly with your God" (Mic. 6:8).

As created, then, the human relational environment vis-à-vis God was one of *šālôm* ("peace, rest, safety, freedom from care, and holistic well-being"). Humans' delight and destiny lies in harmonious relationships with their creator God. As Calvin observed, the chief activity of the soul is to aspire to God, and the perfection of human happiness is to be united with Him.[63] Harmonious relations with God form the basis for right relations with oneself and with other human beings.

## HUMAN RELATIONSHIPS UNDER SIN

We considered the effects of sin on the human intellect, will, emotions, moral capacity, and behaviors (see pp. 238–44). Here we consider sin's effects on all of the relationships into which humans enter. An accurate indicator of the condition of the human heart is the nature of our relationships—how we interact with and respond to others, especially those closest to us. Jesus acknowledged this litmus test of spirituality with the words, "by their fruit you will recognize them" (Matt. 7:20). Sadly, sin has corrupted and ruptured relationships—the high purpose for which human beings were created.

### Relational Effects of Sin for Adam and Eve in the Garden

Adam and Eve's act of eating the forbidden fruit was the external outcome of their internal responses of pride and self-assertion. Sin, Theodore C. Vriezen reminds us, "is man's desire of independence, the desire to shake himself free of the childlike relationship with God, free of true innocence."[64]

---

63. Calvin, *Institutes of the Christian Religion,* 1:192 [1.15.6].
64. Vriezen, *Outline of Old Testament Theology,* 209.

The first couple's disobedience to God's command relative to the Tree of Knowledge of Good and Evil resulted in alienation from the life of their Creator. By heeding the Serpent's bold lies, the first pair lost innocence and experienced estrangement (Gen. 3:8–10, 24). Theologians call breach of relationship with God *spiritual death*. Rebelling against the Creator's wise plan made the first pair acutely conscious of their nakedness (Gen. 3:7), signifying their sense of guilt in the deepest core of their beings. Exchanging loving trust for fretful fear, the couple hid themselves (Gen. 3:8), thus forfeiting the blessing of intimate communion with the Creator. The gravity of the relational breach is seen in God banishing them from the paradise He had prepared for them (Gen. 3:23–24). *In a tragedy of incalculable proportions, Adam and Eve forfeited the very purpose for which they were created.*

Aware of their own nakedness, Adam and Eve covered themselves with fig leaves. This futile attempt to defend their sin-scarred psyches indicates that the first couple experienced shame before one another as male and female. The original shameless relation between the man and the woman was summarily forfeited. Shame in this instance is relational, experienced in the presence of another human being. The relationship between the first couple deteriorated as blame and recrimination mounted. Adam blamed God for providing the woman who offered him the fruit, and the woman blamed the serpent for its seductive insinuations (Gen. 3:12–13).

God's act of cursing the earth in consequence of the primal sin meant judgment for Adam, who must now toil in order to make a living. The resistance offered by a hostile environment to the man's work would lead to interpersonal difficulties. Moving under the tyranny of sin into his demanding world of agriculture and commerce, the man tends to neglect relationships with his wife and children, so he fails to meet their needs. In the case of the woman's relation to the man, "Her *physical attachment* to Adam would lead to moments of excruciating pain (in childbirth) and her *personal attachment* would involve heartache and battle."[65] Larry Crabb summarizes the result, "For Adam, that [i.e., God's judgment] meant struggles as *he moved into his world.* . . . For Eve, that means pain as *she related to Adam.*"[66] The relationship between the man and woman following

---

65. Larry Crabb, *Men and Women: Enjoying the Difference* (Grand Rapids: Zondervan, 1991), 142.
66. Ibid., 158.

the Fall was subject to tension, frustration, and domination. Sin thus ruptured the community and harmony that existed in Eden between Adam, Eve, God, and their surrounding environment.

## Relational Effects of Sin for Adam and Eve's Descendants

We concluded in chapter 7 that sin has negatively impacted human functioning intellectually, volitionally, emotionally, morally, and behaviorally. In the present section we examine how the sin of our first parents (Adam and Eve), examined above, has affected the entire human race in the full range of relationships into which people enter.

### Horizontally: Conflicted Relation with Oneself

All humans in their sinful condition are conflicted within, and alienated from, themselves. Conscious of having violated moral norms, sinners heap upon themselves reproach in the form of self-condemnation that breeds worthlessness, which in turn calls forth the need for self-validation. Estranged from our true selves, we become our worst enemies. The downward spiral of self-deprecation generates anxiety, depression, and in extreme cases loss of the will to live. "'There is no peace,' says my God, 'for the wicked'" (Isa. 57:21). This destructive regression is seen in Judas; overcome with guilt for his shameful betrayal of Jesus, the renegade disciple took his own life.

Unconverted people, moreover, are fundamentally selfish or turned in on themselves. Paul wrote that in the last days, "People will be lovers of themselves . . . proud . . . conceited. . . ." (2 Tim. 3:2–5). Luther expressed sinners' fundamental self-orientation by the phrase, *"curvatus in se"* ("curved in on oneself"). As Jean Vanier puts it, "We are all broken, turned in on ourselves, self-centered, needing success, power, and recognition."[67] The unregenerate's personal desires and comforts selfishly arrogate over the legitimate needs of others. As a consequence, sinners lack significant personal freedom. Crabb notes, "The root of all my problems is not my *personal identity* as an underdeveloped self, but my *moral identity* as a selfish person still driven, in deep ways, by selfish energy."[68]

---

67. Jean Vanier, *Becoming Human* (New York: Paulist, 1998), 156.
68. Crabb, *Men and Women*, 76. Emphasis in original.

## Horizontally: Problematic Relations with Other Persons

Horizontally, human beings experience relational tensions with other persons. The history of the human race is a sad tale of inhumanity, conflict, and misery. Breakdown of the primary relations with God and oneself renders problematic all other relations: with one's spouse, family, neighbors, and the wider community. In biblical times, King David's sinful self-indulgence impelled him to withdraw from social relations, causing anguish and a profound sense of loneliness. "My friends and companions avoid me because of my wounds; my neighbors stay far away" (Ps. 38:11). The "selfism" that pervades contemporary, consumer cultures generates indifference to, and isolation from, other persons, with resulting loneliness. Self-serving impulses are the root cause of "fights and quarrels" among family members, communities, and nations (cf. James 4:1–3).

The Bible candidly chronicles the catalogue of evils that compromise human relationships. Consider, first, disturbances of marital and family relations. Sin incites mistreatment of one's mate, children, or family elder. Such acts include verbal abuse (Ps. 22:7–8; 1 Peter 4:4), where a person is humiliated by cruel words; emotional abuse (Col. 3:19, 21), where love is withheld or one is rejected; physical abuse (Col. 4:1), where bodily harm is inflicted; and sexual abuse (Eph. 5:3), where unnatural sex acts are forced on the unwilling.

Scripture explicitly forbids the relational aberration and moral evil of incest, or sexual intercourse between blood relatives. Leviticus 18:6–15 forbids a man from having sexual relations with his mother, stepmother, sister, stepsister, daughter-in-law, and aunt (cf. Lev. 20:11–12; Deut. 27:20). The apostle Paul sternly rebuked a member of the church at Corinth who was sleeping with his stepmother (1 Cor. 5:1–2).

Scripture also condemns the relational perversion of adultery (Heb. *nāʾap;* Gk. *moicheia),* or unlawful intercourse involving a married or engaged person. The seventh commandment prohibits adultery as a violation of the marriage covenant made before God and His covenantal relationship with the people (Exod. 20:14; Deut. 5:18). The book of Proverbs warns at length against the perilous seductions of the adulterous woman (Prov. 5; 6:20–29; 7) and describes the adulterer as a "fool." Jeremiah inveighs against adulterers in the land, saying, "They have done outrageous [*nᵉbālâ*, "detestable; disgraceful"] things in Israel; they have committed adultery with their neighbors' wives" (Jer. 29:23). So serious was the sin of adultery that the Old Testament penal code (admittedly temporal and cultural) assigned the death penalty to perpetrators (Lev. 20:10).

Polygamous relationships appeared early in Old Testament history, when arrogant Lamech married two women, Adah and Zillah (Gen. 4:19–22). There began the practice that perverted God's plan for monogamous marriage. The subsequent Old Testament history attests the prevalence of polygamy (Gen. 29:21–30; 1 Sam. 25:43; 2 Sam. 5:13) and gives examples of its consequences and God's displeasure. King Solomon was one of the most egregious polygamists, possessing seven hundred wives and three hundred concubines (1 Kings 11:3).

A further distortion of family under sin is that of mixed marriages with those outside covenantal relationship to God. Deuteronomy 7:3–4 explicitly forbids intermarriage with pagans in the lands Israel would occupy. Spiritually mixed marriages became a continuing problem in Israel (Ezra 9:1–2; Neh. 13:23–27; Mal. 2:11–12) that threatened to deflect the hearts of God's people from Him toward idols (Exod. 34:16). Under the gospel, marriage between Christians and unbelievers is forbidden (2 Cor. 6:14) for the fundamental reason that sinners and saints possess wholly different masters.

Also contrary to God's will is breach of the marital relationship in divorce. The Lord through Malachi unequivocally declared, "I hate divorce" (Mal. 2:16; cf. Matt. 19:9). But given the human heart's hardness, God in Old Testament times permitted a man to write a certificate of divorce (Deut. 24:1, 3). Jesus acknowledged that in former times God permitted divorce as a concession to human sinfulness (Matt. 19:8). The Savior Himself elevated the sanctity of marriage above the Old Testament law's requirements by citing God's intention recorded in the Genesis 2:24 creation ordinance. Divorce, Jesus averred, may occur without culpability in cases of "marital unfaithfulness *[porneia]*" (Matt. 5:32).

In our day, as in biblical times, breaches of the marriage covenant are common. Only one-quarter of all children today are raised by a mother and a father in the home.[69] When a marriage is severely stressed, every effort should be expended to repair it. But when the union proves irretrievably broken, the God of grace is able to forgive the sin that causes the divorce

---

69. James Dobson, *Focus on the Family Radio Broadcast*, July 14, 2004.

and allow a new beginning. Divorce and remarriage might be viewed redemptively as a type of death and resurrection experience.[70]

Alienated from God, unregenerate persons often find themselves relationally conflicted against a wider circle of persons. Causes of disordered relationships at this level include deceitfulness (1 Peter 2:1), mistrust (Ps. 49:13), dissension (Prov. 6:19), quarreling (2 Tim. 2:23), strife (Rom. 1:29) and brawling (Eph. 4:31), which in turn lead to betrayal (Matt. 24:10), sexual predation (Matt. 15:19), social oppression (Ezek. 18:12), and ultimately murder (cf. Gen. 4:3–8). Thomas Merton writes, "The spirit of the world, which is selfishness and envy and conspiracy and lust and terror, makes men loud from the fear of their own hollowness. . . . The spirit of the world, which is avarice and oppression, arms men against one another and divides them against themselves and against others: it splits the world into armed camps."[71] The death of relationships that leads to these evils fundamentally constitutes a failure to love one's neighbor as oneself (Matt. 19:19; 22:39).

Sexual sins loom large in relationships between persons in the fallen world. Fornication (Heb. *zānâ*; Gk. *porneia*) denotes any illicit intercourse between a man and a woman: for example, sexual relations outside marriage, aberrant sexual practices, and prostitution. Sexual promiscuity and orgies, even in the context of religious rites, were common in the ancient world. In our day more than 4 million unmarried couples in the United States live together.[72] Scripture describes sexual activity outside of marriage as "a disgraceful *[nᵉbālâ]* thing" (Deut. 22:21). Fornication betrays trust, incurs guilt, and incites God's righteous wrath. Those who sinfully lust after another person lose respect for, and ultimately detest, the object of their perverted desire. Soberly, Scripture states that those who engage in sexual immorality will be held accountable by the holy God. "Marriage should be honored by all, and the marriage bed kept pure, for God will judge the adulterer and all the sexually immoral" (Heb. 13:4).

Rape, assault of another person using sex as a weapon, involves a serious violation of human dignity, as well as physical and emotional harm. Scripture

---

70. See Ray S. Anderson and Dennis B. Guernsey, *On Being Family: A Social Theology of the Family* (Grand Rapids: Eerdmans, 1985), 103.

71. Thomas Merton, *Mornings with Thomas Merton,* selected by John C. Blattner (Ann Arbor, Mich.: Servant Publications, 1998), no. 19.

72. David P. Gusher, "A Crumbling Institution," *Christianity Today,* September 2004, 44.

characterizes Shechem's rape of Dinah, daughter of Jacob, as "a disgraceful [n$^e$bālâ] thing" (Gen. 34:7). Similarly David's son Amnon's rape of his stepsister, Tamar, is described as a "wicked [n$^e$bālâ] thing" (2 Sam. 13:12), and the rapist is depicted as a wicked fool (v. 13).

Prostitution or harlotry (Heb. taznût, z$^e$nûrîm, z$^e$nût; Gk. pornē), the trading of sexual favors for money, was common in biblical times as it is today (Gen. 38:15; Deut. 23:17–18; Ezek. 16:15, 20, 22; Luke 15:30; Heb. 11:31). The Bible strictly forbids prostitution: "Do not degrade your daughter by making her a prostitute, or the land will turn to prostitution and be filled with wickedness" (Lev. 19:29). Male and female cultic prostitution, widely practiced in Canaanite fertility religion, infiltrated Israelite worship (Deut. 23:17–18; 1 Kings 14:24). Paul expressed horror that a believer united to Jesus Christ and indwelt by the Holy Spirit might sexually join with a prostitute (1 Cor. 6:15–20).

Homosexual conduct, or illicit sex between persons of the same gender, represents a serious perversion of human relationships. Genesis 19 relates the account of dissolute men of Sodom who, driven by lust, surrounded Lot's house and cried out, "Where are the men who came to you tonight? Bring them out to us so that we can have sex with them" (v. 5). Lot's offer of his two daughters for sexual gratification represents his flawed attempt to avert a grave moral evil (homosexuality) by proposing another evil (heterosexual fornication). The epistle of Jude offers the following comment on this incident: "Sodom and Gomorrah and the surrounding towns gave themselves up to sexual immorality and perversion. They serve as an example of those who suffer the punishment of eternal fire" (Jude 7; cf. 2 Peter 2:4–6). The word sodomy to this day remains a part of the English language and refers to a form of sexual intercourse practiced by homosexual men. Judges 19 records a similar incident. An elderly man living in Gibeah invited a journeying Levite and his party to spend the night at his home. "While they were enjoying themselves, some of the wicked men of the city surrounded the house. Pounding on the door, they shouted to the old man who owned the house, 'Bring out the man who came to your house so we can have sex with him.'" The elderly man replied, "'No, my friends, don't be so vile. Since this man is my guest, don't do this disgraceful thing.'" (vv. 22–23). Homosexual acts were just one example of the moral depravity of the period, for the record states, "Everyone did as he saw fit" (Judg. 17:6; 21:25).

Mosaic laws against unnatural sexual relations include the prohibition (Lev. 18:22), "Do not lie with a man as one lies with a woman; that is detestable" (*tôʿēbâ*, "abomination"[73]). In the civil code, homosexual practice was a capital offense (Lev. 20:13), indicating how abhorrent such behavior is to God. Homosexual activity was fashionable in the pagan world of Paul's day, and he sets homosexuality among sins to face God's wrath. The apostle gave a reason for unnatural homosexual acts, namely, the natural man's suppression of the knowledge of God afforded by general revelation. "Even their women exchanged natural relations for unnatural ones. In the same way the men also abandoned natural relations with women and were inflamed with lust for one another. Men committed indecent acts with other men, and received in themselves the due penalty for their perversion" (Rom. 1:26–27). With the Levitical code (Lev. 18–20) in mind, Paul wrote to the church at Corinth, "Do not be deceived: Neither the sexually immoral nor idolaters nor adulterers nor male prostitutes [*malakoi*, "passive homosexual partners"] nor homosexual offenders [*arsenokoitai*, "active homosexual partners"] . . . will inherit the kingdom of God" (1 Cor. 6:9–10). The latter Greek word also appears in 1 Timothy 1:9–10: "Law is made not for good men but for lawbreakers and rebels, the ungodly and sinful, the unholy and irreligious; for those who kill their fathers or mothers, for murderers, for adulterers and perverts [*arsenokoitai*]."

Clearly Paul vigorously opposed homosexual practice, albeit not homosexual temptation or "orientation." Persons who engage in homosexual activity can change, as in 1 Corinthians 6:9–11 where Paul recalls that some of the Corinthians *had* changed. Pressured by gay rights groups, the American Psychiatric Association in 1973 removed homosexuality from its list of recognized mental illnesses. Whether a mental illness, homosexual conduct clearly is a grievous sin in God's sight. The Lord clearly hates homosexual behavior as a perversion of His purpose for the race created as male and female. The only God-pleasing response to homoerotic inclination is abstinence (a celibate lifestyle) and pursuit of change.

Jewish tradition in such sources as Philo of Alexandria (20 B.C.– A.D. 50), Flavius Josephus (A.D. 37–101), ancient rabbinical literature, and orthodox Christian moral teaching have universally condemned sodomy and by extension other forms of homosexual expression. The early anonymous church

---

73. "*tôʿēbâ*," in *TWOT*, 2:976.

writing *The Teaching of the Twelve Apostles* (c. A.D. 100) commanded, "Do not murder; do not commit adultery; do not practice pederasty [sex with boys]."[74] *Epistle of Barnabas* 19.4 records the same command. Justin Martyr fought against prostitution, incest, and sodomy.[75] An important early Christian writing characterized homosexual acts as monstrosities, stating that Christians "abhor all unlawful mixtures, and that which is practiced by some contrary to nature, as wicked and impious."[76] Augustine declared that sins against nature constitute the worst sins: "Offenses against nature must everywhere and always be abominated and punished, as were those of the Sodomites."[77] Augustine regarded homosexual conduct as a punishment God visits on a society that departs from His moral law.[78] The preacher John Chrysostom (347–407) emphatically denounced homosexual acts as an insult to God and the ultimate display of corruption.[79] In the medieval era Thomas Aquinas judged that after beastiality sodomy is the most grievous sin of all.[80] In modern times Barth believed that sodomy is a profoundly immoral practice, declaring, "This is the physical, psychological and social sickness, the phenomenon of perversion, decadence and decay."[81]

A few words need to be said about the failure of the community ideal in secular culture. God created humans for relationship and for community, the bond of which is love. When love fails, as it often does in the fallen world, authentic community disintegrates. The self-centeredness that precludes love erects walls of isolation and hostility between persons. This is seen in Western culture's obsession with individualism, self-reliance, autonomy, and privatized religion. The postmodern world heralds the virtue and value of community. But what actually exists in the absence of a viable integrating center, namely Christ, is a collection of micro-communities (e.g., the business community, Hispanic community, gay and lesbian community) that often share little in common with one another. At best, secular community is characterized by *philia* ("brotherly love") and at worst by

74. *Teaching of the Twelve Apostles* 2.2 [*ANF*, 7:376].
75. Justin Martyr, *First Apology* 27 [*ANF*, 1:172].
76. *Constitution of the Holy Apostles* 6.11 [*ANF*, 7:454].
77. Augustine, *Confessions* 3.8.15 [*NPNF*¹, 1:65].
78. Augustine, *On Nature and Grace* 24 [*NPNF*¹, 5:129].
79. John Chrysostom, *Homilies on the Epistle to the Romans* 4 [*NPNF*¹, 11:355–59]; idem, *Homilies on the Gospel of Matthew* 73.3 [*NPNF*¹, 10:440–44]; idem, *Homilies on the Epistle to Titus* 5.4 [*NPNF*¹, 13:535–40].
80. Thomas Aquinas, *ST,* 13:160 [pt. 2, q. 154, art. 12].
81. Karl Barth, *CD*, 3.4.166.

*eros* ("sensual or sexual love"). In the secular world, community in the sense of unconditional caring and selfless giving and receiving remains an unrealized ideal.

### Horizontally: Discordant Relations with the Lower Created Order

Horizontally, discord exists between humans and their material environment. The disobedience of our first parents prompted God to curse the earth (Gen. 3:17–18), subjecting it to disorder and decay (Rom. 8:20–21). Humans rapaciously abuse their environment and its resources, and the environment confounds humans' most strenuous efforts to harness it. A gross example of the relational dysfunction existing between human beings and lower creatures is the practice of beastiality, or sexual relations with animals. This severely unnatural practice transgresses the distinction between human beings and animals. It is strictly forbidden in the Word of God: "Do not have sexual relations with an animal and defile yourself with it. A Woman must not present herself to an animal to have sexual relations with it; that is a perversion" (Lev. 18:23). The Deuteronomist forcefully adds, "Cursed is the man who has sexual relations with any animal" (Deut. 27:21). The Old Testament penal system required death as the punishment for beastiality (Exod. 22:19; Lev. 20:15).

### Vertically: Fractured Relations with God

Vertically, sin causes relational estrangement from God; human beings in sin are cut off from life-giving relationship with the Sovereign One. The sinful human quest for self-autonomy results in forfeiture of communion with the Creator and consequent loneliness and alienation. Following his cruel murder of Abel, Cain became a wanderer on the earth, admitting to the Lord, "I will be hidden from your presence" (Gen. 4:14). According to Isaiah, people "who have forsaken the LORD, who have despised the Holy One of Israel . . . are utterly estranged!" (Isa. 1:4 NRSV). The prophet added the following indictment against the irreligious of his day: "Your iniquities have separated you from your God; your sins have hidden his face from you" (Isa. 59:2; cf. 1:4). Little changed over the centuries. Paul portrayed the unbelieving Gentile world as "separate from Christ, excluded from citizenship in Israel and foreigners to the covenants of the promise" (Eph. 2:12; cf. 4:18). The essence of hell, Jesus insisted, is nothing other than permanent separation from God, when God pronounces the curse, "Away from me, you evildoers!" (Matt. 7:23).

Scripture describes unconverted persons as spiritually obstinate (Isa. 30:1), living not in a state of neutral indifference but of active rebellion against their Maker. "These are rebellious people, deceitful children, children unwilling to listen to the LORD's instruction," intoned Isaiah (30:9; cf. Ezek. 12:2). In their relentless drive for fulfillment without regard for God, humans exhibit what G. C. Berkouwer calls humanity's "apostate autonomy and disobedience."[82] At the human control center of the metaphorical heart, unsaved humans despise God. Jesus said that the unbelieving world, having heard the truth He spoke and having seen the works He performed, chose to love mammon and to hate Him (John 15:18–19, 22–25). The apostle Paul describes unredeemed citizens of this world as "God-haters, insolent, arrogant and boastful" (Rom. 1:30; cf. Rom. 8:7; Col. 1:21). He was confirming the judgment of the psalmist (Ps. 139:21) and of the apostle James (James 4:4). The Heidelberg Catechism (1563) reflects the biblical perspective when it asks in question 5 whether I can live up to the law to love God and neighbor perfectly:

"No.
I am prone by nature to hate God and my neighbor."[83]

A final feature of the relational state of the unsaved vis-à-vis God is forfeiture of the status of sonship. All humans, like their forefather Adam (Luke 3:38), were offspring of God by creation. Having broken fellowship with the loving Lord, humans lost membership in the Father's family and title to the Father's house. Søren Kierkegaard tendered the following lament regarding loss of relationship with the Father: "What is man without Thee! What is all that he knows, vast accumulation though it be, but a chipped fragment if he does not know Thee! What is all his striving, could it even encompass a world, but a half-finished work if he does not know Thee."[84]

---

82. Berkouwer, *Man the Image of God*, 145.
83. G. I. Williamson, ed., *The Heidelberg Catechism* (Phillipsburg, N.J.: Presbyterian and Reformed, 1993), 13.
84. Søren Kierkegaard, *Purity of Heart*, trans. Douglas V. Steere (New York: Harper and Row, 1948), 31.

We acknowledge the biblical truth that the effects of humans' relational brokenness are ameliorated in measure by God's common grace—the goodness that shines on all persons everywhere, even in their alienation and rebellion. Still, we must not mute the clear teachings of Scripture concerning the serious relational consequences of human sinfulness upon family, friends, and the wider circles of neighbors and nations.

## HUMAN RELATIONSHIPS RENEWED IN CHRIST

Through the lifelong process of sanctification, the Holy Spirit renews the mind, will, emotions, moral life, and behaviors of believers (see chap. 7), as well as their social world of interpersonal relationships. Death to the old false self and life to the new true self constitutes the heart of relational transformation. The reorientation of the soul toward God and others offers a challenging undertaking throughout life.

### Horizontally: Integrated Relationship with Oneself

Believers in Jesus Christ, who were formerly liable to self-loathing and self-rejection, accept themselves for who they are as unique images of God by creation and beloved children of God by redemption. Christians accept themselves as imperfect but adopted children who are safe in relationship with the Father (Rom. 8:15–17; Gal. 4:5–7; 1 John 3:1). Believers forgive themselves because they are forgiven by God and love themselves because they are eternally loved by God. With respect to intrapersonal, as well as interpersonal, relations, believers experience God's *šālôm*. One of the redeeming legacies Jesus bequeathed to His followers is "peace" (John 14:27; 16:33)—the inner and outer harmony that, irrespective of life's circumstances, issues from being rightly related to God. Among Jesus' last words while on earth was the comforting benediction "Peace be with you!" (John 20:19, 21, 26). Christ's peace imparts awareness of God's care, release from anxiety, and the freedom and love that forms the bedrock for healthy relationships.

In his classic work *On the Love of God*, Bernard of Clairvaux (1090–1153) outlined four degrees of love. The medieval theologian depicts the first degree as *love of self for self*, meaning that we must love ourselves for our own sake as *imago Dei*. Healthy love of self, Bernard insisted, is psychologically and spiritually foundational, for unless we so relate to ourselves we have nothing wherewith to bless others. Lacking respect and love for oneself, humans will project on others their own inner wounds and anxieties. Bernard designated the first degree of love, love of self for self, as "immature love."[85] This first degree of love is absolutely foundational for personal wholeness and integration, but Christians must move to progressively higher levels of love, including *love of God for self, love of God for God,* and *love of self for God.*

## Horizontally: Trustful Relationships with Spouse and Family

Scripture regards a healthy marriage as a fulfilling feature of the good life. "Enjoy life with your wife, whom you love, all the days of this meaningless life that God has given you under the sun" (Eccl. 9:9). In some countries today, as in much of the ancient world, women are regarded as chattel to be used and abused. But in Christ God views women as spiritual equals with men (Gal. 3:28). In Christ the relationship between men and women has been elevated and restored to God's original design of loving equality.

Three New Testament texts unfold relational expectations within the Christian family. Ephesians 5:21–6:4 establishes the foundational principle of mutual submission between husbands, wives, and children: "Submit to one another out of reverence for Christ" (Eph. 5:21). Rather than insisting on their own rights, husbands and wives must defer to the rights and interests of each other. This means that wives will submit to their husbands as an act of submission to Christ (v. 22) and that husbands will love their wives, "just as Christ loved the church and gave himself up for her" (v. 25). The husband must love his wife as he loves his own body (v. 28), since the two, in fact, are "one flesh" (Gen. 2:24).

Four times in Ephesians 5:25, 28, and 33, the husband's love for his wife is enjoined by means of the strong verb *agapaō* ("unconditional, self-sacrificial love")—a love exemplified by Christ in dying on the cross for His people. Husbands, moreover, must feed (nourish) and care for (cherish; show affection to) their wives. This means that husbands sensitively anticipate their wives' needs, foster their well-being, and help them realize their full potential.

---

85. Bernard of Clairvaux, in James M. Houston, ed., *The Love of God and Spiritual Friendship* (Portland, Ore.: Multnomah, 1983), 154–56.

Moreover, the apostle enjoins dependent children to obey and honor their parents in the Lord (Eph. 6:1) in keeping with the fifth commandment (Exod. 20:12). Finally, fathers are commanded not to "exasperate" their children (Eph. 6:4), which "involves avoiding attitudes, words, and actions which would drive a child to angry exasperation or resentment and thus rules out excessively severe discipline, unreasonably harsh demands, unfairness, constant nagging, and condemnation."[86]

Colossians 3:18–21 condenses the foregoing prescriptions concerning relations between wives, husbands, fathers, and children. "Wives, submit to your husbands, as is fitting in the Lord. Husbands, love *[agapaō]* your wives and do not be harsh with them. Children, obey your parents in everything, for this pleases the Lord. Fathers, do not embitter your children, or they will become discouraged." The verb *erethizō*, "embitter," denotes an overseverity that frustrates a child, leading to despair.

Lastly, consider 1 Peter 3:1–7. Verse 1 enjoins believing wives to submit to their unbelieving husbands, thereby commending to them the Christian faith. Peter's mention of godly women of old, such as Sarah, who submitted to their husbands (vv. 5–6) may suggest a principle that transcends time and culture. "The submission is one of role or function for the orderly operation of the home."[87] Immediately Peter adds, "Husbands . . . be considerate as you live with your wives, and treat them with respect [lit. 'assigning honor or respect'] as the weaker partner and as heirs with you of the gracious gift of life, so that nothing will hinder your prayers." The quality of a person's relation to God will be no better than the quality of his or her relations with significant others.

The building blocks of God-honoring relationships among husband, wife, and children include open communication, honesty, vulnerability, trust, forgiveness, commitment to the well-being of the other, and sacrificial love. Most struggling relationships can be mended by the simple act of seeking forgiveness. Instead of asking, "What has my spouse done for me lately?" husbands should ask, "How have I served my spouse lately?" Each person has immediate control over his or her own behavior and actions; but loving behavior often is reciprocated by one's partner and children. Implementing these basic principles from the Word of God will safeguard and strengthen Christian marriages and families.

---

86. Cleon L. Rogers Jr. and Cleon L. Rogers III, *NLEKGNT,* 446.
87. NIVSB, 1892.

## Horizontally: Harmonious Relationships with Others

Christians have the assignment to sustain loving relationships with all persons created in God's image. An axiom of life, Paul points out, is that "none of us lives to himself alone and none of us dies to himself alone" (Rom. 14:7). Followers of Jesus relate to neighbors with true other-centeredness, genuinely seeking their welfare. Healthy relationships are fostered by self-disclosure (telling you who I am), listening (you telling me who you are), and communication by dialogue, including the sharing of feelings and emotions.

"To the extent that I communicate myself as a person to you and you communicate yourself to me, we share in common the mysteries of ourselves. Conversely, to the extent that we withdraw from each other and refuse mutual transparency, love is diminished."[88] Renewed people relate to others with unfeigned love, which is the unconditional gift of themselves. When asked, "Which is the greatest commandment in the Law?" (Matt. 22:36). Jesus answered, "'Love the Lord your God with all your heart and with all your soul and with all your mind.' This is the first and greatest commandment. And the second is like it: 'Love your neighbor as yourself'" (Matt. 22:37–39). Love of neighbor, Paul adds, "must be sincere ["without hypocrisy"]" (Rom. 12:9). Love that is insincere, or tendered with strings attached, is manipulation. "Presence and availability," Gabriel Marcel reminds us, constitute the essence of love.[89]

Following the teaching and example of Jesus, Christians love their enemies, do good to those who hate them, bless those who curse them, and pray for those who mistreat them (Luke 6:27–28). A notable example of this principle occurred in 1941 at the Auschwitz concentration camp when a group of prisoners were awaiting execution by starvation. Maximilian Kolbe (b. 1894), who had been arrested and sent to Auschwitz as a high-profile Roman Catholic theologian, stepped forward and offered to replace one of the men condemned to death. He then ministered compassionately to the others in the starvation bunker, until the captors quickened his death with an injection. When relationships become strained, followers of Jesus quickly seek to repair the breach. They heed the Lord's command to make

---

88. John Powell, in *Quiet Moments with John Powell*, selected and ed. Nancy Sabbag (Ann Arbor, Mich.: Servant Publications, 2000), no. 2.
89. Ibid., no. 89.

peace with adversaries quickly (Matt. 5:23–25). Christian peacemakers draw upon the power of Christ's saving work, which demolishes barriers between warring factions, whether between Jews and Gentiles in Paul's day (Eph. 2:14–15) or between Palestinians and Israelis or Hutus and Tutsis in our day. The restoration of at-risk relationships requires prayerful intention and faithful effort.

In the arena of sexual relations, renewed persons flee the immorality that may have characterized their former way of life. Paul reminded the Roman Christians of the command, "Do not commit adultery," which the law of love expanded and fulfilled (Rom. 13:9–10). Various members of the church at Corinth had engaged in fornication, adultery, prostitution, homosexual practices, and other relational evils. But having been made clean through Christ's grace, they forsook such destructive practices (1 Cor. 6:9–11). Paul's words, "That is what some of you were" (v. 11a; cf. Eph. 2:1–3), indicate that sexually immoral people can change their patterns of conduct. To Christians at Colosse Paul wrote, "Put to death, therefore, whatever belongs to your earthly nature: sexual immorality, impurity, lust, evil desires and greed, which is idolatry" (Col. 3:5), which call forth God's wrath (v. 6). All forms of sexual misconduct must be excised from the lives of God's redeemed people.

## Horizontally: Loving Relations with Believers in the Body

Christian believers unrelated to one another by blood are brought together by a new birth into the family of God. Paul writes, "You are no longer foreigners and aliens, but fellow citizens with God's people and members of God's household *[oikeios]*" (Eph. 2:19). In the same letter Paul describes the Christian community as the Father's "whole family *[patria]* in heaven and on earth" (Eph. 3:15).

### One Another in Family

The New Testament describes the early church, which often met in homes, in terms of the family or household imagery. As children of the one Father, redeemed people are related to one another as spiritual brothers and sisters (Rom. 8:29; 1 Cor. 15:58; 1 Peter 5:9). As a relational family knit together in Christ, Christians should be committed to each other at an intimate level.

Members of this worldwide spiritual family enter empathically into each other's joys and sorrows (Rom. 12:15), "practice hospitality" (Rom. 12:13; 1 Tim. 5:10), share resources (Rom. 12:13), never take revenge (Rom. 12:19), and live in peace and harmony with everyone (Rom. 12:16, 18; 1 Thess. 5:13).

If estrangement should occur, reconciliation must be sought quickly (Matt. 5:24), illustrated by the reconciliations between Paul and John Mark (cf. Acts 15:37–40 with Col. 4:10 and 2 Tim. 4:11) and between Philemon and Onesimus (Philem. 1–21). Christian believers will be "devoted to one another in brotherly love [*philostorgos*, "authentically loving; tenderly devoted; full of tenderness"]"[90] (Rom. 12:10).

Relations within the Christian family are fortified by the frequent "one another" commands of the New Testament, which include:

> "Be devoted to one another in brotherly love" (Rom. 12:10);
> "honor one another" (Rom. 12:10);
> "serve one another in love" (Gal. 5:13);
> "carry each other's burdens" (Gal. 6:2);
> "[forgive] one another" (Eph. 4:32);
> "encourage one another" (1 Thess. 5:11; Heb. 3:13);
> "live in peace with each other" (1 Thess. 5:13);
> "confess your sins to each other" (James 5:16); and
> "love one another deeply, from the heart" (1 Peter 1:22; cf. 4:8).

These "one another" commands uphold the primacy of mutual caring and self-giving love within the family of God. The regnant, relational principal in the redeemed community is to know the God of love and to relate to one another in loving ways. Restored Peter expressed the matter succinctly: "Love the brotherhood [*adelphotēs*] of believers" (1 Peter 2:17), where *adelphotēs* "has the concrete sense of a band of brothers."[91] The love that believers exude to brothers and sisters in Christ should be akin to the love God has showered on them (1 John 4:19). Love's ultimate commitment, according to Jesus, is to lay down one's life for one's friends (John 15:13; cf. 1 John 3:16). How utterly transformed and empowered the family of God would become if these biblical prescriptions were faithfully followed by all Christians!

---

90. Rogers and Rogers, *NLEKGNT,* 339.
91. Ibid., 572.

The Renaissance championed the sufficiency of the individual, as well as personal rights and freedoms. Postmodernism valiantly promotes the ideal of association and community. Only the church, however, provides the basis on which the elusive ideal of community can be maximally realized. Israel became the community *(qāhāl)* of God as it entered into covenant relation with Yahweh following the miraculous deliverance from Egypt. Israel's psalmist celebrated the excelling grace of a loving and committed community:

> How good and pleasant it is
>   when brothers live together in unity!
> It is like precious oil poured on the head,
>   running down on the beard,
> running down on Aaron's beard,
>   down upon the collar of his robes.
> It is as if the dew of Hermon
>   were falling on Mount Zion.
> For there the LORD bestows his blessing,
>   even life forevermore.
>                                  —Psalm 133

Community lay at the heart of Jesus' program, for his first undertaking was to mold a dozen motley followers into a closely-knit learning and serving community. Following Jesus' departure from earth, the powerful relational bond that existed in the early church was demonstrated by believers sharing meals, possessions, and their very lives (Acts 2:42–47; 4:32–35). The sense of togetherness wrought by the Holy Spirit is witnessed in the twenty occurrences in Acts and the New Testament letters of the word *koinōnia* ("association"; "fellowship"). The strong relational connectedness of the New Testament church is reflected in its representation as a *people* (Titus 2:14; 1 Peter 2:9), a *family* (Gal. 6:10; 1 Peter 4:17), a *flock* (Acts 20:28; 1 Peter 5:2–3), a *body* (1 Cor. 12:27; Eph. 1:22–23), a *living temple* (1 Cor. 3:16–17), and a *nation* (1 Peter 2:9). "In its existential reality, the church is a being-human-with-others in Christ," writes John Schantz.[92] All persons who know and love Jesus become His family (Mark 3:33–35), intimately related to one

---

92. John P. Schanz, *Theology of Community* (Washington, D.C.: University Press of America, 1977), 79.

another as a spiritual brotherhood or sisterhood (cf. Mark 10:29–30). The Holy Spirit poured into forgiven hearts (Rom. 5:5) binds saints to their common Lord and to one another in a community of belonging and intimacy unparalleled in the ancient and contemporary worlds.

How brightly shines the grace of Christian community. The church father Origen testified, "The communities of God, to which Christ has become teacher and guide, are, in comparison with communities of the pagan people among whom they live as strangers, like heavenly lights in the world."[93] Tertullian sharply contrasted communities based on common ancestry with communities rooted in personal knowledge of God and holiness of life. The martyred German theologian Dietrich Bonhoeffer wrote, "Between the death of Christ and the Last Day it is only by a gracious invitation of the last things that Christians are privileged to live in visible fellowship with other Christians."[94] He added, "The more genuine and the deeper our community becomes, the more will everything else between us recede, the more clearly and purely will Jesus Christ and His work become the one and only thing that is vital between us."[95]

The cratered path to wholeness and holiness is found in the safe environments of trust and love. As we are accepted in community, we learn to accept ourselves. As we are forgiven in community, we learn to forgive ourselves. As we are loved in community, we learn to love ourselves. As we know others in community and are known ourselves, we come to know God more fully. The church as the body of Christ functions as a greenhouse for emotional and spiritual growth (Eph. 4:14–16). Jean Vanier puts it that "without community people's hearts close up and die."[96]

### Analogy of the Trinity

God is not an isolated monad but three distinct persons or centers of conscious life and activity in one infinite Spirit Being. In one of his analogies, Augustine depicted the triune God as consisting of Love, the Beloved, and the Love that flows between them. For God to be love, Augustine rea-

---

93. Origen, *Against Celsus* 3.29, cited in Dallas Willard, *Renovation of the Heart: Putting on the Character of Christ* (Colorado Springs, Colo.: NavPress, 2002), 179.

94. Dietrich Bonhoeffer, *Life Together* (San Francisco, Calif.: Harper and Row, 1976), 18.

95. Ibid., 26.

96. Jean Vanier, *Community and Growth* (New York: Paulist, 1989), 8.

soned, there must be a source of love, an object of love, and the love that binds them together. For Augustine, the Holy Spirit was "seen to be the fruit of the mutual love of the Father and the Son, the bond of unity which tied the Trinity together and revealed its essence, which was spirit."[97] The medieval churchman Richard of St. Victor (d. 1173) speculated at length on the social relations within the Trinity. The fullness of true goodness and greatness—divine glory, intimacy, affection, fellowship, delight, joy, and harmony—are reciprocated among the three equally worthy persons of the Trinity. "See how the perfection of one person requires fellowship with another. We have discovered that nothing is more glorious, more magnificent than to wish to have nothing that you do not wish to share."[98]

God invites—indeed commands—Christians to model the loving interrelatedness of the three persons of the Trinity. Let's examine Jesus' prayer recorded in John 17 to gain insight into the relations between the Father, Son, and Holy Spirit that serve as principles for effective, human interpersonal relations. Those principles are:

- *Within the unity of the Trinity, each of the three persons enjoys a unique identity and significance.* Jesus knew Himself to be a person distinct from the Father and from the Holy Spirit. Jesus not only said, "I and the Father are one" (John 10:30), but with not the slightest sense of inferiority He also said, "The Father is greater than I" (John 14:28). The latter saying implies an *economic,* not an *ontological,* subordination of persons.

- *Each person of the Trinity possesses intimate knowledge of the other persons.* Jesus candidly said to His heavenly Father, "I know you" (John 17:25). Elsewhere the Lord said, "No one knows the Son except the Father, and no one knows the Father except the Son" (Matt. 11:27). The verb *know (epignōskō)* connotes a knowledge that is thorough and complete.

- *The persons of the Trinity enjoy intimate, interpersonal communion with one another.* John 1:1-2 describes communion in eternity past:

---

97. G. L. Bray, "Trinity," in *NDT,* 693.
98. Richard of St. Victor, "The Trinity," in *Richard of St. Victor,* The Classics of Western Spirituality, trans. Grover A. Zinn (New York: Paulist, 1979), 379. Cf. ibid., 393: Regarding the three persons of the Trinity, "each is fashioned on account of the other," each "is greatly praised on account of the other," and each "is brought to consummation on account of the other."

"The Word was with God [*pros ton theon*, i.e., in face-to-face communion] . . . He was with God in the beginning." Moreover, during His earthly ministry, Jesus regularly withdrew from the crowds to solitary places in order to commune in prayer with His heavenly Father (Luke 4:42; 5:16; 6:12; 9:18).

- *Open and honest communication occurred between persons of the Trinity.* Through engaging dialogue, Jesus freely shared His struggles, ideals, and hopes. The ease with which Jesus dialogued with the Father is evident in his extended prayer upon leaving the Upper Room, recorded in John 17.

- *Trinitarian life is characterized by mutuality, self-disclosure, and sharing.* With perfect ease, Jesus said to His Father, "All I have is yours, and all you have is mine" (John 17:10). Moreover, to His disciples the Son said, "The Spirit will take from what is mine and make it known to you" (John 16:15; cf. 5:20).

- *A profound allocentricity, or other-centeredness, characterizes intra-Trinitarian relations.* Each divine person perfectly promotes the significance of the other. Within the social life of the Trinity, one finds no cross-purposes, no jealousy, and no complaining. The Father glorifies the Son (John 17:1, 5), and the Son glorifies the Father. Said Jesus, "I have brought you glory on earth by completing the work you gave me to do" (John 17:4). The Spirit, furthermore, brings glory to the Son (John 16:14).

- *Jesus demonstrated humility by consistently living in dependence upon His Father with gratitude to the Spirit.* In His state of humiliation, the Lord acknowledged the sufficiency of the Father's gifts: "Everything you have given me comes from you" (John 17:7).

- *The second person of the Trinity was fully obedient to ordered authority—His Father.* "I love the Father and . . . do exactly what my Father has commanded me" (John 14:31). The zenith of Jesus' obedience was His devoted submission to agonizing death on the cross, where he uttered the pregnant sentence, "It is finished" (John 19:30).

- *Jesus demonstrated unqualified faithfulness by revealing the Father to the world and to His disciples.* "I have made you known to them, and will continue to make you known" (John 17:26). In addition, he shared with His friends the words of life given Him by the Father: "I gave them the words you gave me and they accepted them" (John 17:8; cf. v. 14).

- *Perfect trust existed between the Father and the Son in the outworking of redemption.* Jesus prayed to the Father, "You granted him authority over all people that he might give eternal life to all those you have given him" (John 17:2; cf. v. 9). Earlier Jesus said, "The Father loves the Son and has placed everything in his hands" (John 3:35).
- *Relations within the Trinity are characterized by unconditional love, the essence of which is selfless caring and giving.* The Gospels teach that the Father loves the Son (Matt. 3:17; John 3:35; 5:20; 17:23–24, 26) and the Son loves the Father. Feel the Son's overflowing heart of love for His Father when He uttered these words of longing: "I am coming to you now" (John 17:13a; cf. v. 11).

In relationships with other believers, Christians are summoned to emulate the loving relations that exist among the Trinity. Beyond this obligation to model intra-Trinitarian relations lies the reality that believers are caught up into the relational life of the triune God. The doctrine of "union with Christ" states that at the new birth believers are united with Christ (John 15:5; 1 Cor. 15:22; 2 Cor. 5:17) and Christ with believers (John 15:5; Gal. 2:20). The Epistles express this relational reality by the phrase "in Christ," which occurs 242 times in the writings of Paul and John. Consider also 1 Corinthians 6:17, which states, "He who unites himself with the Lord is one with him in spirit." Second Peter 1:4 teaches the pivotal precept that through Christ's work believers "participate in the divine nature *[theia physis]*." That is, they share in the relational community of love that is the Trinity. Added to this is the Christian doctrine of *perichoresis* (Lat. *circumincession*), which upholds the mutual indwelling of the three persons of the Trinity, such that the supernatural life of each person flows through the others. At its simplest, this is seen in John's assertion that each divine person is "in" the other divine persons. Thus Jesus said with respect to His Father, "Just as you are in me and I am in you." (John 17:21; cf. v. 23), and he added, "The Father is in me, and I in the Father" (John 10:38; cf. 14:10–11).

The mutual indwelling of Father, Son, and Holy Spirit means that Christians are experientially caught up into the loving relational life of the Trinity. Moreover, since each divine person is "in" the others, believers, who are united with Christ's mystical body (1 Cor. 12:13), are inextricably united with one another. All the while, the Spirit's faithful ministry mortifies the old, selfish nature and breathes new, resurrected life into the soul and all its faculties and relations. As a result Christians are empowered by the Spirit to live out the self-giving, self-communicating, always-loving life of the community that is the Trinity. United with Christ, the loving relationality God designed to exist between human image-bearers becomes a blessed reality.

Let it be added that human relationality mirrors the unity and multiplicity of the triune God. The unity of the Trinity corresponds to our human longing to be part of the whole—to connect, to be close, and to merge with another person. The threeness of the Trinity corresponds to our human need to be a part within the whole—to be acknowledged as a distinct and unique person. Too much union, and we humans feel suffocated; too much space and we feel lonely. Every human being needs to discover his or her identity and significance and to be loved unconditionally.

## Horizontally: Harmonious Relation with the Rest of Creation

Christ's death and resurrection began the process of turning cosmic disharmony into harmony and fragmentation into wholeness. Paul writes, "For creation was not rendered futile by its own choice, but by the will of Him who thus made it subject, the hope being that creation as well as man would one day be freed from its thralldom to decay and gain the glorious freedom of God's children" (Rom. 8:20–21 MOFFATT). Ultimately "the whole creation" (meaning "nonrational creation, animate and inanimate"[99]) will be made new, for God's redemption is creation-wide in scope. In the new heaven and the new earth (Rev. 21:1) relations within the subhuman world will be restored to a peaceful state (Isa. 11:6–7; 65:25). The physical environment will no longer resist human efforts to harness and employ it (Isa. 11:8–9; 65:21, 23). Neither will humans any longer abuse the earth or ravage its resources (Isa. 32:16). Lower forms of life no longer will threaten or prey upon human beings (Isa. 35:9). Neither will humans mistreat subhuman species. In the coming great day, humans will dwell in harmony with their physical environment and with lower forms of life. Present discord will give way to universal šālôm as Christ sovereignly rules over the renewed creation.

---

99. John Murray, *The Epistle to the Romans*, 2 vols. The New International Commentary on the New Testament (Grand Rapids: Eerdmans, 1959), 1:302.

## Vertically: Restored Relation with God

Through Christ's redeeming work on the cross, believers experience re-stored relations with God as well as growing intimacy with Him. Formerly separated from God by virtue of sinful thinking and behavior, believers are now reconciled to relationship through their confession of faith and God's forgiveness. Paul writes, "For if, when we were God's enemies, we were rec-onciled to him through the death of his Son, how much more, having been reconciled, shall we be saved through his life! Not only is this so, but we also rejoice in God through our Lord Jesus Christ, through whom we have now received reconciliation." (Rom. 5:10–11; cf. 2 Cor. 5:18). The verb *katallassō* ("reconcile") means to "thoroughly change" the fractured relationship. The apostle adds, "Remember that at that time you were separate from Christ, excluded from citizenship in Israel and foreigners to the covenants of the promise, without hope and without God in the world. But now in Christ Jesus you who once were far away have been brought near through the blood of Christ" (Eph. 2:12–13). The former enmity, it appears, resides on both sides of the relationship—on God's side due to His revulsion against sin and on the sinner's side due to hostility of heart. Millard Erickson judges that in the event of reconciliation the sinner turns to God, "but the process of reconciliation is primarily God's turning in favor to man."[100]

Over time, with intention and spiritual discipline, twice-born people develop a loving relationship with the Lord of creation and redemption. Cultivation of loving communion with God involves a walk of precious intimacy (Mic. 6:8). Psalmists struggled to put into words the longing of the redeemed heart for communion with God. "As the deer pants for streams of water, so my soul pants for you, O God. My soul thirsts for God, for the living God" (Ps. 42:1–2; cf. 63:1). Paul expressed this deep longing for com-munion in Philippians 3:10. "I want to know Christ and the power of his resurrection and the fellowship of sharing in his sufferings, becoming like him in his death."

At the heart of relationship with God is the discipline of prayer. Prayer is as much a meeting with the loving Father as an act of shooting arrows of request to the heavenly benefactor. Prayer is an all-encompassing reality, entered by composure (centering prayer), experienced as communion (con-templative prayer), and expressed as conversation (conversational prayer).

---

100. Erickson, *Christian Theology,* 815.

Fittingly, Calvin wrote, God "ordained [prayer] not so much for his own sake as for our sake."[101] One can enter into prayer at any time, in any place, and under any circumstance. Abraham's servant prayed by a well (Gen. 24:12–14), Elijah under a broom tree (1 Kings 19:4), Jonah in the belly of a great fish (Jonah 2:1), Nehemiah in a king's palace (Neh. 2:4), Jesus on a high mountain (Luke 9:28–29), and Paul in a prison (Col. 1:3, 9–10).

Because we humans are finite and sinful, even Christians may not feel God's immediate presence at every moment or even every day. As in all human relationships, seasons of dryness may dull believers' awareness of God. In the title of Thomas Green's book, *When the Well Runs Dry*,[102] the word *when*, rather than *if*, is appropriate. Absence of God's felt presence, assurance of His love, and delight in prayer constitute the common cold of the spiritual life. Dryness of spirit may be due to physical or mental fatigue that closes down our spiritual responses or to strained or broken relationships with others. Dryness also may be due to our spiritual neglect. We neglect attentive listening, engagement in dialogue, or an authentic response to God's self-communication. The medieval mystic Meister Eckhart (c. 1260– c. 1328) wrote, "God is always ready, but we are very unready; God is near to us, but we are far from Him; God is within, but we are without; God is at home, but we are strangers."[103]

A more severe sense of distance in our relationship with God may be due to what St. John of the Cross (1542–1591) described as the dark night of the soul—a state of spiritual confusion, desolation, or distaste for spiritual things. The dark night may be precipitated by a personal crisis, a difficult life transition, or a movement across a significant spiritual journey boundary (e.g., purgation, illumination, or union). The dark night is described in *The Cloud of Unknowing* and in John of the Cross's works, *Ascent of Mount Carmel* and *Dark Night of the Soul.* John writes: "After a soul has been converted by God, that soul is nurtured and caressed by the Spirit. Like a loving mother, God cares for and comforts the infant soul by feeding it spiritual milk. Such souls will find great delight in this stage." John continues, "At a certain point in the spiritual journey God will draw the person from the beginning stage to a more advanced stage." This is the "time when God will bid them grow

---

101. Calvin, *Institutes of the Christian Religion*, 2:852 [3.20.3].

102. Thomas Green, *When the Well Runs Dry* (Notre Dame, Ind.: Ave Maria, 1979).

103. Meister Eckhart, cited on poetseers.org/spiritual_and_devotional_poets/christian/ meist/me/istp/god (accessed February 11, 2005).

deeper. He will remove the previous consolation from the soul in order to teach it virtue and prevent it from developing vice."[104]

The dark night, then, is the result of God's mysterious initiative—a God-induced desolation. In the dark night God purposefully withdraws His felt presence, creating a spiritual vacuum to the senses or spirit, the purpose of which is to purify fleshly attachments and propel Christians along the path to deeper relationship with Himself. The dark night may be understood in terms of *attachment theory,* in which God causes believers to detach from lesser loves in order to attach more fully to him.

Many dark night experiences are recorded in Scripture, including those of Job (Job 13; 16; 19; and 31), Elijah (1 Kings 19:3–5), David (Pss. 22:1–2, 14–17; 69:1–3, 17), Asaph (Ps. 77:7–9); Jeremiah (Lamentations), and Jonah (Jonah 4:1–3, 8–9). The darkest of all dark nights occurred when God the Father broke relationship with His beloved Son on the cross, prompting the sinless One to cry out in agony, "My God, my God, why have you forsaken me?" (Matt. 27:46). God's purpose for His children in the dark night is indicated early in the biblical revelation. "He humbled you, causing you to hunger and then feeding you with manna . . . to teach you that man does not live on bread alone" (Deut. 8:3). Helpfully, Henry Blackaby and Claude King observe, "The silence of God means that He is ready to bring into my life a greater revelation of Himself than I have ever known."[105]

---

104. John of the Cross, cited in Richard J. Foster and James Bryan Smith, eds., *Devotional Classics* (San Francisco, Calif.: HarperSanFrancisco, 1993), 33–34.
105. Henry T. Blackaby and Claude V. King, *Experiencing God* (Nashville: Broadman and Holman, 1994), 115.

# CHAPTER 11

# RELATIONSHIPS *and* COMMUNITY *in* PSYCHOLOGICAL PERSPECTIVE

## INTRODUCTION

God declared that the creation was good (Gen. 1:4, 10, 12, 18, 21, 25); in fact, all of it, especially one part (the human race), was very good (Gen. 1:31). God was satisfied with the work of His fingers as humans began to function on the spinning planet. We have two accounts of the creation of the human race, and these pronouncements of "good" all appear in the first of the two. In the second account, we learn in more detail about the process God used to create humans. We learn in Genesis 2 that one part of creation was "not good." For a relatively brief span of time, the man Adam was alone. God said, "It is not good for the man to be alone" (Gen. 2:18). Immediately after making the determination to create a mate for Adam, God asked Adam to name all the animals God had created. In the process Adam discovered that he had no companion who corresponded to him. Perhaps God designed the naming exercise to help Adam personally realize that it was not good for him to be alone.

When God had nearly completed the creation of the world, the text of the first creation account records the following statement: "Let us make man in our image, in our likeness" (Gen. 1:26). The plurals in this statement are not an explicit revelation of the Trinitarian nature of the Godhead, but they do hint at a plurality of persons in the Deity and at a social relationship among them. Genesis 2 directly states, however, that God intended humans to function in groups. In the case of Adam and Eve, the group was a marriage. It was not and is not good for any human being to be alone. God created the race to function best when in fellowship with God and with others.

Our study of the human person, then, would be incomplete without looking at the many ways in which humans function in relation to other people. By analogy, we could profitably study a drop of water and learn a great deal about the physics and chemistry that it displays. But our knowledge of water would be very inadequate if we did not also seek to understand how drops of water function when combined with other drops. Only then can we fully understand water, and only when we learn about humans in groups can we hope to understand them completely.

In this chapter we will explore four large categories related to how humans relate to another person or to groups of persons: the capacity to relate self to the other, social competence, individuals in groups, and sexuality. In essence, the area of relationships and community is the interpersonal realm in contrast to the intrapersonal realm we have examined in previous sections of this volume. We use our interpersonal skills to strike up friendships with others, and they use their interpersonal skills to reciprocate. Business, the arts, the many forms of media, politics, education, and counseling all rely on interpersonal interaction without which society, as we know it, would cease to exist. All counselors and psychotherapists get to know their clients by understanding their relationships in both the present and the past.[1]

To explore the varied issues involved in interpersonal psychology, we will be using material from three major approaches in contemporary psychology, which we will first describe before launching into our investigation of the four categories of our chapter.

## Object Relations Theory

While Freud was living he was able almost single-handedly to determine who was "in" the psychoanalytic family and who was "out." But in the latter half of the twentieth century, the psychoanalytic movement began to take on many variations and permutations. One would be hard pressed to find a

---

1. H. A. Bacal and K. M. Newman, *Theories of Object Relations: Bridges to Self Psychology* (New York: Columbia University Press, 1990), 2.

psychoanalyst today who would claim to practice Freudian theory in its pure form as it existed when Freud died in London in 1939. Even the most traditional psychoanalysts have made some adaptations to the Freudian approach.

Among the many theoretical descendants of Freudian thought is a group of object relations theorists. *Object* is a misleading term that unfortunately has been retained by the movement. In essence, object relations theory addresses issues related to how the individual relates to other people (objects). Object relations theory (ORT) builds its psychotherapy approach on developmental events that occur as the infant matures. Freud's interest was in the first five years of life; ORT focuses on the first twenty-four months. The developmental events and tasks of those months, according to ORT, help shape both the normal and the abnormal psychology of individuals. ORT is intensely interested in interpersonal functioning, unlike Freud who focused on drives and instincts.[2] But in spite of their differences, object relations theory "nevertheless derives from Freudian theory."[3] The ORT family of approaches includes both an American and a British branch. They vary to some degree in their emphases.

## Social Learning Theory

Social learning theory (SLT) stems from the work of two Stanford University professors: Robert Sears and Albert Bandura. Sears made an effort to blend psychoanalytic approaches with learning and behavioral theory. Bandura moved away from an emphasis on drive and psychoanalytic concepts and simply built a synthesis of cognitive principles with observational learning.[4] Bandura's main focus of interest was on social development and how it unfolds.[5] Technically, SLT is still a behavior theory, given its retention of reinforcement as a primary means of learning; SLT, along with cognitive-behavior therapy, is now in the mainstream of behavioral therapy. "Behavior change is brought about largely through

---

2. Ibid.

3. J. S. Scharff, "Freud and Object Relations Theory," in *The Psychoanalytic Century: Freud's Legacy for the Future,* ed. D. E. Scharff (New York: Other Press, 2001), 104.

4. Albert Bandura, *Social Learning Theory* (Englewood Cliffs, N.J.: Prentice Hall, 1977).

5. J. E. Grusec, "Social Learning Theory and Developmental Psychology: The Legacies of Robert Sears and Albert Bandura," *Developmental Psychology* 28 (1992): 776–86.

observational learning, a process in which people are influenced by someone else's behavior."[6]

SLT thus shares some interests with ORT: both approaches to interpersonal functioning focus considerable interest on early childhood, and both view these early experiences as influential and shaping in nature. SLT has dedicated a great deal of investigative energy to the study of aggression, an interpersonal theme of importance in contemporary society. The theory is also widely utilized to understand criminal behavior and activity.

## Family Systems Theory

Another cluster of psychotherapeutic approaches utilizes a systems approach to understand interpersonal functioning in organizations and families. Family systems theory (FST) likewise has many expressions and "schools" of thought; but they all share in the conviction that psychological and emotional pathology, dysfunction, and abnormalities reflect pressures from the system in which the individual is operating. FST differs from the prior two approaches in that the systems strategy is to locate the intrapersonal causes of interpersonal problems and to treat them with interpersonal interventions. A major goal of family therapy using a systems approach is to increase personal satisfaction in relationships within the system.[7] The strategies utilized by ORT and SLT are more likely to locate the interpersonal causes of interpersonal problems and to treat them with intrapersonal interventions.

Family systems theory focuses on the family unit as a functioning whole. The system has boundaries and internal dynamics between and among all the members of the system. The system is always configured in such a way that making changes in any one element in the system will push the system into a state of disequilibrium until all members of the unit readjust to the new reality. Therapists who utilize FST do not typically see individual clients, only family groupings (preferably the entire group if at all possible). As the process proceeds, participants in family therapy begin to see the relationship

---

6. D. B. Fishman and C. M. Franks, "The Conceptual Evolution of Behavior Therapy," in *Theories of Psychotherapy: Origins and Evolution,* ed. P. L. Wachtel and S. B. Messer (Washington, D.C.: American Psychological Association, 1997), 142.

7. Suzanne Midori Hanna and Joseph H. Brown, *The Practice of Family Therapy: Key Elements Across Models* (Belmont, Calif.: Brooks Cole, 1999), 60–63.

between the poor functioning of any one member of the group and the pressures that the system are bringing to bear on that person. The therapist then seeks to introduce changes into the system to produce positive changes for everyone in the family. In general, these emphases characterize systems interventions from all of the various types of family therapy: structural, strategic, transgenerational, experiential, or behavioral family therapy.[8]

These three distinct approaches have each contributed to our understanding of interpersonal behavior, a central component of our daily lives. We will now explore four main areas of interpersonal functioning, as psychology currently understands them: self and other relations, social competence, individuals in groups, and sexuality.

## SELF—OTHER RELATIONS

Whereas theology speaks of the soul, psychology speaks of the self. In order for an individual of any age to relate psychologically to another person, the individual must have a sense of self. Interpersonal relationships occur between two or more persons, and participants in these relationships must have at least a rudimentary sense of self that is distinct from a sense of the other. Psychologists have long been interested in tracing the roots of this sense of self, especially as it relates to the other. The interpersonal and relational approach to understanding human functioning and psychopathology is the "most rapidly evolving theoretical orientation within psychoanalysis in the last decade."[9] But no school of thought has been more interested in this pursuit than object relations theorists. Their search begins in the very first month of life for the newborn.

### Infant Development

Many people will be surprised to learn of a new specialty within the field of mental health: infant mental health. The emergence of this effort reflects the growing awareness of most people within the mental health field that psychological problems often display a very early onset and that interven-

---

8. Joseph H. Brown and Dana N. Christensen, *Family Therapy: Theory and Practice,* 2d ed. (Pacific Grove, Calif.: Brooks Cole, 1999).

9. Peter Fonagy and Mary Target, *Psychoanalytic Theories: Perspectives from Developmental Psychopathology* (New York: Brunner-Routledge, 2003), 204.

tions early on can sometimes avert later disaster. Furthermore, many of these problems reflect relationship issues, the subject of our current investigation. "Infant mental health, therefore, focuses on relationships; infant development is conceptualized as always embedded within emergent, active systems of relationships. By definition the infant is born into a social world."[10]

Understanding the psychology of humans by exploring infant development involves processing information through at least four different levels.

1.  The process begins by carefully observing infants as they interact with their caregiver/s and the surrounding environment. Every parent is aware of many features of these early changes in the awareness of the child as well as in the child's responsiveness to others.
2.  The second level involves inferring that these infant behaviors reflect a developing, internal psychology.
3.  Level three infers that the quality of interactions between child and caregiver during this process of growth determines both the normal and abnormal features of that person's later pattern of interaction with others.
4.  Level four claims that therapy can address early deficiencies, correct them, and thus allow the adult to move into relationships of greater interpersonal health. The major difficulty with this fourth level is that all of these shaping events occur during a period of infant amnesia and some of them during a preverbal stage. Thus the therapist must reconstruct these events based on secondary evidence.[11]

Object relations therapists firmly believe in all four levels of this paradigm. Almost everyone agrees with the validity of the first level, and the empirical evidence is strongest there as well. But as we move through the other three levels, the number of adherents gradually shrinks and supporting empirical data likewise diminishes.

At birth the human infant is totally dependent on the care of others.

---

10. H. E. Fitzgerald and L. R. Barton, "Infant Mental Health: Origins and Emergence of an Interdisciplinary Field," in *WAIMH Handbook of Infant Mental Health*, ed. J. D. Osofsky and H. E. Fitzgerald (New York: John Wiley and Sons, 2000), 1:4.
11. Ivri Kumin, *Pre-Object Relatedness: Early Attachment and the Psychoanalytic Situation* (New York: Guilford Press, 1996), 1.

"Human beings are born in a state of marked immaturity."[12] Survival depends on the regular provision of both food and care. The full-term, normal infant is able to utilize all sensory systems, even though they are at different levels of maturation at birth. Babies will react to loud sounds only minutes after birth. The various components of their visual system are intact at birth, but "they are not fully developed and they are not well coordinated."[13] Babies have acute senses of taste and smell from the very beginning. Researchers have identified nine reflexes present at birth. Three of these reflexes are permanent (breathing, eyeblink, and sucking), and the other six disappear between two and twelve months after birth (Babinski, crawling, grasping, startle, rooting, and stepping). Almost immediately the infant appears to possess the ability to differentiate between satiation and need. The child is calmer when fed and dry and considerably less calm when hungry and wet.

Accompanying these many lines of maturation and development are social indicators of change.[14] The infant soon recognizes the mother's voice, is calmer in the presence of the mother, begins to visually explore the mother's face, learns to smile in response to others, senses when someone else is present or absent, and so forth. Object relations theorists take these various steps in social development as indicators of an emerging psychology, the second level of inference referred to above. The observable social changes occurring in the life of the infant, according to ORT, reflect the internal development of the baby's psyche. One of the foremost expositors of the object relations approach (D. W. Winicott) was, in fact, a pediatrician who was fascinated by the many indications of emotional development that he observed during infancy.[15]

The most famous reconstruction of the stages involved in this process comes from the work of Margaret Mahler.[16] Mahler argues that over the

---

12. M. Cole and S. R. Cole, *The Development of Children,* 2d ed. (New York: Scientific American Books, 1993), 128.

13. Ibid., 131.

14. Michael F. Mascolo, Kurt W. Fischer, and Robert A. Neimeyer, "The Dynamic Codevelopment of Intentionality, Self, and Social Relations," in *Action and Self-Development: Theory and Research Through the Life Span,* ed. Jochen Brandtstadter and Richard M. Lerner (Thousand Oaks, Calif.: Sage, 1999), 133–66.

15. D. E. Scharff, *Object Relations Theory and Practice: An Introduction* (Northvale, N.J.: Jason Aronson, 1996), 4.

16. Margaret S. Mahler, Fred Pine, and Anni Bergman, *The Psychological Birth of the Human Infant* (New York: Basic Books, 1975), 39–120.

course of the first twenty-four months of life, the basic psychology of a person forms in interaction with others, primarily the caregiver/s. She described three phases.

1. *Normal autism, 0–2 months.* Most people are familiar with the psychological condition known as autism that sometimes occurs among children. To various degrees the child is unable to make satisfactory contact with other people and seems somehow locked in a private, internal world. Mahler would refer to this condition that we can observe among older children as secondary autism. She argued that all children begin life in a state of primary autism that is normal for the first two months. While in this stage, the infant's physiological processes dominate. The child "seems to be in a state of primitive hallucinatory disorientation. . . ."[17] While this language sounds harsh and uncaring to the adoring parent who is thrilled with the newborn, we can step back and observe that the newborn does not seem very responsive in the first few weeks of life.

2. *Symbiosis, 2–4 months.* Soon, however, the child realizes that life is better when mother is around. The baby is not aware of any boundaries between self and mother, and the child is unable to distinguish between "I" and "not-I." This symbiosis is normal and reflects a major advance over the isolation of the first autistic phase. "The infant develops a sense of unity or symbiosis with that caregiver, especially mediated by physical contact."[18] Theologically we can infer that relationality is indeed an inherent feature of human personhood, even though the infant cannot immediately exercise the capacity. A parallel situation occurs when we posit an inherent capacity to relate to God as a feature of basic human nature, even though infants and small children cannot exercise that capacity in the way they later will be able to do.

3. *Separation-individuation, 5–24 months.* Very early in the baby's life, two concurrent processes begin operation. These processes will eventuate in the psychological separation of the child from the mother and in the individuating of the child. "The infant's visual, tactile, and manual exploration of the mother's face, body, and

---

17. Ibid., 42.
18. Fitzgerald and Barton, "Infant Mental Health," 13.

clothing" show that the infant is beginning to enter the separation-individuation phase.[19] Mahler proposed four subphases in this separation-individuation process: *hatching,* in which the child is much more alert during waking hours; *practicing,* during which the child is able to experiment with separation by crawling or walking away from the mother; *rapprochement,* which is a period of time during which the baby seems to retreat from the full experience of separation he or she was able to enjoy in the second subphase; and *consolidation and the beginnings of object constancy,* a renewed confidence that I am myself even when I am away from my mother because I have an internalized image of her.

Thus the child will have an individuated sense of self apart from the mother and will be able to separate from her as needed without incurring a psychological crisis. "Between 15 and 24 months, infants indicate through the use of personal pronouns, 'me' or 'mine,' and self-recognition in the mirror, that the self has emerged. With its emergence come such capacities as empathy and sharing behaviour, behaviours absolutely necessary for the emergence of relationships."[20]

Object relations theorists thus take the observable events of infancy and infer the internal development of a psychology that deals primarily with self and other. In level three of this process, theorists identify many of the roots of both childhood and adult psychopathology in various segments of the separation-individuation process that have not gone well. "What is wrong with troubled children comes solely from deficiencies in their treatment by others, from inadequate supplies or security."[21] "Even mild or moderate adjustment problems in early infancy may lead to severe maladjustment in adulthood," even though we may not fully understand the processes by which these continuities operate.[22]

---

19. Bacal and Newman, *Theories of Object Relations,* 105.
20. Michael Lewis, "Social Development," in *Introduction to Infant Development,* ed. Alan Slater and Michael Lewis (New York: Oxford University Press, 2002), 223.
21. Scharff, *Object Relations Theory and Practice,* 18.
22. P. deChateau, "Longitudinal Aspects of Early Parent-Infant Interactions and Contacts with Mental Health Agencies," in *WAIMH Handbook of Infant Mental Health,* 86–87.

## Childhood Experience and Adult Psychopathology

One example of an impaired process of social development according to ORT can occur in the third subphase, rapprochement. During this phase the child shrinks back from the exuberance of the practicing subphase. In some ways, returning to the mother is "a regressive return to the merged self- and object representations of the symbiotic phase."[23] As the child returns periodically to the mother, the mother's quiet availability is an important reassurance to the child. An unavailable mother or one who is having difficulty adjusting to the progressing independence of the child will not provide the kind of "object" dependability that the child needs. As a result the child may incorporate into her or his emerging personality certain levels of insecurity and fear of independence.

Some object relations theorists believe that the origins of the borderline personality disorder can be located in inadequate mothering that occurs during this subphase. The child builds a sense of self by interacting with "objects" such as the mother during these crucial months of development and by internalizing a representation of that object. If the mother is a good, reliable, available, and nurturing object, the child will internalize a good object. If the mother is unavailable, resistant, hovering, or abandoning, the child will internalize mother as a bad object.[24] Good and bad internalized objects are related respectively to normal adult functioning and to abnormal adult functioning. "One could regard the entire life cycle as constituting a more or less successful process of distancing from and introjection of the lost symbiotic mother . . . who was at one time part of the self in a blissful state of well-being."[25] An understanding of these roots of borderline conditions can facilitate treatment and therapy that is focused on relationship deficiencies.[26]

---

23. G. Goodman, *The Internal World and Attachment* (Hillsdale, N.J.: The Analytic Press, 2003), 31.

24. M. St. Clair, *Object Relations and Self Psychology: An Introduction* (Monterey, Calif.: Brooks Cole, 1986), 115.

25. M. Mahler, "On the First Three Subphases of the Separation—Individuation Process," in *Essential Papers on Object Relations,* ed. P. Buckley (New York: New York University Press, 1986), 231–32.

26. Donald D. Roberts, "Shorter Term Treatment of Borderline Personality Disorder: A Developmental, Self- and Object Relations Approach," *Psychoanalytic Psychology* 17 (2000): 106–27.

Mahler is just one among many theorists who locate the origins of the more serious psychopathologies in these early months of infancy. The general rule of thumb is that the more serious the emotional pathology is, the earlier is its origin. ORT identifies many negative psychological mechanisms emerging from these early stages of psychological development: distancing, splitting, ambivalence, denial/avoidance, repression, and so forth.[27] These negative mechanisms and experiences can, according to ORT, appear later in life to cause dysfunction.

> The mother who enjoyed closeness with her infant at the symbiotic level, yet wants him to become independent as soon as he begins to explore his separateness, can provoke a fear of object loss. The child, experiencing premature pressure to grow up, may engage in a reaction formation against the recognition of his deeper needs while continuing to have a weakened core. In later life, separations or, paradoxically, successes may reawaken memory traces of being abandoned and produce a sense of profound anxiety or loneliness.[28]

One criticism of the object relations view of how the sense of self and other develops in a young child concerns the pressure the theory exerts on parents, especially mothers, to be "good enough" objects for the growing child. The theory argues that it is not easy to be this "good enough" parent. "The child may demand and reject help simultaneously. He may coerce and control the mother as an extension of himself. He may be negative and obstinate and throw tantrums. The demands on the mother are great."[29] Yet many researchers continue to find evidence supporting the fact that maternal attitudes can influence the physical and emotional health of the infant. These potentially harmful attitudes can reflect attitudinal quality (overt primal rejection, primary anxious overpermissiveness, hostility in the guise of anxiety, oscillation between pampering and hostility, cyclical mood swings, or hostility consciously compensated) as well as issues of attitudinal quantity (partial or complete emotional deprivation).[30] Feminists are

---

27. Mahler, Pine, and Bergman, *The Psychological Birth of the Human Infant,* 24, 108, 117, 194, 211.

28. Bacal and Newman, *Theories of Object Relations,* 106.

29. N. G. Hamilton, *Self and Others: Object Relations Theory in Practice* (Northvale, N.J.: Jason Aronson Inc., 1988), 51.

30. Fitzgerald and Barton, "Infant Mental Health," 14.

quick to wonder whether this approach to understanding adult psychopathology is not just another way of blaming women for all that is wrong in
the world; nonetheless, everyone recognizes the central and crucial role
parents, especially the mother, can play in the development of the child.

The strength of the object relations approach is that it recognizes the
crucial role that the interpersonal realm plays in human functioning. The
ORT approach has moved far away from psychoanalytic approaches that
view core human difficulties as intrapersonal conflicts only. One can find
strong evidence for the central role of interpersonal difficulties in psychopathology by examining the diagnostic criteria for the major adult forms of
mental illness. The definition used by the standard manual for diagnosing
mental disorders requires that the diagnosing process for all conditions must
establish the presence of distress, or disability, or high risk for suffering
before the diagnosis can be applied.[31] The criteria sets for a large number of
disorders specifically require the presence of impairments in occupational
or social functioning (the schizophrenias, manic episodes, dysthymia, bi-
polar I and II disorders, cyclothymia, the specific phobias, social phobia,
obsessive-compulsive disorder, post-traumatic stress disorder, plus many
others).[32] Even if theorists are unwilling to concede interpersonal causal
factors underlying psychopathology, they do recognize that mental illness
has interpersonal consequences.

Other approaches among the many Freudian theoretical descendants
likewise see a strong connection between psychopathology and interpersonal
functioning. John Bowlby's attachment theory views separation, loss, and
threat of loss/separation as key building blocks for psychopathology. When
the processes affecting a child's attachment needs are inadequate or deficient,
various forms of attachment pathology can appear: anxious-ambivalent
attachments, insistent self-reliance, insistent caregiving, or emotional
detachment.[33] These attachment pathologies can all contribute to the
development of agoraphobia, the borderline personality disorder, or
pathological mourning. Leonard Horowitz has been active in developing
an interpersonal approach to psychopathology (both Axis I and Axis II
disorders) from an even broader perspective. "Frustrated interpersonal

---

31. *DSM*-IV, xxxi.
32. Ibid., 312, 362, 381, 388, 397, 400, 449, 456, 463, 468.
33. P. Sable, *Attachment and Adult Psychotherapy* (Northvale, N.J.: Jason Aronson, 2000),
    3, 58–63.

motives (together with biological factors) shape a person's vulnerability, and psychopathology arises in vulnerable people when sensitized motives are frustrated further."[34]

## Schizophrenia

Of the many psychopathologies that display serious interpersonal deficits, schizophrenia is one of the most severe. It is an emotional illness greatly affected by interpersonal deviance.[35] At the heart of the illness are issues reflecting a deficient relationship between self and other. A large number of governmental and nongovernmental researchers have dedicated a great deal of work to understanding this devastating illness. One of the reasons for this enormous effort to unravel the mysteries of the various types of this disease is the high cost to society that schizophrenia causes. A person diagnosed with one of its variations may struggle throughout life with the condition and may sustain disabling consequences that create long-term financial obligations for government. Hence government resources dedicated to this research are investments aimed at curbing this cost to society.

The occurrence rate for schizophrenia is approximately one out of one hundred people, a rate of incidence that tends to be stable cross-culturally. "Most individuals with schizophrenia have an onset in early adulthood, have long periods of illness, are unable to work and have difficulty in sustaining family relationships because of their illness."[36] Most everyone concedes that genetics play a crucial role in the schizophrenic disease process, although people differ in what other factors, if any, contribute to its emergence. Research into the disease seeks to understand causal factors, symptomatology, curative factors, and management issues. Interpersonal functioning is related to all four of these areas, although various theoretical orientations might disagree as to details.

---

34. Leonard M. Horowitz, *Interpersonal Foundations of Psychopathology* (Washington, D.C.: American Psychological Association, 2004), 263.
35. M. J. Zborowski and J. P. Garske, "Interpersonal Deviance and Consequent Social Impact in Hypothetically Schizophrenia-Prone Men," *Journal of Abnormal Psychology* 102 (1993): 482–89.
36. Michael J. Owen and Michael C. O'Donovan, "Schizophrenia and Genetics," in *Behavioral Genetics in the Postgenomic Era,* ed. R. Plomin, J. C. Defries, I. W. Craig, and P. McGuffin (Washington, D.C.: American Psychological Association, 2003), 463.

Current research into the causes of schizophrenia and to those factors that increase a person's level of vulnerability to the onset of the disease include investigations into a wide variety of interpersonal themes. Some studies explore communications patterns used by persons with schizophrenia or those who later develop the disease. These persons display disordered speech that fails to communicate meaning clearly. They differ from the general population in the use of vague and confused references, ambiguous or wrong word meanings, and structural unclarities.[37] Some of these communication problems appear also in patients with other forms of psychosis, but the impaired communication patterns remain stable among people with schizophrenia even when their psychotic symptoms remit. Communication deficits characteristic of schizophrenia probably interact with cognitive deficits to produce an inadequate pattern of interaction with other people.[38] These communication problems in the schizophrenia disease process are thus clearly related to interpersonal impairments. Other research seeks to understand the role of trauma in the development and severity of the disease,[39] the relationship between the disease and the executive function of personality,[40] and how self-esteem issues relate to the disease.[41]

Family systems theory is one orientation that addresses interpersonal issues as causal factors for the development and emergence of schizophrenia among young adults. Murray Bowen, a leading exponent of the family systems approach, argues that each family has a certain quantity of "undifferentiated ego mass" available for the children in that family. Normal children are able to internalize a sufficient quantity of this ego mass to produce a high functioning ego. But sometimes one child will be unable to

37. N. M. Docherty et al., "Stability of Formal Thought Disorder and Referential Communication Disturbances in Schizophrenia," *Journal of Abnormal Psychology* 112 (2003): 469–75.

38. D. M. Barch et al., "Context-Processing Deficits in Schizophrenia: Diagnostic Specificity, Four-Week Course, and Relationships to Clinical Symptoms," *Journal of Abnormal Psychology* 112 (2003): 132–43.

39. S. G. Resnick, G. R. Bond, and J. T. Mueser, "Trauma and Posttraumatic Stress Disorder in People with Schizophrenia," *Journal of Abnormal Psychology* 112 (2003): 415–23.

40. J. G. Kerns and H. Berenbaum, "The Relationship Between Formal Thought Disorder and Executive Functioning Component Processes," *Journal of Abnormal Psychology* 112 (2003): 339–52.

41. C. Barrowclough et al., "Self-Esteem in Schizophrenia: Relationships Between Self-Evaluation, Family Attitudes, and Symptomatology," *Journal of Abnormal Psychology* 112 (2003): 92–99.

appropriate a sufficient amount of this available ego mass and thus will remain immature and undifferentiated. Since persons tend to marry a person with similar levels of ego maturation, this immature adult will tend to marry another similarly immature adult. Their parenting abilities will be weakened, and after several generations, the process will produce a child who suffers from schizophrenia.[42] This paradigm fits some but not all occurrences of the disease.

Because interpersonal factors in the family system contributed to the development of the disease, according to Bowen, he advocated family treatment for the disease. "He decided to admit family units to his inpatient program, requiring parents to live on the ward with the schizophrenic patient. Well siblings who were in school joined the rest of the family in the hospital on weekends."[43] This type of treatment is obviously impractical, but it does illustrate the degree to which Bowen felt systems and interpersonal factors were relevant to the disease.

Samuel Slipp has developed an approach to understanding schizophrenia based on ORT. Slipp found that when families interfered with a child's internal regulation of self-esteem and with the child's ability to differentiate, schizophrenia could be the outcome. "The essential characteristic of this pattern was that each person's self-esteem and ego identity were felt to be dependent on the behavior of the other family members."[44] The vulnerable child thus stayed excessively dependent on family relationships for both self-esteem and for ego identity. The child's symbiotic survival pattern thus prevented individuation and maturation and set the stage, especially during or immediately after adolescence, for the emergence of schizophrenia. Again, interpersonal factors are crucial, in the development of the disease according to Slipp.

Even among theories of schizophrenia that focus on genetics as the fundamental source of the disease, interpersonal factors are still involved. Extensive assessment of people whose schizophrenia has yet to emerge has revealed patterns of neurocognitive deficits in the areas of perception, memory, sustained attention, sensory processing, and problem-solving abili-

---

42. Murray Bowen, *Family Therapy in Clinical Practice* (New York: Jason Aronson, 1985), 45–69.
43. Stephen J. Schultz, *Family Systems Therapy: An Integration* (New York: Jason Aronson, 1984), 34.
44. Samuel Slipp, *Object Relations: A Dynamic Bridge Between Individual and Family Treatment* (New York: Jason Aronson, 1984), 91.

ties. These deficits, in turn, affect the social interactions of the individuals, or their social cognition. Their ability "to perceive emotion in others, the ability to infer what others are thinking, and the ability to understand the individual roles and rules that govern social interactions" are all affected negatively.[45] People who have difficulty with these social skills are likely to have impaired relationships with others. Among children who have a childhood onset of the disease, 44 percent displayed social abnormalities based on prepsychotic developmental data.[46] Thus even theorists who argue that the illness is primarily caused by genetics and brain characteristics acknowledge that interpersonal functioning is at the heart of how the disease manifests itself.

Treatment programs for persons suffering from schizophrenia almost always include efforts to improve the social and interpersonal skills of the client. Investigators are particularly interested in pinpointing the specific social abilities and response patterns that appear to be different from "normals." One such project found that people without a history of schizophrenia responded to a negative life event differently from matched patients diagnosed with chronic schizophrenia. The "normals" tended to use a wide range of cognitive and behavioral strategies for approaching and for avoiding the problem. Those with chronic schizophrenia, however, focused only on strategies for avoiding the problem at hand. Approaching a problem may temporarily increase stress, a result that schizophrenic patients seek to avoid. "Avoidance coping may reduce stress in the short term but may be maladaptive over time, especially in the absence of more active attempts to resolve interpersonal situations that are stressful."[47] Once researchers have identified a specific skill deficit such as this one, the next step is to see whether focused training exercises with schizophrenic patients aimed at stimulating needed skills could improve their social functioning. Any improvements in the social skills of chronic schizophrenics can potentially

45. Michael F. Green, *Schizophrenia Revealed: From Neurons to Social Interactions* (New York: W. W. Norton, 2001), 72–84.

46. S. Kumra, R. Nicolson, and J. L. Rapoport, "Childhood-Onset Schizophrenia," in *The Early Stages of Schizophrenia*, ed. R. B. Zipursky and S. C. Schulz, (Washington, D.C.: American Psychiatric Press, 2002), 175.

47. J. Ventur, K. H. Nuechterlein, and K. L. Subotnik, "Coping with Interpersonal Stressors in Schizophrenia," in *Comprehensive Treatment of Schizophrenia: Linking Neurobehavioral Findings to Psychosocial Approaches*, ed. H. Kashima, I. R. H. Falloon, M. Mizuno, and M. Asai (New York: Springer, 2002), 33.

make a substantial positive change in the quality of their lives and in their ability to function in society.

## SOCIAL COMPETENCE

Social competence is a key component of successful interpersonal functioning for all persons, not just those suffering from schizophrenia. Effective social skills are easier to identify by their absence than by their presence. The socially inappropriate person creates frustration and misunderstanding, but the socially appropriate person often moves through life unnoticed and with ease. A great deal of research within the field of psychology into the nature of sociality is guided by primate research and the principles of evolutionary psychology.[48] Social skills are more easily learned during childhood than they are in the adult years. Parents and educators aim many of their efforts at the development of good social skills while children are malleable and teachable. Theologically, we know that the process of spiritual transformation enhances relational performance even when negative patterns are set and habitual.

### Social Skills

Social skills are "goal-directed actions in interpersonal contexts that are learnable, repeatable, and variable in their quality."[49] When we can accurately understand normal social skills, we have better success at diagnosing, assessing, and correcting social skill deficits. Rating social skillfulness involves exploring how the behavior or interaction in question rates on scales ranging from attractive to unattractive, effective to ineffective, and appropriate to inappropriate.[50] Only by looking at the multidimensional nature of social interactions are we able to do justice to the complexity of human social interactions.

A person's general ability to establish and maintain quality social rela-

---

48. Robert W. Sussman and Audrey R. Chapman, eds., *The Origins and Nature of Sociality* (New York: Aldine de Gruyter, 2004).

49. B. H. Spitzberg and J. P. Dillard, "Social Skills and Communication," in *Interpersonal Communication Research: Advances Through Meta-Analysis*, ed. M. Allen, R. W. Preiss, B. M. Gayle, and N. A. Burrell (Mahwah, N.J.: Lawrence Erlbaum Assocs., 2002), 90.

50. Ibid., 95.

tionships is part and parcel of any general assessment we make of people. People vote for candidates who appear affable as well as astute politically. We hire pastors who are relationally competent as well as theologically sound. And we prefer physicians who can relate to us as well as they can treat our illnesses. We expect leaders in government, business, and society in general to possess high quality social skills. All professionals must likewise function well interpersonally, or their careers are in jeopardy. Effective interpersonal interaction is central to the success of a marriage, to the quality of parenting, and to the functioning of nuclear and extended families. "Important social competencies evade large proportions of the population, however. Estimates indicate that at least 7% to 10% of the population is socially inadequate, although some would estimate the rate at closer to 25%."[51]

We establish relationships with people based on what we observe in others and on how we interpret their motives. Each party to the new relationship displays a self-presentation style that either enhances or hinders the development of a relationship. Relationships develop when the parties have a need for affiliation and a desire to associate with one another. Many social relationships are built when the parties can detect high levels of affinity.[52] The skills needed to establish and maintain a quality interpersonal relationship are many and varied. They include: the abilities to listen, to greet others, to join in, to compliment others, to express anger well and appropriately, to keep friends, to use self-control, to offer assistance when needed, to disagree effectively with others, and to carry on a satisfactory conversation with others.[53] Social relationships are fragile and subject to eventual extinction if not properly maintained and nourished. Some people are better at initiating friendships than maintaining them. Other people possess abilities to do just the opposite.

A central component of effective social interaction is communication skill. Without it, relationships are doomed; with it, relationships can flourish. Studies of the communication process have identified both nonverbal and verbal communication skills that relate to social effectiveness. Eye contact, gestures,

51. B. H. Spitzberg, "Methods of Interpersonal Skill Assessment," in *Handbook of Communication and Social Interaction Skills*, ed. J. O. Greene and B. P. Burleson (Mahwah, N.J.: Lawrence Erlbaum Assocs., 2003), 95.

52. B. M. Gayle and R. W. Preiss, "An Overview of Individual Processes in Interpersonal Communication," in *Interpersonal Communication Research*, 46–52.

53. Martha E. Snee and Rachel Janney, *Social Relationships and Peer Support* (Baltimore: Paul H. Brookes, 2000), 94.

head movements, and verbal statements all contribute to the mix.[54] Our skills in producing a message, communicating it clearly to others, and accurately receiving their messages to us are fundamental components involved in the many verbal skills we need in interpersonal relationships: arguing, persuasion, managing conflict, providing social support, negotiating, relational support, and conversational processes.[55] Each party in the relationship has an effect on and is affected by the other party. Relationships help contribute to our personal sense of identity. "One's role identity is established through interactions with relational partners who provide mutual exchanges of support."[56] Clearly, we can affirm that relating to others is good for the soul.[57]

## Children and Social Skills

Parents, under normal circumstances, have the greatest influence on the developing social competencies of children. This influence can be both positive and negative. While we strive to pass along to the next generation our best social skills, we sometimes find that our children also acquire some of our less desirable social tendencies. "Folk wisdom assigns parents most of the credit for their children's achievements and most of the blame for their weak points."[58] We know, however, that genes and the role of siblings and peers also make an impact on the social development of the child.

At its broadest level, positive parental influence on children helps the next generation adopt the constructive values of society as their own and to develop the individual social skills necessary to function well in society.[59] Christian parents conduct this training within the context of scriptural teach-

---

54. Spitzberg and Dillard, "Social Skills and Communication," 100.

55. Greene and Burleson, *Handbook of Communication and Social Interaction Skills*. See also B. M. Gayle and R. W. Preiss, "An Overview of Interactional Processes in Interpersonal Communication," in *Interpersonal Communication Research*, 214.

56. B. M. Gayle and R. W. Preiss, "An Overview of Dyadic Processes in Interpersonal Communication," in *Interpersonal Communication Research*, 112.

57. Stephen P. Greggo, "The Truth about Relationality: How Others Are Good for the Soul" (paper presented at the annual meeting of the Evangelical Theological Society, San Antonio, Texas, November 2004).

58. Barry H. Schneider, *Friends and Enemies: Peer Relations in Childhood* (London: Arnold, 2000), 72.

59. J. E. Gursec and J. Ungerer, "Effective Socialization as Problem Solving and the Role of Parenting Cognitions," in *Handbook of Dynamics in Parent-Child Relations*, ed. L. Kuczynski (Thousand Oaks, Calif.: Sage, 2003), 211.

ings about how God expects us to behave and conduct ourselves. Rarely do we read statutory laws dealing with theft and robbery to our children, but we do teach them not to steal the toys of their playmates. We do not send our children to law school to study the legal prohibitions regarding the destruction of property, but we do teach them not to throw rocks through windows and not to break the toys of their siblings. As with many other aspects of parenting, the influence between parent and child is bidirectional. Teaching positive social skills to a quiet child is a far different process from training a difficult child to be socially appropriate. When children learn necessary social skills in the home and in their early years, life is smoother and more effective. When basic and necessary social skills are not learned in the home, the school must attempt to fill in the gap.

When children begin their formal schooling, they encounter what often turns out to be their first major set of social challenges. Surrounded by large numbers of peers and several unknown adults in positions of authority, these kindergartners must use every social skill they possess to fit in and function interpersonally. Every child experiences a few rough times, but most school children will soon learn that applying the rules Mom and Dad drilled into them does indeed make things go more smoothly. Their level of social competence soon enables them to engage in "adequate social relations" that produce "desirable social outcomes."[60] These successful adaptors, called resilient children, are cooperative, prone to positive emotions, gregarious, and successful at solving problems and achieving academically.[61] Some children, however, have a difficult time adjusting to the social demands of the school experience with the result that they come to the attention of teachers and administrators as problem students. Sometimes the issue revolves around acquisition deficits (the child has never acquired certain necessary skills), and at other times the problem stems from performance deficits (the child cannot execute the skill effectively).[62]

Most approaches to the assessment of children who have trouble socially

60. Kenneth W. Merrell, *Behavioral, Social, and Emotional Assessment of Children and Adolescents* (Mahwah, N.J.: Lawrence Erlbaum Assocs., 2003), 312.

61. Daniel Hart, Robert Atkins, and Suzanne Figley, "Personality and Development in Childhood: A Person-Centered Approach," *Monographs of the Society for Research in Child Development* 68 (2003): 87.

62. Natalie Rathvon, *Effective School Interventions: Strategies for Enhancing Academic Achievement and Social Competence* (New York: Guilford Press, 1999), 316.

in school focus on their externalizing behaviors, sometimes also called undercontrolled or outer-directed conduct. These actions are aggressive, antisocial, or hyperactive. Teachers also observe a less frequent manifestation of social skill deficits among children who do not externalize their frustration but who internalize it in the form of withdrawal, extreme shyness, or excessive compliance. Social skills are important in all five major dimensions of the school experience:

1.  Peer relationships: social interaction with others, prosocial or anti-social behavior, ability to empathize, leadership, active participation in groups, and general sociability
2.  Self-management: self-control, frustration tolerance, ability to be independent, willingness to follow rules, and willingness to accept responsibility
3.  Academic: social interactions that facilitate or interfere with learning, such as respect for rules and authority, compliance to classroom procedures, and ability to focus on required tasks
4.  Compliance: cooperation with other individuals and the group
5.  Assertion: initiating relationships, activating social exchanges, appropriate assertive behavior[63]

Children who internalize or overcontrol their social frustrations in one or more of these dimensions display an anxiety-withdrawal pattern (fearful, timid, easily hurt, easily frustrated) or a schizoid-unresponsive characteristic (withdrawn, sad, confused, secretive).[64] Children who externalize their social frustrations show undersocialized aggressive conduct toward others (assaultive, destructive, explosive, negative, dishonest), socialized aggressive behavior (truancy, affiliation with delinquent friends, gang membership), or hyperactive behavior (poor concentration, passivity, boredom, or hyperactive motor behavior).[65] Obviously, not all behavioral problems children manifest in school are attributable to social frustration; but social deficits are often a major component among the causal factors.

Educators are well aware that the child who participates in healthy friendships with other children has the best chance of succeeding in school. "Main-

---

63. Merrell, *Behavioral, Social, and Emotional Assessment of Children,* 316.
64. Ibid., 247.
65. Ibid., 219.

taining quality friendships is perhaps the single most salient measure of a child's successful development."[66] Maintaining friendships requires that the child be able to focus on others, not just self; to treat others as equals; and to deal appropriately with conflict. These same skills in adults often determine whether they are able to function well in a marriage or not. Children are sensitive to the acceptance or rejection they perceive coming from peers. Contrary to popular opinion, this social sensitivity is not an exclusive characteristic of the adolescent years. A child's behavior can contribute to acceptance or rejection by peers. Among the behaviors and characteristics of children that facilitate social success are athletic ability, physical attractiveness, friendliness, academic achievement, cooperation, active social interaction, attempts to fit in, and prosocial behaviors such as displaying interest, initiating contacts, and helpfulness. Behaviors that impede the establishment of friendships include shyness and aggression.[67] To the extent that this analysis is correct, teaching children to limit the impeding behaviors and increase the facilitative behaviors should help produce more friendships for the child.

Social skills training in school usually involves whole class lessons (such as how to introduce oneself to another) and small group interactions designed to assist both the socially competent child and those who are struggling socially. This social competence training aims at reducing risk and increasing protective factors in the peer relations of the child.[68] School interventions seek to reduce inappropriate social behaviors (yelling, pushing, arguing, butting into line, emotional outbursts) and to increase social behaviors that will help the child establish good interpersonal relationships (entering into groups, self-control, starting conversations, participating with others, sharing, cooperation, listening).[69] Many educators believe that early intervention is essential since the cycle of ineffective behavior will lead to rejection by teacher and peers that can lead to school and social failure.[70]

The social characteristics of children change as they move through the various stages of development. Mid-adolescents often increase the formation

66. Fred Frankel and Robert Myatt, *Children's Friendship Training* (New York: Brunner-Routledge, 2003), 3.

67. Schneider, *Friends and Enemies*, 95–96.

68. M. L. Bloomquist and S. V. Schnell, *Helping Children with Aggression and Conduct Problems* (New York: Guilford, 2002), 117.

69. Ibid., 118.

70. Rathvon, *Effective School Interventions*, 314.

of cliques that distinguish themselves from others in speech or fashion. These cliques tend to subside in importance as older adolescents become more interested in the opposite sex and in forming couple relationships. Female adolescents often seek after "confidants who can provide social and emotional support," while male adolescents tend to prefer less intense relationships and more group affiliations.[71] In adolescence, friends are allies in the insatiable quest for independence.

## School Violence

Some observers might be tempted to minimize the importance of closely monitoring the social behavior of school children. After all, haven't we always had bullies on playgrounds and in the classroom? Children are supposed to be in school to learn reading, writing, and arithmetic, not all these frilly social skills. If people held such attitudes in the past, they were shocked out of their naiveté by the events in American schools in the 1990s. Consider the following statistics:

- From 1985 to 1999 the homicide rate for fifteen- to twenty-year olds doubled, while the homicide rate for adults over twenty years of age remained stable. "On average, 14 children under the age of 19 died each day due to a firearm-related injury."[72]
- In 1993, sixty-one children and teens were murdered in Chicago.
- In 1994, homicide became the leading cause of death for minority male youths in America.
- From 1997 to 1999 a string of murders perpetrated on school grounds by students against teachers and fellow students shocked the nation: three killed in Pearl, Missouri; three in Paducah, Kentucky; four in Jonesboro, Arkansas; one in Edinboro, Pennsylvania; two in Springfield, Oregon; and thirteen in Littleton, Colorado. The murderers were all middle-class white teens from small towns or suburbs.[73]

---

71. Tina Abbott, *Social and Personality Development* (New York: Taylor and Frances, 2001), 136.
72. K. Bosworth, ed., *Preventing Student Violence: What Schools Can Do* (Bloomington, Ind.: Phi Delta Kappa, 1999), 3.
73. James Garbarino, "Making Sense of School Violence: Why Do Kids Kill?" in *School Violence: Assessment, Management, Prevention*, ed. M. Shafii and S. L. Shafii (Washington, D.C.: American Psychological Assoc., 2001), 3–5.

What factors contribute to a teenager becoming a murderer? Demographic information on minors who kill other persons reveals that they often come from families with a history of criminal violence, have a history of being abused, belong to a gang, and use or abuse drugs or alcohol. The odds triple when a minor has a weapon, has been arrested in the past, has a neurological problem that impairs thinking, and has difficulties in school with poor attendance.[74] The evidence is clear: Ignoring the social struggles of at-risk children can at times lead to violence of proportions unimaginable just a few years ago.

As soon as the initial shock of the school carnage at Paducah, Kentucky and Columbine High School in Littleton, Colorado began to subside, social scientists from many disciplines began exploring how such tragedies could be avoided. One common theme emerged as investigators learned more about these crimes. Bullying—either being bullied or acting as a bully— was often a part of the school murderer's background. Negative emotions and behaviors toward another person take at least three forms.

1.  Anger. Anger is a common emotion among all children, adolescents, and adults. The mature person must learn how to manage this universal response in ways that are constructive and appropriate.
2.  Aggression. This is the urge to hurt another person. This expression of anger can be a spontaneous burst of unplanned action, a methodically executed plan of action, or anything in between. Aggression has constructive outlets and can be appropriately channeled.
3.  Bullying. Bullying is the attempt to intimidate, taunt, or frighten weaker parties for some personal goal such as aggrandizement.[75] It is common among children and adolescents and more socially refined among adults.

Everyone agrees that addressing the issue of bullying early in a child's career is the logical and most efficient way of dealing with this serious issue. Educators, parents, school administrators, and mental health professionals can all work together in teams to develop interventions designed to keep bullying from exploding into violent and perhaps lethal encounters.

---

74. Ibid., 10–11.
75. Peter Sheras, *Your Child: Bully or Victim? Understanding and Ending School Yard Tyranny* (New York: Fireside, 2002), 5.

"Emergency hotlines and support groups have been created for bullying victims and their families. Educators have developed curricula that address issues of cruelty among children, and school administrators have instituted zero-tolerance policies. . . ."[76]

Albert Bandura has long maintained that violence is a learned behavior. "People are not born with preformed repertoires of aggressive behavior; they must learn them in one way or another."[77] Christians ask, however, from whom did Cain learn violence (murder)? Christian theology concludes that one source of violence is fallen human nature itself. But even with this solid biblical conviction, Christians can also agree with Bandura that violence can be learned and that it can escalate to intolerable levels. At one time in the history of the human race, violence was observed, modeled, and learned to such an extent that God chose to destroy the majority of the human race through the mechanism of a widespread flood. God's solution to the level of violence in that case would have been futile if the only source of violence was the intrapersonal, fallen sin nature. All the survivors of the Flood still retained their fallen natures, but what changed in the post-Flood world was a drastic reduction in observable violence.

Bandura identified the conditions necessary for the learning of violence. The child must be exposed to behavioral examples of violence committed by influential people. These people can be real or imaginary. The child must observe the model with certain levels of attention, must retain a memory of the observed behavior, must be able to reproduce the violence in some motoric manner, and must be reinforced or motivated to perform the violent behavior. Then when disinhibition occurs (the lowering of previously learned inhibitions) through various rewards and punishments, a violent response may occur.[78] Bandura's explanation for the childhood acquisition of violent patterns of behavior is only one of several tenable explanations. But they each convincingly point out to us that we dare not ignore the social frustrations of children and the degree to which they observe interpersonal violence lest the results turn tragic.

---

76. Ibid., 2–3.
77. Albert Bandura, *Aggression: A Social Learning Analysis* (Englewood Cliffs, N.J.: Prentice-Hall, 1973), 61.
78. Ibid., 65–68.

## INDIVIDUALS IN GROUPS

### Group Process

Groups are central to the functioning of human lives. Adam and Eve first formed a group (marriage) followed later by a slightly larger group (family). Families clustered into extended groups (clans) that eventually formed nations. Every religious, social, or political movement deals both with individuals and with individuals in groups.[79] "Most social behavior occurs in groups. We live with families, travel in car pools, shop with friends, work as teams, worship in congregations, are entertained as audiences, learn in classes, and decide as juries."[80] Groups are not new, but our understanding of what makes them powerful and effective has increased considerably in recent years.

We know that an aggregate of people is just a collection of unrelated individuals, but a small group is a number of individuals interacting with each other in informal or formal ways for a common purpose. The small group forms its own patterns of communication and can exert a powerful influence on its members.[81] Small groups may have a short or long life span, and they display development phases as they progress through the accomplishment of their task. Successful groups form bonds of interdependence among the members and have capable and effective leaders whose skills match the needs of the task at hand.[82] Group work flourishes in schools, in agencies working with special populations, in work settings, and in the world of public relations and marketing. In the field of mental health,[83] we have witnessed a veritable "surge of interest in group work."[84]

---

79. Max Rosenbaum and Kathleen M. Patterson, "Group Psychotherapy in Historical Perspective," in *Comprehensive Textbook of Psychotherapy: Theory and Practice*, ed. Bruce Bongar and Larry E. Beutler (New York: Oxford University Press, 1995), 173.

80. R. S. Tindale et al., eds., *Theory and Research on Small Groups* (New York: Plenum Press, 1998), ix.

81. D. C. Pennington, *The Social Psychology of Behavior in Small Groups* (New York: Taylor and Francis, 2002), 24.

82. R. S. Tindale and E. N. Anderson, "Small Group Research and Applied Social Psychology: An Introduction," in *Theory and Research on Small Groups*, 4–5.

83. S. T. Gladding, *Group Work: A Counseling Strategy*, 3d ed. (Upper Saddle River, N.J.: Merrill, 1999), 13.

84. Gerald Corey, *Theory and Practice of Group Counseling*, 4th ed. (Pacific Grove, Calif.: Brooks Cole, 1995), 3.

Group work, however, is not for everyone or for every situation. It is a myth that groups are always better than individuals working alone.[85] In the field of mental health, we do know that group treatments are superior to no-treatment control groups and that they are as effective as individual treatments.[86] Some people work better independently; other people function brilliantly as group members. People respond differently to group interactions, and tasks vary as to their suitability for group applications. Group functioning capitalizes on the variety of contributions individual group members can give to the group's task and sometimes produces a synergy that is unmatched by the sum of what members could do as individuals.[87] Other tasks, however, are better performed by individuals. The success of groups revolves around that ability of planners to determine the composition of the group and the task it should seek to perform. Suitable tasks for groups can include problem solving, changing attitudes, influencing members, improving self-understanding, managing conflict, facilitating adjustment, and planning.[88]

## Groups in Education

People look back on their high school and college experience with varying degrees of fondness for classroom group work. Early attempts to include group learning as parts of the educational experience were sometimes clumsy and ineffective. But educators have learned more in recent years about what makes group learning effective or ineffective. Learning teams can be effective when instructors assign group members to groups rather than letting the students select which groups to join, when the group project is not a single paper or project that does not allow for individual accountability, when group members do not all receive the same grade, and when the group work is a consequential part of the course grade.[89]

---

85. Tindale and Anderson, "Small Group Research and Applied Social Psychology," 6.
86. G. M. Gazda, E. J. Ginter, and A. M. Horne, *Group Counseling and Group Psychotherapy* (Boston: Allyn and Bacon, 2001), 84.
87. H. Arrow, J. E. McGrath, and J. L. Berdahl, *Small Groups as Complex Systems: Formation, Coordination, Development, and Adaptation* (Thousand Oaks, Calif.: Sage, 2000), 5.
88. Ibid., 12–20.
89. G. F. Sterling, "Overcoming Initial Mistakes When Using Small Groups," in *Team-Based Learning: A Transformative Use of Small Groups,* ed. L. K. Michaelsen, A. B. Knight, and L. D. Fink (Westport, Conn.: Praeger, 2002), 138.

Some educators have restructured courses so that the central androgogical method is team-based learning. Contemporary students respond better to experiential instruction than to information dumping that sometimes occurs with the exclusive use of the lecture method. These learning teams can be flexible and relatively unstructured. They can lead to cooperation among students and to higher levels of engaged thinking about the course content. Teams work best in courses that seek to teach application and problem solving. The instructor can organize these tasks for the learning teams into the sequential steps that facilitate mastery: preparation, application, and assessment. Teams work well when assessment is directed both at the individuals within the group and at the group itself. Educators recommend allowing all group members to assess the performance or nonperformance of their peers in the group.[90] Taken together, these strategies for including group process into the educational task can create powerful learning tools that enrich the classroom experience for both the learner and the instructor.

## Groups in Business

The business world makes extensive use of groups. The most informal example is the network, a loose association of friendship connections that people mutually utilize to achieve personal goals. Consumers use networks when they need expert advice. ("I need to buy a new printer for my computer. I think I'll call George, who works in computer sales." George meanwhile recommends that I call his friend who repairs printers for advice about which brand and model to purchase.) We use these networks when we want to buy a car, find a reliable plumber, or build a new redwood deck. We tend to have higher levels of trust in the advice we receive from our friends or from their friends; hence the network works well. Consumers are not the only ones who utilize networks. Employees make friends both within their own company and in other firms. Who knows when such an acquaintance will be able to provide valuable help? Individuals who operate in a solitary manner generally will not do as well as those who utilize their interpersonal connections wisely. In some ways, the informal network is the basic building

---

90. L. D. Fink, "Beyond Small Groups: Harnessing the Extraordinary Power of Learning Teams," in *Team-Based Learning*, 4–11.

block of even larger and more structured networks such as alliances, cartels, and federations.[91]

Another use of groups by the business community is the work team. The concept is popular in many social organizations: churches have pastoral teams; hospitals have administrative teams; corporations have executive teams. Some observers estimate that about one half of all workers in American business firms work on teams. As corporations face fierce international competition, a constantly changing world of technology, major demographic shifts in the work force, and governmental regulation and deregulation, they seek to respond by organizing their workers into teams that have the potential to generate synergy and high levels of productivity. These teams often contain six to twenty persons who are given responsibility for a certain job output. The team may even rotate some of their jobs among themselves. The corporations may pay for educational experiences that will enhance the performance of the team. Administrators give little direct supervision and allow the group a considerable amount of latitude in scheduling and making job assignments.[92]

Work teams have a reputation for success that apparently far exceeds empirical evidence. "Research evidence about team performance shows that teams usually do less well—not better—than the sum of their members' individual contributions."[93] This evidence is based on overall averages. Some teams do indeed outperform what the individuals on the team could accomplish on their own. But many teams do not function well and in fact impede productivity. What makes for an effective team? Hackman suggests that the assigned task given to a team should not be a task better performed by individuals, that management should not supervise the team as if the team were merely a collection of individuals, that authority for the project should be shared by management and the team, that teams be given room to work even if it requires the dismantling of previous structures, that teams be given all the organizational support they need, and that management ensure the team contains members with all the skills needed to accomplish

91. B. Dutta and M. O. Jackson, "On the Formation of Networks and Groups," in *Networks and Groups: Models of Strategic Formation*, ed. B. Dutta and M. O. Jackson (New York: Springer, 2003), 1.

92. E. J. Savoie, "Tapping the Power of Teams," in *Theory and Research on Small Groups*, 229–30.

93. J. R. Hackman, "Why Teams Don't Work," in *Theory and Research on Small Groups*, 248.

the goal.[94] Teams can perform brilliantly, but their success is far from automatic.

## Groups in Mental Health

Psychology has not only been interested in understanding groups but also in applying this knowledge of group process as an intervention in the treatment of psychopathology. Groups of many sorts are now found in inpatient hospital units, in community mental health agencies, and in private practice settings. Clinicians sometimes view group therapy as the primary modality of treatment for certain conditions and an ancillary modality for other pathologies. Insurance carriers support the concept of group therapy for financial reasons (groups are often less costly to operate), but solid empirical evidence supports their use for proven curative reasons as well. Groups that function best often utilize pregroup training for the participants, using videos, role play, and written materials to describe the process. Group therapists who use some structure for the group in the initial stages of the group often find that group cohesion occurs more efficiently.[95]

Group psychotherapy owes much of its theoretical foundation to the pioneering work of Irvin D. Yalom at Stanford University. His approach "consolidated much of the theoretical diversity that had long existed in the field, especially in North America. . . ."[96] Yalom's careful research identified a set of eleven therapeutic factors that operate in the group therapy process to effect change. These factors will vary in importance depending on the particular type of group selected for implementation. The factors are interdependent; some are parts of the change process, and others are mechanisms of change. The eleven curative factors he identified are:

1. *Imparting of information.* This is particularly important in educational groups. It may consist of advice from group members or information imparted by the group leader.
2. *Instillation of hope.* This is a factor in all successful psychotherapies but particularly so with group formats. Hope often comes from observing the improvement of other group members.

---

94. Ibid., 248–54.
95. Gazda, Ginter, and Horne, *Group Counseling and Group Psychotherapy,* 84.
96. Rosenbaum and Patterson, "Group Psychotherapy in Historical Perspective," 185.

3. *Universality.* Learning that others have experienced the same difficulties often disconfirms the common feeling that the patient's experience is unique.

4. *Altruism.* When group members are able to engage in altruistic acts toward other group members, movement toward improvement and healing often gets activated in those who are acting in altruistic ways.

5. *The corrective recapitulation of the primary family group.* This is particularly relevant for histories of highly frustrating early experiences with family members. It can be powerfully corrective.

6. *Improvement in socializing skills.* Group members can observe adaptive and maladaptive social interactions among other group members. This is especially helpful in the early phases of treatment.

7. *Imitative behavior.* Clients can learn vicariously and by modeling the behavior of both the group leader and other group members. This group factor is related to the concept of social learning.

8. *Interpersonal learning.* This is an important factor since most pathologies involve interpersonal causes or consequences. The group sometimes provides a corrective emotional experience that is interpersonal in nature.

9. *Group cohesiveness.* This is a critical factor for people who lack a sense of belonging in other social structures. It develops over time but is not an automatic feature of all groups. It is very influential when it does develop, though.

10. *Catharsis.* The experience of telling one's story, releasing pent-up emotion, or learning better how to express certain emotions can be a key component in the healing process.

11. *Existential factors.* This involves the realization that life will inevitably involve injustice, pain, and death and that facing these issues will allow the client to live with more integrity. In short, it is learning to take personal responsibility for one's own life.[97]

Many of these potential healing factors attached to the group process are normally operative in the primary family setting in which persons develop psychologically. The family, after all, is the "ultimate small group."[98] The

---

97. Irvin D. Yalom, *The Theory and Practice of Group Psychotherapy,* 4th ed. (New York: Basic Books, 1995), 1.

98. R. W. Napier and M. K. Gershefeld, *Groups: Theory and Experience,* 5th ed. (Boston: Houghton Mifflin Co., 1993), 493.

family teaches us how to get along with others, and the interpersonal lessons we learn there greatly influence how we later get along in other, larger groups. But when one's early family experience is not positive or is directly negative, people are forced to learn these important lessons elsewhere. Group therapy is one potential source of remediating help.

When a therapy group operates ideally, it becomes a social microcosm if the group is not too heavily structured. "All the patients' interpersonal perceptual distortions, all their pathological interpersonal behavior, will inevitably be exhibited in the here-and-now of the group. Once identified, they become potentially accessible to therapeutic intervention."[99] The group can serve as an influential healing agent in the treatment of mistrust, fear, resistance, loneliness, isolation, dependence, fear of intimacy, depression, lack of meaning, unclear personal goals, and uncertain values.[100] Groups can focus on verbal and affective expression and the experiential atmosphere talking can create. Or groups can utilize other action methods to enhance and supplement what talking only can produce. Creative and dramatic re-enactment, symbolic play, rescripting early family experience, developing ceremonies, rehearsing new and different behaviors, and the use of music and art can all be helpful additions to the group process. Experiences in life, both those that are pleasant and those that are unpleasant, involve all levels of human functioning: cognitive, behavioral, and affective. Thus our efforts to bring healing to those with maladaptive background and experience should give consideration to more than just the verbal level. "Action methods are thus especially appropriate to skills training; role development and expansion; relationship enhancement; and short-term treatment with groups, couples, and families."[101]

Groups are especially helpful in the treatment of survivors of physical or sexual abuse; patients with chronic, severe, or terminal illness; survivors of political torture or ethnic persecution; patients with dissociative conditions; and people who suffer from drug and alcohol problems.[102] One group that responds well to group treatment are people diagnosed with post-traumatic

---

99. Barbara Bollinger and Irvin Yalom, "Group Therapy in Practice," in *Comprehensive Textbook of Psychotherapy,* 192.

100. Corey, *Theory and Practice of Group Counseling,* 442.

101. D. J. Wiener and L. K. Oxford, eds., *Action Therapy with Families and Groups: Using Creative Arts Improvisation in Clinical Practice* (Washington, D.C.: American Psychological Association, 2003), 5.

102. R. H. Klein and V. L. Schermer, eds., *Group Psychotherapy for Psychological Trauma and PTSD* (New York: Guilford Press, 2000).

stress disorder (PTSD). The public is familiar with PTSD because of the many veterans from the Vietnam era that came home from their military service with disabling struggles. At the heart of the PTSD condition is often a highly stressful reaction to interpersonal violence that leads to a lack of trust in others. Other traumas that can induce a PTSD reaction produce a sense of helplessness, fear, or horror. PTSD victims often report a feeling of detachment from other people. Group treatment, therefore, is a logical modality of intervention. "Joining with others in therapeutic work when coping with a disorder marked by isolation, alienation, and diminished feelings" closely matches the major symptoms of the condition with an intervention designed to deal with those symptoms.[103] The group can assist PTSD patients who work in homogeneous groups with an acknowledgment and validation of the original trauma, with helping the patients realize that their reaction to the trauma is understandable and normal, and with displaying nonjudgmental attitudes toward the survival behaviors the patients displayed at the time of the original trauma. Each of these contributions the group makes can aid in the healing and recovery process for traumatized victims.

## HUMAN SEXUALITY

Sexuality is at the heart of God's creative work. God created men and women to function as sexual beings. Sexuality is not and never was individualistic; it is relational in nature. Any consideration of humans in relationship, therefore, is incomplete without a discussion of human sexuality. A fundamental characteristic of human sexuality is its capacity to add immense levels of satisfaction and fulfillment to the lives of individuals or to create great personal pain and suffering. Sexuality is a blessing to many, a bane to some. Sexuality is part of one's life from the cradle to the grave. As it developmentally unfolds toward its full adult expression and beyond, sexuality passes through several critical phases. In each instance, the individual faces opportunities to continue moving toward a mature and healthy sexuality or toward any one of several pathologies that can develop. Sexuality is both powerful and fragile. If exposed to recurrent expressions of deviance, one's sexuality can become attached to an inappropriate object or a patho-

---

103. D. W. Fay, et al, "Group Psychotherapy for PTSD," in *Treating Psychological Traumas and PTSD*, ed. J. P. Wilson, M. J. Friedman, and J. D. Lindy (New York: Guilford Press, 2001), 184.

logical pattern of expression. Extracting oneself from the clutches of sexual pathology can be difficult at best and frustrating at worst. Each of these characteristics of sexuality reflects the veracity of the Bible's instruction regarding sex. God intended sex to be guarded carefully within the boundaries that God has erected around it.

In this chapter we are able to visit this issue only in a cursory fashion, given the breadth and scope of sexuality. We will examine human sexuality as studied by contemporary psychological science in four areas: recent problems on the sexual landscape, sexuality in marriage, sexual disorders, and homosexuality.

## Recent Problems on the Sexual Landscape

Adultery, fornication, and sexual immorality of all stripes are not new features of life. They have characterized all civilizations for millennia and have their roots in ancient human history. But it seems that each generation faces new variations on these old themes. Sexual practice "evolves and changes."[104] And the twenty-first century is no exception. As these new expressions of ancient problems appear, Christians face the challenge of advocating a system of God-honoring morality in the midst of an ever-changing sexual landscape. Psychological researchers continually strive to design investigative efforts that will eventuate in a better understanding of these problems and more effective treatments for them. Consider the following issues:

- *Marital Rape and Coercion.* We are increasingly aware that sexual interaction within a marriage or within a sexually active relationship is not always consensual. This issue is likely not a new problem, but our awareness of it is indeed recent. Sexual coercion often accompanies other forms of partner violence and dysfunction.[105] Marital rape presents challenges for law enforcement and for the court system, but it also represents an insidious problem scarring the contemporary sexual landscape. Designer club drugs have

---

104. Elizabeth Reis, ed., *American Sexual Histories* (Malden, Mass.: Blackwell, 2001), 1.
105. Jill H. Rathus and Eva L. Feindler, *Assessment of Partner Violence: A Handbook for Researchers and Practitioners* (Washington, D.C.: American Psychological Assoc., 2004), 39.

become popular with some party people, and the drugs are sometimes associated with drug-facilitated sexual assaults. Some of these drugs produce anterograde amnesia, a side effect that encourages perpetrators to think that they can escape detection and prosecution if they take sexual advantage of someone suffering from the profound sense of powerlessness that these drugs can also cause.[106]

- *Sexual Addiction.* The American Psychiatric Association does not recognize sexual addiction as a diagnosable mental illness, in spite of the widespread usage of the term by the general public. Current standards do recognize hypoactive sexual desire and aversion to sexual activity as diagnosable conditions;[107] but no provision is yet made for hyperactive sexual desire or sexual preoccupation, both prominent features of most sexual addiction descriptions. Historically, clinicians have viewed excessive sexual behavior as compulsive in nature and have reserved the term *addiction* for substance problems. But excessive sexual behavior or preoccupation shares many of the characteristics of substance addiction. Many clinicians apply treatment principles useful with substance problems to sexual excess with demonstrated success.[108] Sexual addiction, even if unofficial, is a serious and growing problem for both men and women that demands societal attention.[109] Feeding the problem of sexual preoccupation and sometimes central to it is the easy availability of pornography on the Internet. Researchers are only now beginning to understand what impact this new technology will have on the various sexual struggles men, women, teenagers, and perhaps children face.[110]

---

106. Gail Abarbanel, "The Victim," in *Drug-Facilitated Sexual Assault: A Forensic Handbook,* ed. Marce A. LeBeau and Ashraf Mozayani (San Diego: Academic Press, 2001), 19–22.

107. *DSM*-IV, 539–42.

108. Ralph H. Earle and Marcus R. Earle, *Sex Addiction: Case Studies and Management* (New York: Brunner Mazel, 1995), 1.

109. See D. Weiss, *She Has a Secret: Understanding Female Sexual Addiction* (Ft. Worth: Discovery Press, 2000); Rick Ghent and James K. Childerston, *Purity and Passion: Authentic Male Sexuality* (Chicago: Moody, 1994); and Stephen Arterburn and Fred Stoeker, *Every Man's Battle* (Colorado Springs, Colo.: Waterbrook Press, 2000).

110. See Mary Taylor and Ethel Quayle, *Child Pornography: An Internet Crime* (New York: Brunner-Routledge, 2003); and Philip Jenkins, *Beyond Tolerance: Child Pornography on the Internet* (New York: New York University Press, 2001).

- *Sexual Misbehavior in High Places.* Sexual charges against American presidents began with allegations against Thomas Jefferson and have continued episodically from that time to the presidency of William Jefferson Clinton.[111] Sexual impropriety (including proven and unproven allegations) "boldly weaves its way through presidential politics" as a scarlet thread.[112] Some of the other presidents thus affected have included Andrew Jackson, Woodrow Wilson, Warren Harding, Franklin Roosevelt, Dwight Eisenhower, John Kennedy, and Lyndon Johnson.[113] Presidents of the United States are not the only people in high places who sometimes become embroiled in sexual misbehavior, but they are symbols of the pervasive nature of sexual misconduct that characterizes even the leadership of contemporary society.

- *Clergy Sexual Abuse.* The Roman Catholic Church in the United States is reeling from the impact of the sexual crimes committed by priests against both adults and adolescents. The best evidence suggests that 2 percent of priests are pedophiles (sexually attracted to children) and 4 percent are ephebophiles (sexually attracted to adolescents, mostly postpubescent boys).[114] These numbers, if accurate, are staggering. The long-term consequences of this recent scandal could be monumental in scope.

---

111. Richard Shenkman, *Presidential Ambition: How the Presidents Gained Power, Kept Power, and Got Things Done* (New York: Harper Collins, 1999). See also Jerome D. Leven, *The Clinton Syndrome: The President and the Self-Destructive Nature of Sexual Addiction* (Rocklin, Calif.: Forum, 1998).

112. Charles W. Dunn, *The Scarlet Thread of Scandal: Morality and the American Presidency* (Lanham, Md.: Rowman and Littlefield, 2000), 1.

113. Dunn, *The Scarlet Thread of Scandal,* 49, 70–71, 72, 90, 106, 119. For Lyndon Johnson, see Gil Troy, *Mr. And Mrs. President: From the Trumans to the Clintons,* 2d ed., rev. (Lawrence, Kans.: University Press of Kansas, 2000), 139. See also Paul Apostolidis and Juliet A. Williams, eds., *Public Affairs: Politics in the Age of Sex Scandals* (Durham, N.C.: Duke University Press, 2004); Alexander DeConde, *Presidential Machismo: Executive Authority, Military Intervention, and Foreign Relations* (Boston, Mass.: Northeastern University Press, 2000); and Robert Shogan, *The Double-Edged Sword: How Character Makes and Ruins Presidents from Washington to Clinton* (Boulder, Colo.: Westview Press, 1999).

114. Thomas G. Plant, "Introduction: What Do We Know About Roman Catholic Priests Who Sexually Abuse Minors?" in *Bless Me Father for I Have Sinned: Perspectives on Sexual Abuse Committed by Roman Catholic Priests,* ed. Thomas G. Plante (Westport, Conn.: Praeger, 1999), 2.

- *Sexual Coarseness in Public Discourse.* It was only a few years ago when the phrase "shock jock" would have meant nothing to people who love to listen to the radio. But in more recent years, we all have become acquainted with sexual innuendo, sophomoric sex humor, bad-boy "jokes," and other forms of sexual coarseness coming at us through radio broadcasts. The ultimate cause is sin and the penultimate cause is commercialism. Marketers seek to create sexually divided audiences, and they attempt to attract "a young male audience by any means possible."[115] Marketers know exactly what they are doing when they use base sexual themes to attract young adult males.
- *Sex Tourism.* "The term 'sex tourism' is widely associated with organized sex tours, often conjuring up images of middle-aged businessmen being shepherded into state-sanctioned brothels in South Korea or go-go bars in the Philippines and Thailand."[116] Sex tourism involves many countries in the world, both homosexual and heterosexual activity, both domestic and international patrons, and both children and adults as participants in the sexual exchanges.[117] Sex tourism is not a new phenomenon, but it is a burgeoning one facilitated by convenient air travel.

The biblical account of creation clearly teaches us that God gave humans their sexuality as a precious gift and told them to be fruitful and multiply. Sexuality has always been a powerful component of human relationships, but the scarring of sin and unhealthy psychological mechanisms often obscure its original pristine nature.

## Sexuality and Marriage

In our society the marriage of a man and woman occurs under the authority of a license issued by the state and with the blessing of a civil or

---

115. Laruen M. E. Goodlad, "Packaged Alternatives: The Incorporation and Gendering of 'Alternative' Radio," in *Communities of the Air: Radio Century, Radio Culture,* ed. Susan M. Squier (Durham, N.C.: Duke University Press, 2003), 141–44.
116. Julia O. Davidson, *Prostitution, Power and Freedom* (Ann Arbor: University of Michigan Press, 1998), 75.
117. Stephen Clift and Simon Carter, "Tourism and Sex: Critical Issues and New Directions," in *Tourism and Sex: Culture, Commerce and Coercion,* ed. S. Clift and S. Carter (London: Pinter, 2000), 270–73.

religious officiate. Christian morality asserts that sexual intercourse is a right, privilege, and responsibility of both marriage partners. Teaching this standard to adolescents and to young adults anticipating marriage is an ongoing challenge in our sexually-saturated culture. We live in a culture that has separated sexual intercourse from any necessary links to marriage. "With rare exceptions (mostly in certain religious and ethnic communities), sex has become almost entirely divorced from the notion of marriage."[118]

Christian formation with adolescents and unmarried adults thus strives, in contrast with the wider culture, to advocate restraint. The recent movement promoting abstinence among teenagers in America has met with considerable success, although much remains to be done. Churches commonly require a certain amount of premarital counseling for those couples desiring to be married in the church. Pastors and counselors often include pleas for sexual restraint before marriage. In some cases pastors will ask sexually active unmarried couples to refrain from sexual intercourse for a period of time before the wedding date in order to provide a fresh beginning for those who have not confined intercourse to marriage. Sexual restraint is a missing theme in many quarters of contemporary American culture. Sexual intercourse on the first date is a frequent expectation. Observers in the wider, non-Christian circles of American society often view arguments for sexual restraint and abstinence as mere counterculture curiosities.

After marriage, however, Christian morality calls for the expression of sexuality between the husband and wife as an important component of their relationship. Research repeatedly reveals that regular, healthy sexual intercourse within a marriage is a key component in the satisfaction and happiness of the married couple. Conversely, sexual difficulties are either a causal factor of marital distress or an important consequence of other destructive elements of the marital relationship. How do we promote healthy sexual interaction within a marriage? All too often, we assume that it will naturally occur. After all, we have often focused our efforts on restraint; and once the restraint is no longer needed, surely the newly married couple will have no difficulty establishing their sexual relationship as part of their marriage. But that assumption is risky and misleading. All too often, couples (Christian or non-Christian) do indeed struggle as they seek to build a mutually satisfying sexual interaction in their marriage.

---

118. Pamela Paul, *The Starter Marriage and the Future of Matrimony* (New York: Villard, 2002), 18.

Providing remediation for sexual problems (usually called dysfunctions) can involve both medical and psychotherapeutic interventions. Physicians may be able to help the couple with painful intercourse. Psychotherapists can provide help in uncovering issues that may be interfering with the free and fulfilling practice of intercourse in marriage. Helpful strategies for dealing with certain problems such as premature ejaculation are also available and effective.[119] Providing sexual help for couples who are struggling is not the problem; encouraging them to seek out the help is the far bigger issue. Many couples hide their sexual difficulties under a blanket of shame and disgrace.

## Sexual Paraphilias

A paraphilia is sexual interest or activity "without the possibility of a consensual, mutually reciprocal relationship."[120] The paraphilias include attraction to nonhuman objects, interest in sexual activity that results in the suffering or humiliation of self or others, or sexual interest in children or nonconsenting persons. These sexual patterns deviate from the norm and represent a substantial set of problems for society in general and law enforcement in particular. The paraphilias include exhibitionism, voyeurism, transvestism, masochism, sadism, and frotteurism (rubbing against a nonconsenting person). Psychiatry and psychology have been interested in understanding the paraphilias throughout the twentieth century.[121] Each major theoretical school has offered its own etiologic explanation. Behaviorists, for example, find the roots of these disorders in reinforcement and other learning principles. Psychoanalytic authors locate the origin in developmental defects emerging from the early oedipal struggles of the child.[122]

Treatment programs for sexual offenders, whether with inmates or probationers, normally involve a multifocal approach. Therapists work with their clients to foster acceptance of responsibility for the offense, to lower

---

119. John P. Wincze and Michael P. Carey, *Sexual Dysfunction: A Guide for Assessment and Treatment*, 2d ed. (New York: Guilford Press, 2001), 117–18.

120. J. P. Fedoroff, "The Paraphilic World," in *Handbook of Clinical Sexuality for Mental Health Professionals*, ed. Stephen B. Levine (New York: Brunner-Routledge, 2003), 336.

121. As one early example, see Clifford Allen, *The Sexual Perversions and Abnormalities: A Study in the Psychology of Paraphilia*, 2d ed. (Westport, Conn.: Greenwood Press, 1940).

122. Robert J. Stoller, *Perversion: The Erotic Form of Hatred* (Washington, D.C.: American Psychiatric Press, 1975), 215–17.

cognitive distortions that are frequently associated with the paraphilias, and to increase levels of genuine empathy for victims. Other treatment goals include modification of the sexual interests of the offender, enhancement of appropriate social skills, therapy for comorbid substance abuse problems, and development of a relapse prevention program.[123] Therapists also have learned that it is important to assess the offender's procriminal peer associations and work history, including unemployment, as they relate to the crimes.[124]

Considerable controversy exists regarding the effectiveness of sex offender treatment programs. Some people claim that the average relapse rate for sex offenders is 14 percent, a rate better than for most other psychiatric conditions.[125] Conventional wisdom among clinicians, however, is that "sexual preferences are very resistant to change."[126] For every study yielding positive indications that treatment for sex offenders is helpful, one can find another study giving us unclear results. "It is clear from the methodological criticisms of studies concerning sex offender treatment and recidivism that much more study is needed to resolve the question of the effectiveness of treatment and the particular types of treatment that are most effective."[127]

## Homosexuality

Contemporary American culture is embroiled in a debate over this question: Is homosexuality a sexual lifestyle that is within the range of normal options and thus an acceptable sexual alternative? Gay marriage and the ordination of gay and lesbian persons are just two issues in this wide and polarizing debate. Gay and lesbian activists find support in various segments of our society, but those who give a negative answer to the above question are also numerous and influential. The end of this discussion is nowhere in sight. Politicians and denominational leaders struggle to find moderating positions that will satisfy debaters on both sides of the issue,

123. George B. Palermo and Mary Ann Farkas, *The Dilemma of the Sexual Offender* (Springfield, Ill.: Charles C. Thomas, 2001), 142–47.
124. Marnie E. Rice and Grant T. Harris, "What We Know and Don't Know About Treating Adult Sex Offenders," in *Protecting Society from Sexually Dangerous Offenders*, ed. B. J. Winick and J. Q. LaFond (Washington, D.C.: American Psychological Assoc., 2003), 112.
125. Fedoroff, "The Paraphilic World," 351.
126. Ibid., 336.
127. Palermo and Farkas, *The Dilemma of the Sexual Offender*, 151.

but the chasm separating them is wide and deep. Denominations that have survived the divisive potential of numerous other issues may well break up into splinter groups because of this nearly irresolvable issue. Evangelicals, meanwhile, continue to assert that scriptural data clearly identify homosexual practice as immoral and sinful.

Homosexuality is a major issue facing the mental health professions, as well as most other segments of society. In this arena the looming question is more sharply focused: Is homosexuality a psychopathology? Anyone familiar with the current debate will realize that pro-gay arguments nearly always refer to the declassification of homosexuality as pathology by the American Psychiatric Association (APA) prior to 1980. We can trace this change from viewing homosexuality as pathology to dropping it as a diagnosis by examining the various editions of the APA's diagnostic manual.

| Standard Classification of Disease | 1933–1952 | Homosexuality appears as a type of "Psychopathic Personality with Pathological Sexuality." |
|---|---|---|
| DSM-I | 1952–1968 | Homosexuality is a sexual deviation that is a "Sociopathic Personality Disturbance." |
| DSM-II | 1968–1980 | Homosexuality is listed as a sexual deviation in the "Personality Disorders and Certain Other Non-Psychotic Mental Disorders" category. |
| DSM-III | 1980–1987 | Only ego-dystonic homosexuality is diagnosable. Ego-syntonic homosexuality is not a mental disorder. |
| DSM-III Revised | 1987–1994 | Ego-dystonic homosexuality appears in the index as a type of Sexual Disorder Not Otherwise Specified (NOS). ("Persistent and marked distress about one's sexual orientation.") |
| DSM-IV | 1994–2000 | Ego-dystonic homosexuality does not appear in the index. But "Persistent and marked distress about one's sexual orientation" continues to be diagnosable as a Sexual Disorder NOS. |
| DSM-IV Text Revision | 2000– | Same as previous edition |

This evolution of psychiatric thinking about homosexuality both mirrors societal changes and shapes it. The dramatic change occurred as the APA was planning to issue the third edition of the manual in 1980. In 1973 the board of trustees of the APA voted to remove homosexuality from the official list of mental diseases. That decision triggered a massive protest from members who demanded and were granted a referendum of the full APA membership on the question. The mailed ballot contained both a pro and a con statement. Over 10,000 psychiatrists voted on the question, 58 percent in favor of removing homosexuality as a diagnosis and 37 percent opposed to the action.[128] "The result was not a conclusion based on an approximation of the scientific truth as dictated by reason, but was instead an action demanded by the ideological temper of the times."[129] And this would not be the last time ideology would dominate science in public discourse about homosexuality. The ongoing debate often ignores or misuses scientific data for ideological purposes, a weakness probably characteristic of both sides in the discussion but especially of pro-gay advocates.[130] Cultural pressure has always influenced and shaped how medicine views psychopathology, but in this instance the impact was brazen and unmistakable. However, a substantial but quiet residue of practitioners internationally continues to hold the conviction that homosexuality is pathological, even though gay and lesbian groups call such a conviction a homophobic and discriminatory holdover from the past.[131]

Traditional psychoanalytic theory has long argued that homosexuality develops as a result of failure to complete the developmental tasks of childhood. "The widespread incidence of homosexuality is due to the necessity for all human beings to undergo the separation-individuation phase of early childhood."[132] "All psychoanalytic theories assume that adult homosexuality is psychopathologic and assign differing weights to constitutional and experiential determinants. All agree that the experiential determinants are

---

128. Ronald Bayer, *Homosexuality and American Psychiatry: The Politics of Diagnosis* (Princeton, N.J.: Princeton University Press, 1987), 148.

129. Ibid., 3–4.

130. See Stanton L. Jones and Mark A. Yarhouse, *Homosexuality: The Use of Scientific Research in the Church's Moral Debate* (Downers Grove, Ill.: InterVarsity, 2000).

131. Ralph Roughton, "The International Psychoanalytical Association and Homosexuality," in *The Mental Health Profession and Homosexuality: International Perspectives,* ed. V. Lingiardi and J. Drescher (New York: Haworth, 2003), 190–92.

132. Charles W. Socarides, *Homosexuality* (New York: Jason Aronson, 1978), 6.

in the main rooted in childhood and are primarily related to the family."[133] Current psychoanalytic treatment for those wishing to change their homosexual orientation is called reparative therapy.[134] The most common form of psychoanalytic theory used by Christian therapists working in this field is based on the work of Elizabeth Moberly, who views homosexuality as reflective of radical disidentification from the parent of the same sex during early childhood.[135]

---

133. Irving Bieber, *Homosexuality: A Psychoanalytic Study* (New York: Jason Aronson, 1988), 18.

134. See Joseph Nicolosi, *Reparative Therapy of Male Homosexuality: A New Clinical Approach* (Northvale, N.J.: Jason Aronson, 1991); and Joseph Nicolosi, *Healing Homosexuality: Case Stories of Reparative Therapy* (Northvale, N.J.: Jason Aronson, 1993).

135. Elizabeth R. Moberly, *Psychogenesis: The Early Development of Gender Identity* (London: Routledge and Kegan Paul, 1983), ix.

CHAPTER 12

# RELATIONSHIPS *and* COMMUNITY INTEGRATED

WE HAVE OBSERVED IN THE preceding two chapters that both of the disciplines we are exploring (biblical/theological studies and contemporary psychology) give considerable attention to how humans form relationships and how humans function in community. Neither discipline entertains the notion that individual humans are entities to themselves or that we can properly understand humans by exploring only their individuality. Both the consistent witness of Scripture and the findings of modern social science affirm that humans naturally seek out relationships and that they function best when in communities large or small. "Contemporary psychology, in recovering the inner self, is also increasingly seeing that the identity of that self is strongly tied to relationships to others."[1] Postmodernism's emphasis on community in culture and society is serving as an impetus for scholars working in both disciplines to highlight the nurturing role of relationships and people groupings. This clarion call from postmodernism is not uniquely new as much as it is a needed reemphasis of earlier approaches sometimes neglected.

Again, we can clearly see that ancient and contemporary approaches to the investigation of how humans form relationships and function in

---

1. C. Stephen Evans, "The Relational Self: Psychological and Theological Perspectives," in *Judeo-Christian Perspectives on Psychology: Human Nature, Motivation, and Change,* ed. W. R. Miller and H. D. Delaney (Washington, D.C.: American Psychological Association, 2005), 81.

community are significantly distinct from each other. For example, the attention Scripture gives to relationships as they were originally created and designed, as they were tainted by sin, and as they are renewed in Christ is foreign to psychology's sole focus on relationships as we can know and observe them, that is, relationships with their sinful components intact. Nonetheless, we can identify some certainties and areas for future study that emerge from the voluminous attention both disciplines give to relationships and community.

## CHRISTIAN CERTAINTIES

1. *Neither the identity nor the nature of an individual is predicated on that individual's relationship with another or others.* If we were to argue that individuals are only complete humans when they are in relationship with others, how could we ascribe human identity to the neonate, who cannot form a relationship even with its mother in the first few days of postpartum life? How could we affirm full human identity of the Alzheimer's patient who has lost all capacity to form or participate in relationships with other people? And wouldn't we be forced to diminish the full humanity of the profoundly retarded person who is only minimally able to respond to other human beings? Full human identity and full human nature belong to individuals irrespective of their capacity or lack thereof to form relationships with others or to participate in community life.

2. *The formation of relationships with others and participation in community life are natural and wonderful outworkings of an individual's human identity and nature.* Even if human identity is not centered in relational abilities, connecting with other humans is an innate impulse that springs from the core of what it means to be human. Adam's solitary if brief existence as the only human person was divinely declared not good, but the fulfilling existence of Adam and Eve as the first human pair was described by the Creator as very good. Psychology likewise views a person's relational abilities as a central component of maturity, even though few would argue that humans do not possess individual identity, only corporate identity.

3. *The abandonment of the historic, substantialist understanding of human identity in favor of a relational understanding presents us with*

*myriad unsolvable problems.* Relational capacities are components of the whole, but they are not the whole. Placing relational themes at the core of human identity arbitrarily displaces other valuable and helpful means of conceptualizing and describing the human person. We can appropriately highlight relational themes in our anthropology without abandoning other important human core motivations and drives. Expressed otherwise, the traditional substance ontology affirmed by philosophers and theologians need not be abandoned in order to uphold the fact that humans were created to relate with other humans, objects, and ideas.

4. *Relating to oneself in an appropriate, God-honoring manner is a necessary and valid part of human existence.* Too often Christian observers collapse the domain of relations with the self into two categories: pride or self-denial. As we have seen earlier in this volume, such a construal misrepresents scriptural material and ignores valid and replicable findings in contemporary psychology. Scripture and contemporary psychology (not pop psychology) provide for us a wealth of information on how to build a healthy relationship with the self that avoids both narcissism (psychology's language) and pride (Scripture's language) and self-derogation, low self-esteem, self-hatred (psychology's language) and false humility (Scripture's language).

5. *Marriage between a man and a woman is a primary venue for the expression of human relational and community needs.* Scripture teaches that into this foundational relationship God introduces a one-fleshness that is true of no other human relationship. The one-fleshness of a husband and wife represents the unique place marriage occupies in God's economy and in human society.

6. *Both psychology and the Christian Scriptures envision humans participating in relationships ranging in intimacy and intensity from the marital relationship to relationships with strangers and enemies.* Both disciplines argue for a consistency of tone and motive across this broad span of connections with people. In some ways people use a single set of skills in their participation in these relationships, albeit the application of the skills varies according to the occasion and specific nature of the connection one is seeking to make.

7. *Relational aptitude according to contemporary psychology (maturity)*

*and God-honoring relational skills as described in Scripture (Christlikeness) are related and overlapping categories, but they are not coterminous.* In contemporary psychology, psychological maturity results from a complex blend of genetic and environmental influences; and spiritual maturity, according to Scripture, is the by-product of the indwelling Christ and the work of the Holy Spirit. Effective relational capacity for the follower of God is both a psychological and a spiritual issue, not an either-or issue.

8. *Scripture designates the believer's relationship with God as a major component of the God-pleasing life.* By definition, psychology can only give the scantiest attention to this dimension of effective living. Scripture clearly is the major repository of truth regarding how one is to establish, nourish, and maintain a personal relationship with the Creator of the universe and so fulfill his or her destiny.

9. *The pervasive effects of sin on human relational abilities are graphically portrayed in Scripture and are extensively described in psychology's reconstruction of psychopathology.* At times the causal connection between sin and relational ineptitude is immediate, and at other times the connection is mediated. Just as physical disease can be directly related to health behaviors (e.g. smoking and lung cancer) and at other times unrelated to health behaviors (e.g. lung cancer not caused by smoking or secondhand smoke), so can psychopathology be directly caused by sinful behavior (excessive guilt caused by impermissible sexual behavior) or by the sins of generations past (depression unrelated to personal sin).

10. *Homosexual behavior represents a departure from God's creative intention for human sexuality.* People who take the Christian Scriptures seriously and who seek to interpret them in light of the authors' original intent must deal with the conclusion that the Bible does not permit homosexual conduct as an acceptable form of sexual expression. Christian ethics and moral standards thus depart rather sharply from the current social and political approaches of contemporary social science in general and of psychology in particular.

11. *Christian living as described in the New Testament deals directly and intentionally with the restoration, rehabilitation, and development of healthy relationships with God, with self, and with others both within and without the Christian community.* Scripture provides us with

numerous examples of healthy relational living, with frequent ex-
hortations to emulate those examples, and with rich theological foundations supporting these teachings. The very nature of the church,
both in its universal and local expressions, is a prime example of the
deeply relational community life God intends His people to enjoy.

12. *The major psychological approaches to interpersonal relations, while not
exegeted from the pages of Scripture, nonetheless provide us with some
helpful models for partially explaining some of the complexities of relationships and community life.* No single psychological theory is rich or
broad enough to incorporate the full range of Scripture's teaching
about relationships, but each can give us some helpful insights.

13. *Groups are central to church life and to the clinical branches of contemporary psychology.* The exercise of healthy relational skills in group
contexts is an expression of both spiritual maturity in Christ and
psychological/emotional maturity as envisioned by recent social science findings.

## BRIEF INTEGRATION

The theme of relating to God, self, and others represents a large domain
that encompasses a great portion of the drama of redemption as revealed in
the pages of Scripture. The provisions God has made to rebuild shattered
relationships to oneself, God, and others caused by sin form the corpus of
the biblical story. In some ways, one could appropriately describe the Bible
as a manual on relationships. Likewise, the Bible places strong emphasis on
community life as first expressed in patriarchal culture, then in theocratic
Israel, later by the church as the bride of Christ, and eventually in the throng
of worshipers before the throne of God in the eternal state. We also can
summarize much of contemporary psychology by setting forth how the
discipline seeks to understand human relationships and community functioning. Some critics see this set of overlapping interests as proof that the
Bible and psychology are in competition with each other for the allegiance
of twenty-first-century people. We disagree. The overlapping attention both
fields give to relationships and humans in community gives us a rich and
somewhat unprecedented opportunity to work together in collaboration
for mutual benefit. We are convinced that this collaborative work between
theology and psychology can occur without the slightest compromise to

our understanding of the distinction between special and general revelation. Scripture constitutes our benchmark and our rule of truth. Psychology fleshes out some of the details within those divinely ordained boundaries.

## NEEDED RESEARCH

The potential areas for needed integrative study in the areas of human relationships and community life are numerous. For example, we need to articulate more clearly how the sovereign work of God and the Holy Spirit are involved in the maturation and development of persons prior to personal conversion. Can we identify the handiwork of God as the individual infant, child, and adolescent learn how to establish relationships? Likewise, we need to work at clarifying how the sanctifying work of the Holy Spirit that repairs sinful relationships and builds healthier ones in the life of a believer interacts with psychological and emotional processes. The notion that psychological processes predominate before conversion and spiritual processes predominate after conversion is an overly simplistic assessment of the divine working. Other areas for additional exploration include the application of findings from social science investigations of group process to church life, particularly small groups, and invigorating our efforts to understand community as it applies to God's intentions for both local churches and for other forms of Christian community life.

# CONCLUSION

WE HAVE STRIVEN IN THIS VOLUME to explore the profound and perennial question raised initially in the Bible, "What is man . . . ?" (Ps. 8:4). The principal sources of information concerning the human person can be represented as three concentric circles: authoritative Scripture being the inner circle, voices from our Christian past the middle circle, and the social sciences, including psychology, the outer circle, as below.

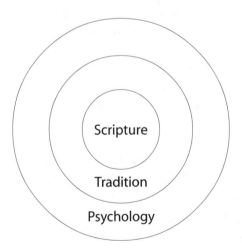

The inspired and infallible source of information concerning the human person is located in the inner circle—the deposit of special revelation contained in the Scriptures. Through the writings of prophets and apostles preserved in sacred Scripture, God graciously tells humans who they are, where they came from, their resemblance to Himself, how they should behave and live, and where their destiny lies. Although it addresses all these issues, the Bible's ultimate focus is humans' relation to their Creator and Redeemer. Hence the Bible is not an encyclopedia of all possible truths about anthropology but is a repository of truthful principles from which encyclopedias may and should be constructed.

The method of engagement practiced by this study humbly and gladly accepts as true and authoritative all that Scripture reveals about humans' origin, material-immaterial nature, functioning, behavior, relations, and final destiny. Moreover, attentive listening to the wisdom of gifted, albeit fallible, voices from Christian history enhances our understanding of the Bible's teaching concerning the human person. The testimonies of learned and godly Christian authorities from the past represent graced commentaries on the Bible's instruction regarding the human person. In addition, we listen seriously to the findings of psychology and other human disciplines concerning many aspects of human functioning and behavior that fruitfully supplement the Bible's anthropology.

The constructive role of psychology and other human disciplines in enlarging understanding of the human person is established on at least three grounds. First, as noted earlier, God's general revelation communicates nonredemptive truth to all persons everywhere, both Christians and non-Christians (Rom. 1:18–21; 2:14–15). Second, God's common grace—his undeserved goodness shed on all people (Matt. 5:45; John 1:9; Acts 14:17)—empowers humans to know and apply truth across the spectrum of human endeavor. All that is proven true in philosophy, psychology, and other disciplines is directly attributable to God's common grace. As a result of general revelation and common grace, the researches of both Christians and non-Christians yield significant truths about the human person that ought not be dismissed. Finally, God via the cultural mandate (Gen. 1:26, 28) commanded His image-bearers to "fill in the blanks" of our knowledge of human nature and functioning through diligent investigation and research. The human disciplines of psychology, anthropology, and sociology wittingly represent the deposit of humans' insatiable hunger to acquire knowledge and often unwittingly fulfill the cultural mandate.

However, given human researchers' presuppositions, worldviews, biases, and limited perspective—particularly if they are not committed Christians—

the results of psychological investigations constitute truth admixed with varying degrees of error. Brunner's law of closeness of relation, cited earlier, highlights this truism. Where the findings of psychology relative to the nature and functioning of human beings contravene explicit teachings or general principles contained in the Scriptures, such must be rejected and more accurate explanations sought. Nevertheless, experience proves that the natural sciences and the human disciplines yield invaluable data that supplement the truthful teachings of Scripture. Again we appeal to the wisdom of Calvin, who wrote that people who have "tasted the liberal arts penetrate with their aid far more deeply into the secrets of the divine wisdom."[1] The editor of the *Institutes* comments, "To Calvin, liberal studies were an aid to comprehension of the divine wisdom conveyed in the Scriptures."[2] Moreover, Frederick W. Faber, the nineteenth-century Huguenot who converted to Catholicism, described the human disciplines as "partial revelations of God."[3] Thus where psychology's researches are soundly established, consistent with Scripture, and practically helpful, they should be accepted and integrated into our helping protocols.

The human person is an incredibly complex organism requiring the joint contributions of infallible Scripture, the wisdom of leading Christian theologians, and valid insights from psychological science. Together these sources maximize our understanding of human beings, the zenith of God's creation. Given the fact that the human person is a complex *whole,* spiritual and psychological aspects of the person cannot be divorced from one another. Richard Lovelace rightly observes, "We cannot isolate 'spiritual' problems from 'psychological' problems and treat the latter nonspiritually, because the human soul is a psychospiritual continuum in which psychological stress, physiological conditions and spiritual states are deeply interrelated."[4] Psychology needs Scripture and Christian tradition to provide the framework of truth, meaning, and purpose. On the other hand, the valid findings of psychological research add detail and specificity to the Bible's more synoptic and religiously-orientated portrait of the human person. At

---

1. John Calvin, *Institutes of the Christian Religion,* ed. John T. McNeill, trans. Ford Lewis Battles, 2 vols., LCC, vols. 20–21 (Philadelphia: Westminster, 1960), 1:53 [1.5.2.].
2. Ibid., 1:53 n. 6.
3. Cited by Bruce Demarest, *Satisfy Your Soul* (Colorado Springs, Colo.: NavPress, 1999), 222.
4. Richard F. Lovelace, *Dynamics of Spiritual Life: An Evangelical Theology of Renewal* (Downers Grove, Ill.: InterVarsity, 1979), 20.

a practical, human level, psychology often abets religious faith and development. Many inner conflicts and anxieties do not yield to simple obedience or vanish as one recites Scripture. Valid psychological interventions often eliminate emotional blockages that impede spiritual growth and maturity. "Psychotherapy may lead persons into a place of readiness for spiritual growth and may even help them take significant steps toward God. However, this is not salvation."[5] Christian psychologist Mark McMinn correctly claims that human development in wholeness and holiness must be founded on a three-legged stool consisting of theology, psychology, and spiritual formation.[6]

An analogue to the relation between Scripture and psychology is the relation of the Bible to medicine. No one denies that Scripture's basic teaching about human health and functioning has been enormously expanded by the findings of modern medicine, represented by specialties such as cardiology, neurology, urology, gerontology, and surgery. Human beings function better and live more fulfilling and longer lives by virtue of the breathtaking discoveries of modern medical research. All people rightly welcome these discoveries with their life-enhancing benefits. But in those few cases where the judgments of medical research conflict with the Bible's teachings or implicit principles, these must be set aside. An example of the latter might include the scientific quest to clone human life, whereas Scripture implies that only God can create the human soul/spirit and thus the human being.

In principle, the disciplines of theology and psychology responsibly undertaken are friends rather than foes. All truth, wherever it is discovered, is God's truth. Calvin wrote with great conviction, "If we regard the Spirit of God as the sole fountain of truth, we shall neither reject the truth itself, nor despise it whenever it shall appear, unless we wish to dishonor the Spirit of God."[7] We repeat our deep-seated conviction that inspired and authoritative Scripture constitutes the center of gravity of truthful information concerning the human person, particularly as it concerns the latter's relation to God. In addition, the writings of Christian authorities, such as Augustine,

5. David G. Benner, *Psychotherapy and the Spiritual Quest* (Grand Rapids: Baker, 1988), 158.

6. Mark McMinn, *Psychology, Theology, and Spirituality in Christian Counseling* (Wheaton, Ill.: Tyndale House, 1996), 9–12.

7. Calvin, *Institutes of the Christian Religion*, 1:273–74 [2.2.15].

Luther, Calvin, and Edwards serve as constructive commentaries on the Bible's teachings. Psychology represents the wider trajectory, which when faithfully undertaken yields additional valuable insights as to how humans function, behave, and relate.

In our ongoing work as scholars and practitioners, particularly as Christians, we are responsible to interpret the Scriptures accurately. We recall that the Roman Catholic Church's Inquisition tried the scientist Galileo in 1633 and judged him guilty for promoting the Copernican (heliocentric) theory of our solar system—that the earth and planets revolve around the sun. Later the church was compelled to admit that scientists were correct in describing the solar system as heliocentric. Thus we must welcome into our integration all research findings of psychology, brain science, genetics, and other fields of inquiry that prove consistent with biblical principles, thereby enlarging our understanding of anthropology and enhancing practical outcomes. Reliable data from psychological research may, in fact, facilitate understanding of the Bible's teaching regarding the human person. How gracious of God to entrust us with the privileged task of investigating the nature and functioning of image-bearers in order to enhance human living.

Investigations in the disciplines of Scripture, psychology, and other disciplines disclose the astonishing complexity of the human person. As the psalmist David wrote, "I praise you because I am fearfully and wonderfully made" (Ps. 139:14). We trust that the interdisciplinary engagement between Scripture, Christian tradition, and psychology undertaken in this book will enhance the reader's understanding of the origin, nature, functioning, relational capacity, and destiny of men and women as glorious images of the Almighty. May the goal of understanding who we are, how we are formed, how we behave, and how we relate be more fully realized for the good of the human community and for the glory of God.

> Thou hast made us for thyself, O Lord; and our heart is restless until it rest in thee.
>
> —St. Augustine

# SELECTED BIBLIOGRAPHY

## BIBLICAL AND THEOLOGICAL RESOURCES

Anderson, Ray S. *On Being Human.* Grand Rapids: Eerdmans, 1982.

————. *Theology, Death and Dying.* Oxford: Basil Blackwell, 1986.

————. *The New Age of the Soul.* Eugene, Ore.: Wipf and Stock, 2001.

Anderson, Ray S., and Dennis B. Guernsey. *On Being Family: A Social Theology of the Family.* Grand Rapids: Eerdmans, 1985.

Bajema, Clifford E. *Abortion and the Meaning of Personhood.* Grand Rapids: Baker, 1974.

Barr, James. *The Garden of Eden and the Hope of Immortality.* Minneapolis, Minn.: Fortress, 1993.

Beckwith, Francis, and Norman Geisler. *Matters of Life and Death.* Grand Rapids: Baker, 1991.

Berdiaev, Nikolai. *The Destiny of Man.* Trans. by Natalie Duddington. New York: Harper, 1960.

Berkouwer, G. C. *Man: The Image of God.* Trans. by Dirk W. Jellema. Grand Rapids: Eerdmans, 1962.

Boyd, Jeffrey H. *Reclaiming the Soul: The Search for Meaning in a Self-Centered Culture.* Cleveland, Ohio: Pilgrim Press, 1996.

————. "Self-Concept: In Defense of the Word *Soul.*" In *Care for the Soul.* Edited by Mark R. McMinn and Timothy R. Phillips. Downers Grove, Ill.: InterVarsity, 2001.

Brown, Warren S., Nancey Murphy, and H. Newton Maloney, eds. *Whatever Happened to the Soul? Scientific and Theological Portraits of Human Nature.* Minneapolis, Minn.: Fortress, 1998.

Brunner, Emil. *Man in Revolt.* Translated by Olive Wyon. Philadelphia: Westminster, 1947, English translation. 1939, German edition.

Buber, Martin. *I and Thou.* Translated by Ronald Gregor Smith. Edinburgh: T. and T. Clark, 1937.

Burns, J. P., ed. *Theological Anthropology.* Philadelphia: Fortress, 1981.

Cairns, David. *The Image of God in Man.* New York: Philosophical Library, 1953.

Carey, George. *I Believe in Man.* London; Grand Rapids: Eerdmans, 1977.

Chapelle, Daniel. *The Soul in Everyday Life.* Albany, N.Y.: State University of New York Press, 2003.

Cooper, John W. *Body, Soul and Life Everlasting: Biblical Anthropology and the Monism-Dualism Debate.* Grand Rapids: Eerdmans, 1989.

Crabb, Larry. *Men and Women: Enjoying the Difference.* Grand Rapids: Zondervan, 1991.

Cullmann, Oscar. *Immortality of the Soul or Resurrection of the Body?* New York: Macmillan, 1958.

Custance, Arthur C. *Man and Adam in Christ.* Grand Rapids: Zondervan, 1975.

Davies, Douglas James. *Anthropology and Theology.* New York: Berg, 2002.

Delitzsch, Franz. *A System of Biblical Psychology.* Reprint, Grand Rapids: Baker, 1977.

Duffy, O. J. *The Dynamics of Grace: Perspectives in Theological Anthropology.* Collegeville, Minn.: Liturgical Press, 1993.

Eichrodt, Walther. *Man in the Old Testament.* Studies in Biblical Theology no. 4. Chicago: H. Regnery, 1951.

Fernandez, Eleazar S. *Reimaging the Human: Theological Anthropology in Response to Systemic Evil.* St. Louis, Mo.: Chalice Press, 2003.

Fornier, Keith, and William D. Watkins. *In Defense of Life: Taking a Stand Against the Culture of Death.* Colorado Springs, Colo.: NavPress, 1996.

Fowler, Paul B. *Abortion: Toward an Evangelical Consensus.* Portland, Ore.: Multnomah, 1987.

Gorman, Michael J. *Abortion and the Early Church.* Downers Grove, Ill: InterVarsity, 1982.

Grenz, Stanley J. *Created for Community.* Grand Rapids: Baker, 1988.

————. *The Social God and the Relational Self*. Louisville, Ky.: Westminster John Knox, 2001.

Gundry, Robert H. *Soma in Biblical Theology*. Grand Rapids: Zondervan, 1987.

Harris, Murray J. *Raised Immortal: Resurrection and Immortality in the New Testament*. Grand Rapids: Eerdmans, 1989.

————. *From the Grave to Glory: Resurrection in the New Testament*. Grand Rapids: Zondervan, 1990.

Haynes, Carlyle B. *Life, Death and Immortality*. Nashville: Southern Publishing, 1952.

Hick, John. *Death and Eternal Life*. San Francisco, Calif.: Harper and Row, 1976.

Hill, Edmond. *Being Human: A Biblical Perspective*. London: Geoffrey Chapman, 1984.

Hoekema, Anthony A. *Created in God's Image*. Grand Rapids: Eerdmans, 1986.

Hughes, Philip Edgcumbe. *The True Image: The Origin and Destiny of Man in Christ*. Grand Rapids: Eerdmans, 1989.

Jenson, Robert W. *On Thinking the Human: Resolutions of Difficult Notions*. Grand Rapids: Eerdmans, 2003.

Jewett, Paul K. *Who We Are: Our Dignity as Human*. Grand Rapids: Eerdmans, 1996.

Johnson, Darrell W. *Experiencing the Trinity*. Vancouver: Regent, 2002.

Kierkegaard, Søren. *Purity of Heart Is to Will One Thing*. Translated by Douglas V. Steere. New York: Harper and Row, 1948.

Kopas, Jane. *Sacred Identity: Exploring a Theology of the Person*. New York: Paulist, 1994.

Kümmel, Werner Georg. *Man in the New Testament*. Philadelphia: Westminster, 1963.

LeFevre, Perry. *Understandings of Man*. Philadelphia: Westminster, 1966.

Levering, Matthew. *On Christian Dying: Classical and Contemporary Texts*. Lanham, Md.: Rowman and Littlefield, 2004.

Machuga, Ric. *In Defense of the Soul: What It Means to Be Human*. Grand Rapids: Baker, 2002.

Macmurray, John. *Persons in Relation*. London: Faber and Faber, 1961.

McDonald, H. D. *The Christian View of Man*. Westchester, Ill: Crossway, 1981.

————. "Biblical Teaching on Personality." In *Psychology and the Christian Faith*. Edited by Stanton L. Jones. Grand Rapids: Baker, 1986.

McFadyen, Alister. *The Call to Personhood: A Christian Theory of the Individual in Social Relationships*. New York: Cambridge University Press, 1990.

Mead, George Herbert. *Mind, Self, and Society*. Chicago: University of Chicago Press, 1934.

Medley, Mark S. *Imago Trinitatis: Toward a Relational Understanding of Becoming Human*. Lanham, Md.: University Press of America, 2001.

Miller, Keith. *The Secret Life of the Soul*. Nashville: Broadman and Holman, 1997.

Moreland, J. P., and Scott Rae. *Body and Soul: Human Nature and the Crisis of Ethics*. Downers Grove, Ill.: InterVarsity, 2000.

Nee, Watchman. *The Spiritual Man*. 3 vols. New York: Christian Fellowship, 1968.

Niebuhr, Reinhold. *Human Nature: A Christian Interpretation*. Vol. 1, *The Nature and Destiny of Man*. New York: Charles Scribner's Sons, 1964.

Orr, James. *God's Image in Man and Its Defacement in the Light of Modern Denials*. Grand Rapids: Eerdmans, 1948.

Pannenberg, Wolfhart. *What Is Man? Contemporary Anthropology in Theological Perspective*. Translated by Duane A. Priebe. Philadelphia: Fortress, 1970.

————. *Anthropology in Theological Perspective*. Trans. by Matthew J. O'Connell. Philadelphia: Westminster, 1985.

Perlman, Helen Harris. *Relationship: The Heart of Helping People*. Chicago: University of Chicago Press, 1979.

Popper, Karl, and John C. Eccles. *The Self and Its Brain*. New York: Springer, 1977.

Rahner, Karl. *Theology, Anthropology, Christology*. Vol. 13, *Theological Investigations*. New York: Seabury Press, 1975.

Reichenbach, Bruce. *Is Man the Phoenix? A Study of Immortality*. Grand Rapids: Christian University Press, 1978.

Roberts, Robert C. *Emotions: An Essay in Aid of Moral Psychology*. Cambridge: Cambridge University Press, 2003.

Robinson, H. Wheeler. *The Christian Doctrine of Man*. Edinburgh: T. and T. Clark, 1926.

Robinson, John A. T. *The Body: A Study in Pauline Anthropology*. Chicago: H. Regnery, 1952.

Scazzero, Peter. *The Emotionally Healthy Church*. Grand Rapids: Zondervan, 2003.

Schanz, John P. *Theology of Community*. Washington, D.C.: University Press of America, 1977.

Schwarz, Stephen D. *The Moral Question of Abortion*. Chicago: Loyola University Press, 1990.

Schwobel, C., and C. E. Gunton, eds. *Persons, Divine and Human*. Edinburgh: T. and T. Clark, 1991.

Sherlock, Charles. *The Doctrine of Humanity*. Downers Grove, Ill: InterVarsity, 1996.

Shores, Steve. *Minding Your Emotions*. Colorado Springs, Colo.: NavPress, 2002.

Shults, F. Leron. *Reforming Theological Anthropology: After the Philosophical Turn to Relationality*. Grand Rapids: Eerdmans, 2003.

Shuster, Marguerite. *Fall and Sin: What We Have Become as Sinners*. Grand Rapids: Eerdmans, 2004.

Singer, Peter. *Practical Ethics*. Cambridge: Cambridge University Press, 1993.

———. *Rethinking Life and Death: The Collapse of Our Traditional Ethics*. New York: St. Martin's Press, 1995.

Singer, Peter, and Helge Kuhse. *Unsanctifying Human Life: Essays on Ethics*. Oxford: Blackwell, 2002.

Smedes, Lewis B. *Mere Morality*. Grand Rapids: Eerdmans, 1983.

———. *Shame and Grace: Healing the Shame We Don't Deserve*. San Francisco, Calif.: Harper and Row, 1993.

Tooley, Michael. *Abortion and Infanticide*. Oxford: Clarendon Press, 1983.

Tozer, A. W. *Man: The Dwelling Place of God*. Harrisburg, Pa.: Christian Publications, 1966.

Vanier, Jean. *Community and Growth*. New York: Paulist, 1989.

———. *Becoming Human*. New York: Paulist, 1998.

Von Balthasar, Hans Ur. *A Theological Anthropology*. New York: Sheed and Ward, 1967.

Wainwright, J. A. *God and Man in the Old Testament*. London: SPCK, 1962.

Ward, Keith. *Defending the Soul*. Oxford: Oneworld Publications, 1992.

Webster, Douglas D. *Soulcraft: How God Shapes Us Through Relationships*. Downers Grove, Ill.: InterVarsity, 1999.

Willard, Dallas. *Renovation of the Heart: Putting on the Character of Christ*. Colorado Springs, Colo.: NavPress, 2002.

Wise, Robert L. *Quest for the Soul: Our Search for Deeper Meaning.* Nashville: Nelson, 1996.

Wolf, Hans Walter. *Anthropology of the Old Testament.* Philadelphia: Fortress, 1974.

## PSYCHOLOGICAL RESOURCES

Abbott, Tina. *Social and Personality Development.* New York: Taylor and Frances, 2001.

Armstrong, D. M. *The Mind-Body Problem: An Opinionated Introduction.* Boulder, Colo.: Westview, 1999.

Baars, B. J., W. P. Banks, and J. B. Newman, eds. *Essential Sources in the Scientific Study of Consciousness.* Cambridge, Mass.: MIT Press, 2003.

Bacal, H. A., and K. M. Newman. *Theories of Object Relations: Bridges to Self Psychology.* New York: Columbia University Press, 1990.

Badcock, C. *Evolutionary Psychology: A Critical Introduction.* Cambridge: Polity Press, 2000.

Bandura, Albert. *Aggression: A Social Learning Analysis.* Englewood Cliffs, N.J.: Prentice-Hall, 1973.

———. *Social Learning Theory.* Englewood Cliffs, N.J.: Prentice-Hall, 1977.

Beck, James R. *Jesus and Personality Theory: Exploring the Five Factor Model.* Downers Grove, Ill.: InterVarsity, 1999.

———. *The Psychology of Paul.* Grand Rapids: Kregel, 2002.

Berkowitz, L. *Causes and Consequences of Feelings.* Cambridge: Cambridge University Press, 2000.

Bieber, Irving. *Homosexuality: A Psychoanalytic Study.* New York: Jason Aronson, 1988.

Bloomquist, M. L., and S. V. Schnell, *Helping Children with Aggression and Conduct Problems.* New York: Guilford, 2002.

Bowen, Murray. *Family Therapy in Clinical Practice.* New York: Jason Aronson, 1985.

Bowers, M. K., E. N. Jackson, and J. A. Knight. *Counseling the Dying.* Northvale, N.J.: Jason Aronson Press, 1975.

Brown, Joseph H., and Dana N. Christensen. *Family Therapy: Theory and Practice.* 2d ed. Pacific Grove, Calif.: Brooks Cole, 1999.

Bunge, M. *The Mind-Body Problem: A Psycho-biological Approach.* Oxford: Pergamon, 1980.

Buss, Arnold. *Psychological Dimensions of the Self.* Thousand Oaks, Calif.: Sage, 2001.

Carter, R. *Mapping the Mind.* Berkeley, Calif.: University of California Press, 1998.

Cole, M., and S. R. Cole. *The Development of Children.* 2d ed. New York: Scientific American Books, 1993.

Cooper, Terry D. *Sin, Pride, and Self-Acceptance.* Downers Grove, Ill.: InterVarsity, 2003.

Corey, Gerald. *Theory and Practice of Group Counseling.* 4th ed. Pacific Grove, Calif.: Brooks Cole, 1995.

Cozolino, L. J. *The Neuroscience of Psychotherapy: Building and Rebuilding the Human Brain.* New York: Norton, 2002.

Dixon, T. *From Passions to Emotions: The Creation of a Secular Psychological Category.* Cambridge: Cambridge University Press, 2003.

Dubin, M. W. *How the Brain Works.* Oxford: Blackwell, 2002.

Dupre, J. *Human Nature and the Limits of Science.* Oxford: Oxford University Press, 2001.

Ellis, R. D., and N. Newton, eds. *The Caldron of Consciousness: Motivation, Affect, and Self-Organization.* Amsterdam: John Benjamin, 2000.

Emmons, R. A. *The Psychology of Ultimate Concerns: Motivation and Spirituality in Personality.* New York: Guilford Press, 1999.

Evans, D. *Emotion: The Science of Sentiment.* Oxford: Oxford University Press, 2001.

Ferguson, E. D. *Motivation: A Biosocial and Cognitive Integration of Motivation and Emotion.* New York: Oxford University Press, 2000.

Fonagy, Peter, and Mary Target. *Psychoanalytic Theories: Perspectives from Developmental Psychopathology.* New York: Brunner-Routledge, 2003.

Foster, J. *The Immaterial Self: A Defense of the Cartesian Dualist Conception of the Mind.* London: Routledge, 1991.

Frankel, Fred, and Robert Myatt, *Children's Friendship Training.* New York: Brunner-Routledge, 2003.

Frijda, N. H., A. S. R. Manstead, and S. Bem. *Emotions and Beliefs: How Feelings Influence Thoughts.* New York: Cambridge University Press, 2000.

Gareth Jones, D. *Our Fragile Brains: A Christian Perspective on Brain Research.* Downers Grove, Ill.: InterVarsity, 1981.

Gazda, G. M., E. J. Ginter, and A. M. Horne, *Group Counseling and Group Psychotherapy.* Boston: Allyn and Bacon, 2001.

Gladding, S. T. *Group Work: A Counseling Strategy.* 3d ed. Upper Saddle River, N.J.: Merrill, 1999.

Goodman, G. *The Internal World and Attachment.* Hillsdale, N.J.: The Analytic Press, 2003.

Green, Michael F. *Schizophrenia Revealed: From Neurons to Social Interactions.* New York: W. W. Norton, 2001.

Greene, J. O., and B. P. Burleson, eds. *Handbook of Communication and Social Interaction Skills.* Mahwah, N.J.: Lawrence Erlbaum, 2003.

Guttenplan, S., ed. *A Companion to the Philosophy of Mind.* Oxford: Blackwell Reference, 1994.

Hamilton, N. G. *Self and Others: Object Relations Theory in Practice.* Northvale, N.J.: Jason Aronson, 1988.

Hanna, Suzanne Midori, and Joseph H. Brown. *The Practice of Family Therapy: Key Elements Across Models.* Belmont, Calif.: Brooks Cole, 1999.

Heilman, K. M. and E. Valenstein, eds. *Clinical Neuropsychology.* 4th ed. Oxford: Oxford University Press, 2003.

Higgins, E. T., and A. W. Kruglenski, eds. *Motivational Science: Social and Personality Perspectives.* Philadelphia: Psychology Press, 2000.

Horowitz, Leonard M. *Interpersonal Foundations of Psychopathology.* Washington, D.C.: American Psychological Association, 2004.

Hwang, Philip O. *Other-Esteem: Meaningful Life in a Multicultural Society.* Philadelphia: Accelerated Development, 2000.

Jeeves, Malcolm. *Mind Fields: Reflections on the Science of Mind and Brain.* Grand Rapids: Baker, 1994.

Jensen, A. R. *The g Factor: The Science of Mental Ability.* Westport, Conn.: Praeger, 1998.

Jones, Stanton L., and Mark A. Yarhouse. *Homosexuality: The Use of Scientific Research in the Church's Moral Debate.* Downers Grove, Ill.: InterVarsity, 2000.

Keshen, Richard. *Reasonable Self-Esteem.* Montreal: McGill-Queen's University Press, 1996.

Kim, Jaegwon. *Philosophy of Mind.* Boulder, Colo.: Westview Press, 1996.

———. *Supervenience and Mind: Selected Philosophical Essays.* Cambridge: Cambridge University Press, 1993.

Kitcher, P. *In Mendel's Mirror: Philosophical Reflections on Biology.* Oxford: Oxford University Press, 2003.

Kumin, Ivri. *Pre-Object Relatedness: Early Attachment and the Psychoanalytic Situation.* New York: Guilford Press, 1996.

Laland, K., and G. R. Brown. *Sense and Nonsense: Evolutionary Perspectives on Human Behaviour.* Oxford: Oxford University Press, 2002.

Larson, E. J., and D. W. Amundsen. *A Different Death: Euthanasia and the Christian Tradition.* Downers Grove, Ill.: InterVarsity, 1998.

Mahler, Margaret S., Fred Pine, and Anni Bergman. *The Psychological Birth of the Human Infant.* New York: Basic Books, 1975.

Matthews, G., M. Zeidner, and R. D. Roberts. *Emotional Intelligence: Science and Myth.* Cambridge, Mass.: MIT Press, 2002.

McCrae, R. R., and P. T. Costa. *Personality in Adulthood.* 2d ed. New York: Guilford Press, 2003.

Merrell, Kenneth W. *Behavioral, Social, and Emotional Assessment of Children and Adolescents.* Mahwah, N.J.: Lawrence Erlbaum, 2003.

Miller, William R., and Harold D. Delaney, eds. *Judeo-Christian Perspectives on Psychology: Human Nature, Motivation, and Change.* Washington, D.C.: American Psychological Association, 2005.

Moberly, Elizabeth R. *Psychogenesis: The Early Development of Gender Identity.* London: Routledge and Kegan Paul, 1983.

Napier, R. W., and M. K. Gershefeld. *Groups: Theory and Experience.* 5th ed. Boston: Houghton Mifflin, 1993.

Nicolosi, Joseph. *Reparative Therapy of Male Homosexuality: A New Clinical Approach.* Northvale, N.J.: Jason Aronson, 1991.

Niemeyer, R. A., ed. *Meaning Reconstruction and the Experience of Loss.* Washington, D.C.: American Psychological Association, 2001.

O'Donohue, W., and K. E. Ferguson, *The Psychology of B. F. Skinner.* Thousand Oaks, Calif.: Sage, 2001.

Penfield, William. *The Mystery of the Mind: A Critical Study of Consciousness and the Human Brain.* Princeton, N.J.: Princeton University Press, 1975.

Pennington, D. C. *The Social Psychology of Behavior in Small Groups.* New York: Taylor and Francis, 2002.

Piedmont, R. L. *The Revised NEO Personality Inventory: Clinical and Research Applications.* New York: Plenum Press, 1998.

Plotkin, H. *Evolution in Mind: An Introduction to Evolutionary Psychology.* Cambridge, Mass.: Harvard University Press, 1998.

Plutchik, R. *Emotions and Life: Perspectives from Psychology, Biology, and Evolution.* Washington, D.C.: American Psychological Association, 2003.

Rathvon, Natalie. *Effective School Interventions: Strategies for Enhancing Aca-*

*demic Achievement and Social Competence.* New York: Guilford Press, 1999.

Rogoff, B. *The Cultural Nature of Human Development.* Oxford: Oxford University Press, 2003.

Rose, H., and S. Rose, eds. *Alas, Poor Darwin: Arguments Against Evolutionary Psychology.* New York: Harmony Books, 2000.

Sable, P. *Attachment and Adult Psychotherapy.* Northvale, N.J.: Jason Aronson, 2000.

St. Clair, M. *Object Relations and Self Psychology.* Monterey, Calif.: Brooks Cole, 1986.

Scharff, D. E. *Object Relations Theory and Practice: An Introduction.* Northvale, N.J.: Jason Aronson, 1996.

Schneider, Barry H. *Friends and Enemies: Peer Relations in Childhood.* London: Arnold, 2000.

Schultz, Stephen J. *Family Systems Therapy: An Integration.* New York: Jason Aronson, 1984.

Slipp, Samuel. *Object Relations: A Dynamic Bridge Between Individual and Family Treatment.* New York: Jason Aronson, 1984.

Snee, Martha E., and Rachel Janney. *Social Relationships and Peer Support.* Baltimore, Md.: Paul H. Brookes, 2000.

Socarides, Charles W. *Homosexuality.* New York: Jason Aronson, 1978.

Staddon, J. *The New Behaviorism: Mind, Mechanism, and Society.* Philadelphia: Psychology Press, 2001.

Sternberg, R. J., and T. Ben-Zeev. *Complex Cognition: The Psychology of Human Thought.* New York: Oxford University Press, 2001.

Stoller, Robert J. *Perversion: The Erotic Form of Hatred.* Washington, D.C.: American Psychiatric Press, 1975.

Storkey, Elaine. *Origins of Difference: The Gender Debate Revisited.* Grand Rapids: Baker, 2001.

Swanson, L. W. *Brain Architecture: Understanding the Basic Plan.* Oxford: Oxford University Press, 2003.

Thiselton, A. C. *Interpreting God and the Postmodern Self: On Meaning, Manipulation, and Promise.* Grand Rapids: Eerdmans, 1995.

Trefil, J. *Are We Unique? A Scientist Explores the Unparalleled Intelligence of the Human Mind.* New York: John Wiley and Sons, 1997.

Uttal, W. R. *The War Between Mentalism and Behaviorism: On the Accessibility of Mental Processes.* Mahwah, N.J.: Laurence Erlbaum, 2000.

Valsiner, J. and K. J. Connolly, eds. *Handbook of Developmental Psychology.* Thousand Oaks, Calif.: Sage, 2003.

Van Leeuwen, Mary Stewart. *The Person in Psychology.* Grand Rapids: Eerdmans, 1985.

Wertheimer, Michael. *Fundamental Issues in Psychology.* New York: Holt, Rinehart and Winston, 1972.

Wilson, E. O. *Sociobiology: The New Synthesis.* Cambridge, Mass.: Harvard University Press, 1975.

Yalom, Irvin D. *The Theory and Practice of Group Psychotherapy.* 4th ed. New York: Basic Books, 1995.

# SUBJECT INDEX

413

# SCRIPTURE INDEX